Sliding Mask

How to Use:

1. When you reach the Sample Oral Questions contained within each task, place the sliding mask over the answers.

2. Read each question carefully and write down your response in the space provided.

3. Once you have answered a question to the best of your ability, uncover the answer provided and compare it to yours.

4. Although your answers may not be as detailed as the answers provided, your response should answer each question thoroughly.

5. If your answer is substantially different, or if you are unable to answer a question, go back and review the information within the task.

JEPPESEN®

A BOEING COMPANY

GUIDED FLIGHT DISCOVERY

PRIVATE PILOT FAA PRACTICAL TEST STUDY GUIDE

AIRPLANE SINGLE-ENGINE LAND

Coordinated with GFD Private Pilot Textbook

Includes:

- Questions, Answers, Explanations, and References
- Knowledge and Skill Areas
- Explanations Adjacent to Questions

Cover Photo: Diamond airplane in flight courtesy of Diamond Aircraft Industries

ISBN 978-0-88487-428-7

Jeppesen
55 Inverness Drive East
Englewood, CO 80112-5498
Web site: www.jeppesen.com
Email: Captain@jeppesen.com

10001390-001
Published 1995, 1996, 1997,1998, 2000, 2002, 2003, 2006, 2015

PREFACE

Thank you for purchasing this *Private Pilot FAA Practical Test Study Guide*. This Study Guide will help you understand the types of tasks you will be required to perform during your Private Pilot Airplane Single-Engine Land (ASEL) practical test, along with some typical questions the examiner might ask. It includes a reprint of the applicable portions of the FAA Practical Test Standards (PTS) at the beginning of each task, with the chapters organized to cover the 12 Areas of Operation. Questions are provided in multiple choice and fill-in-the-blank formats, with answers provided as appropriate. The inclusion of examiner questions offers you the opportunity to take a "mock oral" before actually taking your test. The three-hole punched, perforated pages allow you to remove and study selected sections more effectively, and our unique sliding mask can be used for self-testing. Please note that this Study Guide is intended to be a supplement to your instructor-led flight training, not a stand alone learning tool.

THE JEPPESEN SANDERSON TRAINING PHILOSOPHY

Flight training in the developing years of aviation was characterized by the separation of academics from flight training in the aircraft. For years, ground and flight training were not integrated. There were lots of books on different subjects, written by different authors, which produced a general lack of continuity in training material. The introduction of **Jeppesen Sanderson Training Products** changed all this. Our proven, professional, integrated training materials include extensive research on teaching theory and principles of how people learn best and most efficiently. Effective instruction includes determining objectives and completion standards. We employ an important principle of learning a complex skill using a step-by-step sequence known as the **building block principle**. Another important aspect of training is the principle of **meaningful repetition**, whereby each necessary concept or skill is presented several times throughout the instructional program. Jeppesen training materials incorporate this principle using different teaching tools such as textbooks, videos, exercises, exams, and this Study Guide. When these elements are combined with an instructor's class discussion and the skills learned in the simulator and airplane, you have an ideal integrated training system, with all materials coordinated.

Observation and research show that people tend to retain 10% of what they read, 20% of what they hear, 30% of what they see, and 50% of what they both hear and see together. These retention figures can be increased to as high as 90% by including active learning methods. Video and textbook materials are generally considered passive learning. Exercises, stage exams, student/instructor discussions, and skills in the simulator and airplane are considered to be active learning methods. Levels of learning include rote, understanding, application, and correlation. One of the major drawbacks with test preparation courses, that concentrate only on passing the test, is that they focus on rote learning, the lowest level of learning employed in a teaching situation. Students benefit from Jeppesen's professional approach through standardized instruction, a documented training record, increased learning **and** increased passing rates. Our materials are challenging and motivating, while maximizing knowledge and skill retention. Nearly 3 million pilots have learned to fly using our materials, which include:

MANUALS — Our training manuals contain the answers to many of the questions you may have as you progress through your training program. They are based on the **study/review** concept of learning. This means detailed material is presented in an uncomplicated way, then important points are summarized through the use of bold type and color. The best results can be obtained when the manual is studied as an integral part of the coordinated materials. The manual is the central component for academic study and is cross-referenced to video presentations.

Note: This edition of the Study Guide provides references to the new *Guided Flight Discovery Private Pilot Manual* and videos, which replace previous Jeppesen Sanderson Private Pilot Manuals.

VIDEOS — These motivating, high-quality ground-school videos are professionally produced with actual inflight video and animated graphics. They allow you to review and reinforce essential concepts presented in the manual. The videos are available from flight and ground schools, online pilot supply stores, or wherever Jeppesen Training System products are sold. Call **1-800-621-JEPP** for the names of our Training System dealers in your area.

SUPPORT COMPONENTS — Supplementary items include a training syllabus, exercise book, stage and final exams, FAR/AIM manual, FARs Explained, airmen knowledge test and practical test study guides, test preparation software and videos, question banks and computer testing supplements, an aviation weather book, student record folder, computer, plotter, and logbook. Jeppesen Sanderson's training products are the most comprehensive pilot training materials available. They help you prepare, in conjunction with your instructor, for the FAA exam and practical test; and, more importantly, they help you become a more proficient and safer pilot.

You can purchase our products and services through your Jeppesen dealer. For product, service, or sales information call **1-800-621-JEPP, 303-799-9090, or FAX 303-784-4153**. If you have comments, questions, or need explanations about any component of our Pilot Training System, we are prepared to offer assistance at any time. If your dealer does not have a Jeppesen catalog, please request one and we will promptly send it to you. Just call the above telephone number, or write:

Marketing Manager, Aviation Training
Jeppesen Sanderson, Inc.
55 Inverness Drive East
Englewood, CO 80112-5498

Please direct inquiries from Europe, Africa, and the Middle East to:

JEPPESEN, Gmbh
Frankfurter Strasse 233
63263 Neu-Isenburg
GERMANY
Main Office: +49 6102 507 0
Fax Main: +49 6102 507 999

TABLE OF CONTENTS

PREFACE ..... **iii**

INTRODUCTION ..... **ix**

CHAPTER 1 Preflight Preparation **1-1**
- Task A Certificates and Documents 1-1
- Task B Airworthiness Requirements 1-6
- Task C Weather Information 1-11
- Task D Cross-Country Flight Planning 1-26
- Task E National Airspace System 1-31
- Task F Performance and Limitations 1-37
- Task G Operation of Systems 1-47
- Task J Aeromedical Factors 1-57

CHAPTER 2 Preflight Procedures **2-1**
- Task A Preflight Inspection 2-1
- Task B Cockpit Management 2-5
- Task C Engine Starting 2-7
- Task D Taxiing 2-10
- Task E Before Takeoff Check 2-14

CHAPTER 3 Airport Operations **3-1**
- Task A Radio Communications and ATC Light Signals 3-1
- Task B Traffic Patterns 3-7
- Task C Airport, Runway, and Taxiway Signs, Markings, and Lighting 3-13

CHAPTER 4 Takeoffs, Landings, and Go-Arounds **4-1**
- Task A Normal and Crosswind Takeoff and Climb 4-1
- Task B Normal and Crosswind Approach and Landing 4-7
- Task C Soft-Field Takeoff and Climb 4-14
- Task D Soft-Field Approach and Landing 4-19
- Task E Short-Field Takeoff and Maximum Performance Climb 4-24
- Task F Short-Field Approach and Landing 4-28
- Task G Forward Slip To A Landing 4-32
- Task H Go-Around / Rejected Landing 4-36

CHAPTER 5 Performance Maneuver **5-1**
- Task A Steep Turns 5-1

CHAPTER 6 Ground Reference Maneuvers **6-1**
- Task A Rectangular Course 6-1
- Task B S-Turns 6-6
- Task C Turns Around A Point 6-10

CHAPTER 7 Navigation 7-1
Task A Pilotage and Dead Reckoning 7-1
Task B Navigation Systems and Radar Services 7-7
Task C Diversion 7-16
Task D Lost Procedures 7-18

CHAPTER 8 Slow Flight and Stalls 8-1
Task A Maneuvering During Slow Flight 8-1
Task B Power-Off Stalls 8-5
Task C Power-On Stalls 8-12
Task D Spin Awareness 8-16

CHAPTER 9 Basic Instrument Maneuvers 9-1
Task A Straight-and-Level Flight 9-1
Task B Constant Airspeed Climbs 9-6
Task C Constant Airspeed Descents 9-10
Task D Turns to Headings 9-13
Task E Recovery From Unusual Flight Attitudes 9-16
Task F Radio Communications, Navigation Systems/Facilities, and Radar Services 9-20

CHAPTER 10 Emergency Operations 10-1
Task A Emergency Approach and Landing 10-1
Task B Systems and Equipment Malfunctions 10-5
Task C Emergency Equipment and Survival Gear 10-10

CHAPTER 11 Night Operations 11-1
Task A Night Preparation 11-1

CHAPTER 12 Postflight Procedures 12-1
Task A After Landing, Parking and Securing 12-1

APPENDIX A Abbreviations A-1

INTRODUCTION

Private Pilot Practical Test Standards (PTS) are published by the Federal Aviation Administration (FAA). The Private PTS establishes the standards for the private pilot certification tests for all aircraft categories and classes. FAA inspectors and designated pilot examiners are required to conduct practical tests in compliance with the PTS. The practical test itself includes both oral (knowledge) and flight test (skill) elements. Flight instructors and applicants should be familiar with the established standards.

This *Private Pilot FAA Practical Test Study Guide* is designed to help you prepare for the FAA practical test for a Recreational Pilot or Private Pilot Certificate. It covers a broad range of aeronautical knowledge and the associated skill level requirements that apply to airplanes. Included are pertinent Federal Aviation Regulations (FARs). Information pertaining to rotorcraft, gliders, balloons, and airships is not included.

We recommend that you use this Study Guide along with the Jeppesen Sanderson Pilot Training Course. The Study Guide is organized like the FAA's Airplane Single-Engine Land (ASEL) and Airplane Single-Engine Sea (ASES) *Private Pilot Practical Test Standards*. It is arranged in 12 chapters which correspond to the 12 AREAS OF OPERATION contained in the PTS. Each chapter is divided into Tasks which are aligned with PTS TASKS. As an example, AREA OF OPERATION VI in the PTS is Ground Reference Maneuvers. This is the title of Chapter 6 in the Study Guide. TASK A under this area of operation is Rectangular Course, and this is the title of Task A in Chapter 6 of the Study Guide.

According to the PTS, the AREAS OF OPERATION are phases of flight arranged in a logical sequence. The first AREAS OF OPERATION are concerned with the preparation for flight and the last with the conclusion of the flight. However, you should be aware that the examiner may conduct the practical test in any sequence that results in a complete and efficient test. The TASKS are procedures and maneuvers related to an AREA OF OPERATION.

Each section in the Study Guide begins with a reprint of the TASK as it is published in the PTS. Included are the TASK objectives, followed by a task analysis. Although all of the objectives for Airplane Single-Engine Land (ASEL) and Airplane Single-Engine Sea (ASES) are included in the TASK reprints at the beginning of each section, the task analysis deals only with the TASK objectives that are applicable to Airplane Single-Engine Land (ASEL). You will notice that some TASKS are oriented toward oral or knowledge testing; others tend to emphasize skill, or flight testing. However most TASKS include both knowledge and skill elements.

Knowledge objectives are explained in sufficient depth to cover typical private pilot oral questions. Outline, or abbreviated format, and illustrations are used where appropriate. Skill objectives are covered in a slightly different way, since a specific procedure is often significant. Most maneuver tasks include illustrative figures.

The next segment within each section is the exercises. These normally are in a fill-in-the-blank and True/False format. Answers are included within the task.

Sample oral questions follow the exercise material. These are broad questions that may require a lengthy answer. They are typical examiner questions that simulate a mock oral. Blank spaces are provided for the answers, and synoptic answers are included. However, the page layout for the sample oral questions allows you to cover the answers with a sliding mask which is provided with the Study Guide. This feature is designed so you can complete these self-test questions before you check the answers.

Additional oral questions are added at the end of each section. These questions do not have answers since they are the type of questions that often do not have a specific answer. An example is: "Why did you select this checkpoint for the cross-country?"

As mentioned, the answers to the exercises are provided. These exercise answers follow the additional oral questions in each Task.

References, both Jeppesen and FAA, are also included for all TASKS, for example —

JEPPESEN:

Private Pilot Manual Chap. 6, Sec. C

FAA:

Airplane Flying Handbook (FAA-H-8083-3)

This Jeppesen reference indicates the subject is covered in Chapter 6, Section C, of the *Private Pilot Manual*. If a video reference is applicable, it also is listed. An FAA reference is listed next. Often, more than one Jeppesen and FAA reference is included.

In addition to the 12 chapters covering the 12 practical test AREAS OF OPERATION, an appendix is included at the end of the study guide. The appendix contains a list of common abbreviations used throughout the Study Guide.

HOW TO PREPARE FOR THE PRACTICAL TEST

Pilot applicants often have more trouble with the practical test than they have with the written test. Flight examiners, both FAA inspectors and designated pilot examiners, indicate that, although piloting skills are adequate, many applicants are unable to respond correctly to oral questioning.

This Study Guide is specifically developed to help you with oral portions of the practical test. It covers all AREAS OF OPERATION, TASKS, and Objectives in the Private Pilot Practical Test Standards (ASEL). You should become familiar with all TASKS and Objectives. This way you'll know what criteria apply and what to expect.

For a comprehensive training program, we recommend a structured course with an organized ground school. This will help you complete the course in a timely way, and you will be able to have questions answered. Use this Practical Test Study Guide to test yourself. Where answers are visible, cover them with the sliding mask and fill in your answer. You may want to mark questions you miss for further study and review before you take the practical test. The Jeppesen references are listed to help you find pertinent review material.

WHAT TO EXPECT ON THE PRACTICAL TEST

Important details on the practical test concept are included in the Introduction section of the FAA Private Pilot Practical Test Standards. Read this part carefully. It not only explains the concept, it also tells you about flight instructor/examiner responsibilities concerning the practical test. For example, use of the published PTS is mandatory; however, the examiner may combine or switch the order of AREAS OF OPERATION and TASKS. Some TASKS will only be evaluated orally. Note that the examiner will place special emphasis on areas of aircraft operation which are most critical to flight safety. Among the areas are aircraft control and sound judgment in decision making. The examiner will also emphasize stall/spin awareness, spatial disorientation, collision avoidance, wake turbulence avoidance, low-level wind shear, runway incursion avoidance, and checklist usage.

You also need to be aware of examiners' use of distractions during the practical test. This is to test your ability to divide your attention while maintaining correct control of the airplane. The Introduction also spells out practical test prerequisites, aircraft/equipment requirements, and general satisfactory/unsatisfactory performance standards.

Finally, you should refer to the Applicant's Practical Test Checklist. This is the last item in the PTS. It has a detailed list of personal equipment and records you'll need for the practical test.

THE STOP PROCEDURE

Some examiners may use a procedure called "STOP" to evaluate a given task. The word STOP is an acronym that stands for safety, tolerances, objective, and procedure. If you apply it to a maneuver such as "Turns Around a Point," here is how it may be used during the practical test.

S — Safety. This means the examiner will ask you to verbalize the safety considerations for conducting the maneuver. He or she expects to hear such things as clearing for traffic, selecting a point where terrain is relatively clear of obstructions so an emergency landing can be made if the engine fails, etc.

T — Tolerances. In other words, to what tolerances must the maneuver be performed in order to be satisfactory? In this case, entry is at 600 feet to 1,000 feet AGL, altitude is within +/-100 feet, and airspeed within 10 knots. If you don't know the tolerances, the examiner will indicate what they are. Otherwise, it's like taking a written test without knowing the minimum passing score.

O — Objective. Do you know the purpose of conducting the maneuver? In this case, the purpose is to maintain a constant radius turn around a point by compensating for wind drift and dividing your attention between aircraft control and ground track.

P — Procedure. Do you know how to perform the maneuver correctly, make a downwind entry, compensate for wind, and maintain tolerances?

PREFLIGHT PREPARATION

A. TASK: CERTIFICATES AND DOCUMENTS (ASEL AND ASES)

REFERENCES: 14 CFR parts 43,61,91; FAA-H-8303-3, AC 61-23/FAA-H-8083-25; POH/AFM

Objective: To determine that the applicant exhibits knowledge of the elements related to certificates and documents by:

1. Explaining—

a. private pilot certificate privileges, limitations, and recent flight experience requirements.
b. medical certificate class and duration.
c. pilot logbook or flight records.

2. Locating and explaining—

a. airworthiness and registration certificates.
b. operating limitations, placards, instrument markings, and POH/AFM.
c. weight and balance data and equipment list.

Objective: To determine that the applicant exhibits knowledge of the elements related to certificates and documents by:

1. Explaining –

a. private pilot certificate privileges, limitations, and recent flight experience requirements.
b. medical certificate class and duration.
c. pilot logbook or flight records.

PILOT CERTIFICATES AND DOCUMENTS

PRIVATE PILOT CERTIFICATE

When you receive your private pilot certificate, you are certified under a specific category and class. Typically, most private pilot certificates are issued specifying airplane category and single-engine land class. [Figure 1-1]

PILOT CERTIFICATION		
Category	**Class**	**Type**
Airplane	Single-Engine Land Multi-Engine Land Single-Engine Sea Multi-Engine Sea	Specifies make and model such as: PA-28-161 Hughes 500 Boeing 747
Rotorcraft	Helicopter Gyroplane	
Powered-Lift	----------------------	
Glider	----------------------	
Lighter-Than-Air	Airship Balloon	

Figure 1-1. For purposes of pilot certification, category is the broadest grouping and contains five entries. With the exception of gliders and powered-lift, each category is further broken down into classes. Finally, the type designates the make and model of the aircraft. When you complete your training, your pilot certificate will probably specify airplane single-engine land. The type normally is not listed for small airplanes.

A private pilot certificate is issued without an expiration date; however, there are minimum experience requirements you must meet to remain eligible to fly. For example, you may not act as pilot in command unless within the previous 24 months you have successfully completed a flight review consisting of a minimum of one hour of ground instruction and one hour of flight instruction. However, if within the previous 24 months you satisfactorily complete a pilot proficiency check, an approved flight check for a pilot certificate or rating, or one or more phases of the FAA-sponsored Wings program, you need not accomplish the flight review.

PRIVILEGES AND LIMITATIONS

When you obtain your private pilot certificate you are entitled to certain privileges and restricted by certain limitations. The following is a summary of what you can and can not do according to FAR Part 61.

As a private pilot you may, for compensation or hire, act as pilot in command of an aircraft in connection with any business or employment if the flight is only incidental to that business or employ ment and the aircraft does not carry passengers or property for compensation or hire.

You may also share the operating expenses of a flight with your passengers. The FAA has taken the position that the expenses must be shared equally by all on board the aircraft including the pilot. Your services as pilot cannot be your "share" of the expenses. The expenses that can be shared are those related to the specific flight. Such expenses include fuel, oil, landing fees, tie-down or hangar fees, or rental fees.

If you are an aircraft salesperson with at least 200 hours of logged flight time, you may demonstrate an aircraft in flight to a prospective buyer.

Once you receive your private pilot certificate, you also can act as pilot in command of an aircraft used in a passenger-carrying airlift sponsored by a charitable organization, and for which the passengers make a donation to the organization. However, the sponsor must notify the appropriate FAA Flight Standards District Office at least seven days before the flight, and furnish information required by FAR 61.113. Additional requirements state that the flight must be conducted in VFR conditions from a public airport adequate for the aircraft used, or from another airport that has been approved for the operation by an FAA inspector. Each aircraft used also must have a standard airworthiness certificate and must comply with the 100-hour inspection requirements. Furthermore, you must have logged at least 200 hours of flight time and are prohibited from conducting acrobatic or formation flights.

As a private pilot, your principal limitation is that you may not act as pilot in command of an aircraft that is carrying passengers or property for hire. Nor may you, for compensation, act as pilot in command of an aircraft.

RECENT FLIGHT EXPERIENCE

You must meet certain recent flight experience requirements in order to carry passengers. For example, to act as pilot in command of an aircraft carrying passengers, you must, within the preceding 90 days, have made three takeoffs and three landings as the sole manipulator of the controls in the same category and class of aircraft to be flown. If the aircraft to be flown has a tailwheel, the landings must be made to a full stop.

To carry passengers during the period beginning one hour after sunset to one hour before sunrise, you must, within the preceding 90 days, have made three takeoffs and three landings to a full stop during that period in the same category and class of aircraft to be flown.

MEDICAL CERTIFICATES

To act as the pilot in command of an aircraft, you must have (in your physical possession or readily accessible in the aircraft), a valid medical certificate to exercise the privileges of your pilot's certificate. Required periodic medical examinations are conducted by designated Aviation Medical Examiners (AMEs), who are interested in aviation safety and who have been trained in aviation medicine.

Medical certificates are classified into three categories: first class, second class, and third class. A first-class medical certificate is valid for 6 calendar months when exercising the privileges of an airline transport pilot (ATP) certificate; 12 calendar months when exercising the privileges of a commercial pilot certificate; and 36 calendar months* for private pilot privileges. A second-class medical certificate is valid for 12 calendar months when exercising the privileges of a commercial pilot certificate and 36 calendar months* for private pilot privileges. A third-class medical certificate can only be used when exercising private pilot privileges and is valid for 36 calendar months*.

In simple terms, to exercise the privileges of a private pilot, a first-, second-, or third-class medical certificate is valid for 36 calendar months* after the month of the date of examination shown on the certificate. For example, if a third-class medical certificate is issued to you on May 3, this year, you may exercise private pilot privileges until May 31, 3 years later*.

*24 months if over age 40 on the date of medical examination.

PILOT LOGBOOK

As a pilot, you are required by the FARs to log all aeronautical training and experience required to obtain a pilot's certificate or rating. Furthermore, the flight time used to meet recent flight experience requirements also must be logged.

For each flight and lesson logged, you must enter the date, total time of the flight, the point of departure and arrival, as well as the aircraft type and identification. You must indicate the type of flight experience as pilot in command, solo, flight instruction, instrument flight instruction, or pilot ground trainer. Remember, there could be a combination of some of these elements. For the conditions of flight, an entry is required indicating whether the flight was conducted during the day or at night.

Once you become a private pilot, you may log pilot-in-command time when you are the sole manipulator of the controls of an aircraft for which you are rated, or when you are the sole occupant of the aircraft. You may also log pilot-in-command time when you are acting as pilot in command of an aircraft that requires more than one pilot under the type certification of the aircraft, or the regulations under which the flight is conducted.

As a student pilot, you must carry your logbook with you on every solo cross-country flight. Once you become a private pilot you do not have to carry your logbook; however, you must present it for inspection upon reasonable request by the FAA Administrator, an authorized representative of the National Transportation Safety Board, or any state or local law enforcement officer.

Objective: To determine that the applicant exhibits knowledge of the elements related to certificates and documents by:

2. Locating and explaining—-

a. airworthiness and registration certificates.
b. operating limitations, placards, instrument markings, and POH/AFM.
c. weight and balance data and equipment list.

AIRCRAFT CERTIFICATES AND DOCUMENTS

In addition to the documents you need as a pilot, specific documents are required to be aboard the airplane on every flight. The acronym ARROW can help you remember which documents are required.

A — Airworthiness certificate (required by FAA)

R — Registration certificate (required by FAA)

R — Radio station license (required by FCC — outside U.S.)

O — Operating limitations, pilot's operating hand book, or approved aircraft flight manual (required by FAA)

W — Weight and balance data, as well as equipment list (required by FAA)

AIRWORTHINESS CERTIFICATE

The FAA issues an airworthiness certificate after an aircraft has been inspected to verify it meets the requirements outlined in the Federal Aviation Regulations and is in a safe operating condition. An airworthiness certificate remains valid as long as the aircraft is properly registered in the United States and those maintaining the aircraft comply with all maintenance and airworthiness directives (AD). Prior to every flight you should verify that the airworthiness certificate is displayed so it is visible to passengers and crewmembers.

The airworthiness certificate includes the aircraft registration number, which always begins with the letter "N" in the United States. It also shows the make and model of the aircraft, along with the serial number, and any exemptions from applicable airworthiness standards. The category of certification is also shown, which gives you important information about the flight load factors the airframe is designed to handle. [Figure 1-2]

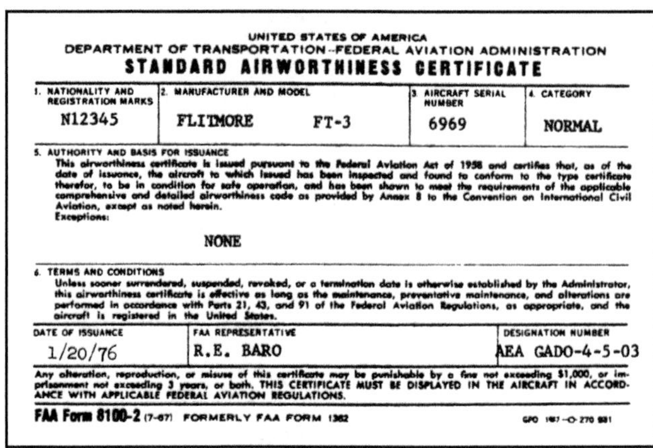

UNITED STATES OF AMERICA
DEPARTMENT OF TRANSPORTATION–FEDERAL AVIATION ADMINISTRATION
STANDARD AIRWORTHINESS CERTIFICATE

1. NATIONALITY AND REGISTRATION MARKS	2. MANUFACTURER AND MODEL	3. AIRCRAFT SERIAL NUMBER	4. CATEGORY
N12345	FLITMORE FT-3	6969	NORMAL

5. AUTHORITY AND BASIS FOR ISSUANCE
This airworthiness certificate is issued pursuant to the Federal Aviation Act of 1958 and certifies that, as of the date of issuance, the aircraft to which issued has been inspected and found to conform to the type certificate therefor, to be in condition for safe operation, and has been shown to meet the requirements of the applicable comprehensive and detailed airworthiness code as provided by Annex 8 to the Convention on International Civil Aviation, except as noted herein.
Exceptions:

NONE

6. TERMS AND CONDITIONS
Unless sooner surrendered, suspended, revoked, or a termination date is otherwise established by the Administrator, this airworthiness certificate is effective as long as the maintenance, preventative maintenance, and alterations are performed in accordance with Parts 21, 43, and 91 of the Federal Aviation Regulations, as appropriate, and the aircraft is registered in the United States.

DATE OF ISSUANCE	FAA REPRESENTATIVE	DESIGNATION NUMBER
1/20/76	R.E. BARO	AEA GADO-4-5-03

Any alteration, reproduction, or misuse of this certificate may be punishable by a fine not exceeding $1,000, or imprisonment not exceeding 3 years, or both. THIS CERTIFICATE MUST BE DISPLAYED IN THE AIRCRAFT IN ACCORDANCE WITH APPLICABLE FEDERAL AVIATION REGULATIONS.

FAA Form 8100-2 (7-67) FORMERLY FAA FORM 1362

Figure 1-2. The standard airworthiness certificate is issued for aircraft in the transport, normal, utility, or acrobatic categories and for manned free balloons.

REGISTRATION CERTIFICATE

The registration certificate is issued to the aircraft owner, and shows the owner's name and address in addition to the make, model, serial number, and registration number of the aircraft. The certificate becomes invalid if the aircraft is registered in a foreign country, the aircraft is destroyed or scrapped, ownership changes, the owner loses U.S. citizenship, or if the owner requests it. The certificate also expires 30 days after the death of the owner. Like the airworthiness certificate, the registration is required to be on board the aircraft. [Figure 1-3]

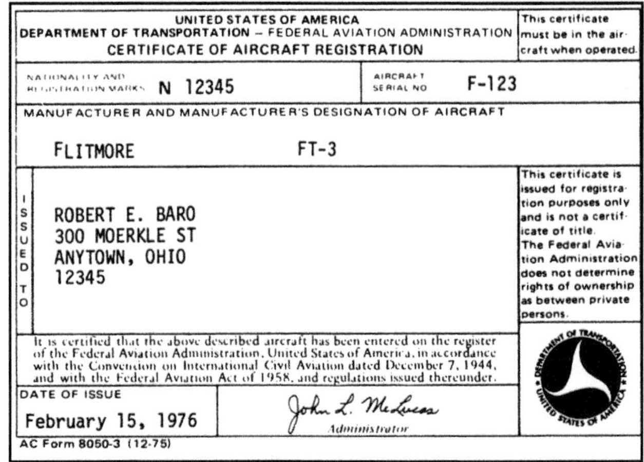

UNITED STATES OF AMERICA
DEPARTMENT OF TRANSPORTATION – FEDERAL AVIATION ADMINISTRATION
CERTIFICATE OF AIRCRAFT REGISTRATION

This certificate must be in the aircraft when operated.

NATIONALITY AND REGISTRATION MARKS	AIRCRAFT SERIAL NO
N 12345	F-123

MANUFACTURER AND MANUFACTURER'S DESIGNATION OF AIRCRAFT

FLITMORE FT-3

ISSUED TO

ROBERT E. BARO
300 MOERKLE ST
ANYTOWN, OHIO
12345

This certificate is issued for registration purposes only and is not a certificate of title. The Federal Aviation Administration does not determine rights of ownership as between private persons.

It is certified that the above described aircraft has been entered on the register of the Federal Aviation Administration, United States of America, in accordance with the Convention on International Civil Aviation dated December 7, 1944, and with the Federal Aviation Act of 1958, and regulations issued thereunder.

DATE OF ISSUE
February 15, 1976

John L. McLucas
Administrator

AC Form 8050-3 (12-75)

Figure 1-3. You can obtain additional information on aircraft registration from an FAA District Office.

FCC RADIO STATION LICENSE

For international flights, or for flights where you communicate with people outside the U.S., the Federal Communications Commission requires that the aircraft have a radio station license. Although the license is not required unless you travel or transmit to someone outside the United States, most U.S. airplanes with radios normally have the license, which must be carried in the aircraft.

The FCC also requires pilots who operate high frequency (HF) radios or fly internationally to have a restricted radiotelephone operator permit. The permit is obtained by completing an FCC application form.

OPERATING LIMITATIONS

The operating limitations and instructions for a particular aircraft are located in an FAA-Approved Airplane Flight Manual or Pilot's Operating Handbook (POH). If the aircraft you are flying was certificated with an approved flight manual, it must be on board the aircraft during flight. For aircraft certified without an approved flight manual, the operating limitations must be on the aircraft through any combination of placards, instrument markings, or approved manual material.

WEIGHT AND BALANCE DATA

As you know, all aircraft do not weigh the same amount. The weight and CG location can vary considerably, even between aircraft of identical make and model, due to the installation of avionics and other equipment. For this reason, current weight and balance information must be kept with every aircraft. Some of the information, such as the aircraft empty weight and CG location, are recorded on FAA Form 337. Other weight and balance information includes an equipment list, which identifies the weight and moment of each accessory added to the basic airplane. After each modification or addition of new equipment, maintenance technicians calculate new weight and balance figures and generate a new Form 337.

EXERCISES:

1. Can you, as a private pilot, fly for compensation or hire under certain circumstances? ________________

2. _____ (True, False) Completing one or more phases of the FAA-sponsored Wings Program satisfies the flight review requirement.

3. List the aircraft documents that must be on board the aircraft.

A ______________________________

R ______________________________

R ______________________________

O ______________________________

W ______________________________

4. A third class medical certificate is good for ________ calendar months.

5. _____ (True, False) As a private pilot, you must carry your logbook with you at all times.

SAMPLE ORAL QUESTIONS

1. As a private pilot, under what circumstances can you act as pilot-in-command of an aircraft for compensation or hire?

____

____

____

____

____

____

____

1. As a private pilot you may, for compensation or hire, act as pilot in command of an aircraft in connection with any business or employment if the flight is only incidental to that business or employment and the aircraft does not carry passengers or property for compensation or hire.

2. Describe the medical certificate classes and duration for private pilots.

____

____

____

____

____

____

____

____

2. For the purpose of exercising the privileges of a private pilot certificate a first-, second-, or third-class medical certificate expires at the end of the last day of the 36th calendar month (24 months if over age 40) after the month of examination shown on the certificate.

3. In order to act as pilot in command of an aircraft carrying passengers during the period beginning one hour after sunset and ending one hour before sunrise, you must, within the preceding 90 days, have made at least three takeoffs and three landings to a full stop during that period in the category and class of aircraft to be flown.

3. Describe the requirements to act as pilot in command of an airplane carrying passengers at night.

4. You are required by the FARs to log all aeronautical training and experience required to obtain a pilot's certificate or rating and meet recent flight experience requirements.

4. What flight time are you required to log?

ADDITIONAL QUESTIONS

5. Is an airworthiness certificate issued with an expiration date?

6. What are the recent flight experience requirements for carrying passengers in a tailwheel aircraft?

7. As a private pilot, are you, for compensation, permitted to act as pilot-in-command of an aircraft?

EXERCISE ANSWERS

1. Yes

2. True

3. Airworthiness Certificate, Registration Certificate, Radio Station License (outside U.S.), Operating Limitations, Weight and Balance data

4. 24 or 36 months, depending on age

5. False

REFERENCES

JEPPESEN:

Private Pilot Manual - Chapter 1A

FAA:

Federal Aviation Regulations
Airplane Flying Handbook (FAA-H-8083-3)
Pilot's Handbook of Aeronautical Knowledge (AC 61-23/FAA-H-8083-25)
Pilots Operating Handbook

B. TASK: AIRWORTHINESS REQUIREMENTS

REFERENCES: 14 CFR part 91; AC-61-23/FAA-H-8303-25.

Objective: To determine that the applicant exhibits knowledge of the elements related to airworthiness requirements by:

1. Explaining —
   a. required instruments and equipment for day/night VFR.
   b. procedures and limitations for determining airworthiness of the airplane with inoperative instruments and equipment with and without an MEL.
   c. requirements and procedures for obtaining a special flight permit.
2. Locating and explaining—
   a. airworthiness directives.
   b. compliance records.
   c. maintenance/inspection requirements.
   d. appropriate record keeping.

Objective: To determine that the applicant exhibits knowledge of the elements related to airworthiness requirements by:

1. Explaining—

a. required instruments and equipment for day/night VFR.

b. procedures and limitations for determining airworthiness of the airplane with inoperative instruments and equipment with and without an MEL.

c. requirements and procedures for obtaining a special flight permit.

REQUIRED INSTRUMENTS AND EQUIPMENT

Certain instruments and equipment are required for flight in all powered aircraft. These requirements are spelled out in 14 CFR part 91.205.

DAY VFR

The shortest list of requirements is for relatively simple aircraft flying in visual meteorological conditions. For a typical single-engine airplane with a fixed pitch propeller and fixed landing gear, only seven instruments are required:

1. Airspeed indicator
2. Altimeter
3. Magnetic direction indicator (usually a compass)
4. Tachometer
5. Oil pressure gauge
6. Temperature gauge (this will be oil temperature for air-cooled engines)
7. Fuel quantity gauge (one that can show the quantity in each tank)

In addition, two pieces of equipment are required:

1. An approved safety belt for each occupant
2. An emergency locator transmitter

Additional requirements are added for more complex airplanes:

1. If the airplane has retractable gear, there must be a landing gear position indicator.
2. If the airplane was manufactured after July 18, 1978, front seats must have approved shoulder harnesses.
3. A manifold pressure gauge is required for each altitude engine.

Finally, if the aircraft is to be operated for hire over water and beyond power-off gliding distance from shore, it must carry approved flotation gear readily available to each occupant, and at least one pyrotechnic signaling device, usually a flare gun.

NIGHT VFR

Besides the equipment required for Day VFR flight, there are some additional equipment requirements for VFR flight at night:

1. Approved position lights.
2. An approved anti-collision light.
3. An adequate source of electrical energy for all installed electrical and radio equipment. (Although this usually refers to the battery, alternator, regulator, and so forth, in some cases a simple battery would be enough, provided it could supply power for the entire duration of the flight.)
4. A spare set of fuses, or three fuses of each kind required, accessible to the pilot in flight.

There is an additional requirement if the aircraft is used for hire: it must have an electric landing light.

These basics apply to all powered aircraft operating with an airworthiness certificate. An important part of your preflight is verifying that these items are functioning.

DETERMINING AIRWORTHINESS

The term airworthiness is not defined in 14 CFR Part 1, and therefore many people have been left to interpret the meaning from various other sources. However, the FAA provides guidance documents that define the term. In many cases, these guidance documents have been developed through case law studies. For example, an accepted definition of airworthiness is found in the Airworthiness Inspector's Handbook, Order 8300.10. In accordance with Chapter 213, Section 1, Paragraph 5A(2), the FAA considers an aircraft to be airworthy when the following two conditions have been met:

1. The aircraft must conform to its type design. Conformity to type design is considered attained when the required and proper components are installed and they are consistent with the drawings, specifications, and other data that are part of the type certificate. Conformity includes applicable supplemental type certificates, and field approved alterations.

2. The aircraft must be in condition for safe operation. This refers to the condition of the aircraft with relation to wear and deterioration. Such conditions could be skin corrosion, window delamination/crazing, fluid leaks, tire wear, etc.

How can you decide if the airplane is legal and safe to fly when some item or piece of equipment is broken or doesn't work? With a simple airplane, virtually everything is necessary for flight. Fortunately, there isn't much to go wrong, so the odds are pretty good that everything will be working on any given day. More complex aircraft have more systems and equipment that can break down, but certain equipment is only used in special circumstances, such as de-icing equipment or oxygen systems. In some cases, it is legal to fly the aircraft with inoperative equipment if specific criteria are met.

INOPERATIVE EQUIPMENT

In general, 14 CFR part 91.213 describes the circumstances under which an aircraft may be operated with inoperative equipment or instruments. Essentially, you must answer four questions to apply this regulation correctly. If the answer to any one of these questions is "yes," the aircraft is not airworthy and maintenance is required. If all four of the questions can be answered "no," it may be possible to operate the aircraft safely with inoperative instruments or equipment. [Figure 1-4]

The first question you must ask is whether the inoperative instrument or item of equipment is part of the list of instruments and equipment prescribed in the applicable airworthiness regulations under which the aircraft was type-certificated. Required instruments or items of equipment are listed in FAR Part 23 and on a Type Certificate Data Sheet that applies to the make and model of your aircraft. You may obtain copies of the data sheet from your local FAA district office or from a qualified maintenance person.

The second question you must ask yourself is if the failed piece of equipment is required by the aircraft's equipment list or Kinds of Operations Equipment List. All civil aircraft of United States registry are required to have an itemized equipment list in the aircraft. Although this information is required by the certification rules, no standard format has been required and the manufacturer may furnish the information in various ways. You can usually find the equipment list for aircraft manufactured after 1975 in the weight and balance section of the POH. This list may specify what is required equipment for FAA certification, what is standard equipment, and what is optional equipment that may replace required items, or standard items which are in addition to required items. All items of equipment listed as required, or installed in substitution for required, must be capable of operating to the original design specifications for all flights.

A Kinds of Operations Equipment List can usually be found in the Limitations section of the POH. This section includes a statement of the kinds of operations allowed when the listed operable equipment is installed. Some examples include: VFR NIGHT, IFR DAY, IFR NIGHT, and FLIGHT INTO ICING CONDITIONS. If any installed equipment affects an operating limitation, the equipment is listed and identified as to which type of operation and where it applies. Some manufacturers may simply reference the applicable regulation that identifies required equipment for different kinds of operations.

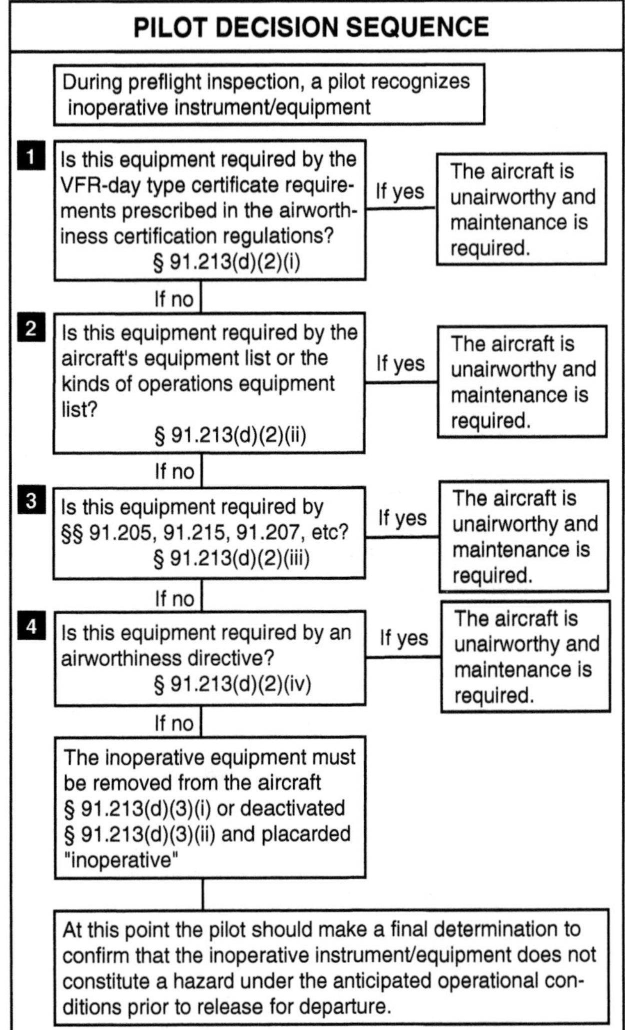

Figure 1-4. If a piece of equipment is not working, this decision tree will help determine if your aircraft is airworthy.

The third question you must ask is whether the item is required by FAR 91.205 or any other rule under Part 91 for the specific kind of flight operation being conducted. There are rules in FAR Part 91 that stipulate instruments and equipment required for certain types and conditions of flight. For example, FAR 91.215 states that an operable transponder with altitude reporting capability is required in Class A, B, and C airspace areas.

The fourth and final question you must ask is if the instrument or item of equipment is required by an airworthiness directive (AD). For example, a second vacuum pump is required by AD to operate a Cessna 210 in instrument meteorological conditions (IMC). To obtain a list of ADs pertinent to the aircraft you're flying, contact a certificated mechanic or your local Flight Standards District Office (FSDO).

If the answer to all of the four questions is no, your next step is to have the inoperative equipment removed [91.213(d)(3)(i)] or deactivated [91.213(d)(3)(ii)] and placarded "inoperative." Placarding can be as simple as writing "Inoperative" on a piece of masking tape and attaching it to the instrument or its cockpit control. The purpose of the placard is to remind you, future operators, and maintenance personnel that the equipment is inoperative.

Removing some equipment may require consultation with and/or the services of qualified maintenance personnel. Removal of any item that affects the airworthiness of the aircraft must be accomplished in accordance with an approved procedure. Pilots certificated under Part 61 may remove items and approve the aircraft for return to service after performing preventive maintenance tasks referenced in FAR Part 43. Any item not listed under preventive maintenance must be removed or deactivated by qualified maintenance personnel. In addition, an entry must be made in the maintenance records in accordance with FAR Part 43.9.

THE FINAL DECISION

You should realize that as PIC you are responsible for the final determination of the aircraft's overall airworthiness. This includes a complete and thorough preflight inspection of the entire aircraft, in addition to examining how the inoperative equipment will affect the intended flight. The pilot in command who accepts an aircraft after preflight inspection issues the final approval for return to service.

SPECIAL FLIGHT PERMITS

If an aircraft is not airworthy due to an inoperative instrument or piece of equipment, you may be able to fly the aircraft if you obtain a special flight permit as specified in FAR 21.197 and 21.199. However, a special flight permit may only be issued for aircraft that are capable of safe flight and for the purpose of flying to a base where repairs, alterations, or maintenance are to be performed, or to a point of storage.

When applying for a special flight permit, you must submit a statement, in a form and manner prescribed by the Administrator, to your local FAA district office. This statement must indicate:

1. The purpose of the flight
2. The proposed itinerary
3. The required crew members needed to fly the aircraft and operate the equipment
4. The ways in which the aircraft does not comply with the applicable airworthiness requirements
5. Any restriction you consider necessary for safe operation of the aircraft
6. Any other information considered necessary by the Administrator for the purpose of prescribing operating limitations

2. Locating and explaining—

- **a. airworthiness directives.**
- **b. compliance records.**
- **c. maintenance/inspection requirements.**
- **d. appropriate record keeping.**

MAINTENANCE RECORDS

AIRWORTHINESS DIRECTIVES

FAR Part 39, Airworthiness Directives (ADs), requires correction of unsafe conditions found in airframes, engines, propellers, and other equipment. ADs also prescribe the conditions under which the equipment may continue to be operated. The list of relevant ADs and the compliance status of an airplane are typically kept with that airplane's maintenance records.

As a private pilot, be aware that airworthiness directives are regulatory and must be complied with, unless a specific exemption is granted. Compliance with ADs is the aircraft owner or operator's responsibility. However, as pilot in command, you are responsible for determining the airworthiness of the aircraft prior to each flight.

MAINTENANCE AND INSPECTION REQUIREMENTS

The inspection of all civil aircraft is required by the FARs to determine overall condition. The time interval between inspections depends upon the type of aircraft operation. To remain airworthy, most aircraft must undergo an annual inspection every 12 calendar months. This type of inspection must be performed by a certificated airframe and powerplant (A&P) mechanic holding an inspection authorization. Airplanes operated for hire must also be inspected every 100 hours, specifically: "no person may operate an aircraft carrying a person (other than a crew member) for hire, or give flight instruction for hire in an aircraft which that person provides, unless within the preceding 100 hours of time in service the aircraft has received an annual or 100-hour inspection." The 100-hour inspection can be conducted by an A&P mechanic without an inspection authorization.

In addition to the airframe and engine, certain components must be inspected at specific intervals. For example, the emergency locator transmitter must be inspected every 12 calendar months. The batteries in an ELT must be replaced after half their useful life has expired, as indicated by a date on the ELT and in the airframe logbook, or after one hour of cumulative use.

APPROPRIATE RECORD KEEPING

The regulations also require the aircraft owner or operator to keep certain maintenance records. You, as the pilot of an aircraft, should have access to the aircraft's logbooks and verify that they contain certain maintenance information. This includes the total time in service for the aircraft and components, the current status of applicable airworthiness directives, records of major repairs and alterations, and the status of all recurring inspections.

You must verify before you fly an aircraft that it has had an annual inspection within the previous 12 calendar months, and, if required, the aircraft has had a 100-hour inspection within the last 100 flight hours. Certain systems and components require periodic inspections. ATC transponders must be tested and inspected every 24 calendar months, and as previously mentioned, ELTs must be inspected every 12 months. In addition, for IFR operations in controlled airspace, altimeter systems and altitude reporting equipment must be tested and inspected every 24 calendar months.

EXERCISES

1. _____ (True, False) Without a Minimum Equipment List (MEL) there is no way you can fly an aircraft if an instrument or piece of equipment fails.

2. _____ (True, False) You, as the pilot in command, are responsible for the final determination of the aircraft's overall airworthiness.

3. How many questions must you ask yourself to determine if an aircraft with an inoperative component is airworthy?

4. All aircraft must go through a(n) _____ inspection to remain airworthy.

SAMPLE ORAL QUESTIONS

1. List the four questions you must ask yourself to determine if an aircraft with an inoperative component is airworthy.

____

____

____

____

____

____

____

2. What items must be contained within an application for a special flight permit?

____

____

____

____

____

____

1. The first question you must ask is whether the inoperative instrument or item of equipment is required for VFR-day as stipulated on all standard U.S. certificated aircraft. If the equipment is not required for VFR-day flights, you must ask yourself if it's required by the aircraft's equipment list or Kinds of Operations Equipment List. The third question you must ask is whether the item is required for the specific kind of flight operation being conducted. The final question you must ask is whether the inoperative instrument or item is required by an Airworthiness Directive (AD).

2. When applying for a special flight permit, you must submit a statement in a form and manner prescribed by the Administrator, indicating:
   1— The purpose of the flight
   2— The proposed itinerary
   3— The required crew members needed to fly the aircraft and operate the equipment
   4— The ways in which the aircraft does not comply with the applicable airworthiness requirements
   5— Any restriction you consider necessary for safe operation of the aircraft
   6— Any other information considered necessary by the Administrator for the purpose of prescribing operating limitations

3. Why does an inoperative piece of equipment have to be placarded inoperative?

3. The purpose of the placard is to remind you, future operators, and maintenance personnel that the equipment is inoperative.

ADDITIONAL QUESTIONS

4. List the required maintenance inspections for your aircraft.

5. Where can you find a list of the equipment required for VFR-day flight?

6. Where can you find the equipment list for an aircraft manufactured after 1975?

7. Where can you find a Kinds of Operations Equipment List for the aircraft you fly?

EXERCISE ANSWERS

1. False

2. True

3. Four

4. Annual

REFERENCES

JEPPESEN:

Private Pilot Manual - Chapter 1A

FAA:

Federal Aviation Regulations
Airplane Flying Handbook (FAA-H-8083-3)
Pilot's Handbook of Aeronautical Knowledge (AC 61-23/FAA-H-8083-25)
Pilots Operating Handbook and FAA-Approved Airplane Flight Manual

C. TASK: WEATHER INFORMATION (ASEL AND ASES)

REFERENCES: 14 CFR part 91; AC 00-6, AC 00-45, AC 61-23/FAA-H-8083-25, AC 61-84; AIM.

Objective: To determine that the applicant:

1. Exhibits knowledge of the elements related to weather information by analyzing weather reports, charts, and forecasts from various sources with emphasis on —
   a. METAR, TAF, and FA.
   b. surface analysis chart.
   c. radar summary chart.
   d. winds and temperatures aloft chart.
   e. significant weather prognostic charts.
   f. convective outlook chart.
   g. AWOS, ASOS, and ATIS reports.
2. Makes a competent "go/no-go" decision based on available weather information.

Objective: To determine that the applicant:

1. Exhibits knowledge of the elements related to weather information by analyzing weather reports, charts, and forecasts from various sources with emphasis on –

a. METAR, TAF, and FA.
b. surface analysis chart.
c. radar summary chart.
d. winds and temperatures aloft chart.
e. significant weather prognostic charts.
f. convective outlook chart.
g. AWOS, ASOS, and ATIS reports.

WEATHER

To make effective use of printed weather reports and forecasts, you need to have a good understanding of weather theory, patterns, and hazards. In addition to being able to apply basic weather theory, you need to develop the ability to interpret weather data. To reinforce your knowledge, we recommend that you review the weather information in your textbook. You will find several sample questions in the EXERCISES and SAMPLE QUESTIONS portions of this task to help you prepare for possible oral questions dealing with weather theory.

METAR, TAF, AND FA

An observation of surface weather that is reported and transmitted is called an **aviation routine weather report** (METAR). A prediction of surface weather expected at an airport is a **terminal aerodrome forecast** (TAF). An **area forecast** (FA) predicts general weather conditions over a wide area, and is a good source of information for enroute weather. Note that a METAR is a report of observed weather that actually exists at that site, while the TAF and FA are forecasts that predict what the weather will be in the next few hours.

METAR

The key to easy interpretation is learning the order in which the information is presented, as well as the common abbreviations, symbols, and word contractions used. After a little practice, you will find the METAR becoming easier to read. The report usually contains ten separate elements, which are discussed in the following paragraphs. [See Figure 1-5 on page 1-12]

TYPE OF REPORT

The two types of weather reports are the scheduled METAR, which is taken every hour, and the aviation selected special weather report (SPECI). The special METAR weather observation is an unscheduled report indicating a significant change in one or more elements.

STATION DESIGNATOR AND DATE/TIME OF REPORT

Each reporting station is listed by its four-letter International Civil Aviation Organization (ICAO) identifier. In the contiguous 48 states, the letter "K" precedes the three-letter domestic location identifier. For example, the domestic identifier for Denver is DEN, and the ICAO identifier is KDEN. In other areas of the world, the first two letters indicate the region, country, or state. Identifiers for Alaska begin with "PA," for Hawaii, they begin with "PH," and for Canada, the prefixes are "CU," "CW," "CY," and "CZ." A list of station designators is usually available at an FSS or NWS office. You can also use the Airport/Facility Directory to decode the identifiers.

Following the station identifier is the date (day of the month) and time of the observation. The time is given in UTC or Zulu, as indicated by the Z following the time.

MODIFIER

When a METAR is created by a totally automated weather observation station, the modifier AUTO will follow the date/time element. These stations are grouped by the type of sensor equipment used to make the observations, and A01 or A02 will be noted in the remarks section of the report. RMK A02 indicates the weather observing equipment used has the capability of distinguishing precipitation type. The modifier COR is used to indicate a corrected METAR that replaces a previously disseminated report. When the abbreviation COR is used, the station type designator, A01 or A02, is removed from the remarks section. No modifier indicates a manual station, or manual input at an automated station.

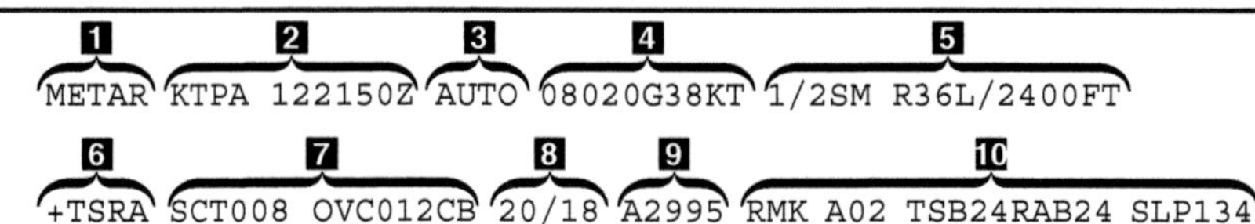

1 Type of Report

METAR Hourly Observation
SPECI Special, unscheduled report

2 Station Designator and Date/Time

Four-letter ICAO location identifier
Date and Time of report in Zulu (UTC)

3 Modifier

Auto = Automated
COR = Corrected

4 Wind Information

First three digits = Direction, or VRB = Variable
Next two digits = Speed in knots (KT), or three digits if speed >99KT. G = highest gust, followed by speed. 00000KT = calm

5 Visibility

Prevailing visibility, statute miles (SM). Runway visual range:
R, runway number, / , visual range in feet (FT).

6 Present Weather

Intensity: -light, +heavy, no sign for moderate.

Proximity: VC = weather 5 to 10 miles from airport center

Descriptor: for precipitation or obstructions to visibility:

TS Thunderstorm	DR low drifting
SH Shower(s)	MI Shallow
FZ Freezing	BC Patches
BL Blowing	PR Partial

Precipitation types:

RA Rain	GR Hail (1/4" increments)
DZ Drizzle	GS Small hail/snow pellets
SN Snow	PE Ice Pellets
SG Snow grains	IC Ice Crystals
	UP Unknown Precipitation (Automated stations only)

Obscurations to visibility:

FG Fog (vsby<5/8SM)	PY Spray
BR Mist (vsby 5/8 to 6SM)	SA Sand
FU Smoke	DU Widespread Dust
HZ Haze	VA Volcanic Ash

Other Phenomena:

SQ Squalls	SS Sandstorm
DS Duststorm	PO Dust/Sand swirls
FC Funnel cloud	+FC Tornado or Waterspout

7 Sky Condition

Amount of sky cover:
SKC Clear (no clouds)
FEW (Less than 1/8 to 2/8 sky cover)
SCT Scattered (3/8 to 4/8 sky cover)
BKN Broken (5/8 to 7/8 sky cover)
OVC Overcast (8/8 sky cover)

Height: three digits in hundreds of feet AGL

Type: towering cumulus (TCU) or cumulonimbus (CB) clouds reported after the height of their base.
Vertical visibility (VV): height into a total obscuration in hundreds of feet.

8 Temperature/Dew Point

Degrees Celsius, two-digit form. Prefixed "M" = minus (below zero)

9 Altimeter

Inches of mercury, prefixed by "A".

10 Remarks

Prefixed by "RMK"
A01 or A02 = Station type (automated)
PK WND 28045/30 = Peak wind from 280, 45 knots, at 30 minutes past the hour.
WSHFT 30 FROPA = Wind shift accompanied by frontal passage beginning at 30 minutes after the hour.
B (Began) or E (Ended) followed by time (minutes after the hour).
TS SE MOV NE = Thunderstorms southeast moving northeast
SLP134 = Sea level pressure in hectoPascals (1013.4 hPa)

DECODED REPORT: Routine observation for Tampa, FL, on the 12th day of the month at 2150 UTC. Automated Station. Wind from 080 at 20 knots with gusts to 38 knots. Prevailing visibility 1/2 statute mile, runway 36 Left visual range 2,400 feet. Thunderstorm with heavy rain. Scattered clouds at 800 feet AGL, overcast cumulonimbus clouds with bases of 1,200 feet AGL. Temperature 20C, dewpoint 18C. Altimeter setting 29.95 inches of mercury. Remarks: Automated station, precipitation discriminator indicated by A02, thunderstorm began 24 minutes past the hour, rain began 24 minutes past the hour, sea level pressure 1013.4 hectoPascals (Note: 1 hPa = 1 millibar).

Figure 1-5. A METAR usually contains most of these elements. If an element cannot be observed at the time of the report, it will be omitted. An item also may be omitted if it is not occurring at the observation time. It may be helpful to refer back to this example as you read the description of each element.

WIND INFORMATION

The wind direction and speed are reported in a five-digit group, or six digits if the speed is over 99 knots. The first three digits represent the direction from which the wind is blowing, in reference to true north. If the direction is variable, the letters "VRB" are used. The next two (or three) digits show the speed in knots (KT). Calm winds are reported as "00000KT."

If the wind direction varies 60° or more and the speed is above six knots, a variable group follows the wind group. The extremes of wind direction are shown, separated by a "V." For example, if the wind is blowing from 020°, varying to 090°, it is reported as "020V090."

In addition to direction and speed, the character, or type, of wind may be reported. Gusty winds are reported with a "G," followed by the highest gust. For example, wind from 080° at 32 knots with gusts to 45 is reported as 08032G45. [Figure 1-6]

VISIBILITY

Prevailing visibility is the greatest distance an observer can see and identify objects through at least half of the horizon. Visibility is reported in statute miles with "SM" appended to it. Examples are 1/2SM for one half statute mile and 7SM for seven statute miles. When **runway visual range (RVR)** is reported, it follows prevailing visibility. It is designated with an "R," followed by the runway number, a "/," and the visual range in feet (FT). For example, R32L/1200FT means runway 32 left visual range is 1,200 feet. Variable RVR is shown as the lowest and highest visual range val-

Coded Data	Explanations
00000KT	Calm
20014KT	Wind from 200 at 14 knots
15010G25	Wind from 150 at 10 knots, gusts to 25 knots
VRB04KT	Wind variable in direction at 4 knots
210103G130KT	Wind from 210 at 103 knots with gusts to 130 knots

Figure 1-6. This figure shows several examples of wind information as it appears on the METAR. The decoded wind direction, speed, and character are shown to the right.

ues separated by a "V." Outside the United States, RVR is normally reported in meters.

PRESENT WEATHER

When weather or obscurations to vision are present at the time of the observation, you will find them immediately after the visibility. The type of precipitation or obscuration is shown in codes, preceded by intensity symbols, proximity, and descriptor. Intensity levels are shown as light (-), moderate (no sign), or heavy (+). Weather obscurations occurring between 5 and 10 statute miles of the airport are shown by the letters "VC." For precipitation, VC applies within 10 statute miles of the observation point.

Next is a descriptor of the precipitation or obscurations to visibility. For example, blowing snow is reported as BLSN, freezing drizzle as FZDZ, and a thunderstorm in the vicinity of the airport with moderate rain is reported as VCTSRA. Some typical obscurations to visibility are smoke (FU), haze (HZ), and dust (DU). Fog (FG) is listed when the visibility is less than 5/8 mile, and when it is between 5/8 and 6 miles, the code for mist (BR) is used. For instance, when fog causes a visibility of 1/4 mile, it is reported as 1/4SM FG. If mist and haze reduce visibility to 1-1/2 miles, it is shown as 1 1/2SM BR HZ. Following the obscurations, other weather phenomena may be listed, such as sandstorm (SS), duststorm (DS), or a funnel cloud (FC).

SKY CONDITION

The extent of clouds covering the sky is reported in eighths of sky cover. A clear sky is designated by SKC in a manual report and CLR in an automated report. FEW is used when cloud coverage is 1/8 to 2/8. However, any amount less than 1/8 can also be reported as FEW. Scattered clouds, which cover 3/8 to 4/8 of the sky, are shown by SCT. Broken clouds, covering 5/8 to 7/8 of the sky, are designated by BKN, while an overcast sky is reported as OVC.

The height of clouds or the vertical visibility into obscuring phenomena is reported with three digits in hundreds of feet above ground level (AGL). To determine the cloud height, add two zeros to the number given in the report. When more than one layer is present, the layers are reported in ascending order. However, the sky cover condition for any higher layers represents total sky coverage, which includes any lower layer. For example, a scattered layer at 900 feet and a broken layer at 3,000 feet AGL would be reported as SCT009 BKN030. In addition, if towering cumulus clouds (TCU) or cumulonimbus clouds (CB) are present, their code is shown following the height of their base, such as BKN040TCU or OVC050CB.

Although not designated by a METAR code, a ceiling is the AGL height of the lowest layer of clouds aloft that is reported as broken or overcast, or the vertical visibility into an obscuration, such as fog or haze. In general terms, a ceiling exists when more than half of the sky is covered.

A ceiling is usually determined with an electronic device called a rotating beam ceilometer. Other means may also be used, such as a ceiling light, cloud detection radar, or by the unobscured portion of a landmark that rises into the ceiling layer. Ceiling heights may also be estimated by the use of pilot reports, balloons, or other measurements. When a ceiling is estimated from a pilot report, the MSL altitude reported by the pilot is converted to an AGL height. Balloon-estimated ceilings are based on the time it takes for the balloon to ascend, and they may be inaccurate because of convective air currents. Other measurements include estimates by meteorologists who must rely on experience and knowledge of cloud formations.

TEMPERATURE AND DEWPOINT

The current air temperature and dewpoint are reported in two-digit form in degrees Celsius and are separated by a slash. For example, "18/09" indicates a surface temperature of 18°C and a dewpoint of 9°C. Temperatures below 0° Celsius are prefixed with an "M" to indicate minus. For instance, 10° below zero would be shown as M10. Temperature and dewpoint also may be added to remarks in an eight-digit format showing tenths of °C.

ALTIMETER

The altimeter setting is reported in inches of mercury in a four-digit group without the decimal point, and is preceded by an "A." An example is A3012, indicating an altimeter setting of three zero point one two inches. Altimeter settings reflect local station pressure.

REMARKS

Certain remarks are included to report weather considered significant to aircraft operations. The types of information that may be included are wind data, variable visibility, beginning and ending times of a particular weather phenomena, pressure information, and temperature/dewpoint in tenths °C. In most cases, you will notice more remarks when the weather is bad and the airport is approved for IFR operations. The remarks section begins with "RMK." The beginning of an event is shown by a "B:" followed by the time in minutes after the hour. The ending time is noted by an "E" and the time in minutes. [Figure 1-7]

Coded Data	Explanations
A02	Automated station with precipitation discriminator
PK WND 20032/25	Peak wind from 200 at 32 knots, 25 minutes past the hour
VIS 3/4V1 1/2	Prevailing visibility variable 3/4 to 1 and 1/2 miles
FRQ LTG NE	Frequent lightning to the northeast
FZDZB45	Freezing drizzle began at 45 past the hour
RAE42SNB42	Rain ended and snow began at 42 past the hour
PRESFR	Pressure falling rapidly
SLP045	Sea level pressure in hectoPascals and tenths, 1004.5 hPa
T00081016	Temperature/dewpoint in tenths C, .8 C/–1.6 C

Figure 1-7. Examples of coded remarks are shown in the left column, with the corresponding explanations on the right.

ADDITIONAL REPORTS

For a more complete picture, you may also refer to separate reports or messages that provide specific information for pilots. These include freezing level reports, notices to airmen, and radar weather reports.

Freezing level data is available at airports where upper air observations are taken. You can identify this information by the letters RADAT, followed by a coded group of numbers. RADATs contain information on the relative humidity at the freezing level or levels. Up to three freezing levels (low, medium, and high) may be reported. "RADAT 87045," for instance, means the relative humidity is 87 percent and the freezing level is at 4,500 feet MSL. Later, you will see that freezing level information is also indicated on some weather forecasts and charts.

Notices to Airmen (NOTAMs) are transmitted as separate lines of information. NOTAMs report changes in the status of airports or airway facilities that could affect your decision to make a flight. They include such information as runway closures, obstructions in the approach and departure paths to airports, and outages or curtailed operation hours of navaids and ATC facilities.

General areas of precipitation, especially thunderstorms, are observed by radar on a routine basis. Most radar stations issue **radar weather reports** (SDs) each hour, with intervening special reports as required. These reports are routinely transmitted on weather service circuits and some are included in FSS weather broadcasts.

SDs not only define the areas of precipitation, they also provide information on the type, intensity, and trend. In addition, these reports normally include movement (direction and speed) of the precipitation areas, as well as maximum height. When the clouds extend to high levels, thunderstorms are likely. This means you can expect turbulence and the possibility of hail.

TAF

Terminal Aerodrome Forecasts (TAFs) normally are scheduled four times a day at 0000Z, 0600Z, 1200Z, and 1800Z. Each forecast is made for a 24-hour period. Each TAF contains these elements: type, location, issuance date and time, valid date and time, and the forecast. With few exceptions, the codes used in the TAF are the same as those used for METAR.

TYPE OF REPORT

The terminal forecast will either be a routine TAF, or an amended forecast (TAF AMD). An amended TAF is issued when the current TAF no longer represents the expected weather. TAF or TAF AMD appears in a header line prior to the text of the forecast. If a TAF is corrected (COR) or delayed (RTD), it will be noted only in the header, which precedes the actual forecast. [Figure 1-8]

LOCATION IDENTIFIER AND ISSUANCE DATE/TIME

The four-letter ICAO location identifier is the same as that used for METAR. The first two numbers of the date/time group represent the day of the month, and the next four digits are the Zulu time that the forecast was issued.

VALID PERIOD

Normally, the forecast is valid for 24 hours. The first two digits represent the valid date. Next is the beginning hour of the valid time in Zulu, and the last two digits are the ending hour. For example, a valid period of 161212 means the forecast is valid for 24 hours, from 1200Z on the 16th to 1200Z the next day. The valid time may be less than 24 hours for an amended, corrected, or delayed TAF. At an airport that is open part time, amendments are not issued after closing time. If an airport closes at 0500Z, for instance, the TAF may include a statement such as, "NIL AMD NOT SKED AFT 0500Z." While part-time airports are closed, the word "NIL" appears in place of the forecast for those locations.

FORECAST

The body of the TAF contains codes for forecast wind, visibility, weather, and sky condition in much the same format as METAR. Weather, including obstructions to visibility, is added to the forecast only when it is significant to aviation. One difference between TAF and METAR is that forecast visibility greater than six miles is reported as P6SM, or plus six statute miles, in the TAF. In addition, TAFs may include the probability of thunderstorms or precipitation events and associated conditions. A PROB group is used when the probability of occurrence is between 30% and 49%, and is followed by a beginning and ending time. For example, PROB40 1923 TSRA forecasts a 40% chance of a thunderstorm with moderate rain between 1900Z and 2300Z.

When a significant permanent change to the weather conditions is expected during the valid time, a change group is used. If a rapid change, usually within one hour, is expected, the code for from (FM) is used with the time of change. A forecast of FM0600 16010KT indicates that around 0600Z, the wind will be from 160 degrees at 10 knots. This wind condition will continue until the next change group or the end of the valid time of the TAF.

A more gradual change in the weather, taking about two hours, is coded as BECMG, followed by beginning and ending times. For instance, the code BECMG 0608 21015KT P6SM NSW SCT040 means that between 0600Z and 0800Z the weather will gradually change, wind becoming 210 degrees at 15 knots, visibility greater than 6 statute miles, no significant weather, sky scattered at 4,000 feet.

Conditions that are expected to last less than an hour at a time are described in a temporary (TEMPO) group,

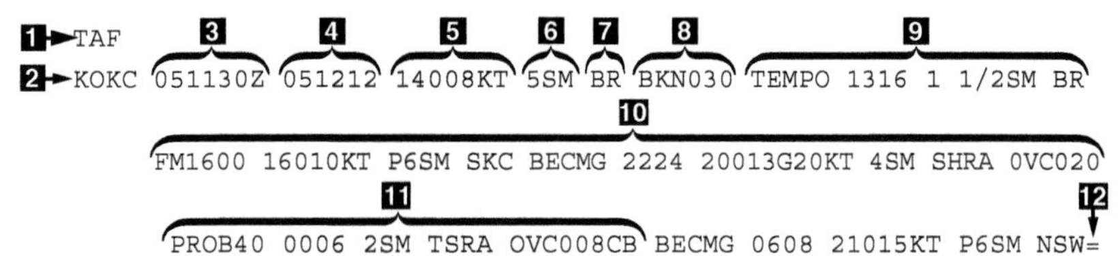

1 **Type of Report** – Routine terminal aerodrome forecast (TAF)

2 **Location Identifier** – ICAO four-letter identifier

3 **Issuance Data and Time** – Two-digit day of the month and the time in Zulu (Z)

4 **Valid Period** – TAF valid time, two-digit date followed by the beginning and ending hours in Zulu

Forecast Elements: Wind/Visibility/Weather/Sky Condition

5 **Wind** – Three-digit direction, two-or three-digit speed in knots (KT)

6 **Visibility** – Expected prevailing visibility in statute miles. Forecast visibility greater than 6 miles is coded as P6SM (plus 6 SM).

7 **Weather** – Significant weather and obstructions to visibility

8 **Sky Condition** – Amount, height (CB) or vertical visibility
Cumulonimbus (CB) is the only type of cloud included in the TAF
North America TAFs will also include nonconvective low-level wind shear (WS), up to 2000 feet. When forecast, WS will appear after the cloud forecast group

9 **Temporary Conditions** – (TEMPO) Fluctuations expected to last less than an hour in each instance and, in aggregate, to cover less than half of the period, two-digit beginning time, in hours, and two-digit ending time, also in hours

10 **Forecast Change Group** – Significant, permanent changes in conditions; from (FM), four-digit hour and minute time the change is expected to begin; or becoming (BECMG) with a four-digit time group to indicate beginning hour and ending hour times

11 **Probability Forecast** – Probability of thunderstorms or precipitation (in percent), along with associated weather conditions (wind, visibility, and sky condition); the four-digit beginning hour and ending hour follows the abbreviation PROB40

12 **End of Report Separator** – (=)

DECODED REPORT:
Routine TAF for Oklahoma City, OK...on the 5th day of the month, at 1130Z...valid for 24 hours from 1200Z on the 5th to 1200Z on the 6th...Wind from 140 at 8 knots...visibility 5 statute miles in mist...broken clouds at 3,000 feet...Temporary condition, between 1300Z and 1600Z, 1 1/2 statue miles visibility in mist...From 1600Z, wind from 160 at 10 knots...visibility greater than 6 miles and sky clear...Becoming, between 2200Z and 2400Z, wind from 200 at 13 knots, gusting to 20 knots, visibility 4 miles with moderate rain showers, sky overcast at 2000 feet...Between midnight (0000Z) and 0600Z, a 40% probability of 2 statute miles visibility with thunderstorms and moderate rain, sky overcast with the bases of cumulonimbus clouds at 800 feet AGL...Becoming, 0600Z to 0800Z, wind 210 at 15 knots, visibility greater than 6 statute miles and no significant weather.

Figure 1-8. TAF codes are similar to those used in the METAR. This example shows the National Weather Service TAF format. The format for TAFs transmitted by FAA weather briefers may be slightly different.

followed by beginning and ending times. An example would be 5 miles of visibility in mist, but between 0100Z and 0500Z visibility of 1 mile in low drifting snow. These conditions would appear in the TAF as: 5SM BR TEMPO 0105 1SM DRSN.

AREA FORECASTS

An **area forecast** (FA) covers general weather conditions over a wide area, and can also help you determine the conditions at airports that do not have terminal forecasts. FAs are issued three times a day in the 48 mainland states. Weather Service Forecast Offices issue FAs for Hawaii and Alaska; however, the Alaska FA utilizes a different format. An additional specialized FA is issued for the Gulf of Mexico by the National Hurricane Center in Miami, FL.

The FA is comprised of four sections: a communications and product header section, a precautionary statement section, and two weather sections; a SYNOPSIS section and a VFR CLOUDS/WX section. Each area forecast covers an 18-hour period. [See Figure 1-9 on page 1-16]

In the heading "SLCC FA 141045," the "SLC" identifies the Salt Lake City forecast area, "C" indicates the product contains a Clouds and Weather forecast, "FA" means area forecast, and "141045" tells you this forecast was issued on the 14th day of the month at 1045 Zulu. Since these forecasts are rounded to the nearest full hour, the valid time for the report begins at 1100Z. The synopsis is valid until 18 hours later, which is shown as the 15th at 0500Z. The Clouds and Weather section forecast is valid for a 12-hour period, until 2300Z on the 14th. The outlook portion is valid for six hours following the forecast, from 2300Z on the 14th to 0500Z on the 15th. The last line of the header lists the states that are included in the Salt Lake City forecast area.

Following the headers are three precautionary statements which are part of all FAs. The first alerts you to check the latest AIRMET Sierra, which describes areas of mountain obscuration that may be forecast for the area. The next statement is a reminder that thunderstorms imply possible severe or greater turbulence, severe icing, low-level wind shear, and instrument conditions. Therefore, when

```
1  SLCC FA 141045
   SYNOPSIS AND VFR CLDS/WX
   SYNOPSIS VALID UNTIL 150500
   CLDS/WX VALID UNTIL 142300...OTLK VALID 142300-150500
   ID MT NV UT WY CO AZ NM

2  SEE AIRMET SIERRA FOR IFR CONDS AND MTN OBSCN.
   TSTMS IMPLY PSBL SVR OR GTR TURBC SVR ICG LLWS
   AND IFR CONDS.

   NON MSL HGTS ARE DENOTED BY AGL OR CIG.

3  SYNOPSIS...HIGH PRES OVER NERN MT CONTG EWD
   GRDLY. LOW PRES OVR AZ NM AND WRN TX RMNG
   GENLY STNRY. ALF...TROF EXTDS FROM WRN MT INTO
   SRN AZ RMNG STNRY..

4  .
   ID MT
   FROM YXH TO SHR TO 30SE BZN TO 60SE PIH TO LKT TO
   YXC TO YXH.
   70-90 SCT-BKN 120-150. WDLY SCT RW-. TOPS SHWRS 180.
   OTLK...VFR
   RMNDR AREA...100-120. ISOLD RW-MNLY ERN PTNS AREA.
   OTLK...VFR

   .
   UT NV NM AZ
   80 SCT-BKN 150-200. WDLY SCT RW-/TRW-. CB TOPS 450.
   OTLK...VFR

   .
   WY CO
   FROM BZN TO GCC TO LBL TO DVC TO RKS TO BZN.
   70-90 BKN-OVC 200. OCNL VSBY 3R-F. AFT 20Z WDLY SCT
   TRW-. CB TOPS 450. OTLK...MVFR CIG RW.
```

1 Heading Section 3 Synopsis

2 Precautionary Statements 4 VFR Clouds and Weather

Figure 1-9. The area forecast has four sections, beginning with a communications and product header, which identifies the area and provides the valid times. Area forecasts contain standard abbreviations and word contractions. The information in this sample forecast is interpreted in the accompanying paragraphs.

thunderstorms are forecast, these hazards are not included in the body of the FA. The third statement reminds you that heights that are not MSL are noted by the letters AGL (above ground level) or CIG (ceiling). All heights are expressed in hundreds of feet.

The synopsis is a brief description of the location and movement of fronts, pressure systems, and circulation patterns in the FA area over an 18-hour period. When appropriate, forecasters may use terms describing ceilings and visibilities, strong winds, or other phenomena. In the example, high pressure over northeastern Montana will continue moving gradually eastward. A low pressure system over Arizona, New Mexico, and western Texas will remain generally stationary. Aloft (ALF), a trough of low pressure extending from western Montana into southern Arizona is expected to remain stationary.

The VFR Clouds and Weather (VFR CLDS/WX) portion is usually broken down by states or geographical regions. It describes clouds and weather which cover an area of 3,000 square miles or more, and that could affect VFR operations. The forecast is valid for 12 hours, and is followed by a six-hour categorical outlook (18 hours in Alaska).

When the surface visibility is expected to be six statute miles or less, the visibility and obstructions to vision are included in the forecast. When precipitation, thunderstorms, and sustained winds of 20 knots or greater are forecast, they will be included in this section. The term OCNL (occasional) is used when there is a 50% or greater probability of cloud or visibility conditions that could affect VFR flight. The percentage of an area covered by showers or thunderstorms is indicated by the terms ISOLD (isolated, meaning single cells), WDLY SCT (widely scattered, less than 25% of the area), SCT or AREAS (25 to 54% of the area), and NMRS or WDSPRD (numerous or widespread, 55% or more of the area). In addition, the term ISOLD is sometimes used to describe areas of ceilings or visibilities that are expected to affect areas of less than 3,000 square miles.

The outlook follows the main body of the forecast, and gives a general description of the expected weather, using the terms VFR, IFR, or MVFR (marginal VFR). Ceilings less than 1,000 feet and/or visibility less than 3 miles is considered IFR. Marginal VFR areas are those with ceilings from 1,000 to 3,000 feet and/or visibility between 3 and 5 miles. Abbreviations are used to describe causes of IFR or MVFR weather. Ceilings are noted by CIG, and restrictions to visibility are described by codes such as TRW, F, L, or BD.

Let's take a look at a portion of the VFR CLDS/WX section in our example. For Wyoming and Colorado, three-letter identifiers outline an area of coverage for the specific forecast. This area extends from Bozeman, MT, to Gillette, WY, to Liberal, KS, to Dove Creek, WY, to Rock Springs, WY, and back to Bozeman. As mentioned previously under the header, the valid time begins on the 14th day of the month at 1100Z for a 12-hour period. A broken to overcast cloud layer begins between 7,000 to 9,000 feet MSL, with tops extending to 20,000 feet. Since visibility and wind information is omitted, the visibility is expected to be greater than six statute miles, and the wind less than 20 knots. However, the visibility is forecast to be occasionally 3 miles in light rain and fog. After 2000Z, widely scattered thunderstorms with light rain showers are expected, with cumulonimbus (CB) cloud tops to 45,000 feet. The 6-hour categorical outlook covers the period from 2300Z on the 14th to 0500Z on the 15th. The forecast is for marginal VFR weather due to ceilings (CIG) and rain showers.

Amendments to FAs are issued whenever the weather significantly improves or deteriorates, based on the judgment of the forecaster. An amended FA is identified by the contraction "AMD" in the header along with the time of the amended forecast. When an FA is corrected, the contraction "COR" appears in the heading, along with the time of the correction.

SURFACE ANALYSIS CHARTS

The surface analysis chart graphically shows fronts, high and low pressure systems, and surface weather conditions for the contiguous 48 states and adjacent areas. The computer-generated chart is issued every three hours. Besides large-scale phenomena such as fronts and pressure systems, the chart provides individual surface weather observations for hundreds of reporting points around the United States.

Lines connecting points of equal atmospheric pressure are called isobars. Where isobars are closer together, the difference in pressure is greater, so wind speeds are higher. Looking at the wind direction indicators, you will note that they point counterclockwise and inward toward a low pressure area. Conversely, the flow of wind is clockwise and outward from areas of higher pressure. In the northern hemisphere, if you stand with the wind at your back, an area of lower pressure will be to your left. [Figure 1-10]

The weather at specific observation stations is shown by individual station model icons. These symbols pack a surprising amount of information into a small space. Interpreting most of the symbols is easy, but you may need a key from an FAA or NWS publication to decode some of them. [See Figure 1-11 on page 1-18]

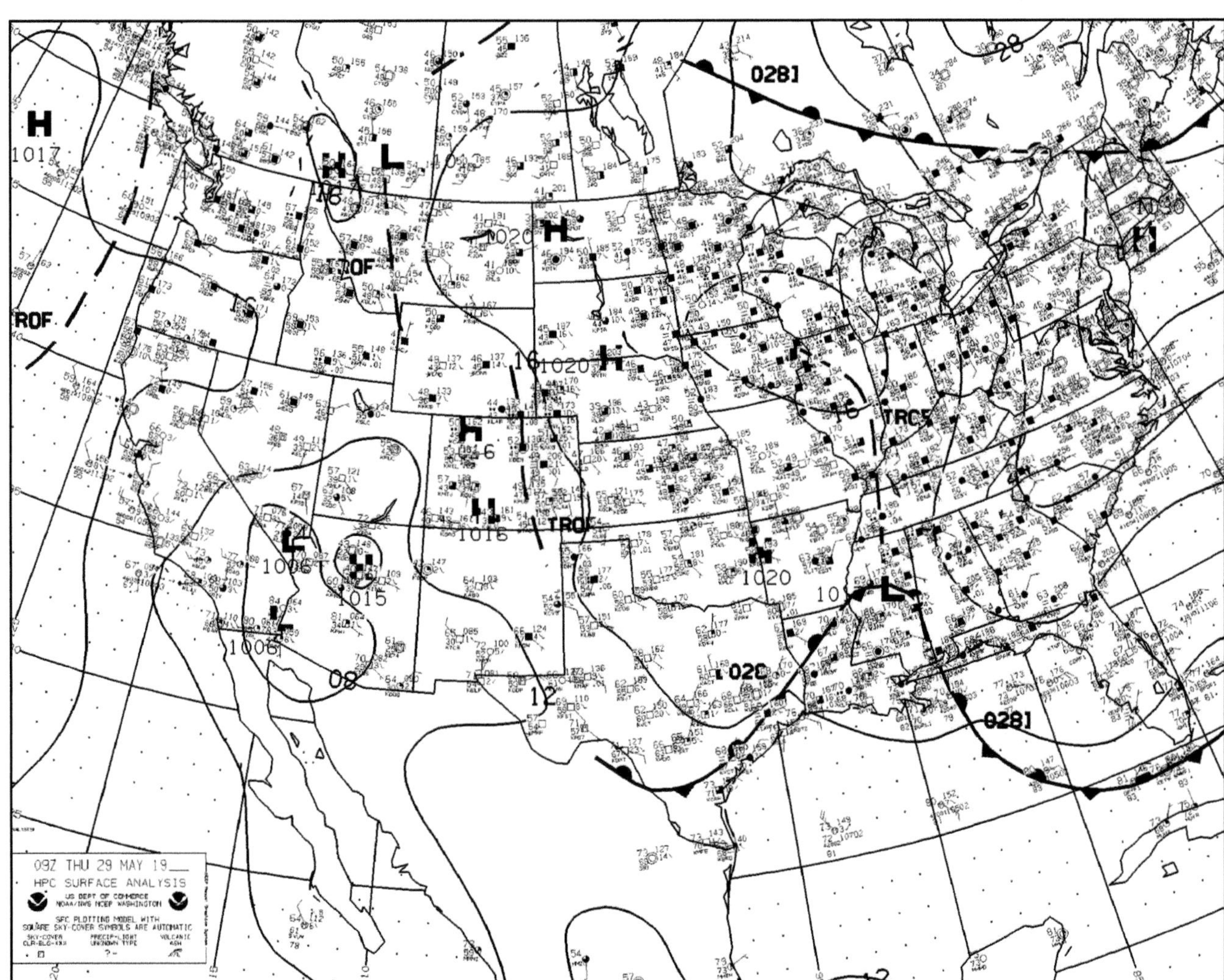

Figure 1-10. You can get a general picture of major weather systems from the surface analysis chart.

RADAR SUMMARY CHARTS

Radar summary charts (SD) are produced hourly at 35 minutes past the hour. By compiling information from weather radar sites across the country, these charts graphically depict areas of precipitation. They are most useful for showing areas of rain, storm cells, and lines of thunderstorms. The radar echoes show the approximate heights of precipitation activity, as well as contour lines to indicate intensity. Added symbols show severe weather watch areas, possible tornados, and the direction of movement of lines and cells. [Figure 1-12]

While radar summary charts are valuable flight planning tools, be sure to keep in mind their inherent limitations. Since radar can only provide information on precipitation of a certain size, these charts can show snow and rain, but may not show clouds, fog, or other weather phenomena. Likewise, the charts show conditions only as they were at the time of issue. By their nature, weather events such as thunderstorms and tornadoes develop and change rapidly, and conditions may be much different than depicted in the chart by the time you arrive in a given area. Always use these charts in conjunction with other weather information.

WINDS AND TEMPERATURES ALOFT

The winds and temperatures aloft forecasts (FD) are available in both chart and tabular form, and provide an estimate of wind direction in relation to true north, wind speed in knots, and the temperature in degrees Celsius at various altitudes. The chart version consists of eight panels, each depicting the winds forecast at a particular altitude, from 6,000 to 39,000 feet in 3,000 foot increments. FDs

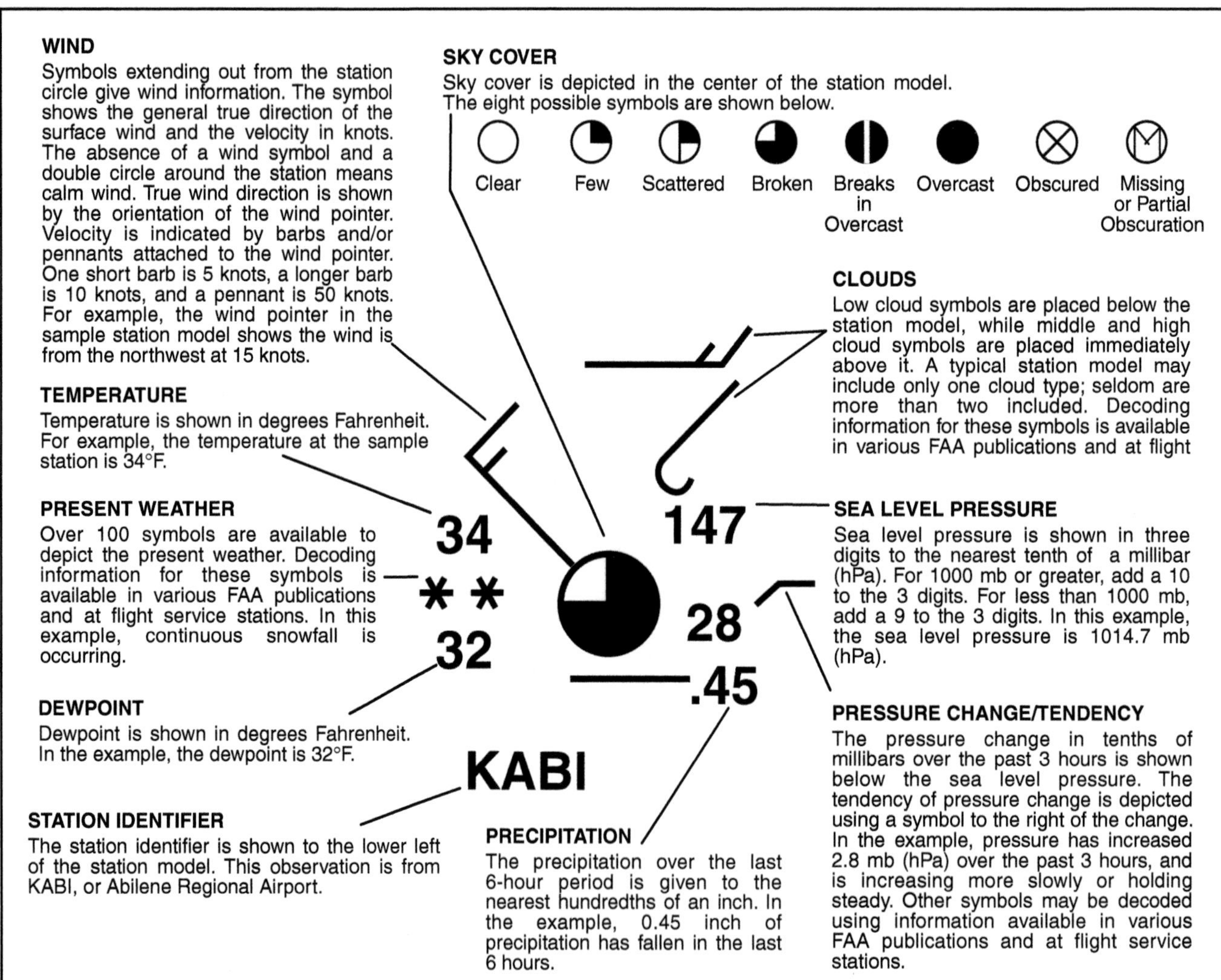

Figure 1-11. Round station symbols indicate that observations were taken by human weather observers, while square station symbols represent automated sites.

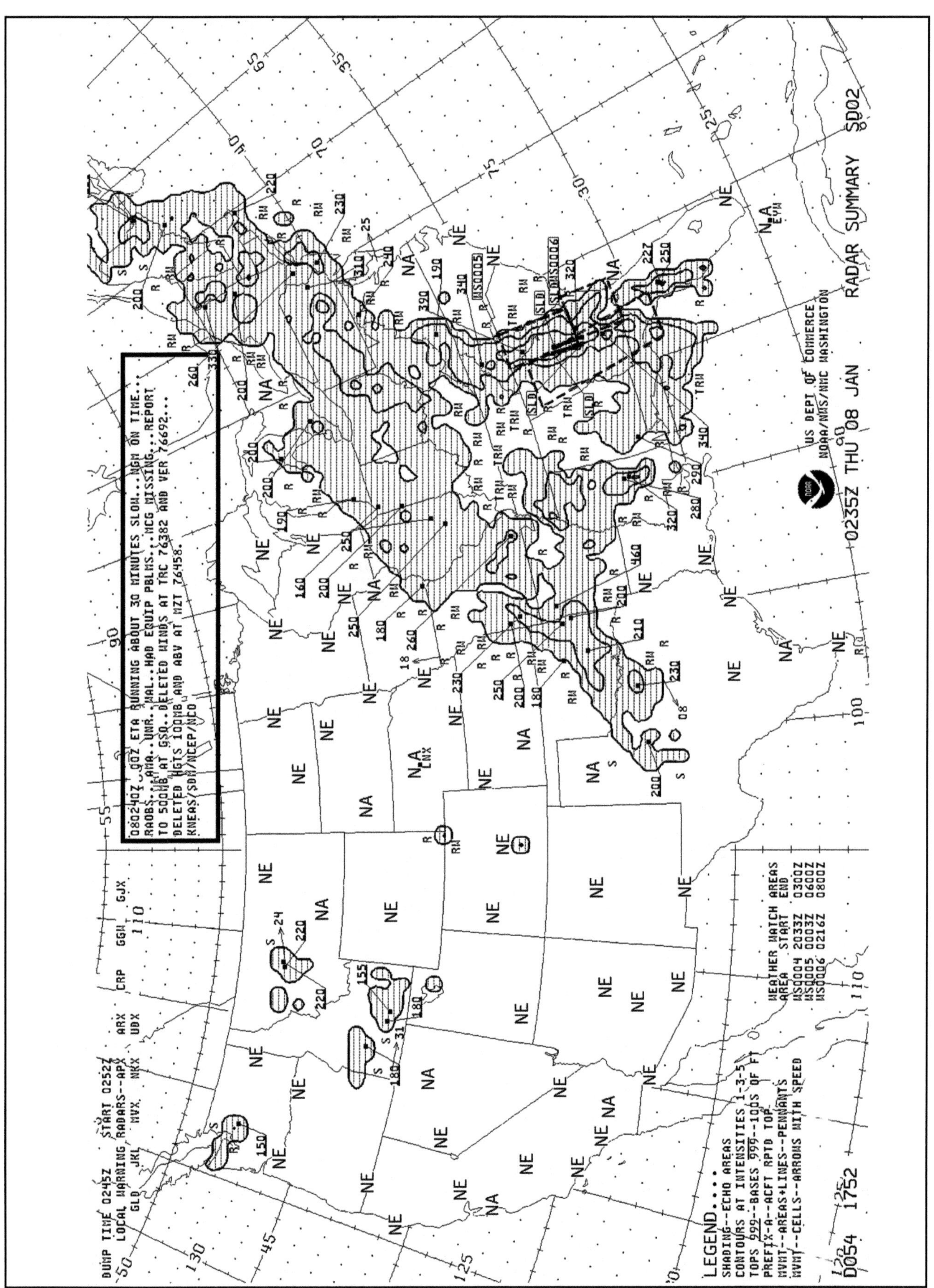

Figure 1-12. Keep in mind that radar summary charts show precipitation, not clouds, so cloud tops may be well above the precipitation heights shown.

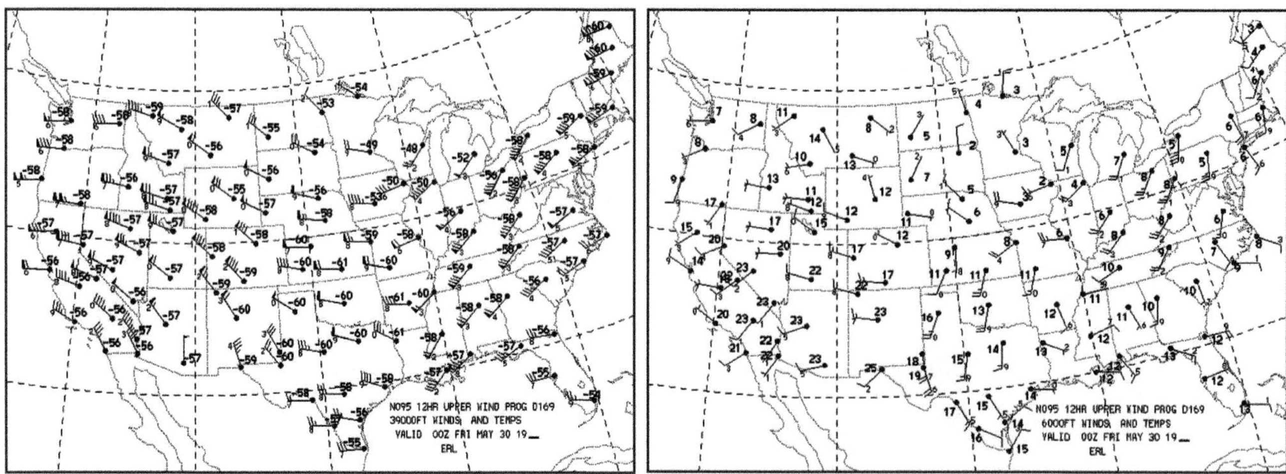

Figure 1-13. The symbology on the winds and temperatures aloft chart is similar to that used on surface analysis charts. Arrows show the wind direction at each station within ten degrees, and the single digit at the tip of the arrow provides the last digit of the direction. The familiar barbs and pennants are used to show wind speed, and the temperature is shown near the station circle in degrees Celsius.

do not include levels within 1,500 feet of the station elevation, and temperatures are not forecast for the 3,000-foot level or for a level within 2,500 feet of the station elevation. [Figure 1-13]

In the tabular format, the wind information is presented almost as it is on other reports and forecasts. Wind speeds between 100 and 199 knots are encoded so direction and speed can be represented by four digits. This is done by adding 50 to the two-digit wind direction and subtracting 100 from the velocity. For example, wind at 140° at 115 knots is indicated as "6415" (14 + 50 = 64 and 115 - 100 = 15). The code 9900 means light and variable.

SIGNIFICANT WEATHER PROGNOSTIC CHARTS

The U.S. low-level significant weather prognostic chart, usually called a prog chart, can give you an idea of general

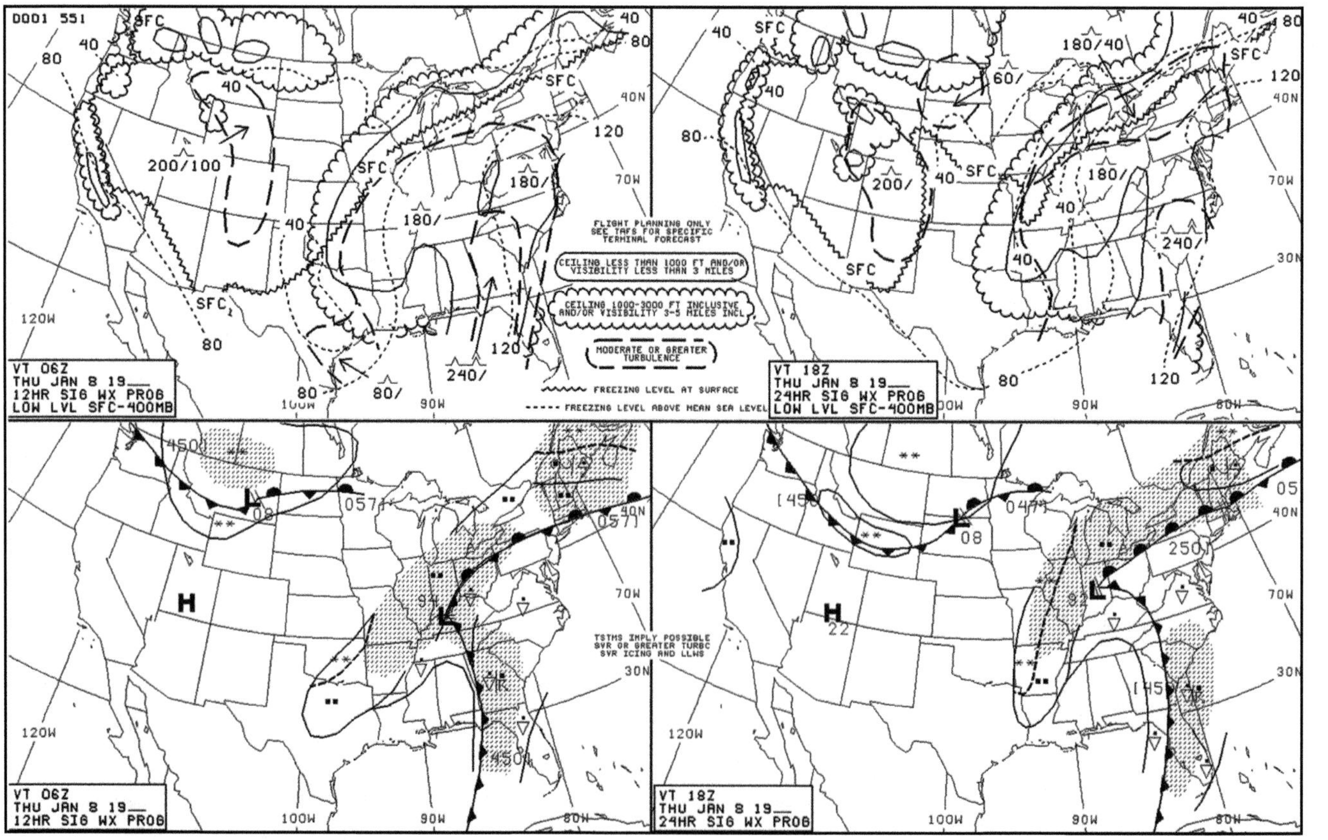

Figure 1-14. Significant weather prog charts are issued at 0000Z, 0600Z, 1200Z, and 2400Z. The two upper panels are the actual significant weather prog charts, showing expected conditions from the surface to 24,000 feet. The lower panels are a surface weather forecast, and show areas of precipitation along with fronts and pressure information.

weather conditions expected in the next 12-24 hours from the surface to 24,000 feet MSL. The two-panel significant weather prog is usually combined with a two-panel surface prog chart to create a four-panel graphic issued four times a day. The left-hand panels show weather that is forecast to exist 12 hours from the valid time, while the right hand panels show the 24-hour forecast. The chart primarily shows where you can expect areas of low visibility in terms of IFR and marginal VFR, as well as forecast areas of turbulence and icing. Note that the chart shows only areas of moderate or greater turbulence. [Figure 1-14]

There are also prognostic charts available for 36-48 hours (Day 2). These are similar to the 12-24 hour charts, except that they also show areas of broken or overcast cloud cover.

CONVECTIVE OUTLOOK CHARTS

To help show you where to expect thunderstorm activity, the Storm Prediction Center generates convective outlook charts (AC). These are issued five times a day, and forecast general as well as severe thunderstorms. They are issued as a two-panel chart, with the Day 1 panel depicting the forecast for the next 24 hours, and Day 2 showing the outlook for the following 24 hours. [Figure 1-15]

AIRMETS AND SIGMETS

When weather conditions develop outside of scheduled reports or forecasts, or a situation warrants particular attention, a special advisory is issued. The most common types of advisories are AIRMETs, SIGMETs, and Convective SIGMETs.

AIRMET (WA) is an acronym for "Airman's Meteorological Information." They are issued every six hours with amendments issued, as necessary, for weather phenomena which mainly concern light aircraft. AIRMETs are issued for moderate icing, moderate turbulence, sustained winds of 30 knots or more at the surface, ceilings less than 1,000 feet and/or visibility less than three miles affecting over 50 percent of an area at any one time, and extensive mountain obscurement. AIRMETs have fixed alphanumeric designators that identify the condition responsible for their issuance. They are: "Sierra," which identifies areas of IFR conditions, and mountain obscuration, "Tango," which indicates turbulence and strong winds/low-level wind shear, and "Zulu," which indicates icing.

The term **SIGMET** (WS) stands for "Significant Meteorological Information," and warns of weather hazards (other than convective activity) that concern pilots of all aircraft. SIGMET criteria include severe icing, severe and extreme turbulence, volcanic eruptions, dust storms, sandstorms, or volcanic ash lowering visibility to less than three miles. Nonconvective SIGMETs use consecutive alphanumeric designators November through Yankee excluding those designators reserved for scheduled AIRMETs.

Convective SIGMETs (WSTs) are issued for hazardous convective weather (existing or forecast) which is significant to the safety of all aircraft. They always imply severe or greater turbulence, severe icing, and low-level wind shear. WSTs are unscheduled and may be issued for any convective situation that the forecaster considers hazardous to all categories of aircraft. Convective SIGMETs include any of the following phenomena: tornadoes, lines of thunderstorms, thunderstorms over a wide area, embedded thunderstorms, hail three-fourths of an inch or more in diameter, and/or wind gusts to 50 knots or greater.

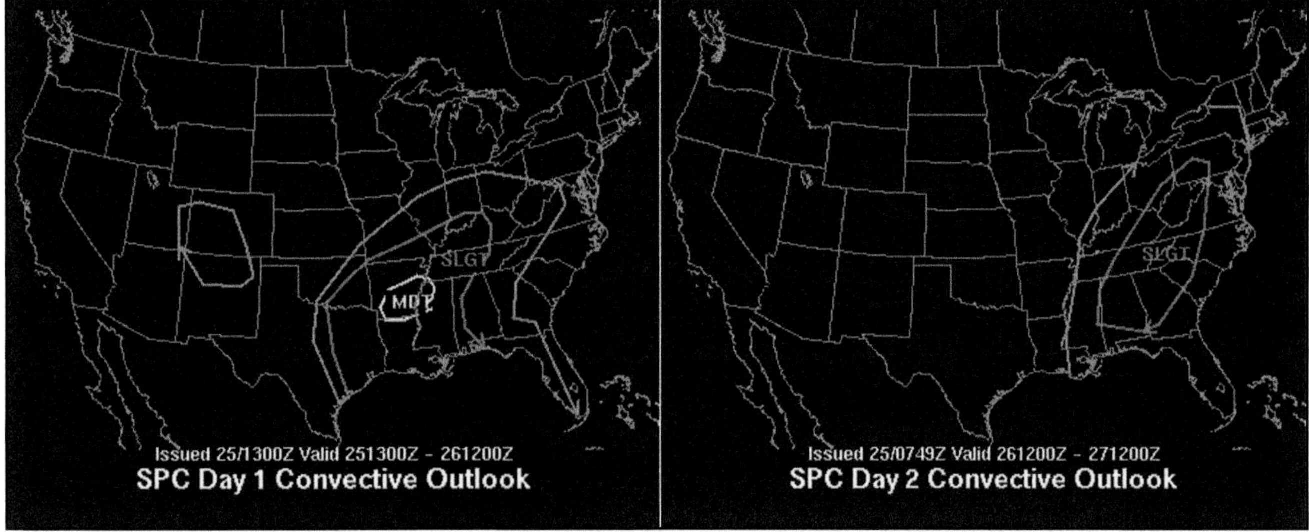

Figure 1-15. A line with an arrowhead shows the general thunderstorm activity forecast. Facing in the direction of the arrow, thunderstorm activity is expected to the right of the line. Areas of greater risk are outlined, and the risk is indicated by an abbreviation inside the outlined area, such as SLGT (slight), MDT (moderate), or HIGH.

PILOT REPORTS

As a pilot, there are some weather observations you can make that are better than even the best ground-based weather observer. When you communicate these observations to an FSS, your observation is known as a pilot report or PIREP.

Pilot reports confirm current weather conditions such as the height of bases and tops of cloud layers, in-flight visibility, icing conditions, and turbulence that are not routinely available from other observation sources. When you encounter unexpected weather conditions, you are encouraged to make a pilot report. Then your report is added to the distribution system, and can be used to brief other pilots or to provide in-flight advisories.

To make a pilot report, call an FSS or ATC facility. You should begin by stating the type of report you would like to make, either a standard PIREP or urgent PIREP. Then continue by reporting your location, the time in Zulu, your current altitude, the type of aircraft you are flying, the existing sky cover, any pertinent weather or restrictions to vision, the temperature in Celsius, the wind direction and velocity if available, any turbulence or icing, and any remarks necessary to clarify the report. Although PIREPs should be complete and concise, do not be overly concerned with strict format or terminology. The important thing is to make the report so other pilots can benefit from it.

WIND SHEAR REPORTS

Wind shear is described as a sudden, drastic shift in wind speed and/or direction that may occur at any altitude in a vertical or horizontal plane. Vertical wind shear can produce violent up and downdrafts, while a horizontal wind shear can result in a sudden change in indicated airspeed. The amount of change is directly related to how fast the wind speed or direction changes. Horizontal wind shear is especially hazardous during climbouts or approaches when your airspeed is low and angle of attack is high. Be alert for a sudden change in airspeed and carry an extra margin of speed if wind shear has been forecast or reported.

Some airports have a low-level wind shear alert system (LLWAS). Wind direction and speed are monitored and compared at several sites on and around the airport, and tower controllers will advise you if there is a significant difference between sensors that could indicate a possible wind shear.

AWOS, ASOS, AND ATIS REPORTS

Various automatic weather observation and reporting systems are available for your use both before and during a flight. You can usually access them by telephone while planning your flight, as well as listening to them on your aircraft radio for fresh updates in flight. They usually provide a 20-30 second weather message updated each minute.

The automated weather observing system (AWOS) uses various weather sensors, a voice synthesizer, and a radio transmitter to provide real-time reports of surface weather at over 700 sites around the country. Depending on the specific system, AWOS stations provide altimeter setting, wind speed, direction, and gusts, temperature, dewpoint, and visibility. The most capable system, AWOS-3, also includes cloud and ceiling information to 12,000 feet.

The Automated Surface Observation System (ASOS) is a somewhat newer system than ASOS, and is operating at more than 800 sites. It provides all the information of an AWOS-3 station, plus variable cloud height, variable visibility, rapid pressure changes, precipitation type, intensity, accumulation, and beginning and ending times, as well as wind shifts and peak winds. Some ASOS stations can determine the difference between liquid and frozen or freezing precipitation. While AWOS stations are either owned privately or by the FAA, ASOS is a joint venture of the National Weather Service, Department of Defense, and FAA.

The primary purpose of the Automatic Terminal Information Service (ATIS) is to provide detailed airport advisories to aircraft arriving and departing from busier airports, but you can also use it as a source of current weather information, whether you plan to use that particular airport or not. ATIS usually gives wind direction and speed, temperature and dewpoint, and altimeter setting. Some weather information may also be included as "remarks" in the broadcast.

2. Makes a competent "go/no-go" decision based on available weather information.

MAKING THE GO/NO-GO DECISION

Normally, you should make a preliminary check of the weather ahead of time to see if your planned flight is feasible. Unfortunately, an FSS usually is unable to issue a forecast beyond 24 to 36 hours. You can, however, assess the current national weather situation in terms of pressure systems and fronts and decide if adverse weather is likely. When you need a long-range forecast, it is best to contact the NWS. Forecasters there can provide reasonably accurate predictions of general weather patterns up to five days into the future. They also can provide a 6- to 10-day outlook, but keep in mind that the longer the forecast period, the less accurate the information. You can use several other sources to get an overall picture. Many areas have local cable television channels devoted to weather. An automated flight service station (AFSS) offers telephone access to recorded weather information, including telephone information briefing service (TIBS). Regardless of what preliminary source you use, be sure to get a standard weather briefing from an FSS specialist before you complete your flight planning on the day of the flight.

After conducting a thorough analysis of all available weather data, you must make a competent go/no-go decision. Typically, any indication of even a chance of IFR conditions warrants a no-go decision.

EXERCISES

1. A close temperature/dewpoint spread typically indicates the formation of ____________ is imminent.

2. You will always experience a change in ________ direction when a front passes.

3. List the three conditions necessary for a thunderstorm to develop.

____

____

____

4. The most severe types of thunderstorms are associated with a _______ _______.

5. _____ (True, False) If turbulence is encountered you should maintain a level flight attitude and not worry about increases or decreases in altitude.

6. _____ (True, False) Frost on a wing is hazardous because it disrupts the smooth flow of air and causes early airflow separation with resulting loss of lift.

7. Match the following abbreviations with the appropriate meanings.

–	_____	A. Partial
FU	_____	B. Scattered sky cover
BR	_____	C. Rain began
BKN	_____	D. Sky clear
SCT	_____	E. Light intensity
VV	_____	F. Broken sky cover
PR	_____	G. Mist
RAB	_____	H. Smoke
SKC	_____	I. Vertical visibility
FG	_____	J. Fog

8. The frequency for contacting Flight Watch is _______.

SAMPLE ORAL QUESTIONS

1. This is an Aviation Routine Weather Report for Pittsburgh Airport taken on the 20th at 1955 Zulu. The wind is 220° at 15 knots gusting to 25. The prevailing visibility is 3/4 statute miles and the runway visual range for runway 28 right is 2,600 feet. There is a thunderstorm with moderate rain occurring. Overcast clouds are present at 1,000 feet consisting of cumulonimbus clouds. The temperature is 18° Celsius and the dewpoint is 16° Celsius. The altimeter setting is 29.92 inches of mercury. The sea level pressure is 1013 hPa (hectoPascals, i.e., 1013 millibars). The temperature is 17.6° Celsius and the dewpoint is 15.8° Celsius.

1. Decode this weather observation:

METAR KPIT 201955Z 22015G25KT 3/4SM R28R/2600FT TSRA OVC010CB 18/16 A2992 RMK SLP013 T01760158

____

____

____

____

____

____

____

____

____

____

____

____

____

____

2. Decode the following Terminal Aerodrome Forecast:

TAF
KPIT 091720Z 091818 22020KT 3SM -SHRA BKN020
FM2030 30015G25KT 3SM SHRA OVC015
PROB40 2022 1/2SM TSRA OVC008CB
FM2300 27008KT 5SM -SHRA BKN020 OVC040
TEMPO 0407 00000KT 1SM -RABR
FM1000 22010KT 5SM -SHRA OV020 BECMG 1315 20010KT P6SM NSW SKC

3. How long are Area Forecasts (FAs) valid, and what are the four sections contained in the forecast?

4. At what altitudes are winds not reported, and at what altitudes are temperatures not reported on a Winds and Temperatures Aloft report (FD)?

2. The Pittsburgh forecast for the 9th was issued at 1720 Zulu. The valid period is the 9th beginning at 1800 Zulu and ending at 1800 Zulu the next day. The wind is forecast to be 220° at 20 knots, and the expected prevailing visibility 3 statute miles. Light rain showers are forecast with broken clouds at 2,000 feet. From 2030 Zulu, the wind is forecast to be 300° at 15 knots gusting to 25, forecast visibility 3 statute miles with rain showers and overcast clouds at 1,500 feet. There is a 40% probability between 2000 Zulu and 2200 Zulu of 1/2 statute mile visibility with thunderstorms and rain, and overcast clouds at 800 feet consisting of cumulonimbus clouds. From 2300 Zulu, the wind is forecast to be 270° at 8 knots, visibility 5 statute miles with light rain showers, broken clouds at 2,000 feet and overcast clouds at 4,000 feet. Temporary changes are expected between 0400 Zulu and 0700 Zulu consisting of calm winds, 1 statute mile visibility, light rain and mist. From 1000 Zulu, the wind is forecast to be 220° at 10 knots, visibility 5 statute miles, light rain showers, and overcast clouds at 2,000 feet. Between 1300 Zulu and 1500 Zulu wind is forecast to become 200° at 10 knots, visibility greater than 6 statute miles, no significant weather, and sky clear.

3. The FA is comprised of four sections: a communications and product header section, a precautionary statement section, and two weather sections; a SYNOPSIS section and a VFR CLOUDS/WX section. Each area forecast covers an 18-hour period.

4. FDs do not include levels within 1,500 feet of the station elevation, and temperatures are not forecast for the 3,000-foot level or for a level within 2,500 feet of the station elevation.

5. AIRMETs are issued every six hours with amendments issued, as necessary, for weather phenomena that mainly concern light aircraft. AIRMETs are issued for moderate icing, moderate turbulence, sustained winds of 30 knots or more at the surface, ceilings less than 1,000 feet and/or visibility less than three miles affecting over 50 percent of an area at any one time, and extensive mountain obscurement. SIGMETs are issued for hazardous weather (other than convective activity) which is considered significant to all aircraft. SIGMET criteria include severe icing, severe and extreme turbulence, volcanic eruptions and dust storms, sand storms, or volcanic ash lowering visibility to less than three miles.

6. To make a pilot report, call an FSS or ATC facility. You should begin by stating the type of report you would like to make, either a standard PIREP or urgent PIREP. Then continue by reporting your location, the time in Zulu, your current altitude, the type of aircraft you are flying, the existing sky cover, any pertinent weather or restrictions to visibility, the temperature in Celsius, the wind direction and velocity if available, any turbulence or icing, and any remarks necessary to clarify the report.

5. What is the difference between a SIGMET and an AIRMET?

____

____

____

____

____

____

____

____

6. What items should be incuded in a PIREP?

____

____

____

____

____

ADDITIONAL QUESTIONS

7. What type of weather is associated with a high pressure system? A low pressure system?
8. What is Coriolis force and how does it affect wind direction?
9. How are clouds and fog formed, and how can the temperature/dewpoint spread be used to predict cloud formation?
10. How would you go about obtaining a Surface Analysis Chart?
11. At what altitudes are winds and temperatures aloft charted?
12. Discuss the different panels on the Significant Weather Prog chart.
13. Explain the significance of the arrowheads on a Convective Outlook Chart.
14. What is the difference between AWOS and ASOS?

EXERCISE ANSWERS

1. fog
2. wind
3. unstable air, high moisture content, and a lifting action
4. squall line
5. True
6. True
7. E, H, G, F, B, I, A, C, D, J
8. 122.0

REFERENCES

JEPPESEN:

Private Pilot Manual/Video – Chapters 6 and 7

FAA:

Aeronautical Information Manual
Aviation Weather (AC 00-6)
Aviation Weather Services (AC 00-45)
Airplane Flying Handbook (FAA-H-8083-3)
Pilot's Handbook of Aeronautical Knowledge (AC 61-23/FAA-H-8083-25)
Role of Preflight Preparation (AC-61-84)

D. TASK: CROSS-COUNTRY FLIGHT PLANNING (ASEL AND ASES)

REFERENCES: 14 CFR part 91; AC 61-23/FAA-H-8083-25, AC-61-84; Navigation Charts; A/FD; AIM.

Objective: To determine that the applicant:

1. Exhibits knowledge of the elements related to cross-country flight planning by presenting and explaining a pre-planned VFR cross-country flight, as previously assigned by the examiner. On the day of the practical test, the final flight plan shall be to the first fuel stop, based on maximum allowable passengers, baggage, and/or cargo loads using real-time weather.
2. Uses appropriate and current aeronautical charts.
3. Properly identifies airspace, obstructions, and terrain features.
4. Selects easily identifiable en route checkpoints.
5. Selects most favorable altitudes considering weather conditions and equipment capabilities.
6. Computes headings, flight time, and fuel requirements.
7. Selects appropriate navigation system/facilities and communication frequencies.
8. Applies pertinent information from NOTAM's, A/FD, and other flight publications.
9. Completes a navigation log and simulates filing a VFR flight plan.

Objective: To determine that the applicant:

1. Exhibits knowledge of the elements related to cross-country flight planning by presenting and explaining a pre-planned VFR cross-country flight, as previously assigned by the examiner. On the day of the practical test, the final flight plan shall be to the first fuel stop, based on maximum allowable passengers, baggage, and/or cargo loads using real-time weather.

CROSS-COUNTRY PLANNING

A large portion of the practical test hinges on your ability to plan a cross-country flight as specified by your examiner. Typically, the route of flight you are assigned to plan will be near the maximum range of the aircraft and at maximum operating weight limits. The examiner may assign your route of flight for the cross-country the night before or the day of your oral examination. Whatever the case, you should obtain and use real-time weather reports to plan the flight. If possible, you should have a printout of all related weather information for the oral examination.

Once you complete your preflight planning, you will be expected to explain how you accomplished the planning. For example, you will be asked why you chose the checkpoints indicated, how you arrived at the performance figures indicated on your flight plan, and what the current forecast weather is along the entire route.

2. Uses appropriate and current aeronautical charts.

AERONAUTICAL CHARTS

Effective cross-country flight planning includes the interpretation and proper selection of current VFR aeronautical charts. The National Aeronautical Charting Office (NACO) publishes several charts including World aeronautical charts, sectional charts, and terminal area charts.

World aeronautical charts (WAC) are typically used for cross-country flights that cover several states. They are appropriate for VFR flights in aircraft that fly at higher speeds or use higher altitudes. These charts have a scale of 1:1,000,000, which equates to one inch representing approximately 14 nautical miles. Because of the small scale, little detail is available making it difficult to identify your exact location.

Sectional charts are used for most VFR cross-country flying. Sectional charts cover the 48 mainland states, plus Alaska, Hawaii, Puerto Rico, and the Virgin Islands. The scale of the sectional chart is 1:500,000. This translates to one inch equaling approximately seven nautical miles, and allows a fairly high level of detail appropriate for VFR navigation. Most sectionals are revised every six months, as indicated by the date printed on the front panel of the chart.

The chart index, also on the front panel, indicates the names of the adjoining charts. If your route of flight is near the edge of a chart, you should always take along the appropriate adjoining charts.

VFR terminal area charts help with orientation and navigation when flying VFR in or around Class B airspace. They have a large scale (1:250,000) and give you a detailed display of topographical features. On sectional charts, the availability of a terminal area chart is indicated by a wide blue band which encloses the Class B airspace and reflects the boundaries of the terminal area chart.

All aeronautical charts have a legend page that identifies the symbols used on the chart. However, prior to taking the practical test you must be familiar with all of the symbols used on aeronautical charts.

It is vitally important that you check the publication date on each aeronautical chart to be used. Obsolete charts should be discarded and replaced by new editions. This is important because revisions to aeronautical information occur constantly. They include changes in radio frequencies, new obstructions, the closing of runways and airports, and other temporary or permanent hazards to flight. You can determine the effective dates of a sectional by referring to the front panel.

LATITUDE AND LONGITUDE

Knowing where you are at any given moment is a fundamental concept of navigation. The system in use today was established centuries ago to define the exact location of any point on the earth. It is based on latitude and longitude coordinates.

To aid in determining locations on a map, a system of lines parallel to the equator was established. These lines are called **lines of latitude**, or parallels. You can locate a position north or south of the equator by using lines of latitude.

Imaginary lines extending from the north to the south pole are called lines of longitude, or meridians. Because they connect the poles, **lines of longitude** are, by definition, true north and south. **The Prime Meridian**, which passes through Greenwich, England, is labeled 0° of longitude. There are 360° of longitude encompassing the earth, with 180° on the east, and 180° on the west side of the Prime Meridian. [Figure 1-16]

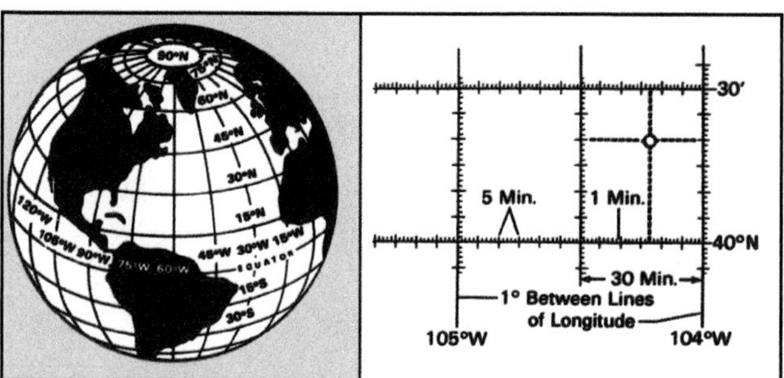

Figure 1-16. The lines of latitude and longitude are printed on aeronautical charts, with each degree subdivided into 60 equal segments called minutes. By specifying the geographic coordinates (or the intersection of the lines of latitude and longitude), you can define any position on the earth. In this example, the airport is located at 40°20'N, 104°13'W.

3. Properly identifies airspace, obstructions, and terrain features.

- Be able to identify each class of airspace, as well as the requirements for entering those classes.
- You must be thoroughly familiar with the symbology used on sectional charts.
- Refresh your understanding by reviewing the chart legend periodically.
- When plotting a course, make it dark enough so it can be seen without obscuring any chart symbology.
- Know how to plot a course that crosses over to the opposite side of the chart.

4. Selects easily identifiable en route checkpoints.

- You need to select checkpoints that are easily identifiable from the air.
- Whenever possible, select a checkpoint that you can compare against a combination of ground features.
- For additional information on selecting checkpoints refer to Chapter 7, Task A on page 7-1 .

5. Selects most favorable altitudes considering weather conditions and equipment capabilities.

- Topographical information such as contour lines, spot elevations, and minimum elevation figures can help you determine an altitude that keeps you well above obstructions.
- Ceiling heights and winds are additional factors that must be considered when choosing a cruising altitude. In general, winds are reduced at lower altitudes, so cruising at higher altitudes can often take advantage of tailwinds along your route.
- If your planned cruising altitude is greater than 3,000 feet AGL and on a magnetic heading between 360° and 179°, you must fly at an odd altitude plus 500 feet. If on a magnetic heading between 180° and 359°, fly an even altitude plus 500 feet.
- Oxygen requirements can also affect the altitude you choose. If flying at a cabin pressure altitude above 12,500 feet MSL up to and including 14,000 feet MSL longer than 30 minutes, you must use supplemental oxygen.
- When above 14,000 feet MSL, you must use supplemental oxygen at all times.
- If flying above 15,000 feet MSL, supplemental oxygen must be available to all passengers.

6. Computes headings, flight time, and fuel requirements.

- Once you determine the winds for your cruising altitude, you can calculate your heading and groundspeed.
- After calculating your groundspeed, calculate your flight time and fuel requirements using the performance data in your POH.
- VFR fuel planning must include enough fuel to fly to the first point of intended landing, plus a reserve.
- Day VFR flights require a 30-minute fuel reserve while night VFR flights require a 45-minute reserve.
- Use your mechanical and electronic flight computer to solve most navigation problems encountered during flight planning and in-flight operations.

7. Selects appropriate navigation system/facilities and communication frequencies.

- Use the navigation and communication facilities available along your route of flight.
- When using a navigation facility, enter the appropriate frequency, identification, and course on your navigation log.
- Communication frequencies can be found on sectional charts and in the Airport/Facility Directory and should be entered on your navigation log.

8. Applies pertinent information from NOTAM's, A/FD, and other flight publications.

NOTAMS

Notices to Airmen (NOTAMs) report changes in the status of airports or airway facilities that could affect your decision to make a flight. They include such information as runway closures, obstructions in the approach and departure paths to airports, and outages or curtailed operation hours of navaids and ATC facilities. NOTAMs are divided into three categories, NOTAM-D (distant), NOTAM-L (local), and Flight Data Center (FDC) NOTAMs.

NOTAM-D information is disseminated for all navigational facilities that are part of the National Airspace System, as well as all public use airports, seaplane bases, and heliports listed in the Airport/Facility Directory. This category of information is distributed automatically and appended to the hourly weather reports. Air traffic facilities, primarily an FSS with telecommunications systems, have access to the entire NOTAM database. These NOTAMs remain available for the duration of their validity or until published in appropriate publications.

NOTAM-L information includes local items like taxiway closures, construction activities near runways, snow conditions, and changes in the status of airport lighting, such as VASI, that do not affect instrument approach criteria. NOTAM-L information is only distributed locally and is not appended to hourly weather reports. A separate file of local NOTAMs is maintained at each FSS for facilities in their area. You must specifically request NOTAM-L information directly from other FSS areas that have responsibility for the airport concerned.

DES MOINES

DES MOINES INTL (DSM) 3 SW UTC–6(–5DT) N41°32.10′ W93°39.64′ **OMAHA**

957 B S4 **FUEL** 100LL, JET A OX 1, 2, 3, 4 LRA ARFF Index C **H–1E, 3G, L–11C**

RWY 13L–31R: H9001X150 (ASPH–GRVD) S–133, D–180, DT–340 HIRL **IAP**

RWY 13L: MALSR. VASI(V4L)—GA 3.0° TCH 56′. Arresting device.

RWY 31R: MALSR. PAPI(P4L)—GA 3.0° TCH 56′. Road. Rgt tfc. Arresting device. 0.8% down.

RWY 05–23: H6501X150 (ASPH–GRVD) S–133, D–169, DT–285 MIRL

RWY 05: REIL. VASI(V4L)—GA 3.0° TCH 51′. Pole. Arresting device.

RWY 23: REIL. VASI(V4L)—GA 3.0° TCH 45′. Pole. Arresting device.

RWY 13R–31L: H3202X100 (ASPH) S–12 MIRL

RWY 13R: REIL. Rgt tfc. **RWY 31L:** REIL. Tree.

AIRPORT REMARKS: Attended continuously. Rwy 13L–31R CLOSED from Jul 14 to Sep 18, 1997. Taxiway M weight restricted to 12,500 lbs. Airport director requires 24 hours notice on transportation of explosives by civil aircraft. No parking south edge terminal ramp without PPR from Aviation Director. Rubber supported arresting cables located 500′ in from thlds of Rwy 13L and Rwy 31R, 1250′ in from thlds of Rwy 05 and Rwy 23 may be in place individually or in combination during military ops. Twr has limited visibility on Twy D between Twy D–5 and D–6. Ramps weight restricted to 60,000 lbs. fixed-base operator. Men and equipment working adjacent all surfaces Apr–Oct Mon–Fri 1330–2230Z‡. mowing ops. Flight Notification Service (ADCUS) avbl. Mon–Fri 1430–2300Z‡. For Sat, Sun Holidays and ngt customs svc, make appointments Mon–Fri 1430–2300Z‡. At least 3 hr advance notice required. NOTE: See Land and Hold Short Operations Section.

WEATHER DATA SOURCES: ASOS (515) 287–1012. LLWAS.

COMMUNICATIONS: ATIS 119.55 (515) 287–3180 **UNICOM** 122.95

FORT DODGE FSS (FOD) TF 1–800–WX–BRIEF. NOTAM FILE DSM.

RCO 122.65 (FORT DODGE FSS)

® **APP/DEP CON:** 123.9 (306°–127° Rwy 13–31) (049°–231° Rwy 05–23) 135.2 (127°–306° Rwy 13–31) (231°–049° Rwy 05–23) 118.6 Utilized as APCH secondary freq, all sectors.

TOWER 118.3 **GND CON** 121.9 **CLNC DEL** 134.15

AIRSPACE: CLASS C svc ctc **APP CON.**

RADIO AIDS TO NAVIGATION: NOTAM FILE DSM.

(H) VORTACW 117.5 DSM Chan 122 N41°26.26′ W93°38.92′ 349° 5.4 NM to fld. 940/7E. **HIWAS.**

FOREM NDB (LOM) 344 DS N41°28.93′ W93°34.85′ 307° 4.2 NM to fld.

ILS 110.3 I–DSM Rwy 31R LOM FOREM NDB.

ILS 108.7 I–VGU Rwy 13L

ILS/DME 111.5 I–DWW Chan 52 Rwy 05. Localizer only.

ASR

Figure 1-17. This sample listing from the A/FD shows the major features. Every volume has a detailed legend in its first few pages.

FDC NOTAMs are used to disseminate information that is regulatory in nature. Examples are amendments to aeronautical charts, changes to instrument approach procedures, and temporary flight restrictions. FDC NOTAMs are kept on file at the FSS until published or cancelled. FSSs are responsible for maintaining unpublished FDC NOTAMs concerning conditions within 400 nautical miles of their facilities. FDC NOTAM information that affects conditions more than 400 miles from the FSS, or that is already published, is provided to a pilot only upon request. Except for Center Area Notams (CANs), FDC NOTAMs are published in the Notices to Airmen publication.

An important part of your preflight planning should be a review of the Notices to Airmen publication. Included are current NOTAM-Ds and FDC NOTAMs available at the time of publication. The Notices to Airmen publication is issued every 28 days and covers notices that are expected to remain in effect for at least seven days after the effective date of the publication. Once published in the Notices to Airmen, this information is taken off the distribution circuits and will not be provided in a pilot weather briefing unless you specifically request it.

AIRPORT/FACILITY DIRECTORY

Published by the National Aeronautical Charting Office, the *Airport/Facility Directory* (A/FD) is a descriptive listing of all airports, heliports, and seaplane bases open to the public. It is divided into seven volumes, each of which covers a specific region of the country. The A/FD is issued every 56 days. [Figure 1-17]

Naturally, you should review the other sources of flight information available. These include *Advisory Circulars* (ACs), NOTAMs, the *Aeronautical Information Manual (AIM)*, and publications such as *JeppGuide*.

9. Completes a navigation log and simulates filing a VFR flight plan.

- All pertinent information for a flight should be recorded on a navigation log.
- Once you complete your navigation log, fill out a flight plan form that the examiner can review.
- You may be asked to simulate filing a flight plan with the examiner or you may file an actual flight plan.

EXERCISES

1. The availability of services at an airport is indicated by _______ _______ extending from the airport symbol.

2. A heavy line surrounding a navaid box indicates

   a. the airport is in Class B Airspace.
   b. TWEB, AWOS, or HIWAS is available at the navaid.
   c. no voice on the frequency.
   d. a flight service station.

3. A visual checkpoint used to identify your position when calling ATC is indicated on sectional charts by a magenta-colored _______.

Answers to the following exercises were derived using an electronic flight computer, and may vary slightly if you use a mechanical flight computer.

4. How long would it take you to travel 275 n.m. at a speed of 110 knots? _______

5. Given the following information, determine your true heading and groundspeed.

   Wind Direction .... 330°
   Wind Speed .... 40 kts.
   True Course .... 180°
   True Airspeed .... 167 kts.

   True Heading _______ Ground Speed _______

6. Isogonic lines printed on sectional charts show _______ _______.

7. The required fuel for a VFR cross-country conducted at night includes enough fuel to reach the first point of intended landing and to fly thereafter for an additional

   a. 15 minutes.
   b. 20 minutes.
   c. 30 minutes.
   d. 45 minutes.

SAMPLE ORAL QUESTIONS

1. List the three types of aeronautical charts and briefly explain the differences between them.

1. The three most common aeronautical charts are the world aeronautical chart (WAC), sectional chart, and terminal area chart. A WAC chart is typically used on cross-country flights that cover several states. Its scale is 1:1,000,000 giving it little detail. A sectional chart has a scale of 1:500,000 and is typically used for VFR flights. A terminal area chart has a scale of 1:250,000 and is used for navigating in the vicinity of Class B airspace.

2. What factors must be considered when choosing a cruising altitude?

2. When choosing a cruising altitude you must consider things such as terrain, weather conditions, aircraft performance, and equipment requirements. Furthermore, if flying above 3,000 feet AGL, regulations require that you adhere to VFR cruising altitudes.

3. Explain VFR cruising altitudes specified in FAR Part 91.

3. Anytime you operate an aircraft under VFR in level cruising flight more than 3,000 feet AGL and on a magnetic course of 360° through 179°, you must fly at an odd altitude plus 500 feet. If on a magnetic heading of 180° through 359°, an even altitude plus 500 feet is required.

4. Briefly explain when you must use supplemental oxygen.

4. When flying at a cabin pressure altitude above 12,500 feet MSL up to and including 14,000 feet MSL you, as pilot in command, must use supplemental oxygen during that time in excess of 30 minutes. At pressure altitudes above 14,000 feet MSL, supplemental oxygen must be used at all times. If flying above a pressure altitude of 15,000 feet MSL, supplemental oxygen must be available to all passengers.

ADDITIONAL QUESTIONS

5. What are the minimum fuel reserve requirements for day and night VFR flights?
6. Describe how to properly complete each numbered block of an FAA flight plan form.
7. Describe how the Airport/Facility Directory is used in conjunction with aeronautical charts.

EXERCISE ANSWERS

1. tick marks
2. d
3. flag
4. 2:30:00
5. 187° 200 kts.
6. magnetic variation
7. d

REFERENCES

JEPPESEN:

Private Pilot Manual/Video - Chapters 4C, 4D, 8A, 8C, 9A, and 11A

FAA:

FEDERAL AVIATION REGULATIONS
Aeronautical Information Manual
Airport/Facility Directory
Navigation Charts
Airplane Flying Handbook (FAA-H-8083-3)
Pilot's Handbook of Aeronautical Knowledge (AC 61-23/FAA-H-8083-25)
Role of Preflight Preparation (AC-61-84)

E. TASK: NATIONAL AIRSPACE SYSTEM (ASEL AND ASES)

REFERENCES: 14 CFR part 71, 91; Navigation Charts, AIM.

Objective: To determine that the applicant exhibits knowledge of the elements related to the National Airspace System by explaining:

1. Basic VFR weather minimums — for all classes of airspace.
2. Airspace classes — their operating rules, pilot certification, and airplane equipment requirements for the following —
   a. Class A
   b. Class B
   c. Class C
   d. Class D
   e. Class E
   f. Class G
3. Special use and other airspace areas.

Objective: To determine that the applicant exhibits knowledge of the elements related to the National Airspace System by explaining:

1. Basic VFR weather minimums - for all classes of airspace.

VFR WEATHER MINIMUMS

VFR cloud clearance and visibility requirements are designed to help you avoid flying into clouds, as well as maintain adequate forward visibility in flight. They are also designed to meet other practical requirements, such as seeing and avoiding other air traffic and navigating to your destination. The altitude at which you fly in controlled airspace usually is the determining factor for the specific cloud clearance and visibility that you must maintain. [Figure 1-18]

As you can see, VFR minimums in Class G airspace below 10,000 feet MSL allow for operations with 1 mile visibility during the day and 3 miles visibility at night. However, as a student pilot, you must maintain a minimum surface visibility of 3 statute miles during the day and 5 statute miles at night. Once you become a private pilot you may conduct VFR operations in Class G airspace as specified in the table. Furthermore, when the visibility is less than 3 statute miles but not less than 1 statute mile at night, you may operate an aircraft clear of clouds in the airport traffic pattern when within one-half mile of the runway. However, you may not operate an aircraft beneath the ceiling under VFR operations within the lateral boundaries of Class B, C, D, and E airspace that extends to the surface when the ceiling is less than 1,000 feet.

SPECIAL VFR

Normal VFR airport operations in Class B, C, D, and E airspace require at least three miles ground visibility and a cloud ceiling of at least 1,000 feet. However, when the weather is below VFR minimums and there is no conflicting IFR traffic, a Special VFR clearance may be obtained from ATC if the visibility is at least one mile and you can remain clear of clouds. At uncontrolled airports with ASOS/AWOS automated weather broadcast capability, if ATC service is required for special VFR or requested for VFR, you should monitor the broadcast frequency, advise the controller that you have the one-minute weather, and state your intentions.

As a private pilot, you may obtain a special VFR clearance only during the daytime unless you are instrument rated and your aircraft is equipped for instrument flight. Some major airports do not allow special VFR clearances to be issued to fixed-wing aircraft. These airports are noted on sectional charts with the phrase "NO SVFR."

2. Airspace classes — their operating rules, pilot certification, and airplane equipment requirements for the following —

a. Class A **d. Class D**
b. Class B **e. Class E**
c. Class C **f. Class G**

AIRSPACE

In order to properly operate in the National Airspace System you must know the various airspace segments and classifications, as well as their associated operational requirements. Furthermore, you also need to be aware of any special flight restrictions or aircraft equipment requirements that apply.

In general, there are two broad classifications of airspace that cover the U.S. They are: controlled and uncontrolled. Additional classifications of airspace include special use airspace and other airspace areas. [Figure 1-19]

CONTROLLED AIRSPACE

The important thing to remember about operating in controlled airspace is that you may be subject to air traffic control (ATC). As a VFR pilot, your contact with ATC typically is limited to terminal areas. For example, when you take off or land at controlled airports, you must contact the control tower, and you will often use radar approach and departure control services.

Separation of air traffic is the primary function of air traffic control, and radar is one of the controller's principal tools. Because of this, the regulations require you to use the aircraft transponder (if your aircraft is so equipped) whenever you fly in controlled airspace. Furthermore, a transponder with altitude encoding equipment is required when flying in controlled or uncontrolled airspace at or above 10,000 feet MSL and when above 2,500 feet AGL

BASIC VFR WEATHER MINIMUMS		
Airspace	**Flight Visibility**	**Distance from Clouds**
Class A	Not Applicable	Not Applicable
Class B	3 statute miles	Clear of Clouds
Class C	3 statute miles	500 feet below 1,000 feet above 2,000 feet horizontal
Class D	3 statute miles	500 feet below 1,000 feet above 2,000 feet horizontal
Class E Less than 10,000 feet MSL	3 statute miles	500 feet below 1,000 feet above 2,000 feet horizontal
At or above 10,000 feet MSL	5 statute miles	1,000 feet below 1,000 feet above 1 statute mile horizontal
Class G 1,200 feet or less above the surface (regardless of MSL altitude). Day, except as provided in section 91.155(b). Night, except as provided in section 91.155(b).	1 statute mile 3 statute miles	Clear of Clouds 500 feet below 1,000 feet above 2,000 feet horizontal
More than 1,200 feet above the surface but less than 10,000 feet MSL. Day	1 statute mile	500 feet below 1,000 feet above 2,000 feet horizontal
Night	3 statute miles	500 feet below 1,000 feet above 2,000 feet horizontal
More than 1,200 feet above the surface and at or above 10,000 feet MSL.	5 statute miles	1,000 feet below 1,000 feet above 1 statute mile horizontal

Figure 1-18. VFR weather minimums vary depending on the class of airspace you are in, your altitude, and the time of day.

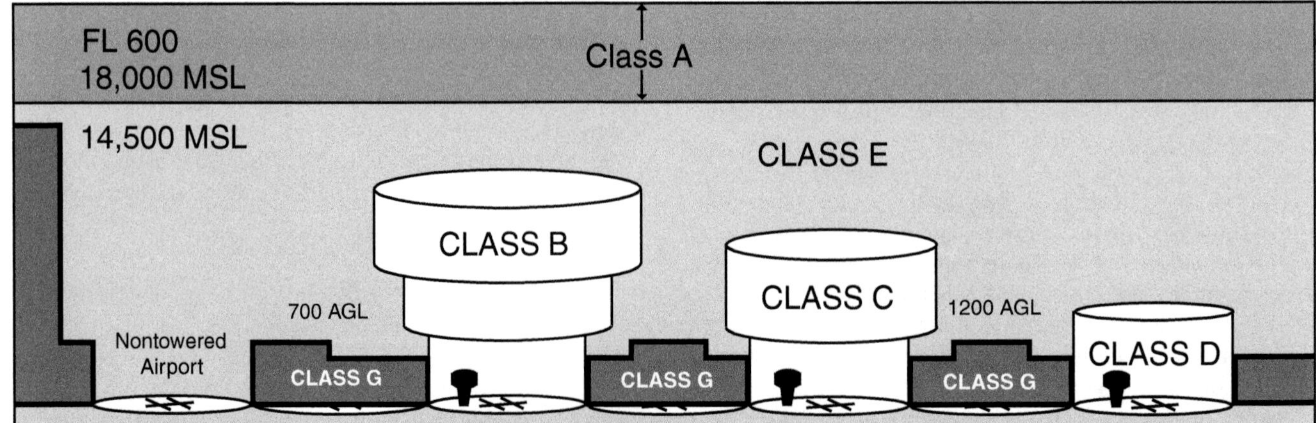

Figure 1-19. The airspace that covers the U.S. is divided into controlled and uncontrolled airspace. Operational requirements depend on the type of airspace you are flying in, as well as your altitude. Along with these requirements, you also must be aware of the minimum flight visibilities and cloud clearance requirements that apply at various altitudes in controlled and uncontrolled airspace.

The subdivisions of controlled airspace include Class A, B, C, D, and E airspace areas.

CLASS A AIRSPACE

This airspace extends from 18,000 feet MSL up to and including 60,000 feet MSL, and covers the majority of the conterminous U.S. out to 12 nautical miles beyond the coast. To operate in Class A airspace you must be instrument rated and all aircraft must be controlled by ATC, transponder equipped, and operated under Instrument Flight Rules (IFR).

Within Class A airspace, pilots are required to set their altimeters to the standard setting of 29.92 in. Hg. This ensures that all pilots maintain their assigned altitudes using the same altimeter reference.

At 18,000 feet MSL and above, altitudes are expressed as flight levels (FL), and are prefaced by the letters "FL," with the last two zeros omitted. As an example, 27,000 feet is referenced as FL 270.

CLASS B AIRSPACE

At some major airports safety dictates that all arriving and departing traffic be under positive radar control. To accomplish this, Class B airspace is typically designated for a large terminal area. Each Class B airspace layer is designated by an upper and lower altitude, referred to as the ceiling and floor respectively. Each layer is a building block for controlling the airspace in the area and for funneling air traffic into the terminal area.

To operate within Class B airspace, your aircraft must have two-way radio communications capability and a transponder with Mode C (altitude reporting) capability. With certain exceptions, a Mode C transponder is required within 30 nautical miles of the Class B area's primary airport from the surface to 10,000 feet MSL. In addition, a VOR or TACAN is required for IFR operations.

In order to fly within Class B airspace, or to take off or land at an airport within that airspace, you must possess at least a private pilot certificate. However, student pilots may be permitted to conduct flight operations within specified Class B areas by obtaining training and a logbook endorsement from a certified flight instructor. You should refer to part 91 in the regulations for specific rules pertaining to student pilot operations within Class B airspace.

Before entering Class B airspace, you must obtain ATC permission even after a departure from an airport that is other than the primary airport. Some Class B areas have VFR corridors designated to permit flight through the area without contacting ATC. Within a VFR corridor, you are not actually in Class B airspace, so you do not have to meet the operational and equipment requirements.

FAA regulations specify a speed limit of 200 knots (230 miles per hour) indicated airspeed when flying in the airspace underlying Class B airspace or in a designated VFR corridor for a Class B area. Furthermore, the speed within Class B airspace below 10,000 feet is restricted to 250 knots. The FAA encourages aircraft which are not required to operate in a Class B area to avoid it whenever practical. The boundaries of Class B areas are clearly shown on sectional and terminal area charts.

CLASS C AIRSPACE

Within a Class C area, ATC services are provided to ensure traffic separation for all IFR and VFR aircraft. Participation in this service is mandatory. Most Class C areas are similar to one another, and consist of two circles of airspace surrounding the primary airport. The airspace immediately around the airport consists of a five nautical mile radius area starting at the surface and extending up to 4,000 feet above airport elevation. Beyond this core lies a 10 n.m. radius shelf area that extends from 1,200 feet to 4,000 feet above the airport elevation.

An "outer area" usually extends out to 20 n.m. from the primary airport. As a VFR pilot, you are not required to contact ATC prior to entering the outer area, but it is helpful to do so. For approach, departure, or overflights, ATC normally provides the same radar services for you in the outer area as it does within the Class C airspace.

Before entering either the five nautical mile surface area or ten nautical mile radius shelf of Class C airspace, you must establish two-way communications with the ATC facility having jurisdiction and maintain it while operating within the airspace. When you depart the primary airport, you must maintain radio contact with ATC until you are clear of the Class C airspace. When departing a satellite airport without an operating control tower, you must contact the control tower for the primary airport as soon as practicable after takeoff.

In addition to the two-way radio requirement, all aircraft operating in a Class C area and in all airspace above it to 10,000 feet MSL, must be equipped with an operable transponder with encoding altimeter (Mode C). Aircraft operating in the airspace beneath a Class C area are not required to have a transponder with Mode C. An airspeed limit of 200 knots applies in Class C airspace when operating at or below 2,500 feet above the surface within 4 nautical miles of the primary airport.

ATC facilities may not operate full-time at some Class C locations, so radar service may not be available at all times. Although Class C services may be part-time, communication and transponder requirements are in effect at all times. Hours of operation for ATC facilities are listed in the Airport/Facility Directory.

CLASS D AIRSPACE

When an airport has an operating control tower, but is not associated with Class B or C airspace, it is surrounded by Class D airspace. The control tower provides separation between aircraft and an orderly flow of traffic in and out of the airport. The airspace at an airport with a part-time control tower is designated as Class D only when the tower is in operation. To find out what type of airspace exists after the tower closes, refer to the Airport/Facility Directory.

Class D airspace normally extends up to and including 2,500 feet above the airport elevation, and may include extensions for approaches and departures. However, the vertical and lateral limits of Class D airspace areas can vary widely depending on the type of operations conducted.

If the control tower is operating, you must establish two-way communications with the tower prior to entering Class D airspace and for all operations to, from, or on that airport. You also must comply with the prescribed speed limitation of 200 knots when at or below 2,500 feet AGL within 4 nautical miles of the primary airport, as well as any established approach and departure procedures applicable to the airport.

In some Class D airspace areas, a non-towered satellite airport may be located within the airspace designated for the primary airport. In this situation, you must establish contact with the primary airport's control tower. When departing a nontower satellite airport in Class D airspace, contact the controlling tower as soon as practicable after takeoff.

CLASS E AIRSPACE

The majority of Class E airspace includes that extending from 14,500 feet MSL up to 18,000 feet MSL, and covers the 48 contiguous states plus 12 nautical miles beyond the coastlines. The only exceptions are restricted and prohibited areas and airspace within 1,500 feet of the surface.

Federal airways constitute another segment of Class E airspace. They normally begin at 1,200 feet above the surface, extend upward to 18,000 feet MSL, and include the airspace within four nautical miles each side of the airway centerline. The airspace between airports and the airway route system are also designated Class E airspace. This allows IFR traffic to remain in controlled airspace while transitioning between the enroute and airport environments. These segments of Class E airspace usually begin at 1,200 feet AGL if they are associated with an airway. This airspace is not outlined on sectional charts unless it borders uncontrolled airspace.

At nontower airports which have an approved instrument approach procedure, Class E airspace often begins at 700 feet above the surface. At some nontower airports, Class E airspace extends upward from the surface, and usually encompasses airspace surrounding the airport, including extensions to accommodate arrivals and departures. Both of these types of Class E airspace are depicted on aeronautical charts. [Figure 1-20]

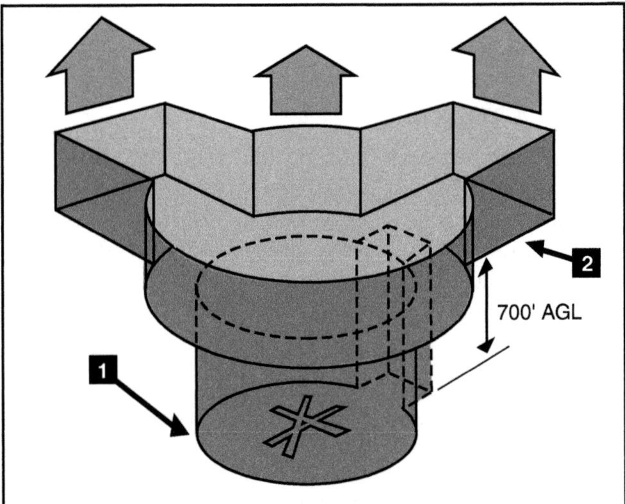

Figure 1-20. This nontowered airport is surrounded by Class E airspace which extends from the surface (item 1) and adjoins Class E airspace which begins at 700 feet AGL (item 2).

CLASS G (UNCONTROLLED AIRSPACE)

Class G, or uncontrolled airspace, is that airspace that has not been specified as Class A,B,C,D, or E. ATC does not control air traffic in Class G airspace. Uncontrolled airspace typically extends from the surface to the base of the overlying Class E airspace, which is normally 700 or 1,200 feet AGL. In some areas of the western U.S. and Alaska, uncontrolled airspace may extend upward to 14,500 feet MSL. An exception to this rule occurs when 14,500 feet MSL is lower than 1,500 feet AGL. In that event, uncontrolled airspace continues up to 1,500 feet above the surface.

3. Special use and other airspace areas.

SPECIAL USE AIRSPACE

Segments of controlled and uncontrolled airspace have been designated as special use airspace. Civilian flight operations within special use airspace are considered hazardous, so there are some limitations and prohibitions.

Prohibited Areas — For reasons of national security, aircraft are not permitted to fly in prohibited areas. Prohibited areas are depicted on aeronautical charts.

Restricted Areas — Designated restricted areas often have invisible hazards to aircraft, such as artillery firing, aerial gunnery, or guided missiles. Permission to fly through restricted areas may be granted by the controlling agency.

Warning Areas —Airspace that may contain hazards to aircraft over domestic and international waters is called a warning area. It may contain many of the same operations that are found in restricted areas, except that they are conducted outside U.S. coastal borders.

Military Operations Areas (MOAs) — MOAs are blocks of airspace in which military training and other military maneuvers are conducted. MOAs usually have specified floors and ceilings to contain military activities. As a VFR pilot, it is wise to avoid active military operations areas.

Alert Areas — These areas are shown on aeronautical charts to inform you of unusual types of aerial activities or high concentrations of student pilot training. You should be especially cautious when flying through them.

Controlled Firing Areas — CFAs contain activities that could be hazardous to nonparticipating aircraft. CFA activities are suspended when spotter aircraft, radar, or ground lookout positions indicate an approaching aircraft.

National Security Areas — NSAs are established at locations where there is a requirement for increased security and safety of ground facilities. You are requested to voluntarily avoid flying through an NSA. If authorities decide that greater security is necessary, a NOTAM is issued to prohibit flight within an NSA.

OTHER AIRSPACE AREAS

Other airspace areas primarily consist of airport advisory areas and military training routes. Other segments of airspace in this category may be designated by temporary flight restrictions or flight limitations/prohibitions. Parachute jump areas are also classified as other airspace areas.

Airport Advisory Area — Airport advisory areas extend 10 s.m. from airports where there is a nonautomated flight service station (FSS) located on the field and no operating control tower. You normally contact the FSS on the published CTAF frequency. The FSS provides local airport advisory service, which includes advisories on wind direction and velocity, favored runway, altimeter setting, and reported traffic in the area.

Military Training Routes (MTRs) — Low-level, high-speed military training flights are conducted on military training routes. Generally, MTRs are established below 10,000 feet MSL for operations at speeds in excess of 250 knots. Check with an FSS within 100 n.m. to obtain the current information regarding MTR activity in your area. MTRs are marked on sectional charts and are classified as "VR" where VFR operations apply and "IR" where IFR operations apply.

Temporary Flight Restrictions — Temporary flight restrictions are imposed by the FAA to protect people and property that might be jeopardized by unnecessary flight activity. They may be issued to provide a safer environment for rescue/relief operations or to prevent unsafe congestion of sightseeing or other aircraft near an event that generates high public interest. Examples might include volcanic eruptions, forest-fire-fighting activities, toxic chemical spills, floods, or other natural disasters.

Flight Limitations/Prohibitions — Flight limitations may be imposed by the FAA to restrict flights in certain situations. Flights near space launch and landing operations are routinely prohibited, and are designated by NOTAM. These restrictions help protect space flight crews and prevent costly delays. NOTAMs are issued to create flight restrictions in the proximity of the President, Vice President, foreign heads of state, and other persons who may attract large numbers of people. When such NOTAMs are issued, they are considered to be regulatory.

Parachute Jump Areas — To help you see and avoid parachute jump activity, selected jump sites are tabulated in the Airport/Facility Directory. Times of operation are local, and MSL altitudes are listed unless otherwise specified. They may also be depicted on sectional charts with an open parachute symbol.

EXERCISES

1. _______ (True, False) The floor of Class E airspace can extend to the surface.

2. The normal radius of the outer area of Class C airspace extends out to _______ nautical miles.

3. _______ (True, False) The upper limit of Class C airspace is typically 4,000 feet above the primary airport elevation.

4. With a special VFR clearance, you must maintain a visibility of _______ miles and remain clear of clouds.

SAMPLE ORAL QUESTIONS

1. What are the VFR weather minimums and equipment requirements for flying in Class B airspace?

1. The VFR weather minimums for flying in Class B airspace are 3 miles visibility and remain clear of clouds. In addition, to operate in Class B airspace, your aircraft must have two-way radio communication capability and a Mode C transponder.

2. What are some operational considerations when flying in the "outer area" of Class C airspace?

2. As a VFR pilot, you are not required to contact ATC prior to entering the outer area of Class C airspace, which usually extends from 10 n.m. to 20 n.m. from the primary airport. However, it is helpful for you to contact ATC in the outer area because they normally provide the same radar services that are available within the Class C airspace.

3. What are the limitations to a VFR pilot desiring to fly through Military Operations Areas (MOAs)?

3. As a VFR pilot, you may fly through MOAs. It is wise, however, to avoid active MOAs. Flight Service Stations within 100 n.m. of an MOA have information regarding the hours of operation. If you need to fly through an MOA, contact the controlling agency for traffic advisories.

4. Explain the implications of flying in Class A airspace.

4. To operate in Class A airspace you must be instrument rated and all aircraft must be controlled by ATC, transponder equipped, and operated under instrument flight rules. In addition, pilots are required to set their altimeters to 29.92 in. Hg.

ADDITIONAL QUESTIONS

5. What are the VFR weather minimums for Class C air space? Class D? Class E? Class G?
6. What pilot qualifications are required to fly in Class B airspace?
7. What is the maximum speed you can fly below 10,000 feet MSL? Beneath Class B airspace? Within Class D Airspace?
8. Describe the types of Special Use Airspace and Other Airspace Areas.
9. How can you tell if a special VFR clearance is not permitted at an airport?
10. What equipment is required to fly in Class C airspace?

EXERCISE ANSWERS

1. True
2. 20
3. True
4. 1

REFERENCES

JEPPESEN:
Private Pilot Manual/Video - Chapters 4C and 4D

FAA:
Federal Aviation Regulations
Aeronautical Information Manual
Navigation Charts

F. TASK: PERFORMANCE AND LIMITATIONS (ASEL AND ASES)

REFERENCES: AC 61-23/FAA-H-8083-25, FAA-H-8083-1, AC 61-84, POH/AFM.

Objective: To determine that the applicant:

1. Exhibits knowledge of the elements related to performance and limitations by explaining the use of charts, tables, and data to determine performance and the adverse effects of exceeding limitations.
2. Computes weight and balance. Determines the computed weight and center of gravity is within the airplane's operating limitations and if the weight and center of gravity will remain within limits during all phases of flight.
3. Demonstrates use of the appropriate performance charts, tables, and data.
4. Describes the effects of atmospheric conditions on the airplane's performance.

Objective: To determine that the applicant:

1. **Exhibits knowledge of the elements related to performance and limitations by explaining the use of charts, tables, and data to determine performance and the adverse effects of exceeding limitations.**

PERFORMANCE

To become a safe and competent private pilot, you need to develop your ability to predict performance. You must be able to explain to the examiner how you can use performance charts and other information to determine, for example, how much runway you need for takeoff, how long it will take you to reach your destination, how much fuel is required, and how much runway you will need for landing.

Operating Limitations — You must also comply with the operating limitations that establish the boundaries within which the aircraft can be flown. These operating limitations define what is called the performance envelope. By regulation, operating limitations may be found in the approved aircraft flight manual; approved manual materials, markings, and placards; or any combination.

CHART PRESENTATIONS

Performance charts are typically presented in either a table or graph format. The table format usually contains several notes to help you adjust for various conditions not accounted for in the body of the chart. Graph presentations usually incorporate more variables, reducing the adjustments required. Both tables and graphs specify a set of conditions under which the chart is valid. Therefore, you should always check the chart conditions before using it.

2. **Computes weight and balance. Determines the computed weight and center of gravity is within the airplane's operating limitations and if the weight and center of gravity will remain within limits during all phases of flight.**

WEIGHT AND BALANCE

The location of the aircraft's center of gravity (CG) directly affects its performance and stability. When determining aircraft weight and balance, you must have the aircraft's weight and balance records. These include the aircraft's empty weight, center of gravity, total moment, and a list of all optional equipment. When equipment is removed, replaced, or added, or major repairs are made to the aircraft, revised weight and moment information is created, and the old records are marked "superseded.'

AIRCRAFT WEIGHT

Your weight and balance computations begin with the weight of the airplane before passengers, cargo, and fuel are added. The term **basic empty weight** includes the weight of the aircraft, optional equipment, unusable fuel, and full operating fluids, including full engine oil.

Aviation gasoline (avgas) weighs 6 pounds per gallon, while oil weighs 7.5 pounds per gallon. Remember that engine oil capacity is usually given in quarts, so be sure to convert to gallons to determine its weight.

Useful load is the difference between maximum takeoff weight and basic empty weight, and is the upper limit for the combined weight of people, usable fuel, and baggage or cargo that the airplane can safely carry.

There are several other terms you need to understand in order to discuss weight and balance. **Ramp weight** describes the airplane loaded for flight before engine start. Subtracting the fuel burned during engine start, taxi, and runup yields the **takeoff weight**. **Landing weight** is the takeoff weight minus the fuel burned enroute.

The aircraft manufacturer determines the maximum weight allowable for each stage of flight. The "Limitations" section of the POH will list the **maximum ramp weight, maximum takeoff weight,** and **maximum landing weight**. Often these weights will be nearly the same, and may be combined as the **maximum weight** in the POH. When you add the weight of the pilot, passengers, fuel, and baggage to the basic empty weight of the airplane, the total must not exceed the maximum weight stated in the POH.

Weight limitations are necessary for aircraft structural integrity, and enable you to predict aircraft performance accurately. Overloading can lead to structural deformation or failure during flight, should you encounter high load factors, strong wind gusts, or turbulence. Landing gear damage or failure could result from exceeding the maximum landing weight. Operating in excess of the maximum weight also affects performance. It results in a longer takeoff roll, reduced climb performance, reduced cruising speed, an increase in fuel consumption, an increase in stall speed, and an increase in the landing roll.

AIRCRAFT BALANCE

Center of gravity (CG) limitations affect where weight should be located within the airplane. This aspect of weight and balance calculations deals with computing the center of gravity of the loaded airplane and checking to be sure that it falls within the limits given in the POH. If your calculations show that the CG will be outside these limits, you must relocate, or possibly reduce, the weight of fuel, passengers, or cargo in order to move the CG within acceptable limits. The weight of the airplane changes during flight as fuel is used. The fuel tanks of most general aviation airplanes are located to minimize CG changes as fuel is burned, but you must make sure that the CG remains within limits throughout the flight. Any movement of passengers or cargo during the flight will also change the CG location.

COMPUTING WEIGHT AND BALANCE

Your results can only be as accurate as the information you use, so avoid using estimates or guesses in your computations. Ask passengers what they weigh, and weigh baggage on a scale. If you have to make an estimate, be conservative and overestimate the weight.

The CG location is typically expressed in inches aft of a defined reference datum. The reference datum is an imaginary vertical plane, arbitrarily established along the longitudinal axis of the aircraft, from which all horizontal distances are measured for weight and balance purposes. Reference datum location is established by the manufacturer and defined in the POH or the aircraft's weight and balance papers.

The horizontal distance from the reference datum to any aircraft component or object located within the aircraft is called the arm. If the component or object is located aft of the datum, it is measured as a positive number and referred to as inches aft of the datum. If the component or object is ahead or forward of the datum, it is indicated as a negative number and is referred to as inches forward of the datum.

When you multiply the weight of an object by its arm, the result is known as its **moment**. If you think of the arm as a lever, moment is the force that results from the object's weight acting on the lever. You can also think of moment as a measure of the tendency of the weight of an object to cause rotation around a fulcrum, in this case the datum. The further an object is from a pivotal point, the greater its force.

Each part of the aircraft, as well as each object it carries, exerts a moment proportional to its weight and distance from the designated reference datum. By totaling the weights and moments of all components and objects, you can determine the point where a loaded airplane would balance on an imaginary fulcrum. This is the aircraft's CG. There are three primary methods to determine an aircraft's CG. They are the computational, graph, and table methods.

COMPUTATIONAL METHOD

With the computational method, you use simple arithmetic to solve weight and balance problems. The first step is to look up the basic empty weight and total moment for the aircraft you are going to fly. If the center of gravity is given, it should also be noted. The empty weight CG can be considered the "arm" of the empty airplane. This information is contained in the aircraft's weight and balance records, and it is the first item on the weight and balance form.

Write down the weight of fuel, pilot, passengers, and baggage. It is extremely important to record each weight in its proper location to obtain an accurate CG calculation. Add all of the weights together to determine the total weight of the loaded aircraft.

Next, verify that the total weight does not exceed the maximum allowable weight under existing conditions. If it does, you must reduce the total weight. You might reduce the amount of fuel and plan an extra fuel stop. When you are satisfied that the total weight is within prescribed limits, multiply each individual weight by its associated arm to determine its moment. Then, add the moments together to arrive at the total moment for the aircraft. Then find the center of gravity of the loaded aircraft by dividing the total moment by the total weight. [Figure 1-21]

WEIGHT and BALANCE FORM			
ITEM	WEIGHT (pounds)	ARM (inches)	MOMENT (pound-inches)
BASIC EMPTY WT.	1,398	38.75	54,173
FUEL (38 gal.)	228	48.0	10,944
PILOT & PASSENGER	350	36.5	12,775
REAR PASSENGER	190	73.0	13,870
BAGGAGE	34	95.0	3,230
TOTAL	2,200		94,992
CG = 43.2 INCHES			

Figure 1-21. In this example of a completed weight and balance form, the appropriate weight has been recorded next to each item. The amount of fuel in gallons also has been recorded on the fuel line. The CG, filled in at the bottom of the form, is determined by dividing the total moment of the airplane by its total weight.

You then need to determine if the CG is within acceptable limits by referring to the aircraft's center of gravity limits graph. If the CG falls outside acceptable limits, you must adjust aircraft loading. To determine if the center of gravity is within limits, plot the point at which the aircraft's total weight and CG meet. If this point is within the acceptable limits on the graph, the aircraft is considered to be properly loaded. [Figure 1-22]

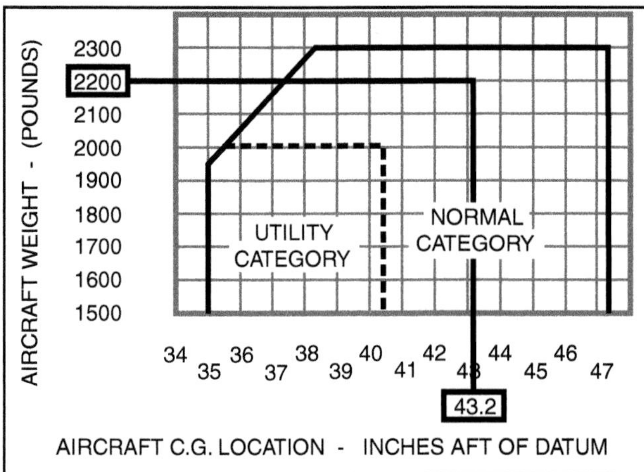

Figure 1-22. In this example, the weight of 2,200 pounds and CG location of 43.2 inches are within acceptable limits for operations in the normal category. However, note that the airplane is too heavy and the CG is too far aft for operations in the utility category.

GRAPH METHOD

A simplification of the computational method is called the graph method. With this method, you use a graph supplied by the manufacturer to determine moment. When this method is used, the graph that shows center-of-gravity limits usually reflects weight and moment instead of weight and CG. This saves you the step of dividing the total moment by the weight.

To use the graph method, record the basic empty weight and moment of your airplane. Then add fuel, pilot, passenger, and baggage weight on the weight and balance worksheet and determine the total weight of the aircraft. If the weight is within prescribed limits, compute the moment for each weight and for the loaded aircraft. Do this using the manufacturer's loading graph. For example, let's assume the pilot and front seat passenger have a combined weight of 340 pounds. [Figure 1-23]

After recording the basic empty weight and moment of the airplane and the weight and moment for each item, total and record all weights and moments. Next, plot the listed takeoff weight and moment on the manufacturer's moment envelope graph to determine if your aircraft is properly loaded for flight.

TABLE METHOD

A derivative of the computational and graph methods is called the table method. With this method, you locate a given weight on the appropriate table, then look up its corresponding moment. Often, however, the exact weight you are looking for is not found on the table. In these situations, look up two smaller weights which add up to the total

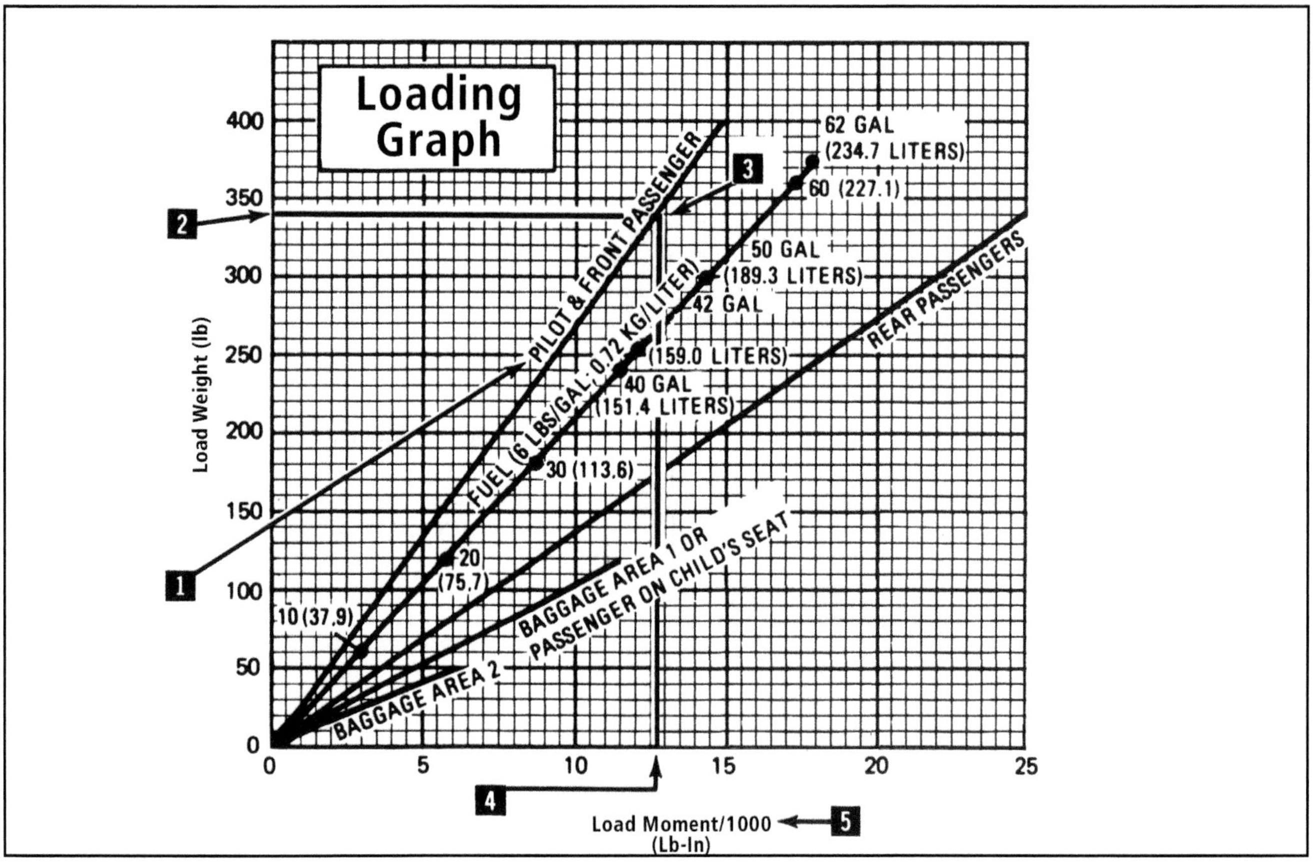

Figure 1-23. First, find the line that is labeled "pilot & front seat passenger" (item 1). Now, enter the graph from the left side at a weight of 340 pounds (item 2), and proceed horizontally to the appropriate line (item 3). Next, drop straight down and read the moment of 12.6 (item 4). Notice that numbers on this scale represent the load moment/1,000 (item 5). This is referred to as a reduction factor. In this case, the moment of 12.6 actually represents a moment of 12,600 pound-inches.

weight you want, and add their corresponding moments. [Figure 1-24]

	FRONT SEATS			3RD AND 4TH SEATS	
	FWD POS.		AFT POS.	BENCH SEAT	SPLIT SEAT
	ARM 104	ARM 105	ARM 112	ARM 142	ARM 144
WEIGHT	MOM/100	MOM/100	MOM/100	MOM/100	MOM/100
120	125	126	134	170	173
130	135	137	146	185	187
140	146	147	157	199	202
150	156	158	168	213	216
160	166	168	179	227	230
170	177	179	190	241	245
180	187	189	202	256	259
190	198	200	213	270	274
200	208	210	224	284	288

Figure 1-24. Note that this table uses a reduction factor of 100 and the highest weight given is 200 pounds. To determine the moment/100 for 340 pounds, look up the moments for 200 pounds and 140 pounds (200 lb. + 140 lb. = 340 lb.). In this case, the moment/100 is 354 pound-inches (146 lb.-in. + 208 lb.-in.).

When you complete the weight and balance worksheet, you must check to see if the aircraft is loaded within acceptable limits. You can do this by referring to the manufacturer's gravity moment envelope or a "moment limit versus weight" table. To use this table, find the aircraft loaded weight, then check to see if the loaded moment falls within the minimum and maximum values given for that weight.

WEIGHT SHIFT

During weight and balance computations, you may find that the aircraft weight or its CG location is outside acceptable limits. Usually, you can solve this problem by simply decreasing weight, especially if you do it before you calculate the aircraft's CG. However, if you change the load in order to adjust the CG, the computations are more complex. [Figure 1-25]

Weight Shift Formula

$$\frac{\text{Weight of Cargo Moved}}{\text{Weight of Airplane}} = \frac{\text{Distance CG Moves}}{\text{Distance Between Arm Locations}}$$

Figure 1-25. Use this formula to determine changes in CG when weight must be shifted. An easy way to remember this formula is to note that the small values are on top of the formula and the large values are on the bottom.

The easiest way to apply this formula is to work several different weight shift problems. You do this by inserting known values into the formula and solving for the unknown. For example, assume a loaded airplane weight of 2,100 pounds and a CG of 43 inches. A box weighing 30 pounds is moved from cargo area "B," which has an arm of 123 inches, to cargo area "A," where the arm is 95 inches. Solving this problem results in an answer of 42.6 inches.

3. Demonstrates use of the appropriate performance charts, tables, and data.

TAKEOFF CHARTS

Assume you are planning to depart an airport under the following conditions. Use the sample chart in Figure 1-26 to determine the ground roll and total distance required to clear a 50-foot obstacle.

Pressure altitude .... 3,000 ft.
Temperature .... 20°C
Flaps .... 10°
Runway .... Paved, level, and dry
Wind .... Calm
Weight .... 1,670 lbs.

In the example, the wind condition was calm, but how would the problem change with a headwind? You can find the answer in the notes listed for the chart. According to note number 3, the distance decreases by 10% for each nine knots of headwind. For example, with a 9 knot headwind, the ground roll is reduced by 10%, to 900 feet (1000 - 100 = 900). With a dry grass runway surface, note number 4 applies. In this case, the ground roll increases by 15%.

For the next sample chart, assume you are planning to depart under the following conditions. This time you are only concerned with the distance required to clear a 50-foot obstacle. Use the sample chart in figure 1-27 for this exercise.

Pressure altitude .... 1,500 ft.
Temperature .... 27°C.
Flaps .... Up
Runway .... Paved, level, and dry
Wind .... 15 kts. headwind
Weight .... 2,316 lbs.

Since a graphic chart often incorporates more variables into a single chart, you must exercise extra care when using it. You may be tempted to estimate where two lines meet on the chart, or to "eyeball" values rather than drawing your lines carefully. This can lead to substantial errors.

TIME, FUEL, AND DISTANCE TO CLIMB CHART

The sample chart in Figure 1-28 is a little different from the others. First, you determine the time, fuel, and distance to climb from sea level to your cruise altitude, then subtract the time, fuel, and distance to climb from sea level to the departure airport. What remains is the time to climb from the departure airport to your cruising altitude. For this example, assume the following conditions, and determine the time, fuel, and distance required to climb from the airport elevation of 2,000 feet to 8,000 feet.

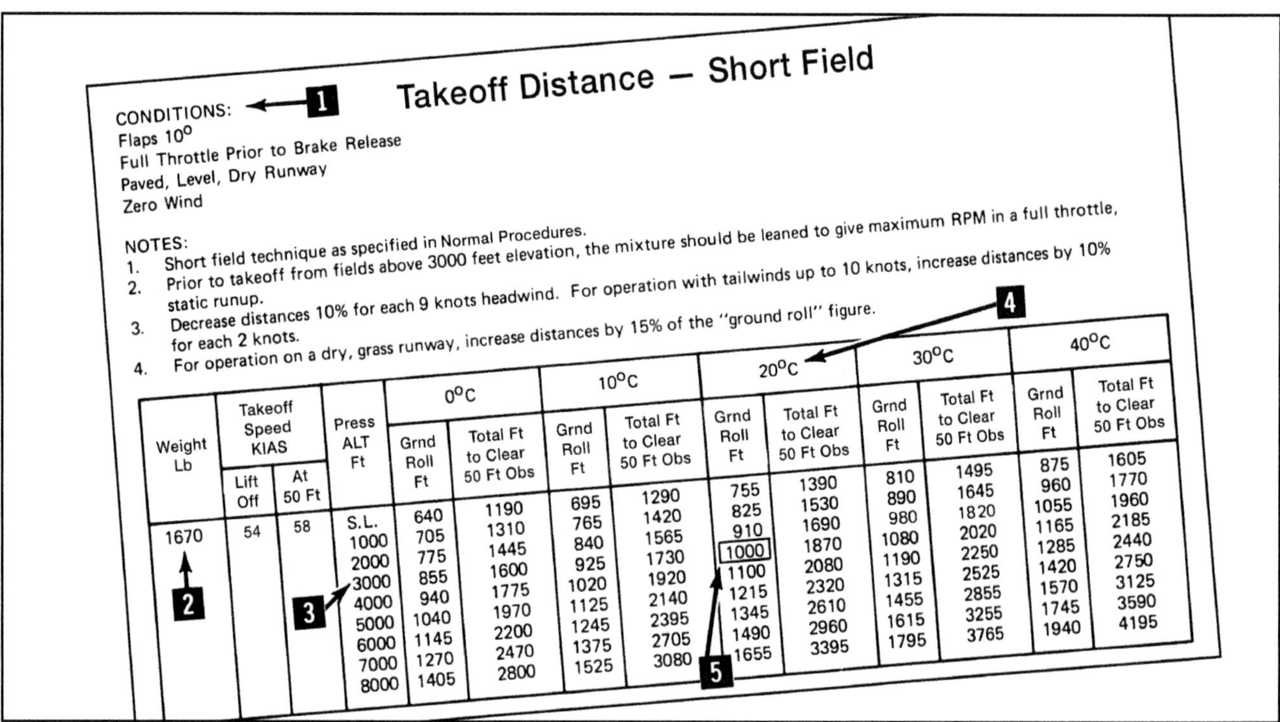

Takeoff Distance — Short Field

CONDITIONS:
Flaps 10°
Full Throttle Prior to Brake Release
Paved, Level, Dry Runway
Zero Wind

NOTES:
1. Short field technique as specified in Normal Procedures.
2. Prior to takeoff from fields above 3000 feet elevation, the mixture should be leaned to give maximum RPM in a full throttle, static runup.
3. Decrease distances 10% for each 9 knots headwind. For operation with tailwinds up to 10 knots, increase distances by 10% for each 2 knots.
4. For operation on a dry, grass runway, increase distances by 15% of the "ground roll" figure.

Weight Lb	Takeoff Speed KIAS Lift Off	Takeoff Speed KIAS At 50 Ft	Press ALT Ft	0°C Grnd Roll Ft	0°C Total Ft to Clear 50 Ft Obs	10°C Grnd Roll Ft	10°C Total Ft to Clear 50 Ft Obs	20°C Grnd Roll Ft	20°C Total Ft to Clear 50 Ft Obs	30°C Grnd Roll Ft	30°C Total Ft to Clear 50 Ft Obs	40°C Grnd Roll Ft	40°C Total Ft to Clear 50 Ft Obs
1670	54	58	S.L.	640	1190	695	1290	755	1390	810	1495	875	1605
			1000	705	1310	765	1420	825	1530	890	1645	960	1770
			2000	775	1445	840	1565	910	1690	980	1820	1055	1960
			3000	855	1600	925	1730	1000	1870	1080	2020	1165	2185
			4000	940	1775	1020	1920	1100	2080	1190	2250	1285	2440
			5000	1040	1970	1125	2140	1215	2320	1315	2525	1420	2750
			6000	1145	2200	1245	2395	1345	2610	1455	2855	1570	3125
			7000	1270	2470	1375	2705	1490	2960	1615	3255	1745	3590
			8000	1405	2800	1525	3080	1655	3395	1795	3765	1940	4195

Figure 1-26. A quick check of the conditions (item 1) and the takeoff weight (item 2) indicate you are using the correct chart. Enter the tabular data at the pressure altitude of 3,000 feet (item 3) and proceed horizontally to the column for 20°C (item 4). The ground roll distance is 1,000 feet (item 5).

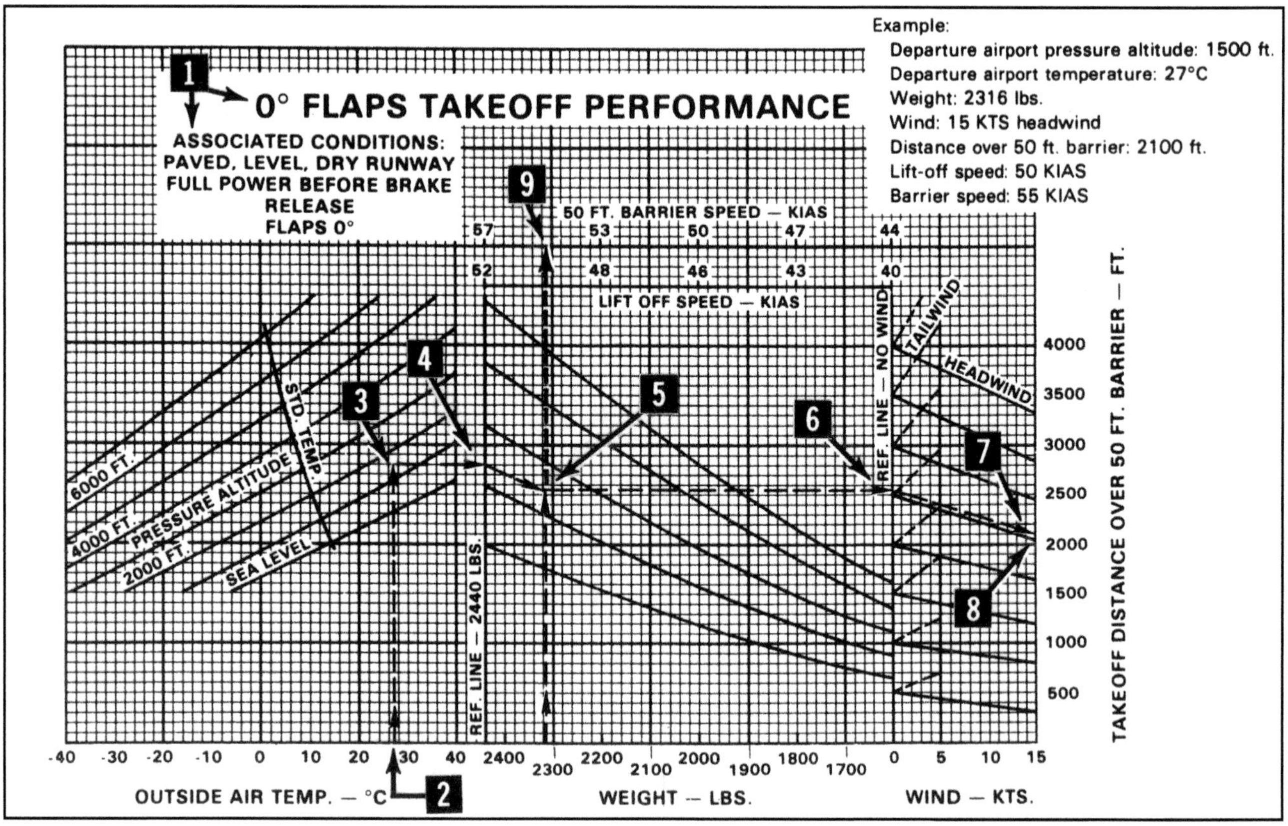

0° FLAPS TAKEOFF PERFORMANCE

ASSOCIATED CONDITIONS:
PAVED, LEVEL, DRY RUNWAY
FULL POWER BEFORE BRAKE RELEASE
FLAPS 0°

Example:
Departure airport pressure altitude: 1500 ft.
Departure airport temperature: 27°C
Weight: 2316 lbs.
Wind: 15 KTS headwind
Distance over 50 ft. barrier: 2100 ft.
Lift-off speed: 50 KIAS
Barrier speed: 55 KIAS

50 FT. BARRIER SPEED — KIAS: 57 53 50 47 44
LIFT OFF SPEED — KIAS: 52 48 46 43 40
6000 FT. 4000 FT. 2000 FT. PRESSURE ALTITUDE SEA LEVEL STD. TEMP
REF. LINE — 2440 LBS. REF. LINE — NO WIND TAILWIND HEADWIND
OUTSIDE AIR TEMP. — °C: -40 -30 -20 -10 0 10 20 30 40
WEIGHT — LBS.: 2400 2300 2200 2100 2000 1900 1800 1700
WIND — KTS.: 0 5 10 15
TAKEOFF DISTANCE OVER 50 FT. BARRIER — FT.: 500 1000 1500 2000 2500 3000 3500 4000

Figure 1-27. After checking the associated conditions (item 1), you can see that this chart is appropriate. Enter the graph at a temperature of 27°C (item 2) and proceed vertically to the pressure altitude of 1,500 feet (item 3). Next, proceed horizontally to the first reference line (item 4), then diagonally down until you intercept the takeoff weight of 2,316 pounds (item 5). Continue across to the second reference line (item 6), and correct for the headwind by paralleling the diagonal line downward until you intercept the 15-knot mark (item 7). The takeoff distance is 2,100 feet on the right side of the graph (item 8). To determine the appropriate takeoff speed, proceed vertically up from the takeoff weight (item 5) to the speeds listed at the top of the chart (item 9). The takeoff speed is 50 knots.

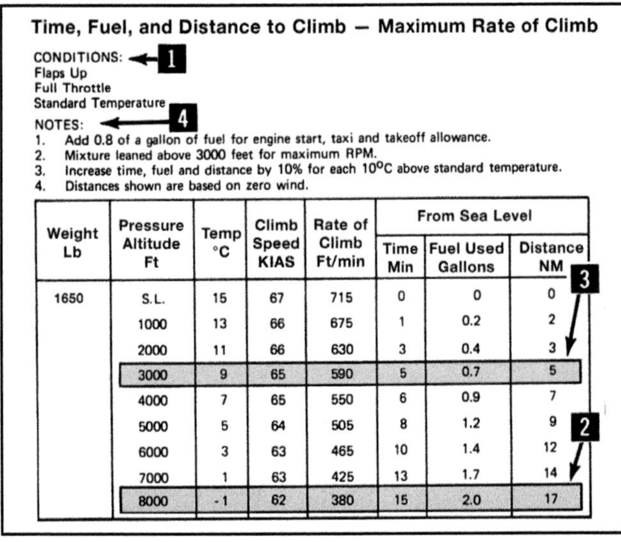

Time, Fuel, and Distance to Climb — Maximum Rate of Climb

CONDITIONS: 1
Flaps Up
Full Throttle
Standard Temperature

NOTES: 4
1. Add 0.8 of a gallon of fuel for engine start, taxi and takeoff allowance.
2. Mixture leaned above 3000 feet for maximum RPM.
3. Increase time, fuel and distance by 10% for each 10°C above standard temperature.
4. Distances shown are based on zero wind.

Weight Lb	Pressure Altitude Ft	Temp °C	Climb Speed KIAS	Rate of Climb Ft/min	From Sea Level Time Min	Fuel Used Gallons	Distance NM
1650	S.L.	15	67	715	0	0	0
	1000	13	66	675	1	0.2	2
	2000	11	66	630	3	0.4	3
	3000	9	65	590	5	0.7	5
	4000	7	65	550	6	0.9	7
	5000	5	64	505	8	1.2	9
	6000	3	63	465	10	1.4	12
	7000	1	63	425	13	1.7	14
	8000	-1	62	380	15	2.0	17

Figure 1-28. First, check the conditions (item 1). Then, read the time, fuel, and distance to climb to 7,000 feet of 13 minutes, 1.7 gallons, and 14 miles, respectively (item 2). Next, determine the time, fuel, and distance credits to be applied for departing an airport at 3,000 feet. These values are 5 minutes, 0.7 gallons, and 5 miles (item 3). After you subtract the credits, the net values are 8 minutes, 1.0 gallon, and 9 miles. A check of the notes, however, indicates that you must add an additional 0.8 gallons of fuel for the engine start, taxi, and takeoff allowances (item 4). The final values of time, fuel, and distance to climb from 3,000 feet to 7,000 feet are 8 minutes, 1.8 gallons (1.0 + .8), and 9 miles.

Cruise altitude .... 7,000 ft.
Airport elevation .... 3,000 ft.
Flaps .... Up
Power .... Full throttle
Temperature .... Standard
Weight .... 1,670 lbs.

CRUISE PERFORMANCE CHART

Cruise performance charts vary considerably. Before you use a particular chart, make sure you understand how the information is portrayed. Temperatures for cruise may include International Standard Atmosphere (ISA) values, as well as colder and warmer temperatures. For instance, temperature categories may specify 20°C below standard temperature, standard temperature, and 20°C above standard temperature. Assume you are planning a flight under the following conditions, and use the chart in figure 1-29 to determine the percent brake horsepower (%BH), true airspeed, and fuel flow in gallons per hour.

Pressure altitude .... 8,000 ft.
Temperature .... 20°C below std.
Power .... 2,400 r.p.m.
Weight .... 2,300 lbs.

LANDING DISTANCE CHART

Landing distance charts are similar to takeoff distance charts. For this sample of a graph-style performance chart, use the following conditions to determine the distance to land over a 50-foot obstacle and bring the airplane to a complete stop. [Figure 1-30]

Cruise Performance

CONDITIONS:
2300 Pounds
Recommended Lean Mixture

Pressure Altitude Ft	RPM	20°C Below Standard Temp % BHP	KTAS	GPH	Standard Temperature % BHP	KTAS	GPH	20°C Above Standard Temp % BHP	KTAS	GPH
2000	2500	---	---	---	75	116	8.4	71	115	7.9
	2400	72	111	8.0	67	111	7.5	63	110	7.1
	2300	64	106	7.1	60	105	6.7	56	105	6.3
	2200	56	101	6.3	53	100	6.1	50	99	5.8
	2100	50	95	5.8	47	94	5.6	45	93	5.4
4000	2550	---	---	---	75	118	8.4	71	118	7.9
	2500	76	116	8.5	71	115	8.0	67	115	7.5
	2400	68	111	7.6	64	110	7.1	60	109	6.7
	2300	60	105	6.8	57	105	6.4	54	104	6.1
	2200	54	100	6.1	51	99	5.9	48	98	5.7
	2100	48	94	5.6	46	93	5.5	44	92	5.3
6000	2600	---	---	---	75	120	8.4	71	120	7.9
	2500	72	116	8.1	67	115	7.6	64	114	7.1
	2400	64	110	7.2	60	109	6.8	57	109	6.4
	2300	57	105	6.5	54	104	6.2	52	103	5.9
	2200	51	99	5.9	49	98	5.7	47	97	5.5
	2100	46	93	5.5	44	92	5.4	42	91	5.2
8000	2650	---	---	---	75	122	8.4	71	122	7.9
	2600	76	120	8.6	71	120	8.0	67	119	7.5
	2500	68	115	7.7	64	114	7.2	60	113	6.8
	2400	61	110	6.9	58	109	6.5	55	108	6.2
	2300	55	104	6.2	52	103	6.0	50	102	5.8
	2200	49	98	5.7	47	97	5.5	45	96	5.4
10,000	2650	76	122	8.5	71	122	8.0	67	121	7.5
	2600	72	120	8.1	68	119	7.6	64	118	7.1
	2500	65	114	7.3	61	114	6.8	58	112	6.5
	2400	58	109	6.5	55	108	6.2	52	107	6.0
	2300	52	103	6.0	50	102	5.8	48	101	5.6
	2200	47	97	5.6	45	96	5.4	44	95	5.3
12,000	2600	68	119	7.7	64	118	7.2	61	117	6.8
	2500	62	114	6.9	58	113	6.5	55	111	6.2
	2400	56	108	6.3	53	107	6.0	51	106	5.8
	2300	50	102	5.8	48	101	5.6	46	100	5.5
	2200	46	96	5.5	44	95	5.4	43	94	5.3

Figure 1-29. Begin by moving to 8,000 in the pressure altitude column (item 1). Next, move laterally to the RPM column and locate the desired RPM setting of 2,400 (item 2). From this point you must proceed to one of the three temperature columns, 20°C below standard temperature, standard temperature, or 20°C above standard temperature. In this case, use the figures in the 20°C below standard temperature column (item 3). The percent brake horsepower is 61%, your true airspeed is 110 knots, and the fuel burn is 6.9 gallons per hour.

Pressure altitude .... 2,500 ft.
Temperature .... 24°C
Flaps .... 40°
Runway .... Paved, level, and dry
Wind .... 0 kts. headwind
Weight .... 2,179 lbs.
Braking .... Maximum

INTERPOLATION

Interpolation is the process of finding an unknown value between two known values. Often this is necessary when you use charts with tabular information. So far, the sample problems have used altitudes and temperatures that permitted you to extract answers directly. To see how to solve a problem when this is not the case, use the chart in figure 1-31 to work another landing performance problem. In this example, assume you need to know the ground roll requirement under the following conditions.

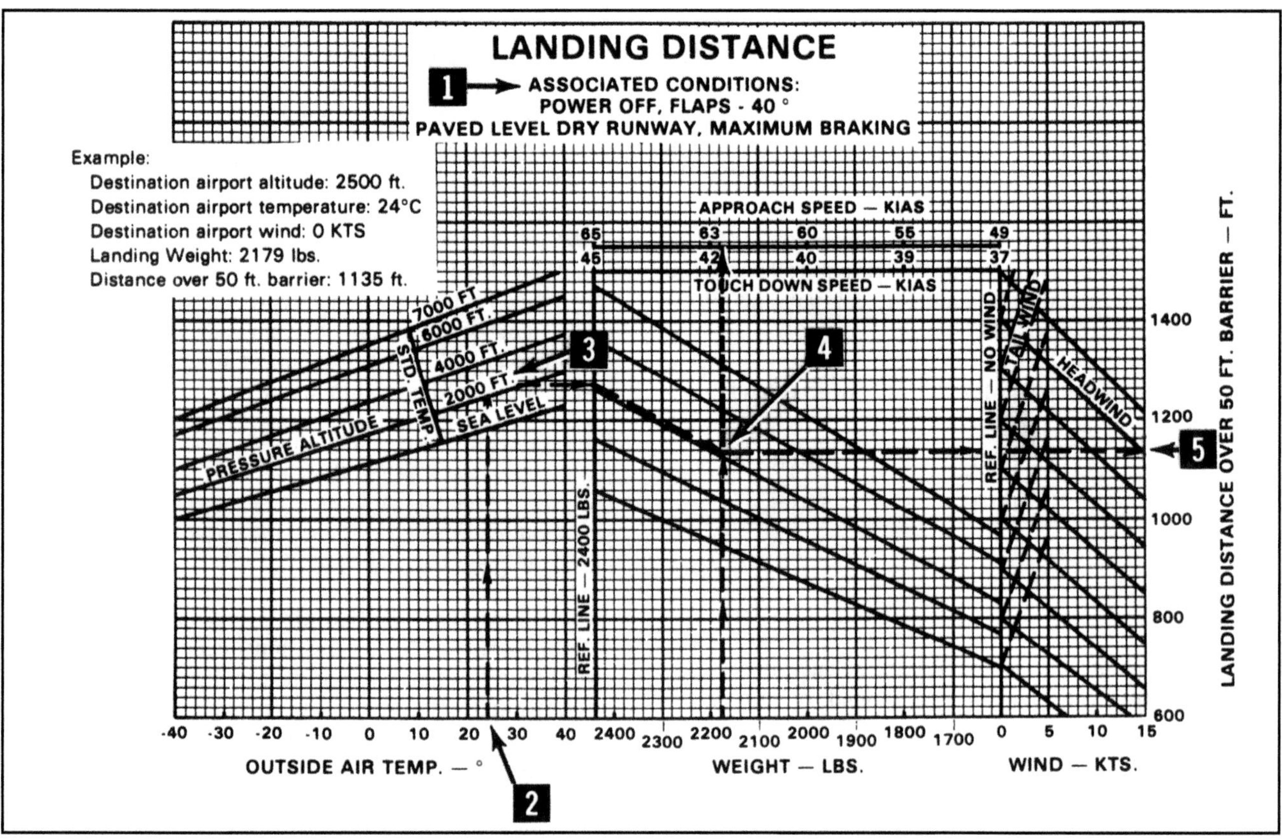

Figure 1-30. First, check the associated conditions listed on the sample chart (item 1). Next, enter the chart at the given temperature of 24°C (item 2) and proceed vertically up to the pressure altitude of 2,500 feet (item 3). Proceed horizontally to the first reference line, then diagonally down to a weight of 2,179 pounds (item 4). Continue horizontally to the reference line. Note that since the reported wind is calm, no correction is required. Read the distance required of 1,135 feet on the right side of the chart (item 5).

Landing Distance

CONDITIONS:
Flaps 40°
Power Off
Maximum Braking
Paved, Level, Dry Runway
Zero Wind

NOTES:
1. Short field technique as specified in Normal Procedures.
2. Decrease distances 10% for each 9 knots headwind. For operation with tailwinds up to 10 knots, increase distances by 10% for each 2 knots.
3. For operation on a dry, grass runway, increase distances by 45% of the "ground roll" figure.

Weight Lb	Speed At 50 Ft KIAS	Press Alt Ft	0°C		10°C		20°C		30°C		40°C	
			Grnd Roll	Total Ft to Clear 50 Ft Obs	Grnd Roll	Total Ft to Clear 50 Ft Obs	Grnd Roll	Total Ft to Clear 50 Ft Obs	Grnd Roll	Total Ft to Clear 50 Ft Obs	Grnd Roll	Total Ft to Clear 50 Ft Obs
2300	60	S.L.	495	1205	510	1235	530	1265	545	1295	565	1330
		1000	510	1235	530	1265	550	1300	565	1330	585	1365
		2000	530	1265	550	1300	570	1335	590	1370	610	1405
		3000	550	1300	570	1335	590	1370	610	1405	630	1440
		4000	570	1335	590	1370	615	1410	635	1445	655	1480
		5000	590	1370	615	1415	635	1450	655	1485	680	1525
		6000	615	1415	640	1455	660	1490	685	1535	705	1570
		7000	640	1455	660	1495	685	1535	710	1575	730	1615
		8000	665	1500	690	1540	710	1580	735	1620	760	1665

Figure 1-31. Looking at the sample landing chart excerpt, you can see that the given pressure altitude of 2,500 feet falls between the 2,000- and 3,000-foot pressure altitude values. This means your ground roll distance will fall between 590 and 610 feet. Interpolation is required.

Pressure altitude .... 2,500 ft.
Temperature .... 30°C.
Flaps .... 40°
Runway .... Paved, level, and dry
Wind .... Calm
Weight .... 2,300 lbs.

In this case, you know the ground roll figures for 2,000 and 3,000 feet and want to determine the ground roll for 2,500 feet. The first step in interpolation is to compute the differences between known values.

	Pressure Altitude	Ground Roll
	3,000 ft.	610 ft.
	2,000 ft.	590 ft.
Difference	1,000 ft.	20 ft.

The 2,500-foot airport pressure altitude is halfway between 2,000 and 3,000 feet. Therefore, the ground roll also is half of the difference between 590 and 610 feet. The answer then, is 600 feet. (20-foot difference X .5) + 590 feet = 600 feet.

4. Describes the effects of atmospheric conditions on the airplane's performance.

FACTORS AFFECTING PERFORMANCE

There are numerous things that affect aircraft performance. Some of these include the airport elevation, temperature, humidity, surface winds, aircraft weight, and the slope and condition of the runways.

The **elevation** you takeoff from can significantly affect performance. As altitude increases, the amount of air available for engine combustion and the production of lift decreases. This decrease in air density results in a loss of performance that is most evident during takeoff and climbout. As air density decreases it is referred to as an increase in density altitude. By the same token, if air density increases, density altitude decreases.

Another performance-related item you must be familiar with is air **temperature**. As the temperature rises, the density of the air decreases, resulting in a decrease in engine power output, propeller efficiency, and aerodynamic lift.

Most performance charts do not require you to compute density altitude, since it is built into the chart. You must enter the correct pressure altitude and the temperature. Older charts, however, may require you to determine density altitude, or calculate it with a flight computer. Conditions that cause high density altitude are "high, hot, and humid."

The amount of water vapor contained in the atmosphere is referred to as **humidity**, and it is expressed as a percentage of the maximum amount of water vapor the air can hold. Humidity affects aircraft engine performance by taking up space that is normally available for vaporized fuel. As humidity increases, less air enters the engine. This has the effect of causing a small increase in density altitude. The moist air also tends to retard even fuel burning in the cylinder. When the relative humidity is high, engine power loss may be as high as seven percent, and the airplane's total takeoff and climb performance may be reduced by as much as 10 percent. You can also expect a higher landing speed and a longer landing roll in less dense, humid air.

Surface winds also can have a significant impact on airplane operations. When they are used to your advantage, they reduce takeoff and landing distances. Because of this you should always takeoff and land on a runway that is most closely aligned into the wind.

Aircraft **weight** significantly affects performance. As weight increases, the aircraft must accelerate to a higher speed to generate sufficient lift for flight. This means the aircraft requires more runway for takeoff. The additional weight also reduces acceleration during the takeoff roll, and this adds to the total takeoff distance. Increases in weight also reduce climb performance. This is because excess power and thrust are limited.

Runway conditions relating to aircraft performance data normally specify a paved and level runway with a smooth dry surface. If any one of these conditions do not exist, the takeoff and landing distances will not agree with the values listed in the performance charts.

Runway surfaces which are not hard, smooth, and dry increase takeoff roll. Impediments such as mud, water, snow, or grass prevent the aircraft from rolling smoothly on the runway, and reduce aircraft acceleration. At times, the reduction in acceleration may make it impossible for you to attain takeoff speed.

Runway **gradient,** or **slope** refers to the amount of change in runway height over its length, and is usually expressed as a percentage. A gradient of two percent means the runway height changes two feet for each 100 feet of runway length. A positive runway gradient reduces takeoff performance by slowing the rate of acceleration, but decreases the landing roll. A negative gradient shortens the takeoff roll, but increases the landing distance. Runway gradient is listed in the Airport/Facility Directory.

Braking Effectiveness refers to how much braking power you can apply to the tires. If the runway is wet, less friction between the tires and runway is available and the length of the landing roll increases. In some cases, you can lose all braking effectiveness due to a thin layer of water that separates the tires from the runway. This is known as hydroplaning. Braking effectiveness may be completely lost on ice-covered runways. Ensure that you have adequate runway length and favorable surface winds under these conditions.

EXERCISES

1. As aircraft weight increases, the airspeed required for liftoff _______.

2. Using Figure 1-26 on page 1-41, determine the ground roll under the given conditions.

Pressure altitude .... 3,500 ft.
Temperature .... 20°C
Flaps .... 10°
Runway .... Paved, level, and dry
Wind .... 9 kts. headwind
Weight .... 1,670 lbs.

The ground roll is _______ feet.

3. Given the following conditions, determine the time, fuel, and distance to climb using Figure 1-28 on page 1-42.

Cruise altitude .... 8,000 ft.
Airport elevation .... 1,000 ft.
Flaps .... Up
Power .... Full throttle
Temperature .... Standard
Weight .... 1,670 lbs.

Time _______ Fuel _______ Distance _______

4. What item is not included in the basic empty weight of the aircraft?

   1. Usable fuel
   2. Full engine oil
   3. Standard equipment
   4. Optional equipment

5. Useful load includes payload plus _______ fuel.

6. Given the following weight and balance form, determine the aircraft's total weight, total moment, and center of gravity.

WEIGHT and BALANCE FORM			
ITEM	WEIGHT (pounds)	ARM (inches)	MOMENT (pound-inches)
BASIC EMPTY WT.	1,405	37.50	52,687.5
FUEL (40 gal.)	240	46.0	
PILOT & PASSENGER	360	37.0	13,320
REAR PASSENGER	180	73.0	13,140
BAGGAGE	40	100.0	
TOTAL			
CG = _______ INCHES			

SAMPLE ORAL QUESTIONS

1. Conditions on the ground which affect aircraft performance include the surface winds, aircraft weight, and the condition and slope of the runway. Atmospheric conditions affecting performance include the density altitude, temperature, and humidity.

2. The amount of change in runway height over its length is referred to as runway gradient or slope. A gradient of one percent means the runway height changes one foot for each 100 feet of runway length. Keep in mind that this figure is an overall gradient, and it does not reflect variations along the runway. A positive runway gradient indicates the slope of the runway increases, which reduces takeoff performance, but decreases landing roll. A negative gradient shortens the takeoff roll, but increases the landing distance. Runway gradient is listed in the Airport/Facility Directory.

1. List the conditions on the ground and the atmospheric conditions that affect aircraft performance.

2. Describe runway gradient, or slope, and how it affects aircraft performance.

3. Describe the significance of weight as it relates to take-off performance.

3. Aircraft weight significantly affects performance. As weight increases, the aircraft must accelerate to a higher speed to generate sufficient lift for flight. This means the aircraft requires more runway for takeoff. The additional weight also reduces acceleration during the take-off roll, and this also adds to the total takeoff distance.

4. Describe density altitude and its affect on aircraft performance.

4. Density altitude significantly affects your aircraft's performance capability. Density altitude is pressure altitude corrected for nonstandard temperature, and at a given level it is equal to pressure altitude only when standard atmospheric conditions exist. With normally aspirated engines, increased density altitude results in decreased engine power, propeller efficiency, and aerodynamic lift. Most performance charts do not require you to compute density altitude. The conditions which cause a high density altitude are "high, hot, and humid."

ADDITIONAL QUESTIONS

5. You must know how to use the performance charts listed in your aircraft's POH.

6. What do the terms arm, moment, and CG mean, and how are they determined?

7. The examiner will ask you to calculate weight and balance for your aircraft.

EXERCISE ANSWERS

1. increases

2. 945

3. 14 minutes, 2.6 gallons, 15 n.m.

4. 1

5. usable

6. Total weight: 2,225 lbs; total moment: 94,187.5 lb/in; CG: 42.3 inches.

REFERENCES

JEPPESEN:

Private Pilot Manual/Video - Chapters 8A and 8B

FAA:

Airplane Flying Handbook (FAA-H-8083-3)
Pilot's Handbook of Aeronautical Knowledge (AC 61-23/FAA-H-8083-25)
Role of Preflight Preparation (AC-61-84)
Pilot's Weight and Balance Handbook (FAA-H-8083-1)
Pilot's Operating Handbook and FAA-Approved Airplane Flight Manual

G. TASK: OPERATION OF SYSTEMS (ASEL AND ASES)

REFERENCES: AC 61-23/FAA-H-8083-25, POH/AFM.

Objective: To determine that the applicant exhibits knowledge of the elements related to the operation of systems on the airplane provided for the flight test by explaining at least three (3) of the following systems:

1. Primary flight controls and trim.
2. Flaps, leading edge devices, and spoilers.
3. Water rudders (ASES).
4. Powerplant and propeller.
5. Landing gear.
6. Fuel oil and hydraulic.
7. Electrical.
8. Avionics.
9. Pitot-static, vacuum pressure and associated flight instruments.
10. Environmental.
11. Deicing and anti-icing.

Objective: To determine that the applicant exhibits knowledge of the elements related to the operation of systems on the airplane provided for the flight test by explaining at least three (3) of the following systems:

1. Primary flight controls and trim.

FLIGHT CONTROLS

The primary flight controls consist of the ailerons, rudder, and elevator. Mechanical linkages extend from each control surface to the rudder pedals and control yoke (stick) inside the cockpit. When a control surface is deflected, the camber, and angle of attack of its associated wing or stabilizer changes, creating new lift and drag characteristics.

AILERONS

The ailerons are attached to the outboard portion of the wing's trailing edge. They move up and down, alternately, to **bank** the aircraft. Because of their aerodynamic shape, they can enhance lift when lowered and create drag when raised. When an aileron is lowered, it increases the angle of attack on a wing and increases lift. On the other hand, when an aileron is raised, the angle of attack on a wing decreases resulting in a corresponding loss of lift. This allows you to bank (roll) an aircraft around its longitudinal axis.

RUDDER

The tail section is referred to as the **empennage** and consists of a vertical stabilizer and a horizontal stabilizer. The rudder is attached to the vertical stabilizer and controls movement about the vertical axis of the aircraft. This movement is referred to as yaw and is controlled by the rudder pedals. When the left rudder pedal is depressed, the rudder also is deflected to the left, allowing the airflow to push the tail to the right and the nose to the left.

ELEVATOR

The elevator is also part of the empennage, but is attached to the horizontal stabilizer. The elevator controls **pitch**, or movement about the lateral axis. Movement of the elevator is controlled by pushing or pulling on the control yoke. When the yoke is pulled back, the elevator deflects upward and decreases the angle of attack on the horizontal stabilizer. This forces the tail down resulting in the nose pitching up and an increase in the angle of attack on the wings. When the yoke is pushed forward, the elevator deflects downward and increases the angle of attack on the horizontal stabilizer. This causes the tail to rise, decreasing the wing's angle of attack.

STABILATOR

Some empennage designs have a one-piece horizontal stabilizer that pivots up and down from a central hinge point. This type of design, called a **stabilator**, functions as both an elevator and horizontal stabilizer. You move the stabilator using the control wheel, just as you would the elevator. An **antiservo tab** is mounted at the back of the stabilator, to provide you with a control "feel" similar to what you experience with an elevator. Without the antiservo tab, control forces from the stabilator would be so light that you might over-control the airplane or move the control wheel too far to obtain the desired result.

TRIM

Most airplanes have small hinged, aerodynamic surfaces, called trim tabs. These devices can be attached to the trailing edge of an elevator, rudder, and aileron and are used to relieve control pressures. A trim tab is moved opposite the direction of travel of the control surface it is attached to. For example, if you want to relieve, or neutralize, pressure when holding an upward deflected elevator, the trim tab is deflected down. This results in the flow of air striking the trim tab exerting an upward force on the elevator. [Figure 1-32]

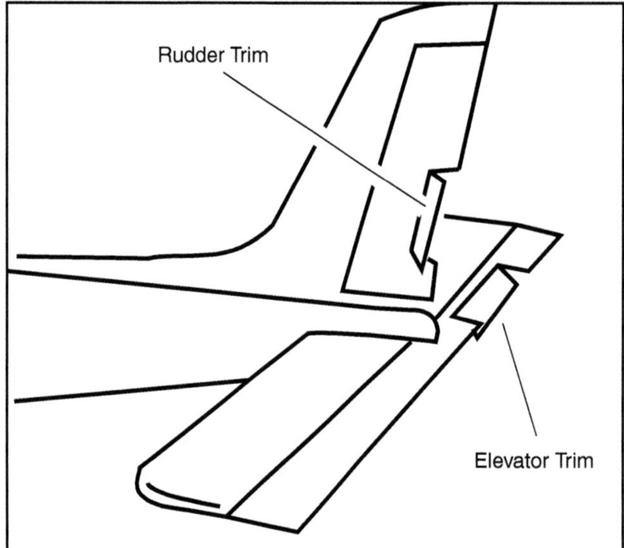

Figure 1-32. Aircraft are equipped with trim devices for the purpose of relieving control pressures. Most training aircraft have elevator trim that can be adjusted in the cockpit and a flexible trim tab on the rudder that is adjusted on the ground.

2. Flaps, leading edge devices, and spoilers.

FLAPS

One of the primary purposes of flaps is to allow the aircraft to make steeper approaches without increasing airspeed. When properly used, flaps increase lift and decrease stall speed. This allows you to fly at a reduced speed while maintaining sufficient control for sustained flight. Flaps also can be used to shorten the takeoff run and steepen the climb path.

There are several common types of flaps, including the **plain flap**, the **split flap**, the **slotted flap**, and the **Fowler flap**. You should be familiar with the type installed on your aircraft as well as the differences between types. [Figure 1-33]

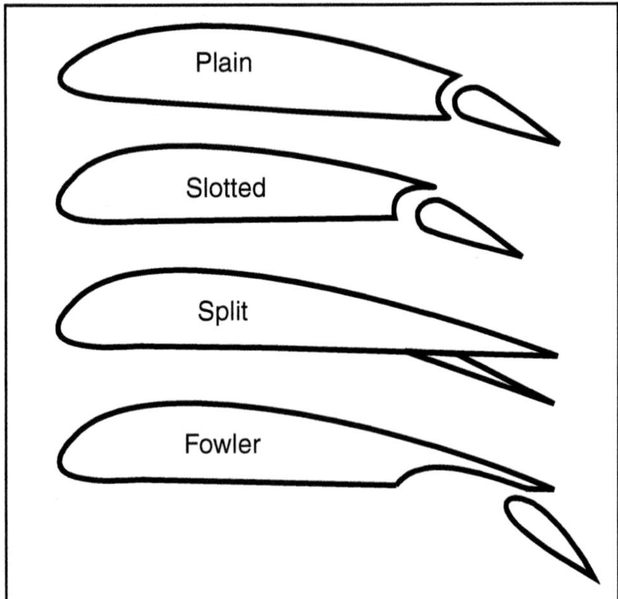

Figure 1-33. Flap types include plain, split, slotted, and Fowler. Although some flaps increase the wing's surface area, most change only the effective camber and the chord line.

Although the amount of lift and drag created by a specific flap setting varies, you can make a few general assumptions. When flaps are partially extended, they produce a relatively large amount of lift for a small increase in drag. However, once flap extension reaches approximately the midpoint, this relationship reverses. Now, a significant increase in drag occurs for a relatively small increase in lift. Because of this, most manufacturers limit the takeoff setting to half flaps or less.

SLOTS AND SLATS

In addition to flaps, some wings incorporate leading edge devices to further increase lift. Two of these devices that you should be aware of are **slots and slats**. A leading edge slot is an actual space between the leading edge and the rest of the wing. The slot allows a smooth flow over the top of the wing at higher angles of attack. Slots are usually placed near the wingtip to allow aileron control to be maintained throughout a stall. Slats, on the other hand, are moveable leading edge devices that produce slots.

SPOILERS

Up to this point, we've looked at ways to increase the amount of lift a wing can generate. However, at times it's advantageous to decrease the amount of lift produced. One way this is done is with spoilers. Spoilers are mounted flush with the top of the wing. When activated, they extend or pivot upward into the airflow on top of the wing and decrease lift. On larger aircraft, spoilers are used at lower speeds, in conjunction with the ailerons, to bank the aircraft and to increase the rate of descent.

4. Powerplant and propeller.

THE ENGINE

Most training airplanes are powered by horizontally opposed, reciprocating engines, which get their name from the back and forth movement of the internal engine components. The reciprocating motion is caused by the ignition and controlled burning of the fuel/air mixture in a four-stroke cycle. [Figure 1-34]

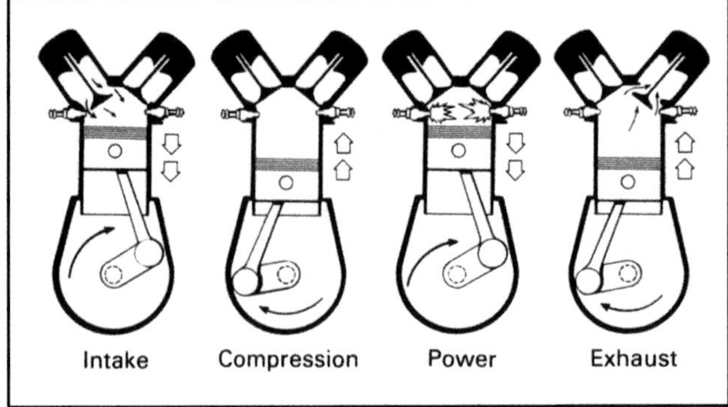

Figure 1-34. The arrows in this illustration indicate the direction of motion of the crankshaft and piston during the four-stroke cycle.

In the first of the four strokes, the **intake** stroke, the downward movement of the piston draws the fuel/air mixture into the cylinder. In the **compression** stroke, the piston moves upward, compressing the mixture. The beginning of the power stroke occurs when the spark plugs ignite the fuel/air mixture. As the mixture burns, rapidly increasing pressure forces the piston downward. During this stroke the mechanical energy is delivered to the crankshaft. Finally, in the **exhaust** stroke, the piston travels upward and expels the burned mixture. These events are very precisely timed and allow the four-stroke cycle to be repeated several hundred times per minute.

When the engine is operating optimally, the fuel/air mixture burns in a controlled manner. This type of combustion causes a smooth buildup of temperature and pressure.

Detonation, on the other hand, is an uncontrolled explosive ignition of the mixture that causes excessive temperatures and pressure to be exerted on the piston, cylinder, and valves. Initial indications of detonation include excessive engine temperatures, engine roughness, and loss of power. Detonation can happen any time you allow the engine to overheat or if an improper grade of fuel is used.

In a properly functioning engine, ignition of the fuel/air mixture occurs at precisely the right moment. In contrast, **preignition** occurs when the mixture ignites too soon due to residual hot spots on the cylinder or carbon deposits. This can cause serious engine damage if not corrected.

INDUCTION SYSTEM

The induction system brings outside air into the engine, mixes it with fuel in the proper proportion, and delivers it to the cylinders where combustion occurs. The **carburetor** is the device that actually mixes the incoming air with fuel. Most light aircraft use a float-type carburetor system. When the air enters the carburetor it passes through a venturi. This increases its velocity and decreases its pressure.

Carburetors are calibrated at sea level, and the correct fuel-to-air mixture ratio is established at that altitude with the mixture control set in the FULL RICH position. However, as altitude increases, the density of air entering the carburetor decreases while the density of the fuel remains the same. To maintain the correct fuel/air mixture, you must use the mixture control to adjust the amount of fuel that is mixed with the incoming air.

Most mixture adjustments are required during changes of altitude or during operations at airports with field elevations well above sea level. A mixture that is too rich can result in engine roughness. The roughness is normally due to spark plug fouling from excessive carbon buildup on the plugs. On the other hand, if you fail to enrich the mixture during a descent from high altitude, it normally will become too lean. This can cause high engine temperatures resulting in excessive engine wear or even failure. The best way to avoid this situation is to monitor the engine temperature gauges regularly and follow POH guidelines for maintaining the proper mixture.

CARBURETOR ICING

The effect of fuel vaporization and decreasing air pressure in the venturi causes a sharp drop in temperature in the carburetor. If the air is moist, the water vapor in the air may condense. When the temperature in the carburetor is at or below freezing, **carburetor ice** may form on internal surfaces. Icing can occur even on warm days with temperatures as high as 38°C (100°F) and humidity as low as 50%. However, it is more likely to occur when temperatures are below 21 °C (70°F) and the relative humidity is above 80%.

Typically, your first indication of carburetor icing is a decrease in engine r.p.m. followed by engine roughness and possible fuel starvation. The **carburetor heat** system prevents or eliminates the ice by routing air across a heat source before it enters the carburetor. Generally, you should use full carburetor heat whenever you reduce engine r.p.m. below the normal operating range for your airplane or when you suspect the presence of carburetor ice. Carburetor heat tends to decrease engine power output and increase the operating temperature of the engine. Normally, you do not use it continuously when full power is required, particularly during takeoff. Be sure to check your pilot's operating handbook for specific recommendations.

THE PROPELLER

The propeller supplies the thrust that drives the airplane through the air. Because of its shape, each blade of the propeller acts as a rotating wing or airfoil. However, unlike a wing, which moves through the air at a uniform speed, the tip of the propeller rotates at a much greater speed than the hub. To compensate for this, the propeller is shaped to give the blades a low angle of attack at the tips and a high angle of attack at the hub. This allows the propeller to provide uniform thrust along most of its length. [Figure 1-35]

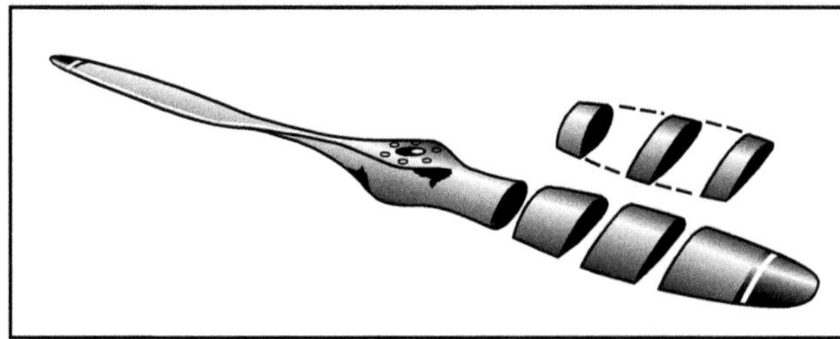

Figure 1-35. The cross sections of this propeller blade illustrate the well-defined airfoil shape. The front surface of the blade is cambered, or curved, while the back is comparatively flat. The leading edge is the thicker part of the blade that meets the air during rotation. Notice how the shape of the airfoil cross-sections changes along the length of the propeller. Near the hub, the cross section is a thick, low-speed airfoil with a high angle of attack, while the tip is a thin, high-speed airfoil with a very low angle of attack.

Light airplanes have either **fixed-pitch** or **constant-speed** propellers. A fixed-pitch propeller's blade angle cannot be changed and its speed is controlled by the throttle setting. A constant-speed propeller allows you to change the pitch of the blades to the most efficient angle for different phases of the flight. This allows the propeller to convert a high percentage of the engine's power into thrust.

An airplane with a constant-speed propeller has two power controls — the throttle and the propeller control. The throttle adjusts the power output of the engine, which is directly indicated on the manifold pressure gauge. The propeller control changes the pitch of the propeller blades and regulates the r.p.m. of the engine and the prop, as indicated on the tachometer.

5. Landing gear.

LANDING GEAR

The landing gear supports the aircraft when it is on the ground. Landing gear can either be fixed or retractable. Both types typically use three wheels. The main gear are positioned on each side of the fuselage, while the third wheel may be located either under the nose or under the tail. If it is located at the tail, it is said to be a **tailwheel** or **conventional** gear aircraft. If the third wheel is under the nose it is termed a **tricycle** gear airplane.

The landing gear includes the brakes, which are somewhat similar to automobile brakes, except that each brake can be controlled separately, and only the main gear wheels are equipped with brakes. Using one brake more than the other is referred to as differential braking, and is quite helpful in steering the airplane on the ground.

RETRACTABLE LANDING GEAR

Retractable landing gear is intended to increase performance by reducing drag. Gear retraction systems are classified according to the power source used for retraction and extension. Electrical and hydraulic actuating mechanisms are used most frequently. If the airplane you fly is equipped with retractable landing gear, you must be thoroughly familiar with the type of system used, as well as the procedure used to manually extend the gear.

6. Fuel, oil, and hydraulic.

FUEL SYSTEM

Fuel systems vary from airplane to airplane, but all consist of some combination of tanks, vents, valves, pumps, drains, gauges, and lines. There are two general types of fuel systems found in light airplanes æ those that require a fuel pump and those that feed by gravity. The **fuel pump system** is usually found in low-wing airplanes, and in most high-performance airplanes with fuel-injected engines. An engine-driven pump provides fuel under pressure to the engine. Because engine-driven pumps operate only when the engine is running, a **boost pump** is used to provide fuel pressure for engine starting and as a backup. In a **gravity feed system**, fuel flows by gravity from the fuel tanks to the engine. This type of system is typically used in high-wing airplanes where the fuel is stored above the engine allowing gravity to pressurize the system.

FUEL SYSTEM COMPONENTS

The fuel tanks are usually located in the wings and contain vents that allow air pressure inside the tank to remain the same as that outside the tank. The vents may be located in the filler caps, or the tank may be vented through a small tube extending through the wing surface.

To allow you to draw fuel from either tank, a fuel selector is incorporated in most aircraft fuel systems. A selector typically has at least three positions: LEFT, RIGHT, and OFF. With this type of system, you must monitor fuel consumption closely to ensure that you don't run a tank completely out of fuel. Other selectors may have a BOTH position that lets fuel flow to the engine from both tanks simultaneously.

After the fuel selector valve, the fuel passes through a strainer. The strainer removes water droplets and other sediments that might be in the system. To prevent these contaminants from building up in the strainer, it is generally recommended that you drain it before each flight. In addition, you should take a fuel sample from the sump drains located on each wing tank. When doing this, you should be checking for the proper fuel grade and the presence of water or other contaminants.

REFUELING

When refueling an aircraft, be aware that a small spark can ignite fuel vapors. The most probable cause of a spark is static electricity. To reduce the possibility of sparking, you should ground the aircraft with a grounding wire.

FUEL GRADES

In addition to using the proper refueling technique, you must also be sure you are using the proper grade of fuel. Airplane engines are designed to operate with a fuel that meets certain specifications. The recommended fuel grade and authorized substitutes are in the pilot's operating handbook for your airplane. Fuel grades are identified according to octane, or performance number, and each grade is dyed a standard color to assist in identification. You should be familiar with the colors of the most common aviation fuels, including:

Grade	Color
80	Red
100LL	Blue
100	Green
Turbine Fuel	Colorless

OIL SYSTEM

Aircraft oil systems are designed to lubricate and cool the engine. The correct oil grade and quantity is specified by the manufacturer and is listed in the pilot's operating handbook (POH). You should check oil quantity before each flight. To allow you to monitor the oil system, oil temperature and oil pressure gauges are installed in the aircraft. Both of these gauges have a normal operating range indicated with a green arc. If you should observe other than normal indications, follow the appropriate instructions in your POH.

HYDRAULIC SYSTEM

On many light training aircraft, the wheel brakes are the only hydraulic system. The brake system has independent master cylinders that are mechanically connected to each of the brake pedals. When you press the brake pedals, you supply pressure to the system causing the brake calipers to apply pressure to the brake pads, which in turn slow the wheels. Prior to flight, you should always test the braking system by depressing the brake pedals to check for proper operation. If the airplane you fly has other hydraulically operated equipment, be sure you understand the system and its operation.

7. Electrical.

ELECTRICAL SYSTEM

Aircraft electrical systems typically consist of at least an alternator or generator, battery, circuit breakers, fuses, and buses. On most light airplanes, electrical energy is supplied by a 14- or 28-volt direct-current system, which usually is powered by an engine-driven alternator.

Alternators produce alternating current (AC), which must be converted to direct current (DC) for use in the system. Direct current is delivered to a bus bar, which serves to distribute the current to the various electrical components on the aircraft. The various devices connected to the bus bar are protected from excessive electrical loads or surges by circuit breakers. However, you should still make sure all electrical equipment is turned off before you start the engine. This protects sensitive components, particularly the radios, from damage that may be caused by random voltages generated during the starting process.

The battery is another essential part of the electrical system. Its main purpose is to provide power to start the engine. It also permits limited operation of electrical components without the engine running. Finally, the battery is a valuable source of standby or emergency electrical power in case of alternator malfunction.

An ammeter is used to monitor the electrical current, in amperes, within the system. Actually, there are two types of ammeters. One reflects current flowing to or from the battery. The other type simply displays the load placed on the alternator and is often referred to as a loadmeter.

The ammeter normally shows charging (needle on the plus side) following an engine start, since the battery power lost during starting is being replaced. After the battery is charged, the ammeter should stabilize near zero as the alternator supplies the electrical needs of the system. A discharging ammeter means the electrical load is exceeding the output of the alternator, and the battery is helping to supply system power. In this situation, you should reduce the electrical load to conserve battery power and land as soon as practicable.

With a loadmeter, you can tell immediately if the alternator is operating normally because it reflects the amount of current being drawn by the electrical equipment. The POH will tell you the normal load to expect. Loss of the alternator will cause the loadmeter to indicate zero.

The engine's ignition system is independent of the airplane's electrical system, since magnetos operate whenever the engine is rotating. The ignition switch controls the magnetos by grounding their output when the ignition is turned off. The master switch controls the entire electrical system, except for the magnetos. The engine's starter won't operate unless the master switch is ON because power for the starter comes from the electrical system, not the magnetos.

Most aircraft master switches have two sides: a battery side and an alternator side. During normal operations, both sides of the master switch are ON. The split switch lets you isolate the alternator from the rest of the system in case of malfunction. This type of master switch also allows you to check equipment on the ground before you start the engine by turning on just the battery side.

8. Avionics.

AVIONICS

Avionics is a contraction of the words "aviation" and "electronics." In training airplanes, avionics include the radios used for navigation and communication, as well as transponders, audio panels, and intercoms. An autopilot is also considered an avionics system.

These systems vary widely from one aircraft to another. You are expected to be familiar with the operating procedures and limitations of each piece of avionics equipment installed in your aircraft.

Information on specific pieces of equipment is usually found in section nine of the pilot's operating handbook.

9. Pitot-static, vacuum pressure and associated flight instruments.

PITOT-STATIC SYSTEM

The pitot-static system includes a pitot tube and one or more static ports. Three instruments are commonly connected to the pitot-static system. The airspeed indicator uses pressures from both the pitot tube and the static port, but the altimeter and vertical speed indicator use only static pressure. [Figure 1-36]

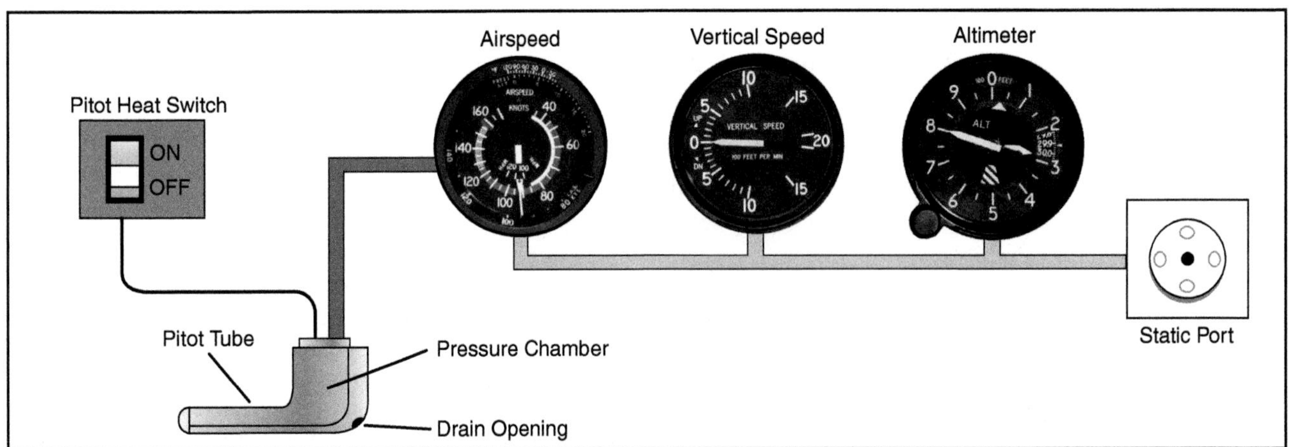

Figure 1-36. Ram air pressure enters the system through a hole in the forward end of the pitot tube. Electrical heating elements may be installed to remove ice from the pitot head, and a drain opening normally is located near the aft portion of the pressure chamber. Ram air pressure is supplied only to the airspeed indicator, while all three instruments use static pressure.

AIRSPEED INDICATOR

The airspeed indicator senses the difference between ram and static air pressure and is the only instrument connected to the pitot tube. Ram air pressure enters the airspeed indicator and moves a pressure-sensitive diaphragm that is mechanically linked to the pointer on the face of the airspeed indicator. As the diaphragm moves, the needle of the airspeed indicator responds to display the aircraft's speed.

The airspeed indicator is divided into color-coded arcs that define speed ranges for different phases of flight. For example, the white arc represents the flap operating range, while the green arc identifies the speed range for normal operations. The yellow arc indicates the speed the aircraft can be flown in smooth air and the red line represents the maximum, or never-exceed speed.

AIRSPEEDS

In addition to knowing what each of the color arcs on the airspeed indicator represent, you must know the V-speeds associated with your aircraft. These include:

V_{SO} _____ kts. — stalling speed or minimum steady flight speed in the landing configuration.

V_{S1} _____ kts. — stalling speed or minimum steady flight speed in a specified configuration.

V_A _____ kts. — design maneuvering speed

V_{FE} _____ kts. — maximum flap extended speed

V_{NO} _____ kts. — maximum structural cruising speed

V_{NE} _____ kts. — never-exceed speed

V_X _____ kts. — best angle-of-climb speed

V_Y _____ kts. — best rate-of-climb speed

Best Glide Speed — _____ kts.

If you are flying a retractable-gear airplane you must also know V_{LO} and V_{LE}. V_{LO} is the maximum speed you can safely fly while raising or lowering the landing gear. V_{LE} is the maximum speed you can safely fly with the landing gear in the fully extended position.

Once you are familiar with your aircraft's V-speeds, you need to understand the four types of speed you will deal with during flight. They are indicated airspeed, calibrated airspeed, true airspeed, and groundspeed.

Indicated airspeed (IAS) is the airspeed read directly from the airspeed indicator.

Calibrated airspeed (CAS) is indicated airspeed corrected for installation and instrument errors.

True airspeed (TAS) represents the true speed of the airplane through the air. It is calibrated airspeed corrected for altitude and nonstandard temperature.

Groundspeed (GS) represents the actual speed of the airplane over the ground.

ALTIMETER

The altimeter uses small, sealed containers to sense pressure changes. As air pressure outside the containers changes, they react by expanding or contracting. The tiny movements drive mechanical pointers to display the altitude in feet. Altimeters usually have three pointers to indicate the altitude. Most also have an adjustable barometric scale to compensate for changes in pressure.

ALTITUDE DEFINITIONS

Altitude is the measure of vertical elevation above a given reference point. The reference may be the surface of the earth, sea level, or some other point. There are several different types of altitude, depending on the reference point used. The five most common types are: indicated, pressure, density, true, and absolute.

Indicated altitude is the altitude read directly from the altimeter when it is correctly adjusted to the local altimeter setting.

Pressure altitude is the height above the standard datum plane when the altimeter is adjusted to the standard sea level atmospheric pressure of 29.92 in. Hg. The standard datum plane is a theoretical plane where the air pressure is equal to 29.92 inches of Mercury. Pressure altitude is used with existing temperature to compute density altitude and other values.

Density altitude is pressure altitude corrected for nonstandard temperature. It is a theoretical value computed from existing temperature and is an important factor in determining airplane performance.

True altitude is the actual height of an object above mean sea level. On aeronautical charts, the elevation figures for fixed objects, such as airports, towers, and TV antennas, are true altitudes. You can calculate approximate true altitude with a flight computer. In two cases, true and indicated altitude are equal. One case occurs during flight, when you have the correct altimeter setting and atmospheric conditions match ISA values. The other occurs on the ground. When the altimeter is set to the local atmospheric pressure setting, it indicates the field elevation, which is a true altitude.

Absolute altitude is the actual height of the airplane above the earth's surface. Absolute altitude is commonly referred to as height above ground level.

ALTIMETER ERRORS

The most common altimeter error occurs when you fail to keep the altimeter set to the local altimeter setting. For example, assume your altimeter is set to 30.00 in. Hg. and you are flying at a constant altitude of 3,500 feet. If you fly into an area where the atmospheric pressure is 29.50 in. Hg, the altimeter will sense this decrease in pressure as an increase in altitude and will display a higher reading. Your response will be to lower the nose of the airplane and descend to maintain your "desired" altitude. If you fly from an area of high pressure to an area of low pressure, your actual altitude will be lower than you intended. A good memory aid is, "When flying from high to low or hot to cold, look out below."

Another type of error occurs if the static port becomes blocked. Since the altimeter must sense changes in pressure as you climb or descend, a blocked static port results in the altimeter remaining at a constant altitude.

VERTICAL SPEED INDICATOR

The vertical speed indicator (VSI) also uses static pressure to sense a climb or descent. The instrument measures the speed at which ambient air pressure changes when the airplane climbs or descends. The VSI displays two types of information. The first is trend information, which is an immediate indication of an increase or decrease in the aircraft's rate of climb or descent. The second is rate information, which represents a stabilized rate of change. For example, when maintaining a constant 500 f.p.m. climb and you lower the nose, the VSI senses and displays the reduced rate of climb. After a period of six to nine seconds, the VSI stabilizes and displays the new rate of climb.

Since the vertical speed indicator is connected to the static system, any blockage of the static system also affects the VSI. If the static system is completely blocked, the VSI continually indicates zero.

GYROSCOPIC INSTRUMENTS

Most training aircraft are equipped with an engine driven vacuum pump that provides suction to drive the gyroscopes in the attitude indicator, heading indicator, and, in some cases, the turn coordinator. However, in most airplanes, the turn coordinator is electrically driven to provide redundancy. The basic vacuum system includes an engine-driven or electrical vacuum pump, a relief valve, a suction gauge, and an air filter. Air is drawn through a filter under the instrument panel to the appropriate instruments and the suction gauge, then through the relief valve and vacuum pump, and is finally pumped overboard. The gyroscope wheels inside these instruments have fins or scoops on the edges to catch the air being drawn through the instrument, causing them to spin rapidly.

CHARACTERISTICS OF GYROS

Any rotating body exhibits certain gyroscopic properties. One of these properties — rigidity in space — means that once a gyroscope is spinning, it tends to remain in a fixed orientation in space and resists external forces applied to it.

Another characteristic of the gyro is precession, which is the tilting or turning of a gyro in response to pressure. Unfortunately, it is not possible to mount a gyro in a frictionless environment; therefore, a small force is applied to a gyro whenever the airplane changes direction. The reaction to this force occurs in the direction of rotation, approximately 90° past the point where the force was applied. This causes slow drifting and minor erroneous indications in the gyro instruments.

ATTITUDE INDICATOR

The attitude indicator gives a pictorial view of the airplane's pitch and bank attitude. The dot at the center of the miniature airplane indicates the position of the nose above

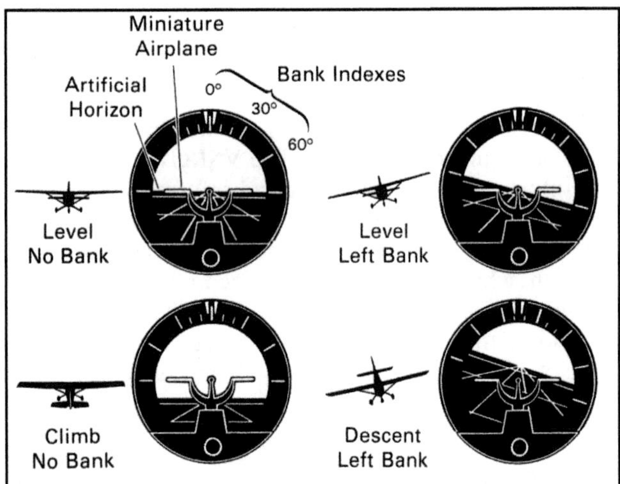

Figure 1-37. The attitude indicator shows the airplane as it would appear from behind. Prior to flight, you should set the miniature airplane symbol so that it is level with the horizon bar. The angle of bank is shown both by the relationship of the miniature aircraft to the horizon reference and by the alignment of the pointer with the bank scale at the top of the instrument. Pitch is indicated by the position of the "nose," or center, of the miniature airplane with respect to the horizon bar. The attitude indicator is the only instrument to supply both pitch and bank information.

or below the horizon, while the rotation of the artificial horizon shows the angle of bank. [Figure 1-37]

HEADING INDICATOR

The heading indicator, also called a directional gyro (DG), senses motion about the vertical axis and displays this information as an aircraft heading based on a 360° azimuth. When properly set to correspond with your magnetic compass, the heading indicator should be your primary source for heading information.

Due to internal friction within the instrument, precession is common in heading indicators. Precession causes the selected heading to drift from the set value. For this reason, you must regularly realign the indicator with the magnetic compass.

TURN COORDINATOR

The turn coordinator senses yaw and roll movement about the vertical and longitudinal axes. It has two main elements: a miniature airplane to indicate the rate of turn and an inclinometer to indicate coordinated flight. You can use the turn coordinator to establish and maintain a standard-rate turn by aligning the wing of the miniature airplane with the turn index. This means the turning rate is three degrees per second. At this rate, you will complete a 360° turn in two minutes.

The inclinometer consists of a liquid-filled, curved tube with a ball inside. The ball is used to determine coordinated use of aileron and rudder. During coordinated, straight-and-level flight, the force of gravity causes the ball to rest in the lowest part of the tube, centered between the references lines. During a coordinated turn, forces are balanced, which also causes the ball to remain centered in the tube.

The position of the ball tells you whether you are using the correct angle of bank for the rate of turn. In a **slip**, the rate of turn is too slow for the angle of bank, and the ball moves to the inside of the turn. In a **skid**, the rate of turn is too great for the angle of bank, and the ball moves to the outside of the turn.

10. Environmental system.

ENVIRONMENTAL SYSTEM

The environmental system refers to controlling the climate inside the cabin. In most light aircraft, cabin cooling is accomplished by pulling the CABIN AIR knob, which allows outside air to enter the cockpit through air inlets and ducting. The degree of airflow depends on how far the knob is pulled out. On some aircraft, additional vents may be mounted in the upper corner of the glare shield, side windows, or in the passenger seating area.

On the other hand, cabin heating is typically accomplished by drawing air through a shroud that surrounds the muffler. Although this type of system is reliable, a crack in the exhaust system could result in carbon monoxide gas entering the cabin and asphyxiating you.

More sophisticated airplanes are equipped with air conditioners and heaters. If this is the case with your aircraft, you must know how each system operates.

11. Deicing and anti-icing

DEICING AND ANTI-ICING

Deicing refers to systems that remove ice after it has accumulated, while anti-icing describes systems that prevent the formation of ice.

If the aircraft used for the practical test has either an anti-icing or deicing system, you must be able to describe how the system works.

EXERCISES

1. The ailerons, elevator, and rudder control movement around the _______, _______, and _______ axes respectively.
2. The explosive burning of the fuel/air mixture is known as _______.
3. Typically, the formation of carburetor ice is indicated by a(n) _______ (increase/decrease) in r.p.m.
4. The color of 100LL fuel is _______.
5. The three instruments that are connected to the pitot-static system include the _______, _______, and _______.
6. VA represents _______ speed.
7. A standard-rate turn changes the aircraft's heading at a rate of _______ per second.

SAMPLE ORAL QUESTIONS

1. What is preignition?

1. Preignition is the premature burning of the fuel/air mixture. The source of preignition is usually a hot spot on the cylinder wall from carbon deposits or a cracked ceramic spark plug insulator. Preignition creates high temperatures and a rough running engine. The two conditions, detonation and preignition, can coexist.

2. Explain why the angle of attack varies along the length of a propeller blade.

2. Unlike a wing, which moves through the air at a uniform speed, the tip of a propeller moves through the air at a much greater speed than the portion of the blade near the hub. To compensate for this, the propeller is made with a low angle of attack at the tips and a high angle of attack at the hub. This allows the propeller to provide fairly uniform thrust along most of its length.

3. What is density altitude?

3. Density altitude is pressure altitude corrected for nonstandard temperature. It is a theoretical value that is computed from existing temperature, and it is an important factor in determining airplane performance.

4. What do the colored arcs on the airspeed indicator represent?

4. The color-coded arcs define speed ranges for different phases of flight. For example, the white arc represents the flap operating range, while the green arc identifies the speed range for normal operations. The yellow arc indicates the speeds the aircraft can be flown in smooth air and the red line represents the maximum, or never-exceed speed.

5. How does a slip differ from a skid?

5. Both a slip and skid indicate an uncoordinated flight condition. In a slip, the ball of the turn coordinator is on the inside of the turn, which indicates that too much bank is being applied for the amount of rudder used. Correcting for this condition involves reducing the bank, or increasing the rate of turn by increasing rudder. In a skid, the ball is on the outside of the turn. This indicates that not enough bank is being applied for the amount of rudder being used. You correct for this by increasing the bank or decreasing the rate of turn by reducing rudder.

ADDITIONAL QUESTIONS

6. List all the V-speeds for your aircraft.

7. How long will it take to make a 360° standard-rate turn?

8. What is precession?

9. How does trim work?

10. What instrument errors can be expected with a blocked pitot tube? Static port?

11. Describe each of the systems on your airplane.

EXERCISE ANSWERS

1. longitudinal, lateral, vertical
2. detonation
3. decrease
4. blue
5. airspeed indicator, altimeter, vertical speed indicator
6. maneuvering
7. 3°

REFERENCES

JEPPESEN:
Private Pilot Manual/Video - Chapter 2

FAA:
Airplane Flying Handbook (FAA-H-8083-3)
Pilot's Handbook of Aeronautical Knowledge (AC 61-23/FAA-H-8083-25)
Pilot's Operating Handbook and FAA-Approved Airplane Flight Manual

J. TASK: AEROMEDICAL FACTORS (ASEL AND ASES)

REFERENCES: AC 61-23/FAA-H-8083-25, AIM.

Objective: To determine that the applicant exhibits knowledge of the elements related to aeromedical factors by explaining:

1. The symptoms, causes, effects, and corrective actions of at least three (3) of the following—
   a. hypoxia.
   b. hyperventilation.
   c. middle ear and sinus problems.
   d. spatial disorientation.
   e. motion sickness.
   f. carbon monoxide poisoning.
   g. stress and fatigue.
   h. dehydration.
2. The effects of alcohol, drugs, and over-the-counter medications.
3. The effects of excess nitrogen during scuba dives upon a pilot or passenger in flight.

Objective: To determine that the applicant exhibits knowledge of the elements related to aeromedical factors by explaining:

1. The symptoms, causes, effects, and corrective actions of at least three (3) of the following—

a. hypoxia.

HYPOXIA

Hypoxia results from a lack of oxygen in the bloodstream and impairs the functions of the brain and other organs. The onset typically results from the reduced barometric pressures encountered at high altitudes. Although night vision begins deteriorating at a cabin pressure altitude as low as 5,000 feet, other significant effects of altitude hypoxia usually do not occur in a normal, healthy pilot below 12,000 feet. From 12,000 to 15,000 feet, judgment, memory, alertness, coordination and ability to make calculations are impaired. You may also experience headache, drowsiness, dizziness and either a sense of well-being (euphoria) or belligerence. There are four recognized types of hypoxia: hypoxic, anemic, stagnant, and histotoxic.

Hypoxic hypoxia is associated with a lack of available oxygen in the atmosphere. It can occur very suddenly, as in a rapid decompression; or very slowly at lower altitudes when the body is deprived of available oxygen for extended periods of time. Anemic hypoxia occurs when there is sufficient oxygen in the lungs, but the blood has lost some of its capacity to carry it. This type of hypoxia is commonly associated with carbon monoxide poisoning. However, smoking and donating blood can also put you at a greater risk for this type of hypoxia. Stagnant hypoxia results when the appropriate amount of oxygen is in the blood, but circulation is below normal. Stagnant hypoxia can result from the high positive G-forces associated with aerobatic flight. Histotoxic hypoxia is caused by the body's inability to take the oxygen it needs from the blood. This happens primarily when you are under the influence of drugs or alcohol.

SYMPTOMS

The effects of hypoxia are usually quite difficult to recognize, especially when they occur gradually. Since symptoms of hypoxia vary from individual to individual, your ability to recognize hypoxia can be greatly improved if you are familiar with several of the symptoms. Some of the common symptoms include:

— Headache

— Sweating

— Sleepiness

— Cyanosis, or blue fingernails and lips

— Lightheadedness or dizziness

— Increased breathing rate

— Tingling or warm sensations

— Personality changes (aggressiveness)

— Reduced visual acuity

— Feelings of euphoria

— Impaired judgement, including slow decision-making

CORRECTIVE ACTIONS

Training yourself to be aware of your body's personal response to hypoxia can only come from experiencing it firsthand. Visiting an altitude chamber is an excellent way to determine how you respond to hypoxia.

If you suspect hypoxia when flying, your immediate reaction should be to make a controlled descent to a lower altitude, or begin using supplemental oxygen immediately, if available. For optimum protection, you are encouraged to use supplemental oxygen above 10,000 feet during the day, and above 5,000 feet at night. The FAR's require that flight crews be provided with and use supplemental oxygen after 30 minutes of exposure to cabin pressure altitudes between 12,500 and 14,000 feet MSL and immediately on exposure to cabin pressure altitudes above 14,000 feet MSL. Every occupant of the aircraft must be provided with supplemental oxygen at cabin pressure altitudes above 15,000 feet MSL.

b. hyperventilation.

HYPERVENTILATION

Hyperventilation is the term used to describe a breathing rate that is too rapid and too deep. This process forces too much carbon dioxide from your body and creates a chemical imbalance in the blood.

Hyperventilation usually is an involuntary response to a stressful situation. Emotions that can induce hyperventilation include tension, anxiety, apprehension, or fear. Flight situations that lead to these emotions include receiving confusing ATC instructions, entering marginal weather conditions, or experiencing an engine failure.

SYMPTOMS

Since many of the symptoms of hyperventilation are similar to those of hypoxia, it is important to correctly diagnose and treat the proper condition. Some of the symptoms of hyperventilation include:

- Drowsiness
- Hot and cold sensations
- Muscle spasms
- Rapid heart rate
- Dizziness and tingling extremities
- Weakness and numbness
- Confusion
- Nausea
- Loss of consciousness

CORRECTIVE ACTION

If you experience hyperventilation, your first goal should be to slow down your breathing rate to restore carbon dioxide to your body. This can be accomplished in a variety of ways. For example, breathing into a paper bag forces you to rebreathe your own expired carbon dioxide. Speaking out loud is also useful because it is impossible to talk aloud and breathe quickly. Recovery is typically rapid when the proper balance of carbon dioxide is restored.

c. middle ear and sinus problems.

PRESSURE EFFECTS

Atmospheric pressure changes associated with ascending and descending can cause pain and discomfort if air becomes trapped in your ears or sinus cavities. An upper respiratory infection, such as a cold or sinusitis, or a nasal allergic condition can produce congestion that can trap air. This "sinus block" occurs most frequently during descent.

CORRECTIVE ACTION

If your ears or sinuses become blocked, climb or descend as required to help equalize pressure. Since descending usually presents a greater problem it may be necessary to climb to a higher altitude and make a very gradual descent. Climbing and descending in a "stair-step" fashion is also helpful. Additional things that may help clear congestion include using the Valsalva technique, chewing gum, swallowing, and yawning. Some pilots find the use of nasal drops and sprays help reduce congestion, however, check with an Aviation Medical Examiner prior to using these medications for flying.

d. spatial disorientation.

DISORIENTATION

When the brain receives messages that contradict what the body perceives, spatial disorientation can occur. When disoriented, you have an incorrect mental image of your position in relation to what is actually happening to the airplane.

During the day, in good weather, you typically orient yourself primarily through your vision. Because of this, spatial disorientation rarely occurs during the day in good weather conditions. However, at night or in marginal weather conditions fewer visual cues exist, and you rely upon the vestibular and kinesthetic senses to supplement your visual sense. The probability of spatial disorientation occurring is quite high during these times. Correctly interpreting your flight instruments is extremely important, because they are your only sources of accurate information under these conditions.

Everyone is subject to spatial disorientation, and even experienced pilots feel its effects. Some situations are more disorienting than others. An awareness of the conditions that are more likely to produce spatial disorientation and the illusions they create helps you guard against their occurrence.

GRAVEYARD SPIRAL

During a prolonged, constant-rate turn, the fluid in the semicircular canals eventually stops moving. This can create the illusion that you are no longer turning. A loss of altitude in this situation may be interpreted as a wings-level descent, which can lead you to increase elevator back pressure. This action tightens the turn and increases the loss of altitude. A recovery to wings-level flight may produce the illusion that the airplane is in a turn in the opposite direction, prompting the pilot to re-enter the spiral.

CORIOLIS ILLUSION

If you tilt your head down in a prolonged, constant-rate turn to change fuel tanks or pick up a pencil, the rapid head movement puts the fluid in more than one semicircular canal in motion. This creates an overwhelming sensation of rotating, turning, or accelerating in an entirely different plane. An attempt to stop the sensation by maneuvering the airplane may put it into a dangerous attitude. To avoid this, do not move your head too fast in limited visibility or darkness.

LEANS

The leans occur when an abrupt recovery or a rapid correction is made to a bank. If you make such a recovery, your semicircular canals sense a roll in the opposite direction. This may cause you to re-enter the original attitude. When you return the aircraft to a wings-level condition, you will tend to lean in the direction of the incorrect bank until the semicircular canal fluids return to normal. Maintaining a level attitude for a minute or two generally will stop the leans.

FALSE HORIZONS

Another illusion, that of a false horizon, occurs when the natural horizon is obscured or not readily apparent. It can be generated by confusing bright stars and city lights or while flying toward the shore of an ocean or a large lake. Because of the relative darkness of the water, the lights along the shoreline can be mistaken for the stars in the sky. Flying above a sloping cloud deck can produce another illusion of a false horizon. The natural tendency in this case is to level the aircraft with the clouds.

e. motion sickness.

MOTION SICKNESS

Motion sickness, or airsickness, is a common experience for many passengers and some inexperienced pilots. The same types of factors that cause spatial disorientation also bring on airsickness. Airsickness comes in many forms. The most common symptoms are dizziness, nausea, and sweating. Other symptoms include general discomfort, paleness, and vomiting.

Specific remedies for airsickness can vary among people, but there are some actions that generally seem to help. You can suggest that your passengers put their heads back and attempt to relax. Since anxiety and stress can contribute to motion sickness, keep unsure or nervous passengers informed on how the flight is progressing, and explain unusual noises such as flap or landing gear retraction. Another suggestion that can reduce the possibility of airsickness is to focus on objects outside the aircraft.

f. carbon monoxide poisoning.

CARBON MONOXIDE

Carbon monoxide (CO) attaches itself to the hemoglobin in blood about 200 times more easily than does oxygen. In fact, carbon monoxide prevents oxygen from attaching to the hemoglobin and can produce anemic hypoxia. Because carbon monoxide poisoning is a form of hypoxia, you are more susceptible to its effects as altitude increases. Carbon monoxide poisoning can result from a faulty aircraft heater. Tobacco smoke contains CO, so smoking also causes a mild case of carbon monoxide poisoning. The effects of cigarette smoke are especially apparent by a reduction in visual acuity during a night flight. Smoking three cigarettes during a night flight can dramatically reduce the sharpness of your vision.

SYMPTOMS

Since CO poisoning causes hypoxia, the symptoms are the same, and can result in loss of muscle power, a headache, nausea, confusion, and dizziness. If the poisoning is severe enough it can result in death.

CORRECTIVE ACTIONS

If you suspect carbon monoxide poisoning, immediately turn off the heater and open the air vents and windows. Use supplemental oxygen, if available. It may take several hours for your body to completely purge itself of the poison, so consult a doctor as soon as possible. You may want to purchase a carbon monoxide detector, a small patch that can be attached to the instrument panel that turns black when exposed to abnormal amounts of carbon monoxide.

g. stress and fatigue.

STRESS

Stress can be defined as the body's response to any demand made on it by physical, physiological, or psychological factors. Anything that is perceived as a threat to the body's equilibrium causes a reaction. These reactions include the release of chemical hormones (such as adrenalin) into the body and the speeding of the metabolism to provide energy to the muscles.

A certain amount of stress is good for you. It keeps you on your toes and prevents complacency. However, stress effects are cumulative and can eventually add up to an intolerable burden, unless you cope with them adequately. Performance generally increases with the onset of stress, but peaks and then begins to fall off rapidly as stress levels exceed your ability to cope.

You need to be able to recognize the symptoms of stress overload in yourself and to learn how to manage stress. Several techniques can help prevent the accumulation of stresses. The first involves a program of physical fitness. Second, learn to recognize and avoid the heavy pressures imposed by getting behind schedule and not meeting deadlines. Plan your schedule to accomplish those tasks that are important and necessary, and don't worry about those that are not. Allow time in your schedule for relaxation. Third, take a realistic assessment of yourself. What are your capabilities and limitations? Strengths and weaknesses? Set your goals accordingly. Fourth, whenever possible, avoid stressful situations and encounters.

h. dehydration.

DEHYDRATION

Many factors can contribute to dehydration in pilots, including wind, insufficient fluid intake, loss of body moisture due to reduced humidity at higher altitudes, hot cabin temperatures, and diuretic drinks like coffee and soft drinks. Some of the effects of mild dehydration include nausea, dizziness, headaches, and cramps. Fatigue or sleepiness may also be experienced. The progression can be rapid from mild discomfort to incapacitating heat stress, heat exhaustion, or heat stroke. Dehydration is easily prevented by drinking plenty of water throughout your flight, especially in warm temperatures or at high altitudes.

2. The effects of alcohol, drugs, and over-the-counter medications.

ALCOHOL AND DRUGS

Your physical and mental skills must be in top shape when flying an aircraft. Alcohol dulls these senses and can reduce your performance to a dangerous level. Illness and disease also can affect the functioning and performance of your body, as can the drugs that are meant to treat these illnesses.

ALCOHOL

Extensive research has provided a number of facts about the hazards of alcohol consumption and flying. As little as one ounce of liquor, one bottle of beer, or four ounces of wine can impair flying skills, and remain detectable in your blood for at least 3 hours. Even after the body completely metabolizes a moderate amount of alcohol, you can still be severely impaired for many hours by a hangover. There is simply no way of increasing the metabolization rate of alcohol or alleviating a hangover. Alcohol also renders you much more susceptible to disorientation and hypoxia.

A consistently high rate of alcohol related fatal aircraft accidents serves to emphasize that alcohol and flying are a lethal combination. The FARs prohibit you from flying within 8 hours after drinking any alcoholic beverage or when your blood alcohol content is .04% or greater. However, due to the slow metabolization of alcohol, you may still be under the influence 8 hours after drinking a moderate amount of alcohol. Therefore, an excellent rule is to allow at least 12 to 24 hours between "bottle and throttle," depending on the amount of alcohol consumed.

DRUGS

Pilot performance can be seriously degraded by both prescribed and over-the-counter medications, as well as by the medical conditions for which they are taken. Many medications, such as tranquilizers, sedatives, strong pain relievers, and cough-suppressant preparations, have primary effects that may impair judgment, memory, alertness, coordination, vision, and the ability to make calculations. Others, such as antihistamines, blood pressure drugs, muscle relaxants, and agents to control motion sickness, have side effects that may impair the same critical functions. In addition, any medication that depresses the nervous system, such as a sedative, tranquilizer, or antihistamine can make you much more susceptible to hypoxia.

The FARs prohibit pilots from performing crewmember duties while using any medication that affects the faculties in any way contrary to safety. The safest rule is not to fly while taking any medication, unless approved to do so by the FAA. If you have any question as to how a specific medication will effect your ability to fly, you should consult an Aviation Medical Examiner (AME).

3. The effects of excess nitrogen during scuba dives upon a pilot or passenger in flight.

SCUBA DIVING

If you or a passenger intends to fly after scuba diving you must allow the body sufficient time to rid itself of excess nitrogen absorbed during diving. If not, decompression sickness can occur during exposure to low atmospheric pressure, creating a serious in-flight emergency.

The recommended waiting time before going to flight altitudes of up to 8,000 feet is at least 12 hours after a dive which has not required a controlled ascent (nondecompression stop diving), and at least 24 hours after a dive which required a controlled ascent (decompression stop diving). The waiting time before going to flight altitudes above 8,000 feet should be at least 24 hours after any SCUBA dive. These recommended altitudes are actual flight altitudes above mean sea level (AMSL) and not pressurized cabin altitudes. This takes into consideration the risk of decompression of the aircraft during flight.

EXERCISES

1. If you suspect you are hypoxic, you should _______ immediately.

2. Hyperventilation decreases the amount of _______ in your blood.

3. _______ (True, False) If you are planning to fly an aircraft and are congested due to a cold, take a decongestant prior to taking off to avoid ear block and sinus problems.

4. _______ (True, False) Experienced pilots are not susceptible to spatial disorientation.

SAMPLE ORAL QUESTIONS

1. What is the difference between hypoxia and hyperventilation?

2. How long must you wait to fly after consuming alcohol?

3. What are the implications of flying after SCUBA diving?

4. What is the most common source of in-flight carbon monoxide poisoning?

1. Hypoxia is a condition in which the body is not receiving enough oxygen and the symptoms are marked by a feeling of well-being, sleepiness, and dizziness. Hyperventilation, on the other hand, indicates a lack of carbon dioxide. This is indicated by feelings of drowsiness, dizziness, and confusion. The symptoms of hypoxia and hyperventilation can be quite similar, so it is important to know your own personal responses.

2. The FAR's prohibit you from flying within 8 hours after drinking any alcoholic beverage or when your blood alcohol content is .04% or greater. However, due to the slow elimination of alcohol, you may still be under the influence 8 hours after drinking a moderate amount of alcohol. Therefore, an excellent rule is to allow at least 12 to 24 hours between "bottle and throttle," depending on the amount of alcohol you have consumed.

3. The recommended waiting time before going to flight altitudes of up to 8,000 feet is at least 12 hours after a dive which has not required a controlled ascent (non-decompression stop diving), and at least 24 hours after a dive which required a controlled ascent (decompression stop diving). The waiting time before going to flight altitudes above 8,000 feet should be at least 24 hours after any SCUBA dive.

4. Damaged exhaust manifolds are usually to blame in carbon monoxide poisoning incidents. Most aircraft heaters draw fresh air across the hot exhaust manifold and vent it into the cabin. In a faulty system, the cracked exhaust manifold leaks poisonous gas into the cockpit.

ADDITIONAL QUESTIONS

5. What is spatial disorientation and when is it most likely to occur?

6. What senses are disturbed when experiencing spatial disorientation? How do you overcome it?

7. List some things that can cause stress and explain how stress can affect your flying.

EXERCISE ANSWERS

1. descend

2. carbon dioxide

3. False

4. False

REFERENCES

JEPPESEN:

Private Pilot Manual/Video - Chapters 1C and 10A

FAA:

Medical Handbook for Pilots
Airplane Flying Handbook (FAA-H-8083-3)
Aeronautical Information Manual
Federal Aviation Regulations

CHAPTER 2

PREFLIGHT PROCEDURES

A. TASK: PREFLIGHT INSPECTION (ASEL and ASES)

REFERENCES: FAA-H-8083-3; POH/AFM

Objective: To determine that the applicant:

1. Exhibits knowledge of the elements related to preflight inspection. This shall include which items must be inspected, the reasons for checking each item, and how to detect possible defects.
2. Inspects the airplane with reference to an appropriate checklist.
3. Verifies the airplane is in condition for safe flight.

Objective: To determine that the applicant:

1. Exhibits knowledge of the elements related to preflight inspection. This shall include which items must be inspected, the reasons for checking each item, and how to detect possible defects.

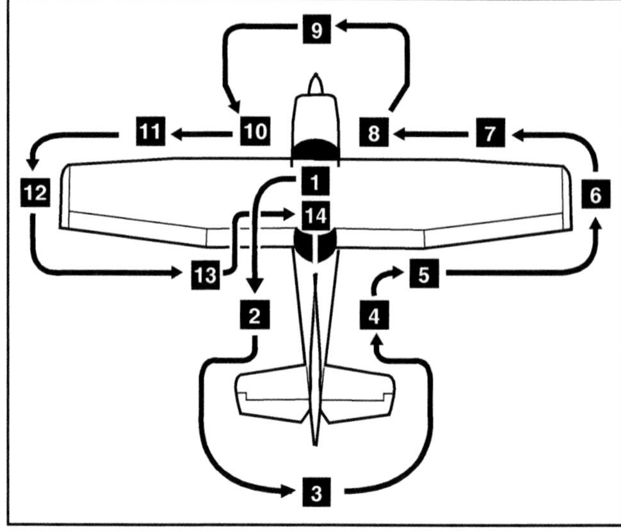

Figure 2-1. During the preflight inspection, you methodically check the aircraft in a planned sequence. The steps for a typical aircraft are outlined in the text with a numbered callout for each position.

PREFLIGHT INSPECTION

The accomplishment of a safe flight begins with a careful visual inspection. According to the Federal Aviation Regulations, you, as pilot in command, are responsible for making the decision as to whether an aircraft is in a safe condition to fly. Any defects discovered during your inspection must be evaluated and corrected prior to flight.

Preflight procedures can vary widely between aircraft, so the techniques presented here are intentionally general in nature. For specific information on the aircraft you are flying, consult the pilot's operating handbook.

The preflight inspection must be carried out according to a written checklist. Listed below is the proper sequence for a typical preflight inspection. [Figure 2-1]

CABIN

Once you have unlocked the cabin door and entered the aircraft, place the key to the ignition on the glare shield so it remains in full view from the front of the aircraft. This allows you to easily verify that the ignition is in the off position prior to inspecting the propeller later in the preflight inspection. Check the aircraft cabin (position 1) to verify all required documents are on board. The memory aid **ARROW** can be used to help you remember the required documents.

A — Airworthiness certificate (required by FAA)
R — Registration certificate (required by FAA)
R — Radio station license (required by FCC—outside U.S.)
O — Operating limitations, pilot's operating handbook, or approved aircraft flight manual (required by FAA)
W — Weight and balance data, as well as equipment list (required by FAA)

Although the engine and aircraft logbooks are not required to be on board the aircraft, they must be available to the examiner for the practical test.

After you verify the required documents are in the aircraft, remove the control lock so the controls can be checked for freedom of movement. Then, make sure no one is standing near the propeller, and turn the master switch ON. With the electrical power on, check the fuel quantity gauges to ensure proper operation and note the amount of fuel in each tank. Next, place the wing flaps in the full-down position, so you can examine the internal flap components, and then turn the master switch OFF.

Check the windshield, or windscreen, and cabin windows for cleanliness and general condition. Inspect the instrument panel for any irregularities, such as cracked glass, and for any instruments or radios which have been removed for maintenance.

Once you have completed all cabin checks, verify that the magneto switch, master switch, mixture control, and throttle are in the appropriate OFF positions. Then, continue with the exterior part of the preflight check.

LEFT FUSELAGE

As you move to the left side of the fuselage (position 2), check for wrinkles, dents in the skin, and loose rivets. Examine the lower surface of the fuselage for dents, rock damage, cleanliness, and evidence of excessive engine oil leakage.

EMPENNAGE

Several items on the tail section (position 3) must be inspected. Remove any gust lock, if installed, before you check the tail assembly. Inspect the tail surfaces for general condition, and look closely for dents, skin wrinkles, and loose rivets. Check the underside and leading edge of the horizontal stabilizer (or stabilator) for rock damage. Examine the elevator (or stabilator) and rudder for damage, loose hinge bolts, and freedom of movement. Inspect the control cables and stops for damage and the surface skin for dents and wrinkles. At this time, inspect the trim tab for security and general condition, the tail and beacon lights for damage, and the VOR navigation antenna. Then, remove the tail tiedown chain or rope. If the tiedown ring is bent, it may indicate internal structural damage to the tail section. If this is the case, you should have it checked by an aircraft mechanic prior to flight. If the airplane is equipped with a tailwheel, check the steering arms, cables, and springs for wear. In addition, inspect the tire for wear, proper inflation, cuts, and abrasions.

RIGHT FUSELAGE

Inspect the right side of the fuselage (position 4), repeating the same procedures used on the left side. In addition, ensure the emergency locator transmitter (ELT) antenna is secure.

RIGHT WING

As you move to the trailing edge of the right wing (position 5), inspect the flap and flap tracks. Check the flap control for movement and wear. Next, inspect the aileron for freedom of movement and the corresponding hinges for security and wear. In addition, check the aileron pushrod or control cable for damage and tension. If the aileron is equipped with counterweights, check to make sure they are secure. Check the right wingtip (position 6) for damage and secure attachment. Then, inspect the right navigation light for damage. If you are flying past sunset, all navigation lights must be operational. Examine the leading edge of the right wing (position 7) for dents or other damage. Then, check the upper wing surface for signs of stress and frost or snow accumulation.

While the aircraft is resting on a flat, level, surface, check the fuel quantity level by removing the cap and looking into the tank. The quantity in the tank should agree with the fuel gauge reading you observed earlier. After checking the fuel level, inspect the fuel vent in the filler cap for obstructions. If no obstructions exist, replace the filler cap and tighten it securely.

Check the fuel tank drain before every flight for obstructions, security, and leakage. If the airplane is equipped with a quick-drain device, take a fuel sample and check it for water and other contaminants. If water or other contaminants are found, continue draining fuel until there is no evidence of contamination. Water can form in the fuel tanks from condensation of moisture in the air, or it may be present in fuel added to the tanks. Because of this, you should take a sample before every flight. If the aircraft was just fueled, allow some time before taking a sample. This allows any contamination to settle to the bottom of the fuel tank where it can be detected.

Inspect the attachment points of the main landing gear (position 8) for dents and wrinkles. Check the tire for wear, cuts, abrasions, and proper inflation. Inspect the wheel fairing, if installed, for cracks, dents, and general security. Check the brake pads for wear and the brake lines for security and leaks. If the aircraft is equipped with oleo struts on the main gear, pay particular attention to proper strut inflation. Finally, remove the tiedown chain or rope.

NOSE

Open the cowl access door and inspect the engine compartment for loose wires and clamps, worn hoses, and oil or fuel leaks. Determine the oil quantity by removing and reading the dipstick. Add oil if the level is below the minimum recommended by the manufacturer. Then, replace the dipstick and tighten it securely. Drain the fuel strainer (if located within the engine compartment) for several seconds to eliminate any water or other contaminants that may have collected. Because the fuel strainer is often the lowest point in the fuel system, any water that may exist should accumulate in the strainer. Finally, close and secure the access door.

Some aircraft may have a fuel drain directly below the fuel selector on the underside of the aircraft. If this is the case, you should take a fuel sample and check for contamination.

The cowl flaps, if installed, should be checked for security and obstructions. As you move to the front of the aircraft, check the front cowl openings (position 9) for obstructions. At the same time, inspect the alternator belt for cracks or excessive wear. Before inspecting the propeller, verify the key is out of the ignition. Check the propeller blades and tips for nicks and scratches and ensure the spinner is secure. Propeller nicks can cause excessive stress in the metal of the propeller. They should be repaired by a certificated mechanic prior to flight. If your aircraft has a constant-speed propeller, check it for oil leakage. You can generally detect leakage by the presence of oil streaks along the backside of the propeller blades. In cold weather, you should carefully pull the propeller through two or three revolutions in the direction of normal propeller rotation. This procedure loosens the congealed oil and makes engine starting easier.

If a landing light is mounted in the cowl, check it for cleanliness and operation. On aircraft with carbureted engines, inspect the carburetor air filter for obstructions such as dirt or other foreign matter. Check the nose strut for proper inflation and fluid leakage and the steering linkages and shimmy dampener for security. In addition, inspect the nose wheel for wear, cuts, abrasions, and proper inflation.

As you move to the left side of the cowling, (position 10) it's important that you ensure the static port is open so the airspeed, altimeter, and vertical speed indicators function properly. Check the windshield and cabin windows for cleanliness and general condition. Do not use a dry rag to clean the windshield because it can scratch the surface. Only a cloth and cleaning compound specifically designed for airplane windshields should be used.

LEFT WING

Inspect the left wing structure (position 11) in the same manner used on the right wing. Then, remove the tiedown chain or rope. Next, inspect the fuel tank vent opening. Perform the checks on the fuel tank drains, vents, and fuel quantity in the same manner described for the right wing. Finally, check the communications antenna for general condition and security.

Remove the pitot tube cover, if installed, and check the tube opening for obstructions. A plugged pitot tube causes the airspeed indicator to malfunction. The pitot tube should show no signs of damage and should not be bent out of alignment. On some aircraft, the static port also is located on the pitot tube. Check the stall warning vane on the leading edge of the wing for freedom of movement. It is a good practice to turn the master switch on just prior to the stall warning vane inspection. This enables you to check the stall warning signal when the vane is deflected upward. Remember to turn the master switch OFF immediately after making this inspection. If your aircraft is equipped with a pneumatic stall warning device, check the leading edge opening for obstructions.

Examine the left wingtip (position 12) in the same manner as the right. As you move to the back of the wing, inspect the left aileron, flap, and left main gear (position 13), repeating the same steps that were used for the right.

After loading any baggage, close the baggage door and make sure it is secure (position 14).

2. Inspects the airplane with reference to an appropriate checklist.

- You must always use a written checklist and follow it step-by-step to ensure that all necessary items are accomplished in a safe, logical sequence.
- Written checklists are used because of variations in aircraft types and models, and because it is unwise to rely on your memory.
- The FAA stresses the use of checklists during the practical test.

3. Verifies the airplane is in condition for safe flight.

- As the pilot in command, you must conduct the preflight inspection before every flight to ensure that the aircraft is in a safe condition to fly.
- If you discover any defects during the inspection, you should evaluate them and, if required, correct them prior to your flight.

EXERCISES

1. Checking the lower surface of the fuselage can help reveal evidence of excessive engine _____ leakage.

2. For the airspeed, altimeter, and vertical speed indicators to function properly, the small static air source must be _____ (open, closed).

3. If the pitot tube opening is plugged, it causes the ______ ______ to malfunction.

4. ___ (True, False) It is sufficient to check for fuel contamination only on the first flight of the day.

5. Check the propeller blades and tips for nicks and scratches because they can cause excessive _____ in the metal.

SAMPLE ORAL QUESTIONS

1. What certificates and documents must be on board the aircraft?

1. To help you remember what documents are required on board the aircraft, the acronym ARROW can be used. The "A" stands for airworthiness certificate, which must be on board as well as visible to all passengers. The first "R" stands for registration certificate and is required by the FAA. The second "R" stands for radio station license and is required for international flights and communications by the Federal Communications Commission. The "O" stands for operating limitations which are contained in the approved aircraft flight manual or POH. Finally, the "W" stands for weight and balance data for the specific airplane you are going to fly.

2. Explain why you should use a checklist.

2. A written checklist ensures that all necessary items are checked in a logical sequence. Checklists are also used because of variations in types and models of aircraft and because it is unwise to rely on your memory. The use of a checklist is required when taking the practical test.

3. What are you looking for when you take a fuel sample?

3. When checking a fuel sample, the first thing you should check for is proper color and type. You should also check the sample for water or contamination. If contaminants exist, continue draining fuel until there is no evidence of contamination.

ADDITIONAL QUESTIONS

4. List the preflight inspection items for wing flaps and ailerons.
5. List the important items to inspect on aircraft tail surfaces.
6. During the preflight inspection, the examiner may ask you to explain what you are checking for.

EXERCISE ANSWERS

1. oil
2. open
3. airspeed indicator
4. False
5. stress

REFERENCES

JEPPESEN:

Private Pilot Maneuvers/Video – Maneuver 1

FAA:

Airplane Flying Manual (FAA-H-8083-3)
Pilot's Operating Handbook and FAA-Approved Airplane Flight Manual
Federal Aviation Regulations

B. TASK: COCKPIT MANAGEMENT (ASEL and ASES)

REFERENCES: FAA-H-8083-3; POH/AFM

Objective: To determine that the applicant:

1. Exhibits knowledge of the elements related to cockpit management procedures.
2. Ensures all loose items in the cockpit and cabin are secured.
3. Organizes material and equipment in an efficient manner so they are readily available.
4. Briefs occupants on the use of safety belts, shoulder harnesses, doors, and emergency procedures.

Objective: To determine that the applicant:

1. Exhibits knowledge of the elements related to cockpit management procedures.

COCKPIT MANAGEMENT

Effective cockpit management begins with your initial flight planning and knowing what resources are available to you. For example, when planning a flight you must make a conscious effort to think and plan ahead. As you prepare for departure, ask yourself if you have considered alternate courses of action should something arise enroute.

Once you are in the airplane, take time to organize the cockpit. The lack of effective cockpit organization can make even a simple flight complicated, especially if you must divert your attention from flying the aircraft. Remember the saying "A place for everything and everything in its place."

Pilot decision making is another important element of cockpit management. It refers to how you assess and respond to problems you encounter. Risk assessment becomes necessary when you detect a change or problem and the need to react to the change. The five elements of risk assessment are: pilot, aircraft, environment, operation, and situation. Assessing the first element, the **pilot**, can be difficult because it requires an objective self evaluation. This is extremely critical in single-pilot operations because there isn't that extra safety margin available when operating with more than one crewmember. The **aircraft** refers to the condition of the aircraft and the amount of equipment that is available. The **environment** includes situations outside the aircraft that might limit, modify, or affect the aircraft, pilot, or operational elements. The **operation** element of risk assessment pertains to the way a flight is conducted and **situation** is best explained as the overall combination of the first four risk assessments.

2. Ensures all loose items in the cockpit and cabin are secured.

- Secure all items in the cockpit and baggage area.
- Items in the cockpit can be secured with seatbelts or placed in seat pockets and storage areas.
- All items in the baggage compartment should be secured with a cargo net or approved tiedown.

3. Organizes material and equipment in an efficient manner so they are readily available.

- Organize items in a logical manner so you can retrieve and replace them efficiently during the flight.
- Always keep frequently used items within easy reach so you are not distracted when retrieving them.
- It is helpful to keep your flight case nearby for easy access to additional items.

4. Briefs occupants on the use of safety belts, shoulder harnesses, doors, and emergency procedures.

PASSENGER BRIEFINGS

You are required under FAR 91.107, as pilot in command, to brief each person on board prior to take off on how to fasten and unfasten their safety belts and, if installed, their shoulder harness. Furthermore, before the aircraft moves on the surface, you must also notify all passengers to fasten their safety belts and their shoulder harness.

Regulations also require that you thoroughly brief your passengers on emergency procedures relevant to the aircraft prior to take off. At a minimum, this briefing should include the general steps used to cope with an emergency off-airport landing. You should also brief your passengers on the operation of door handles and make sure they understand how to properly latch and unlatch them.

EXERCISES

1. ___ (True, False) All items should be secured in the cockpit even when no reports of turbulence exist.
2. Loose items in the cockpit are a safety hazard in flight because they can _____ the pilot.
3. Cockpit management is enhanced by organizing items in a logical _____.

SAMPLE ORAL QUESTIONS

1. Describe some of the key items related to cockpit management.

1. Effective cockpit management skills include: organizing information and equipment in a logical flight sequence, thorough preflight planning, securing all items in the cockpit, briefing passengers, and utilizing checklists.

2. What items must you brief passengers on prior to flight?

2. You are required under FAR 91.107 to brief each person on board prior to takeoff on how to fasten and unfasten their safety belt and shoulder harness. You should also explain how to operate the doors and door latches. Furthermore, before the aircraft moves on the surface, you must also notify all passengers to fasten their safety belts and shoulder harness. Regulations also require that you thoroughly brief your passengers on emergency procedures relevant to the aircraft.

ADDITIONAL QUESTIONS

3. What are some benefits of cockpit management?
4. What are the five elements of risk assessment, and what should you evaluate about each?

EXERCISE ANSWERS

1. True
2. distract
3. sequence

REFERENCES

JEPPESEN:

Private Pilot Manual/Video – Chapters 1C and 10B
Private Pilot Maneuvers/Video – Maneuver 1

FAA:

Airplane Flying Handbook (FAA-H-8083-3)
Federal Aviation Regulations
Pilot's Operating Handbook and FAA-Approved Airplane Flight Manual

C. TASK: ENGINE STARTING ASEL and ASES)

REFERENCES: FAA-H-8083-3, AC 61-23/FAA-H-8083-25, AC 91-13, AC 91-55; POH/AFM

Objective: To determine that the applicant:

1. Exhibits knowledge of the elements related to recommended engine starting procedures. This shall include the use of an external power source, hand propping safety, and starting under various atmospheric conditions.
2. Positions the airplane properly considering structures, surface conditions, other aircraft, and the safety of nearby persons and property.
3. Utilizes the appropriate checklist for starting procedure.

Objective: To determine that the applicant:

1. **Exhibits knowledge of the elements related to engine starting. This shall include the use of an external power source, hand propping safety, and starting under various atmospheric conditions, as appropriate.**

ENGINE STARTING

After completing the preflight inspection, you can prepare to start the engine. When doing this, safety dictates the use of a checklist. [Figure 2-2]

STARTING THE ENGINE

- Carburetor heat – COLD
- Mixture – RICH
- Primer – AS REQUIRED (up to 6 strokes, none if engine is warm)
- Throttle – OPEN 1/2 INCH (CLOSED if engine is warm)
- Propeller area – CLEAR
- Master switch – ON
- Ignition switch – START (release when engine starts)
- Oil pressure – CHECK (30 seconds summer, 60 seconds winter)

Figure 2-2. This checklist is typical for a single-engine airplane. Follow the recommendations of the airplane manufacturer for the best engine-starting method.

Although starting procedures differ from airplane to airplane, there are some safety precautions that are common to all aircraft. For example, prior to starting any aircraft engine, you must be aware of the aircraft's position. If the tail is pointing toward vehicles, people, or an open hangar, you should move or turn the aircraft by hand so debris picked up by the aircraft's prop blast doesn't injure people or damage property. When operating from unimproved airports you should inspect the ground under the propeller before starting the engine. Any rocks, pebbles, or loose debris that can be picked up by the propeller and forced backward could damage the aircraft. If the debris cannot be cleared, move the airplane to another location before starting the engine.

When ready to start the engine, you should look in all directions to make sure nothing is near the propeller. In addition to yelling "clear,'' you should visually clear the area before engaging the starter.

Once the engine starts, disengage the starter motor immediately and check for oil pressure. Under normal conditions, oil pressure should be obtained within 30 seconds. If oil pressure isn't obtained immediately, shut down the engine and have it checked.

EXTERNAL POWER SOURCE

To aid in starting the engine, most aircraft have a ground service receptacle which permits the use of an external power source. The receptacle is typically located on the aft section of the aircraft or near the cowling. To determine the exact location and procedures for using an external power source, you should always consult the pilot's operating handbook for your aircraft.

Although the procedures for using an external power source can vary from aircraft to aircraft, there are some general precautions that relate to all aircraft. For example, you should never use an external power source to start an aircraft that has a dead battery. In this situation the battery should be removed and charged or replaced.

When utilizing an external power source, the avionics power switch and all electrical equipment are usually turned off to prevent damage to the electrical system from power fluctuations. To prevent arcing, the external power unit is typically turned off when connecting to the aircraft. Furthermore, after the aircraft engine starts, engine r.p.m. is reduced to idle, and the external power unit is turned off prior to disconnecting.

HAND PROPPING SAFETY

There is great potential for serious injury during hand propping. Never attempt to start an engine by hand without a qualified person familiar with the airplane at the controls, as well as out front handling the propeller. Be sure both of you thoroughly understand the procedures and communications you will use. Verify that the wheels are chocked and the brakes set. Often it is a good idea to tie the tail down as well. If the ground area near the prop has mud, oil, snow, ice, wet grass, or other potentially slippery contaminants, move the airplane to a dry area. Look around carefully and remove any loose dirt or gravel that could cause your feet to slip. When pulling the prop through to bring fuel to the cylinders or to position the blades for starting, be certain that the ignition is off before moving the propeller. When the engine is ready to start, tell the person at the controls "BRAKES and CONTACT." When you get confirmation from the cockpit, position yourself not quite arm's length from the prop blade. You may want to push against the propeller hub to satisfy yourself that the brakes are applied. Pull down quickly with the palms of both hands, stepping back and away from the prop disc as you do. Keep your fingers on the front of the propeller if possible, without wrapping them over the trailing edge, in case the engine should kick backward. After the engine starts, be especially careful around the spinning propeller. When removing chocks, external power cables, etc., always approach from behind the propeller.

ATMOSPHERIC CONDITIONS

In addition to starting an aircraft engine in standard atmospheric conditions, you also must be familiar with the unique starting procedures associated with cold and hot weather. The following discussion looks at some general procedures used to start an engine in either cold or hot conditions. For more specific information consult the pilot's operating handbook for your aircraft.

COLD WEATHER OPERATIONS

During cold weather the oil in your aircraft's engine thickens, making starting difficult. There are several things you can do to overcome this. For example, your first step should be to verify that the engine contains the manufacturer's recommended viscosity oil for the temperature range in which you are operating.

If the aircraft is exposed to outside air temperatures below 20°F, you may need to preheat the engine. Preheating helps loosen up the oil which reduces engine wear. The simplest method of preheating is to store the aircraft in a heated hangar. If this is not possible, portable heaters may be used to direct warm air to the engine and cabin.

Some aircraft manufacturers recommend pulling the propeller through several times by hand to " limber up" the oil before starting on cold days. This helps conserve battery energy. For safety purposes, when pulling the propeller through by hand, ensure that the ignition is off, the throttle closed, and the mixture is in the cutoff position. Furthermore, the parking brake should be set, the wheels chocked, and the propeller area clear.

The pilot's operating handbook for most light aircraft recommends priming the engine prior to starting in cold temperatures. However, overpriming can result in poor compression and difficulty starting the engine.

Once the engine starts, you should see oil pressure within the time specified by the manufacturer. A good rule of thumb to use is that if you don't obtain oil pressure within the first 60 seconds or the pressure drops after a few minutes, shut the engine down and check for broken oil lines or oil cooler leaks.

Allow the engine to idle at a low r.p.m. setting for two to five minutes prior to taxiing. This allows the oil to warm up and begin circulating before high r.p.m. loads are placed on the engine. If the aircraft is equipped with cowl flaps, close them to retain engine heat.

Under extremely cold temperatures, you may have no indication on the oil temperature gauge for several minutes; however, if the engine accelerates smoothly, with steady, normal oil pressure, the aircraft should be ready for takeoff.

HOT WEATHER OPERATIONS

When starting an engine in hot weather or one that has just been shutdown, many pilots tend to flood the engine. To avoid this, make sure you follow the manufacturer's recommendations for hot weather operations. If the correct procedures are not followed, excess fuel could accumulate and create a fire hazard. After starting, you should avoid prolonged ground operations to reduce the risk of overheating the engine. If the aircraft has cowl flaps, open them during all ground operations.

Excessive engine cranking also can cause the starter to overheat. To avoid this, it's often recommended that you allow the starter to cool for at least two minutes for every thirty seconds it's engaged.

2. Positions the airplane properly considering structures, surface conditions, other aircraft, and the safety of nearby persons and property.

- Always be aware of where the tail of your aircraft is pointing to avoid causing damage to persons or property.
- If there is any chance that the aircraft's prop blast could cause damage, you should tow or move the aircraft by hand to an area that is clear of objects.
- Always yell "clear" and carefully look in all directions before starting the engine.

3. Utilizes the appropriate checklist for starting procedure.

- It is essential that you carefully follow the checklists in the pilot's operating handbook and FAA-Approved Airplane Flight Manual.
- You must refer to a checklist during the starting sequence.

EXERCISES

1. The primer is used to pump fuel into the engine ______, to aid in starting.

2. ___ (True, False) A thorough look around the propeller area before starting eliminates the need to open a window or door and shout, "Clear!"

3. ___ (True, False) Releasing the starter as soon as the engine starts helps avoid damage to the starter motor.

4. You should shut down the engine if oil pressure does not register properly within ______ seconds in warm weather, or _____ seconds in cold weather.

SAMPLE ORAL QUESTIONS

1. There are many items to consider to safely start an engine. Some of these include: position of the aircraft in relation to people and property, clearing the propeller area, surface conditions, and weather conditions.

2. When pulling a propeller through by hand you must make sure the ignition is off, the throttle closed, and the mixture in the idle cutoff position. Furthermore, the parking brake should be set, the wheels chocked, and the propeller area clear.

1. List key engine starting safety precautions.

____

____

____

____

____

2. Describe the procedure for pulling the propeller through by hand.

____

____

____

____

____

____

ADDITIONAL QUESTIONS

3. Describe how you would use an external power source to start an aircraft engine.

4. What are some of the considerations of starting an engine in hot weather?

5. Explain why a written checklist is essential to the engine starting process.

EXERCISE ANSWERS

1. cylinders
2. False
3. True
4. 30, 60

REFERENCES

JEPPESEN:

Private Pilot Manual/Video – Chapter 2B

Private Pilot Maneuvers/Video – Maneuver 2

FAA:

Airplane Flying Handbook (FAA-H-8083-3)

Pilot's Operating Handbook and FAA-Approved Airplane Flight Manual

D. TASK: TAXIING (ASEL)

REFERENCES: FAA-H-8083-3; POH/AFM

Objective: To determine that the applicant:

1. Exhibits knowledge of the elements related to safe taxi procedures.
2. Performs a brake check immediately after the airplane begins moving.
3. Positions the flight controls properly for the existing wind conditions.
4. Controls direction and speed without excessive use of brakes.
5. Complies with airport/taxiway markings, signals, ATC clearances, and instructions.
6. Taxies so as to avoid other aircraft and hazards.

Objective: To determine that the applicant:

1. Exhibits knowledge of the elements related to safe taxi procedures.

TAXIING

During the private pilot practical test, you must be able to explain and demonstrate safe taxi procedures. The procedures you are tested on include: directional control, taxi speeds, throttle use, taxiing in wind, and brake usage.

In addition, you must comply with ATC instructions, airport requirements, and be alert for other aircraft, equipment, and hazards.

DIRECTIONAL CONTROL DURING TAXI

Most light training aircraft have a steerable nosewheel which is linked to the rudder pedals. Since the amount you can turn the nosewheel varies from aircraft to aircraft, you should consult the POH for your particular aircraft.

When you depress the rudder pedal it also deflects the rudder, so the airflow from the propeller slipstream produces a small additional force to assist you in turning the aircraft. Furthermore, the application of brakes in the direction of the turn allows you to reduce the radius of a turn even further.

USE OF THE THROTTLE

Smooth and precise power adjustments are important when taxiing. Erratic throttle movement leads to directional control problems. When taxiing, control your speed primarily with the throttle and secondarily with the brakes. Use the brakes only when a reduction in power is not sufficient. Taxi speeds should be no faster than a brisk walk. When operating in confined areas, keep your speed slow enough to allow you to stop safely without using the brakes. A useful suggestion for developing proper taxi speed control is to assume the brakes are inoperative. This allows you to learn proper use of power for taxiing.

ENGINE COOLING DURING TAXIING

Since most air-cooled engines are tightly cowled, extended ground operations, especially in warm weather, can cause engine overheating before the oil temperature gauge indicates a significant temperature rise. If your aircraft has a cylinder head temperature gauge, use it to monitor engine temperature. In addition, if the aircraft is equipped with cowl flaps, you should use them as engine temperatures dictate.

2. Performs a brake check immediately after the airplane begins moving.

- Conduct a brake check by coming to a complete stop almost immediately after you begin moving.
- Once you've completed your brake check, ask your instructor or examiner to check their brakes as well.

3. Positions the flight controls properly for the existing wind conditions.

EFFECTS OF WIND ON TAXI TECHNIQUES

When taxiing in moderate to strong winds, you must use special taxi techniques to maintain aircraft control. When strong winds get under the upwind wing, they create a tipping tendency toward the downwind side. You can counteract this tendency with proper use of the flight controls. As the speed of air flowing over the control surfaces increases, aileron, rudder, and elevator (or stabilator) control effectiveness also increases. For example, if you taxi an airplane at 10 knots into a 15-knot wind, the controls experience 25 knots of airflow over them and respond accordingly. On the other hand, if you taxi an airplane at 5 knots in a tailwind of 5 knots, the taxi speed and wind speed cancel each other out, and the controls respond as though no wind exists.

TAXIING IN HEADWINDS

When taxiing an airplane straight into the wind there is no tendency for the aircraft to tip. This is because the wind flows over both wings equally. Under these conditions, you should hold the ailerons in the neutral position and the elevator (or stabilator) near neutral, or slightly forward.

Holding too much forward pressure during strong headwinds results in the wind striking the bottom of the elevator (or stabilator), which forces the tail section up and the nose down. This places additional weight on the nose gear, compresses the nose strut, and decreases propeller ground clearance. To avoid propeller damage when taxiing over rough ground into strong headwinds, you should hold back on the control wheel so the elevator (or stabilator) is raised. This forces the tail down and the nose up, which increases propeller clearance.

TAXIING IN TAILWINDS

To prevent strong tail winds from striking the underside of the horizontal stabilizer when taxiing, you should place the control wheel in the full-forward position. This causes the wind to strike the upper surface of the elevator (or stabilator) creating a downward force on the tail. This prevents the wind from raising the tail and causing the airplane to nose over.

TAXIING IN CROSSWINDS

Proper response to crosswinds is vital to maintaining precise aircraft control. Although the crosswind lifting effect on one wing usually will not overturn an aircraft, a strong crosswind and improper control positioning can upset and cause aircraft damage. For this reason, there are specific control deflections that must be used when taxiing in any type of crosswind.

QUARTERING HEADWIND

To counter the effects of quartering headwinds, you must apply neutral elevator (or stabilator) pressure and turn the control wheel full into the wind. This counters the tipping tendency created by allowing the wind to exert pressure on the raised aileron, and force the wing down. For example, when taxiing in a right quartering headwind, the elevator remains in the neutral position and the upwind aileron is deflected upward to keep the right wing from rising. [Figure 2-3]

QUARTERING TAILWIND

The most critical taxiing situation occurs when you are in a tricycle-gear, high-wing aircraft with a strong quartering tailwind. With a quartering tailwind, you must place the elevator in the down position. In addition, you must counteract the tipping tendency by rotating the control wheel away from the wind. For example, when the wind is from the left rear (a left quartering tailwind), the control wheel should be pushed forward and turned to the right. This helps prevent strong winds from striking the underside of the horizontal stabilizer and results in a downward pressure on the left wing. In a right quartering tailwind, full left aileron deflection and full forward elevator (or stabilator) is used.

When you are beginning a turn with a strong quartering tailwind, you must be cautious. The tailwind component, combined with the normal tendency to tip during the turn, makes the aircraft especially vulnerable to overturning. Slow taxi speeds and slow turns minimize this danger. Furthermore, you should avoid sudden throttle increases and sharp braking when turning.

PROP AND JET BLAST

When taxiing behind other aircraft, be aware of the wind effects created by their engines. Large prop and jet engines can produce significant airflow even at low power settings. When taxiing behind these types of aircraft, it's best to allow extra room and position your controls appropriately.

TAXIING TAILWHEEL AIRCRAFT

Tailwheel aircraft have a tendency to weathervane, or turn into the wind. This tendency is greatest when taxiing in a direct crosswind. To help compensate for a crosswind, tailwheel airplanes are taxied with the ailerons held the same as for a tricycle-gear airplane; however, the elevator must be positioned to help keep the tailwheel on the ground. For

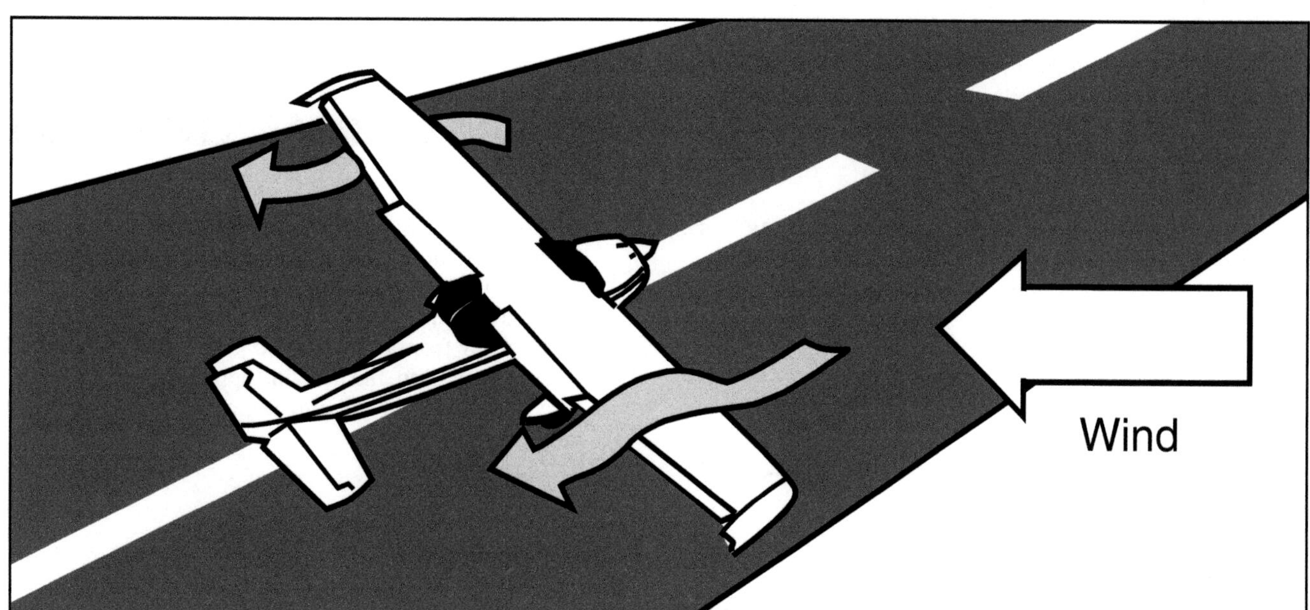

Figure 2-3. In a right quartering headwind, apply neutral elevator (or stabilator) and turn the control wheel full right to raise the right aileron and lower the left aileron. In a left quartering headwind, apply neutral elevator and turn the control wheel full left.

example, in a headwind, you must hold the elevator control aft (elevator up). In a tailwind, hold the elevator control forward (elevator down).

4. Controls direction and speed without excessive use of brakes.

- Taxi speed is controlled by the throttle. Use the brakes only when a reduced engine r.p.m. will not slow the aircraft.
- For safety and operational reasons, keep your taxi speed no faster than a brisk walk.
- In confined ramp areas, keep your speed slow enough so you can stop safely without using the brakes.

5. Complies with airport/taxiway markings, signals, ATC clearances, and instructions.

- You must demonstrate that you can maintain aircraft control while adhering to airport markings and complying with ATC instructions.

6. Taxies so to avoid other aircraft and hazards.

- Be alert at all times to avoid stationary aircraft, moving aircraft operating nearby, and any hazards while taxiing.
- Keep your eyes outside, and avoid doing things inside the cockpit such as looking for a sectional chart or navlog.

EXERCISES

1. It takes more power to ______ (start, keep) the airplane moving during normal operations than to _____ (start, keep) it moving.

2. Recommend using a taxi speed that is no faster than a _____ _____.

3. If you are taxiing at 5 knots into a 20-knot headwind, the total airflow velocity over the wings is

   a. 10 knots.
   b. 15 knots
   c. 20 knots
   d. 25 knots

4. If you are taxiing with a right quartering tailwind, your controls should be positioned with the elevator

   a. up, and the right aileron down.
   b. down, and the right aileron up.
   c. up, and the right aileron up.
   d. down, and the right aileron down.

5. Assume you are taxiing in a tricycle-gear airplane with the elevator up and the left aileron up. For a left quartering headwind, your controls are placed ________ (correctly, incorrectly).

SAMPLE ORAL QUESTIONS

1. What wind situation is most critical when taxiing?

1. In a tricycle-gear, high-wing aircraft, a strong quartering tailwind is most critical because the tail and upwind wing are susceptible to being lifted by the wind. To counter this, you must rotate the control wheel away from the wind and push it full forward. In this configuration, the tailwind applies an aerodynamic force on the top of the elevator and tends to push the tail down.

2. To respond to a quartering headwind, apply neutral elevator and turn the control wheel fully into the wind to counteract the wing tipping tendency. With the controls in this position, the wind flows over the upwind wing and exerts pressure against the raised aileron, forcing the wing down.

2. What control response should be taken to counteract a quartering headwind?

3. Taxi speed is controlled primarily with throttle movements requiring only minimal braking. Excessive brake usage increases wear and can cause the braking system to overheat.

3. How should brakes be used to control taxi speed?

ADDITIONAL QUESTIONS

4. Describe the effect of airflow velocity over the wings when taxiing in a tailwind.
5. How do you position the controls when taxiing with a left quartering headwind?
6. How do you position the controls when taxiing with a right quartering tailwind?

EXERCISE ANSWERS

1. start, keep
2. brisk walk
3. d
4. d
5. incorrectly

REFERENCES

JEPPESEN:

Private Pilot Manual/Video – Chapters 4A and 4B

Private Pilot Maneuvers/Video – Maneuver 3

FAA:

Airplane Flying Handbook (FAA-H-8303-3)

Pilot's Operating Handbook and FAA-Approved Airplane Flight Manual

F. TASK: BEFORE TAKEOFF CHECK (ASEL and ASES)

REFERENCES: FAA-H-8083-3; POH/AFM

Objective: To determine that the applicant:

1. Exhibits knowledge of the elements related to the before takeoff check. This shall include the reasons for checking each item and how to detect malfunctions.
2. Positions the airplane properly considering other aircraft/vessels, wind and surface conditions.
3. Divides attention inside and outside the cockpit.
4. Ensures that engine temperature and pressure are suitable for run-up and takeoff.
5. Accomplishes the before takeoff checklist and ensures the airplane is in safe operating condition.
6. Reviews takeoff performance airspeeds, takeoff distances, departure, and emergency procedures.
7. Avoids runway incursions and/or ensures no conflict with traffic prior to taxiing into takeoff position.

Objective: To determine that the applicant:

1. Exhibits knowledge of the elements related to the before takeoff check. This shall include the reasons for checking each item and how to detect malfunctions.

BEFORE TAKEOFF

The before-takeoff check is a systematic procedure for making a last minute check of the engine, controls, systems, instruments, and radio prior to flight. When doing the takeoff check you must use a written checklist provided by the airplane manufacturer or operator. This ensures that each item is checked in the proper sequence and that nothing is omitted. While each item is checked, it's important for you to be able to detect malfunctions. Most inflight mechanical problems have a precursor on the ground, which an alert pilot can detect.

After taxiing the airplane to the runup area, position it so the propeller blast is directed away from any buildings or other aircraft. If possible, point the nose into the wind to improve engine cooling. To prevent damage to the propeller and other parts of the airplane, avoid engine runups on loose gravel and sand.

Although aircraft have different features and equipment requiring a specific checklist, there are several items that are common to all aircraft. The following is a typical before-takeoff checklist:

1. Before you begin the runup, the parking brake should be set. Furthermore, you must divide your attention between the cockpit and the area round the airplane. If the parking brake slips, the airplane can move forward while your attention is inside the cockpit.

2. Check all cabin doors and windows to determine that they are securely closed and locked.

3. The seats, seat belts, and shoulder harnesses must be secure. It is important to check the seats carefully to ensure that they are securely locked into position so they do not slide at anytime.

4. The flight controls must be checked for full movement and direction of travel. This check should include the elevator, rudder, ailerons, and flaps.

5. Check and set the flight instruments.

   a. Verify the airspeed indicator reads zero.

   b. The attitude indicator should be erect with the miniature airplane aligned with the horizon.

   c. Set the altimeter to the current altimeter setting or to the correct field elevation. If the altimeter does not indicate the field elevation within 75 feet, you should consider postponing the flight.

   d. The miniature airplane in the turn coordinator should be level and the ball in the inclinometer centered.

   e. Set the heading indicator to coincide with the magnetic compass.

   f. Check that the vertical speed indicator (VSI) is pointing at zero. If the VSI is not pointing at zero, you may fly the aircraft and use the indicated value as the zero indication.

6. Set the elevator trim to the TAKEOFF position. If this is not done, excessive control wheel pressures could make it extremely difficult to lift off the runway or cause the aircraft to pitch up sharply immediately after takeoff.

7. Set the throttle to the r.p.m. recommended by the manufacturer for the power check, and lean the mixture as required.

   a. Move the carburetor heat to the ON position and note the power loss, then return it to the OFF position. With hot air entering the carburetor, the engine r.p.m. should decrease, indicating the carburetor heat is functioning.

   b. Test the magnetos by noting the r.p.m. with the magneto switch in the BOTH position, then move the magneto switch to the RIGHT position and note the r.p.m. drop. Next, return the magneto switch to BOTH, then switch to the LEFT position and again note the r.p.m. drop. Finally, return the magneto switch to the BOTH position for takeoff. The airplane manufacturer specifies the maximum permissible r.p.m. reductions for each magneto, as well as the maximum differential.

c. Check the engine instruments. With the exception of the oil temperature gauge, they should register operation in the green arcs. In cold weather, oil temperature might not indicate in the normal range until after takeoff. However, the airplane is considered ready for takeoff if the engine accelerates normally, the oil pressure remains steady and normal, and the other engine instruments continue to register normally.

d. Check the suction gauge for a normal indication. A low reading may indicate a dirty air filter. Unreliable gyro indications may result if sufficient suction is not maintained.

e. Check the ammeter for a normal indication. A discharge or low voltage light indicates a faulty alternator or broken alternator belt or excessive electrical load.

8. Check and set the radios and navigation equipment.

   a. Set the radios to the desired frequencies.

   b. Set the course selectors to the desired courses or radials.

2. Positions the airplane properly considering other aircraft, wind and surface conditions.

- Prior to beginning the before-takeoff check, position the aircraft so the prop blast is not directed toward other aircraft, buildings, or vehicles.
- If safety permits, try to point the aircraft into the wind. This improves engine cooling.
- Avoid doing the before-takeoff check in areas of loose rock or soft ground.

3. Divides attention inside and outside the cockpit.

- During the before-takeoff check, you must divide your attention between systems and procedures inside the cockpit and any activity outside the cockpit.
- It's a good idea to look outside on every other check list item. When doing the power check, be especially alert to ensure the aircraft does not move.

4. Ensures that engine temperature and pressure are suitable for runup and takeoff.

- As you initiate the before-takeoff check, verify that the oil pressure is " in the green.''
- If manifold pressure or cylinder head temperature gauges are installed, check for operation in normal range.
- In cold weather, there might not be an indication of oil temperature during the runup.

5. Accomplishes the before takeoff checklist and ensures the airplane is in safe operating condition.

- Complete the before-takeoff check using the appropriate checklist.
- If all systems are normal, you can proceed to the runway and prepare for takeoff.
- If any deviation is identified that could endanger your flight, you should taxi the aircraft back to parking and report the discrepancy.

6. Reviews takeoff performance airspeeds, takeoff distances, departure, and emergency procedures.

- Prior to takeoff you should review the pertinent takeoff and climb speeds.
- You also should review takeoff performance figures and the appropriate departure procedure.
- A good habit to develop is to mentally review the appropriate responses to the various emergencies that could arise on takeoff. As a minimum, this should include the procedures for an engine failure both before and after liftoff.

7. Avoids runway incursions and/or ensures no conflict with traffic prior to taxiing into takeoff position.

- After receiving a clearance to taxi onto the runway, you should carefully scan the final approach path for conflicting traffic.
- At nontowered airports, it's recommended that you scan the entire traffic pattern prior to taxiing onto the runway.
- If the airport utilizes a CTAF, you should listen carefully so that you are aware of other aircraft in the airport vicinity.
- You also should announce your intentions prior to taxiing onto the runway.

EXERCISES

1. If you notice an abnormal condition during the before-takeoff check, you should
   a. attempt a takeoff.
   b. return the airplane for maintenance.
   c. run the engine at 2,000 r.p.m. to see if the condition improves.
   d. let the engine idle until it is warmed up and try the check again.

2. When you apply carburetor heat during the before-takeoff check, proper operation is indicated by a(n) _____ (increase, decrease) in engine r.p.m.

3. __ (True, False) You will always get an oil temperature indication before doing a runup.

4. ___ (True, False) When you have been cleared by the tower to taxi into takeoff position, you do not need to check for any traffic conflicts on final approach to your departing runway.

SAMPLE ORAL QUESTIONS

1. Describe the significance of a negative ammeter reading during the before-takeoff check.

1. The ammeter indicates the amount of electrical current going from the alternator to the battery, or from the battery to the aircraft electrical system. A negative ammeter reading indicates a battery discharge, which may result from a malfunction in the alternator, or an electrical load in excess of the alternator output. If a higher engine r.p.m. does not result in a normal indication, have the problem corrected before flight.

2. Describe the procedures for checking the altimeter prior to takeoff.

2. Prior to takeoff, the current altimeter setting should be placed in the altimeter. Once this is done, the altimeter should indicate the field elevation within 75 feet. If this isn't the case, you may want to consider postponing the flight. If no altimeter setting is available, you should set the altimeter to the correct field elevation.

3. Prior to taxiing onto any runway you should position the aircraft so you can carefully scan the final approach course. At nontowered airports, it's wise to scan the entire traffic pattern and utilize the CTAF.

3. Describe how you avoid conflicting traffic prior to taxiing onto an active runway.

____

____

____

____

____

____

____

ADDITIONAL QUESTIONS

4. Why should you try to position the aircraft heading into the wind during the before-takeoff check?

5. Describe the specific checks you should make on the flight instruments prior to take off.

6. What should you be checking for during the magneto check?

EXERCISE ANSWERS

1. b
2. decrease
3. False
4. False

REFERENCES

JEPPESEN:

Private Pilot Manual/Video – Chapters 4B and 5B
Private Pilot Maneuvers/Video – Maneuver 4

FAA:

Federal Aviation Regulations
Airplane Flying Handbook (FAA-H-8033-3)
Pilot's Operating Handbook and FAA-Approved Airplane Flight Manual

CHAPTER 3

AIRPORT OPERATIONS

A. TASK: RADIO COMMUNICATIONS AND ATC LIGHT SIGNALS (ASEL and ASES)

REFERENCES: 14 CFR part 91; AC61-23/FAA-H-8083-25; AIM.

Objective: To determine that the applicant:

1. Exhibits knowledge of the elements related to radio communications and ATC light signals.
2. Selects appropriate frequencies.
3. Transmits using recommended phraseology.
4. Acknowledges radio communications and complies with instructions.

Objective: To determine that the applicant:

1. **Exhibits knowledge of the elements related to radio communications and ATC light signals.**

USING THE RADIO

Talking on the radio should be done in a professional manner. Incorrect radio procedures compromise your safety and the safety of others. One of the most important items in radio communication is to speak clearly so others understand what you are saying. Before speaking on the radio, think of what you are going to say. As a guideline, you should state the name of the facility you are calling, your callsign, where you are, and what type of service you are requesting.

When you are ready to talk, ensure the volume control is turned up, and speak in a normal, conversational voice. When using a microphone, hold it close to your lips and make sure the noise cancelling port is unobstructed. It may take a few moments for the facility you called to respond. If you do not get a response, verify you have the correct frequency, check your radio to see if it is working properly, and try again.

COMMUNICATIONS AT NONTOWERED AIRPORTS

When flying in the vicinity of a nontowered airport, there are three ways you can obtain airport and/or traffic information as well as informing others of your intentions. The most common is by making a self-announce broadcast using the **common traffic advisory frequency** (CTAF). The other two methods involve communicating with a Flight Service Station (FSS) or UNICOM operator.

SELF-ANNOUNCE PROCEDURES

At nontowered airports, you must utilize self-announce procedures. When doing this, you are responsible for determining which runway to use and how to enter the pattern. You also must see and avoid other air traffic and maintain proper spacing in the pattern. In these situations, you should use the common traffic advisory frequency (CTAF) to receive advisories and to broadcast your intentions. When available, advisories usually include wind direction and speed, favored runway, and known traffic. To achieve the highest degree of safety, it's essential that all aircraft use the same frequency. The designated CTAF varies with the type of airport and its facilities.

Anytime you are operating within ten miles of an airport without an operating control tower, you should monitor and communicate on the common traffic advisory frequency. When transmitting, the five "W" approach to self-announce procedures should be followed. You begin with stating WHO you intend to address, followed by WHO you are, WHERE you are located, WHAT you want or what you are going to do, and then conclude by repeating WHO you are addressing. For example, "*Front Range Traffic, Skyhawk 19620, taxiing to runway two-six, Front Range.*" A position report would sound like this, "*Front Range Traffic, Skyhawk 19620, 10 miles south, inbound for landing, Front Range.*"

When in the traffic pattern you should announce your position on every leg including entering the pattern, downwind, base, final, and when clear of the runway. Furthermore, you should announce whether you intend on making a touch-and-go or a full stop landing. For example, "*Front Range Traffic, Skyhawk 19620, entering left downwind, runway two-six, full stop, Front Range.*"

FLIGHT SERVICE STATIONS

At some nontowered airports that have a Flight Service Station on the airport, you may be able to obtain a local airport advisory (LAA). An LAA typically provides wind direction and velocity, favored runway, altimeter setting, known traffic, and NOTAMs, and may include airport taxi routes, traffic pattern information, and instrument approach procedures. An inbound aircraft should report approximately 10 miles from the airport, reporting altitude and aircraft type, location relative to the airport, whether landing or overflight, and request an airport advisory. A typical request for airport information would sound like this: "*Vero Beach Radio, Centurion six niner delta-delta, is 10 miles south, two thousand, landing Vero Beach. Request airport advisory.*"

Departing aircraft should state the aircraft type, full identification number, type of flight planned (VFR or IFR), and the planned destination or direction of flight. Report before taxiing and before taking the runway for departure. If communications with a UNICOM are necessary after your initial report to FSS, return to the FSS frequency for a traffic update. A typical request would sound like this: "*Vero Beach Radio, Centurion six niner delta-delta, ready to taxi, VFR, departing to the southwest. Request airport advisory.*"

UNICOM

UNICOM facilities are nongovernment radio communication stations which often provide airport information at public use airports where there is no tower or FSS. Some UNICOMs offer only an advisory service and are not the CTAF. In this case, after receiving an airport advisory, you must return to the designated CTAF to listen for other aircraft and self-announce your position and intentions.

At other airports, the UNICOM may be the designated CTAF and you do not have to change frequencies to get advisory information. Announcing your position and intentions is standard procedure at airports where the designated CTAF is the UNICOM frequency. Since UNICOMs are privately operated, you can also request other information or services through these facilities. For example, you may call UNICOM to request fuel or a taxicab.

If your flight takes you to an airport that does not have a tower, an FSS, or a UNICOM, the CTAF will be the **MULTICOM** frequency, 122.9 MHz. At airports where MULTICOM is the CTAF, pilots are responsible for determining the favored runway and self-announcing their position and intentions. For example, "*Frederick traffic Cessna eight-zero-one Tango-Foxtrot departing runway three-six to the northeast, Frederick.*"

ATC FACILITIES AT TOWER-CONTROLLED AIRPORTS

The following discussion covers the various ATC communications procedures in the normal order you would use them. Departure procedures for a large airport will be covered first. Following that, arrival procedures at the same airport will be described. For these examples we will use the Colorado Springs Municipal Airport.

AUTOMATIC TERMINAL INFORMATION SERVICE

To improve controller effectiveness and to reduce frequency congestion, busy airports utilize **automatic terminal information service** (ATIS). ATIS is prerecorded and broadcast on its own frequency. It includes routine information usually available in an airport advisory. ATIS broadcasts are labeled with successive letters from the phonetic alphabet, such as "Information Alpha" or "Information Bravo."

CLEARANCE DELIVERY

After listening to ATIS, you may be required to contact **clearance delivery**. A clearance delivery facility is established at busy airports mainly for ATC to relay IFR clearances to departing IFR traffic. However, when the ATIS message includes instructions for VFR departures to contact clearance delivery, you should contact them and inform them of your intentions.

On your initial callup, state your N-number and aircraft type, the current ATIS letter, and VFR departure intentions. Most important, you should advise them of your destination and/or direction of flight. Your initial callup should sound like this, "*Colorado Springs Clearance Delivery, Skyhawk 19620, Information Echo, VFR to the southeast.*"

The controller will respond by giving you a departure clearance, which includes a heading and an altitude, along with a transponder code and the departure control frequency. Your clearance may sound something like this, "*Skyhawk 19620, after departure, fly heading 120, climb and maintain 7,500 feet, squawk 3504, departure frequency will be 124.0, contact ground control 121.7 when ready to taxi.*"

GROUND CONTROL

After talking with clearance delivery, call **ground control**. Before leaving the parking area, you must receive a clearance to taxi to the active runway. When you call ground control, you should say, "*Colorado Springs Ground, Skyhawk 19620, at the general aviation ramp, ready to taxi to runway 35 left for departure.*" The controller will respond with something like, "*Skyhawk 620, taxi to runway 35 left.*" When taxiing at unfamiliar airports, you can inform the controller that you are not familiar with the airport, and you will be given specific instructions.

A clearance to "*taxi to*" your assigned takeoff runway authorizes you to cross any runways (except the active runway) intersecting your taxi route, but not to taxi onto the departure runway. If you are asked to "*hold short*" of a runway, you must read back the "*hold short*" clearance to the controller, stop at the hold lines preceding the runway, check for traffic, and continue only after cleared to do so. After taxiing to the departure runway and completing your before-takeoff checklists, taxi to the hold line, switch to the control tower frequency, and say, "*Colorado Springs Tower, Skyhawk 19620, ready for takeoff, runway 35 left.*" If the final approach path is clear and you are next for departure, the controller might say, "*Skyhawk 19620, cleared for takeoff.*" You should then make a final check for traffic before you taxi onto the runway for takeoff. You might also be asked to "*. . . line up and wait.*" This means that you may position yourself on the runway for takeoff while waiting for another aircraft to clear the runway or to provide takeoff separation.

DEPARTURE CONTROL

Shortly after takeoff, the tower controller might say "*. . . right turn approved, contact departure control, 124.0.*" When you initiate contact with **departure control**, you should say, "*Colorado Springs Departure, Skyhawk 19620, climbing through 6,500 for 7,500.*" The controller may respond, "*Skyhawk 19620, radar contact, report reaching 7,500.*" The term **radar contact** means your aircraft has been radar identified and flight following will be provided. **Flight following** means the controller is observing the progress of your aircraft while you provide your own navigation. When clear of the departure control airspace, the controller will inform you that "*. . . radar service is terminated, frequency change is approved, squawk 1200.*"

ARRIVAL PROCEDURES

When returning to Colorado Springs, listen to the current ATIS as soon as you can receive it. While you are outside of the approach control airspace, contact approach control over a designated visual checkpoint or other prominent landmark, or provide your distance and direction from the airport. **Approach control** provides separation and sequencing of inbound aircraft as well as traffic advisories or safety alerts when necessary.

Approach control frequencies are published on sectional charts and broadcast over ATIS. A typical call to an approach facility might be: "*Colorado Springs Approach, Skyhawk 19620, over Ellicott, with Sierra, at 8,500, landing.*" Usually, approach control will provide a transponder code and ask you to "*. . . squawk ident.*" After radar contact is established, the controller may say, "*. . . radar contact, 15 miles east of Colorado Springs Airport, turn right, heading 220 for a right base to runway 35 right.*" The controller will tell you to "*. . . contact tower on 119.9*" at the appropriate time. After contacting the tower, continue your approach and follow any other instructions given to you by the tower controller. On your approach, the tower controller will tell you when you are "*. . . cleared to land runway 35 right.*" Be sure you understand land and hold short operations (LAHSO), and available landing distance (ALD).

There may be times when you want to stay in the traffic pattern to practice landings. You should advise approach control or the tower on initial contact that you will be "*. . . remaining in the pattern.*" The tower controller may ask you to "*. . . make closed traffic . . . .*" This means you should remain in the traffic pattern unless you are otherwise instructed. On your last time around the pattern, request a "*full-stop*" landing. During your roll-out, the tower should instruct you to "*. . . turn left on the next available taxiway and contact ground, point niner.*" Ground control, on 121.9 MHz, will provide a taxi clearance to the parking area. You should not switch to ground control before the tower instructs you to do so.

LOST COMMUNICATIONS PROCEDURES

As you are aware, establishing two-way radio communications with the control tower is required before you enter Class D airspace. If your communications radios become inoperative, it is still possible to land at a tower-controlled airport by following the lost communication procedures. Anytime you believe your radio has failed, set your transponder to Code 7600. This alerts ATC if you are in an area of radar coverage. If you have reason to believe that only the receiver is inoperative, remain outside or above the Class D surface area until you can determine the direction and flow of the traffic; then advise the tower of your aircraft type, position, altitude, intention to land, and request that you be controlled with light signals. If you have reason to believe that either the transmitter only, or both the transmitter and receiver are inoperative, remain outside or above the Class D surface area until you can determine the direction and flow of traffic; then, join the airport pattern and maintain visual contact with the tower.

ATC LIGHT SIGNALS

Air traffic control tower light signals are used to control aircraft with which radio contact cannot be established. The light gun that emits these signals utilizes an intense narrow light beam that is directed at aircraft. [Figure 3-1]

COLOR AND TYPE OF SIGNAL	MEANING	
	On the Ground	In Flight
Steady Green	Cleared for takeoff	Cleared to land
Flashing Green	Cleared for taxi	Return for landing (to be followed by steady green at proper time)
Steady Red	Stop	Give way to other aircraft and continue circling
Flashing Red	Taxi clear of landing area (runway) in use	Airport unsafe — do not land
Flashing White	Return to starting point on runway	(No assigned meaning)
Alternating Red and Green	Exercise extreme caution	Exercise extreme caution

Figure 3-1. Located in the cab of the control tower is a powerful light that controllers can use to direct light beams of various colors toward your aircraft. Each color or color combination has a specific meaning for an aircraft in flight, or on the airport surface.

ACKNOWLEDGING LIGHT SIGNALS

If you receive light signals during the daytime, you should acknowledge tower transmission or light signals by rocking your wings. When on the ground, acknowledge light signals by moving the ailerons or rudder. At night, acknowledge any light signals by blinking your landing light or navigation lights to indicate that you understand the signal and will comply.

It may be more convenient to land at a nearby nontowered airport rather than a tower-controlled airport. If so, you should also determine the landing direction by observing other traffic and the wind direction indicator prior to entering the pattern.

2. Selects appropriate frequencies.

- During your preflight, it is a good idea to write down the frequencies of all facilities you may use during your flight.
- Valuable sources for determining frequencies include sectional charts and airport facility directories.

3. Transmits using recommended phraseology.

- Proper phraseology is important to maintain a safe level of understanding during all communications.
- You should use the phonetic alphabet whenever you state individual characters in your N-number or when spelling out words.
- When stating altitude figures below 10,000 feet, indicate hundreds and thousands in round numbers. For example, 3,500 feet is: "THREE THOUSAND FIVE HUNDRED FEET."
- When stating altitudes between 10,000 feet and 18,000 feet, indicate the separate digits of the thousands followed by the word "THOUSAND." For example, 11,000 is "ONE ONE THOUSAND."
- Numbers such as headings and speeds are stated by pronouncing each digit. For example, 320 is stated as " THREE TWO ZERO."

4. Acknowledges radio communications and complies with instructions.

- You should acknowledge all callups or clearances. It is advisable to repeat any instructions given by ATC, especially headings and altitudes.
- Comply with appropriate instructions received from ATC. If any clearance would compromise the safety of the flight, you should inform ATC that you can not comply.

EXERCISES

1. At nontowered airports, you typically must utilize ______ ______ procedures.

2. You should announce your position anytime you are operating within ______ miles of an airport without an operating control tower.

3. ____ (True or False) A clearance to "taxi to" your assigned takeoff runway authorizes you to cross all runways (except the active runway) intersecting your taxi route.

4. Aircraft equipped with a transponder should be set to squawk ______ when a radio failure is experienced.

5. A flashing red light from the tower when you are in flight indicates the airport is ________.

6. The MULTICOM frequency is ______.

SAMPLE ORAL QUESTIONS

1. The three forms of radio communication include: making self-announced broadcasts on the CTAF frequency, obtaining airport advisories from an FSS located on the field, and obtaining information from a UNICOM operator.

2. You begin by stating WHO you are talking to, followed by WHO you are, WHERE you are located, WHAT you want or what you are going to do, and conclude by repeating WHO you are talking to.

3. During the day, while on the ground, acknowledge light signals by moving the ailerons or rudder, and when in flight, by rocking your wings. At night, acknowledge all light signals by blinking your landing or navigation lights.

4. You should first listen to ATIS to obtain weather and airport information. Then, if indicated on ATIS, contact clearance delivery and provide your N-number, aircraft type, destination, direction of flight, and indicate you are VFR and have received ATIS. After talking with clearance delivery, contact ground control to receive your taxi clearance. Once you've completed your runup and are ready for takeoff, contact tower for your takeoff clearance. Shortly after takeoff, the tower will direct you to contact departure.

1. What are the three forms of radio communication associated with airports without an operating tower?

2. What is the five "W" approach to self-announce procedures at nontowered airports?

3. How do you acknowledge a light gun signal when on the ground or in the air?

4. Explain the sequence of communications when departing a tower-controlled field.

ADDITIONAL QUESTIONS

5. Describe, in detail, radio failure procedures.
6. Where can you find the CTAF and UNICOM frequencies for an airport?
7. When would you use the MULTICOM frequency?

EXERCISE ANSWERS

1. self-announce
2. 10
3. True
4. 7600
5. unsafe
6. 122.9

REFERENCES

JEPPESEN:

Private Pilot Manual/Video – Chapters 5A and 5B

FAA:

Federal Aviation Regulations (14 CFR part 91)

Pilot's Handbook of Aeronautical Knowledge (AC 61-23/FAA-H-8083-25)

Aeronautical Information Manual

B. TASK: TRAFFIC PATTERNS (ASEL and ASES)

REFERENCES: FAA-H-8083-3, AC 61-23/FAA-H-8083-25, AC 90-66; AIM.

Objective: To determine that the applicant:

1. Exhibits knowledge of the elements related to traffic patterns. This shall include procedures at airports with and without operating control towers, prevention of runway incursions, collision avoidance, wake turbulence avoidance, and wind shear.
2. Complies with proper traffic pattern procedures.
3. Maintains proper spacing from other traffic.
4. Corrects for wind drift to maintain the proper ground track.
5. Maintains orientation with the runway/landing area in use.
6. Maintains traffic pattern altitude, ±100 feet (30 meters), and the appropriate airspeed, ±10 knots.

Objective: To determine that the applicant:

1. **Exhibits knowledge of the elements related to traffic patterns. This shall include procedures at airports with and without operating control towers, prevention of runway incursions, collision avoidance, wake turbulence avoidance, and wind shear.**

TRAFFIC PATTERNS

At most airports, traffic pattern altitudes for propeller driven aircraft are generally between 600 feet AGL and 1,000 feet AGL. Normally, turns in the traffic pattern are made to the left. This type of pattern is called a left-hand or "standard" pattern. However, you will find variations from a standard pattern at different airports due to noise abatement, obstacles, or when multiple runway patterns would interfere. In these situations a right-hand or "nonstandard" pattern may be designated.

TRAFFIC PATTERN LEGS

The traffic pattern typically has six segments or legs. They are: upwind, crosswind, downwind, base, final, and departure. This terminology is used by ATC and by pilots making position reports at nontowered airports. [Figure 3-2]

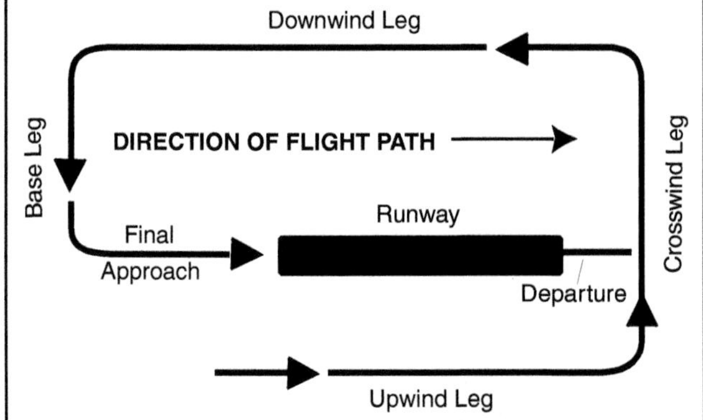

Figure 3-2. This diagram illustrates the individual legs of the traffic pattern.

The departure leg normally consists of the airplane's flight path after takeoff. When on this leg, fly the airplane directly above the runway or on the imaginary extension of the runway centerline and do not permit it to drift to one side or the other. Normally, you continue along this leg, without turning, until you reach an altitude within 300 feet of pattern altitude. Under certain conditions, such as high density altitudes or the existence of special airport procedures, you may need to start a turn at a somewhat lower altitude. However, never start a turn at an altitude which is unsafe.

Begin the crosswind leg after you pass the departure end of the runway and have achieved a safe altitude. Also, be sure to check for other traffic in the pattern before starting your turn to crosswind, since you may have to extend your departure leg to follow another aircraft. If flying a standard pattern, this leg is referred to as a left crosswind. In a nonstandard pattern, the leg would be called a right crosswind.

Ideally, as you turn from crosswind to downwind, the airplane is once again at the appropriate traffic pattern altitude. The downwind leg is a flight path parallel to the landing runway and is also designated as a left or right downwind, depending on the pattern. Fly the downwind leg parallel to the runway and at the designated traffic pattern altitude. For most training airplanes, the appropriate distance from the runway is about one-half to one mile. If it becomes necessary to maneuver to maintain spacing with another airplane, only shallow "S" turns should be used.

Normally, you turn onto the base leg when the touchdown point is approximately 45° behind the inside wing tip. However, the base leg must be adjusted according to other traffic and wind conditions. One important objective of the base leg is to allow the airplane to roll out on final approach at a distance no closer than one-quarter mile from the end of the runway, at an altitude appropriate to the glide path being flown.

The final approach is the path the airplane flies immediately prior to touchdown. Since it is flown along an imaginary extension of the centerline of the runway, you must compensate for any crosswind conditions.

The upwind leg consists of a flight path parallel to the landing runway in the direction of landing. Normally, this leg is flown on the side of the runway opposite the airport traffic pattern and is not to be confused with normal traffic pattern entry procedures.

TRAFFIC PATTERN OPERATIONS

When approaching the traffic pattern at a non towered airport, it is important to use the appropriate advisory frequency to obtain local weather, traffic, and landing information prior to entering the pattern. At a nontowered airport, you may be the one to determine which runway to use, depending on the type of services available.

Furthermore, at nontowered airports, traffic pattern altitudes and entry procedures may vary according to established local procedures. Usually, you enter the pattern at a 45° angle to the downwind leg, abeam the midpoint of the runway, and at pattern altitude.

Traffic pattern entry procedures at an airport with an operating control tower are specified by the tower operator. ATC may instruct you to enter the pattern at different points depending on your direction of arrival. When landing at an airport with a control tower, you must be cleared to land before you touch down. Also, you should remain on the tower frequency until directed to change to the ground frequency.

When a control tower is in operation, you can request and usually will receive approval for just about any type of departure. At airports without an operating control tower, you must comply with the departure procedures established for that airport. These procedures usually are posted so you can familiarize yourself with the local rules. The standard procedure is either to fly straight-out or to make a 45° turn in the direction of the pattern after you reach pattern altitude.

SEGMENTED CIRCLE

At nontowered airports, a wind sock, wind tee, or wind cone is usually placed in the middle of a segmented circle at a central location on the airport. The **segmented circle** has two purposes. First, it helps to identify the location of the wind direction indicator. Second, extensions on the segmented circle indicate the direction to turn in the traffic pattern. [Figure 3-3]

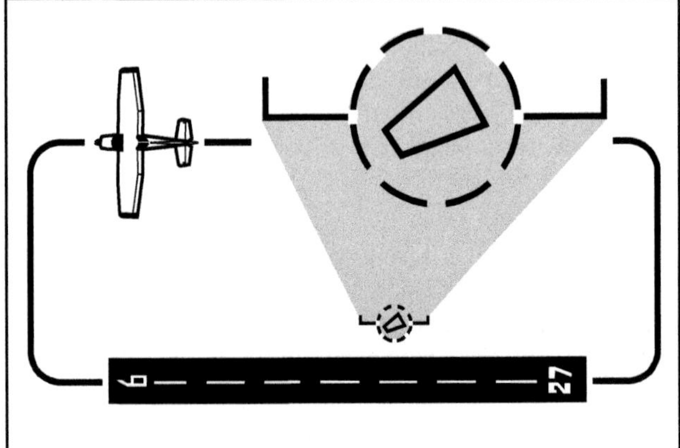

Figure 3-3. This segmented circle indicates that Runway 9 uses left traffic and Runway 27 utilizes right traffic.

The " L-shaped" extensions are placed so they indicate the direction you should turn in the traffic pattern for a given runway. You can think of the " L" as your base and final legs to the runway. If the " L," indicates a right turn, then you need to make a right-hand pattern on your approach When approaching an unfamiliar airport without an operational control tower, you should overfly the airport at 500 to 1,000 feet above the traffic pattern altitude to observe the flow of traffic and to locate the segmented circle. If no traffic is observed, follow the directions indicated by the segmented circle extensions and land on the runway indicated by the wind direction indicator. If there is no segmented circle, use a standard pattern for all runways.

COLLISION AVOIDANCE

A primary factor in flight safety is your ability to see and avoid other aircraft. When flying, you should spend at least 70% of your time looking outside the airplane. However, for scanning to be effective, you must develop a pattern that is compatible with how your eyes function. For example, your eyes require time to refocus when switching from the instrument panel to distant objects outside the airplane. Another characteristic of the eye is that only a small area in the back of the eye can send sharply focused images to the brain. Since the eyes require time to focus on this narrow viewing area, scanning is most effective when you use a series of short, regularly spaced eye movements. This helps bring successive areas of the sky into your central visual field. The FAA recommends that you scan in 10° increments and that you focus for at least one second on each segment.

Effective scanning habits help you compensate for a phenomenon called **empty field myopia.** This condition usually occurs when you are looking at a featureless sky that is devoid of objects or contrasting colors, such as flying in haze or reduced visibility. In these situations, your eyes tend to focus 10 to 30 feet in front of the aircraft. With empty field myopia, an aircraft must be two or three times larger (closer) before you are able to see it. To counter the effects of empty field myopia, you should consciously increase your scan rate and focus your eyes alternately far and near.

Your peripheral vision also plays an important role in spotting other aircraft because it is especially effective in detecting relative movement. Relative movement usually is your first perception of a collision threat. Remember, however, that you should be especially alert for an aircraft which shows no movement in relation to your airplane. In this situation, it is likely that the aircraft is on a collision course with you, requiring you to take evasive action.

If you take evasive action, watch the other aircraft to see if it makes any unusual maneuvers and, if so, plan your reaction accordingly. The more time you spend on developing your scan throughout your flight training, the more natural it will become later.

Scanning is especially important when near airports where there are large concentrations of traffic and increased cockpit duties. It is important that you do not sacrifice your scanning to complete a checklist or perform cockpit duties. Another part of collision avoidance is to increase the visibility of your aircraft. This is accomplished by turning on your landing or taxi light, especially when near an airport. Finally, your aircraft will be seen more readily if your aircraft is where other pilots expect to find it. Therefore, you should avoid unexpected maneuvers when in the area of the airport. For example, at nontowered airports, other pilots will be expecting you to enter the traffic pattern at a 45° angle on downwind.

RUNWAY INCURSIONS

A runway incursion refers to an occurrence at an airport involving an aircraft, vehicle, person, or object on the ground that created a collision hazard or resulted in loss of proper separation with an aircraft taking off, intending to take off, landing or intending to land. To avoid being involved in a runway incursion, you need to maintain a constant awareness of your position relative to other traffic, ensure that you understand and comply with ATC instructions, and scan your surroundings.

To help you maintain situational awareness, it is recommended that you take time to familiarize yourself with the airport layout by studying the airport diagram for any unfamiliar airport. To maintain an awareness of other aircraft, always monitor the transmissions of controllers and other aircraft.

In addition to knowing where you and other aircraft are, you must understand and comply with ATC instructions. To facilitate this, you should read back all clearances with restrictions and numbers. Furthermore, if there is a misunderstanding, do not hesitate to request clarification.

Another factor in avoiding a runway incursion is to utilize your collision avoidance skills on the ground. For example, before crossing any taxiway or runway you should carefully scan the surrounding area. Before taxiing onto an active runway for takeoff, you should scan the final approach to verify that it is clear of traffic. When operating out of a nontowered airport, it is a good idea to make a 360° circle to check the entire pattern. When on final, avoid staring at one end of the runway. Instead, you should watch for other aircraft at both ends of the runway as well as on intersecting runways.

WAKE TURBULENCE

Before you can successfully avoid wake turbulence, you must understand what it is and how it is created. Wake turbulence is caused by wingtip vortices and jet and prop blast. Wingtip vortices form whenever lift is generated and are the result of high pressure air below a wing spilling over the wingtips to the lower pressure areas above the wing. The greatest vortex danger is produced by large, heavy aircraft operating at low speeds, high angles of attack, and in a clean configuration.

Wake turbulence trails behind all aircraft. Vortices produced in flight typically descend at a rate of several hundred feet per minute and tend to level off 500 to 1,000 feet below the generating aircraft's flight path. However, when near the ground, wingtip vortices sink until they reach the ground and then begin to move laterally outward at two to three knots. In light winds of three to seven knots, the vortices may stay in the touchdown area, sink into your takeoff or landing path, or drift over a parallel runway. The most dangerous condition for landing is a light, quartering tailwind. It can move the upwind vortex of a landing aircraft over the runway and forward into the touchdown zone.

AVOIDING WAKE TURBULENCE

Wingtip vortices begin when an aircraft is generating lift. Therefore, vortices are present from the moment an aircraft rotates for takeoff to the time it touches down for landing. To help avoid flying through wingtip vortices when taking off behind a large aircraft, lift off prior to the large aircraft's rotation point, and stay above its flight path. When your aircraft's climb performance won't permit this, you can avoid the wake turbulence by choosing a flight path upwind of the large aircraft's flight path. When landing behind a large aircraft, stay above the large airplane's glide path and plan to touch down beyond its touchdown point. [Figure 3-4]

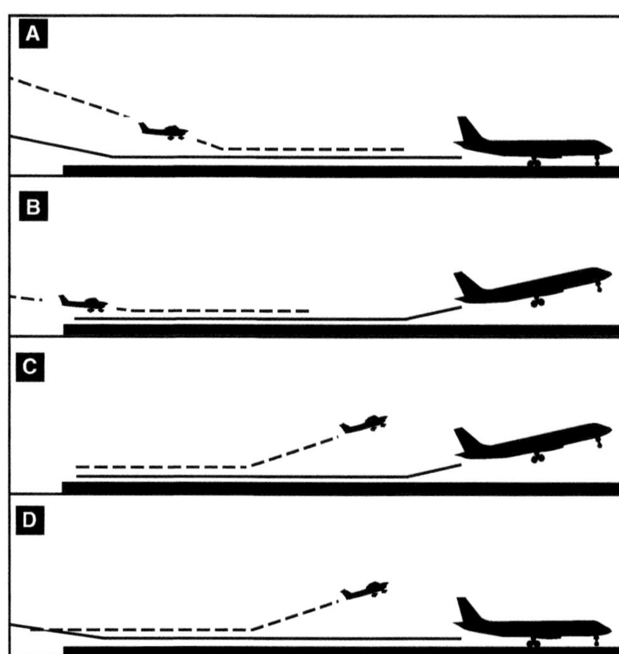

Figure 3-4. To avoid turbulence when landing behind a large aircraft, stay above the large airplane's glide path and touch down beyond its touchdown point (part A). If a large airplane has just taken off as you approach to land, touch down well before the large aircraft's liftoff point (part B). When taking off behind a large aircraft, lift off before the large airplane's rotation point and climb out above or upwind of its flight path (part C). When departing after a large aircraft has landed, lift off beyond its touchdown point (part D).

WIND SHEAR

Wind shear is a sudden, drastic shift in wind speed and/or direction that may occur at any altitude in a vertical or horizontal plane. It can subject your aircraft to sudden updrafts, downdrafts, or extreme horizontal wind components, causing loss of lift or violent changes in vertical speeds or altitudes. The best way to counter the effects of wind shear is to avoid it. You should never try to conduct any flight operations, especially traffic pattern work, in the proximity of wind shear. You should anticipate wind shear when frontal systems and thunderstorms are in the area. It also may occur during a temperature inversion when cold, still surface air is covered by warmer air which contains winds of 25 knots or more.

Some airports now have a low-level wind shear alert system (LLWAS). This system measures the difference in wind speeds between sensors at various locations around the airport. If a significant difference is noted, tower controllers will alert you by advising you of the wind velocities at two or more of the sensors.

If you happen to be conducting an approach and the possibility of experiencing wind shear is present, consider flying the approach at a slightly higher airspeed and power setting. A typical guideline to follow is to add one-half of the existing wind gust factor to your approach speed. If at anytime you get an indication of wind shear such as a sudden decrease in airspeed or increased rate of descent, initiate a go-around immediately.

MICROBURSTS

A microburst is an intense, localized downdraft which spreads out in all directions when it reaches the surface. This creates severe horizontal and vertical wind shears which pose serious hazards to aircraft, particularly those near the surface. A microburst typically covers less than two and a half miles at the surface, with peak winds as high as 150 knots and lasting only two to five minutes. Any convective cloud can produce this phenomenon. Microbursts commonly occur during heavy precipitation in thunderstorms and can be identified by a dark area consisting of a heavy rain shaft that spreads out at the surface. However, microbursts also are associated with **virga**, or streamers of precipitation that trail beneath a cloud but evaporate before they reach the ground. If there is no precipitation, your only visual cue may be a ring of blowing dust at the surface.

Because unexpected changes in wind speed and direction can be hazardous to aircraft operations at low altitudes on approach and departure, pilots are urged to promptly volunteer reports to controllers of wind shear conditions they encounter. An advance warning of this information will assist other pilots in avoiding or coping with a wind shear on approach or departure. When describing wind shear conditions for a PIREP, you should avoid using the terms "negative" or "positive" windshear on final. Instead, state the loss or gain of airspeed and/or describe the effects of the windshear on the aircraft.

2. Complies with proper traffic pattern procedures.

- Prior to entering the traffic pattern, you must know if a left- or right-hand pattern is applicable.
- When entering the traffic pattern you should be at the appropriate altitude and enter the pattern at a 45° angle on downwind, or as directed by ATC.
- At non towered airports, you should make the appropriate self-announced position reports.
- At towered airports, you should enter the traffic pattern as directed by ATC and comply with instructions.

3. Maintains proper spacing from other traffic.

- When in the pattern, you must be aware of other aircraft and maintain separation.
- At non towered airports you may have to do shallow S-turns or a 360° turn on downwind to maintain separation.
- You are always responsible for seeing and avoiding other traffic.

4. Corrects for wind drift to maintain the proper ground track.

- You should maintain a rectangular traffic pattern by properly anticipating and correcting for current wind conditions.
- The procedure for flying a traffic pattern is identical to that used for flying a rectangular course. Refer to Chapter 6, Task A on page 6-1.

5. Maintains orientation with the runway in use.

- You must always know where you are in the traffic pattern.

6. Maintains traffic pattern altitude, ± 100 feet (30 meters), and the appropriate airspeed, ± 10 knots.

- Once established at the proper altitude, use outside references to maintain the appropriate pitch attitude. Periodically check the altimeter to verify you are maintaining pattern altitude.
- Use a combination of pitch and power to maintain the desired speeds in the pattern.

COMMON ERRORS

1. **Traffic pattern not square.**

   Cause: Failure to compensate properly for wind drift.

   Solution: After establishing a crab angle, check the aircraft's ground track and modify the crab angle as necessary.

2. **Not maintaining pattern altitude, excessive gain or loss of altitude.**

   Cause: Failure to divide your attention between visual and instrument references.

   Solution: Use outside references to set the correct pitch attitude, and periodically check the altimeter to verify your altitude.

EXERCISES

1. The traffic pattern altitude for propeller driven aircraft is generally between ____ feet and ____ feet AGL.

2. When flying a standard traffic pattern, all turns are made to the _____.

3. The ______ (upwind, downwind) leg is the flight path parallel to the landing runway in the direction of the landing.

4. At airports without an operational control tower, you normally enter the pattern at a ____ angle on downwind and at pattern altitude.

5. Near the ground, wingtip vortices sink until they reach the ground and then begin to move laterally outward at about _____ knots.

SAMPLE ORAL QUESTIONS

1. A segmented circle serves two purposes: it helps identify the location of the wind direction indicator, and the circle itself indicates the direction (left-hand or right-hand) of traffic pattern used for each runway.

2. You should overfly the airport at 500 to 1,000 feet above the traffic pattern altitude to observe the flow of traffic and to locate the segmented circle. If no traffic is observed, follow the directions indicated by the segmented circle extensions and land on the runway indicated by the wind direction indicator. The " L'' shaped pextensions are placed so they indicate the direction to turn in the traffic pattern for a given runway. You can think of the " L'' as your base and final legs. If there are no extensions for the runways, they all have standard left-hand traffic patterns.

1. What is the purpose of a segmented circle?

____

____

____

____

____

2. How do you use a segmented circle for determining how to land at an airport without an operating control tower or UNICOM?

____

____

____

____

____

____

____

____

____

____

____

____

3. What are some indications of a microburst?

3. Microbursts commonly occur during heavy precipitation in thunderstorms and can be identified by a dark area consisting of a heavy rain shaft that spreads out at the surface. However, microbursts also are associated with virga, or streamers of precipitation that trail beneath a cloud but evaporate before they reach the ground. If there is no precipitation, your only clue may be a ring of blowing dust at the surface.

4. Describe the recommended technique you should use when scanning for traffic.

4. Since the eyes require time to focus, scanning is most effective when you use a series of short, regularly spaced eye movements. This helps bring successive areas of the sky into your central visual field. The FAA recommends that you scan in 10° increments and that you focus for at least one second on each segment.

ADDITIONAL QUESTIONS

5. Describe the procedures you should use to avoid wake turbulence.
6. What is the best way to counter the effects of wind shear?
7. What three things can you do to help avoid being involved in a runway incursion?

EXERCISE ANSWERS

1. 600, 1,000
2. left
3. upwind
4. 45°
5. 2-3

REFERENCES

JEPPESEN:

Private Pilot Manual/Video – Chapters 4A, 4B and 6C

Private Pilot Maneuvers/Video – Maneuver 12

FAA:

Airplane Flying handbook (FAA-H-8083-3)

Pilot's Handbook of Aeronautical Knowledge (AC 61-23/FAA-H-8083-25)

Recommended Standards Traffic Patterns for Aeronautical Operations at Airports without Operating Control Towers (AC 90-66)

Aeronautical Information Manual

C. TASK: AIRPORT/SEAPLANE BASE, RUNWAY, AND TAXIWAY SIGNS, MARKINGS, AND LIGHTING (ASEL and ASES)

REFERENCES: AC 61-23/FAA-H-8083-25; AIM.

Objective: To determine that the applicant:

1. Exhibits knowledge of the elements related to airport/seaplane base, runway, and taxiway operations with emphasis on runway incursion avoidance.
2. Properly identifies and interprets airport/seaplane base, runway, and taxiway signs, markings, and lighting.

Objective: To determine that the applicant:

1. **Exhibits knowledge of the elements related to airport, runway, and taxiway operations with emphasis on runway incursion avoidance.**

RUNWAY MARKINGS

Since you normally fly magnetic courses and headings, the numbers on runways correlate to a magnetic heading and are rounded to the nearest 10°, with the last zero omitted. At some airports, there may be two parallel runways with the same runway number. In this situation, one runway is labeled the left runway and the other the right runway; for example, "36L" and "36R." If there is a third parallel runway, the middle one is labeled the center runway, or "36C."

Runway markings vary depending on the type of operations conducted to the runway. For example, a basic VFR runway will have only the runway number and a dashed white centerline. If a runway is used in conjunction with a nonprecision instrument approach, threshold markings are added. Touchdown zone markers, aiming point markings, and side stripes are added when the runway is used in conjunction with a precision instrument approach. Occasionally, you may see fixed distance markings and side stripes on a nonprecision runway. [Figure 3-5]

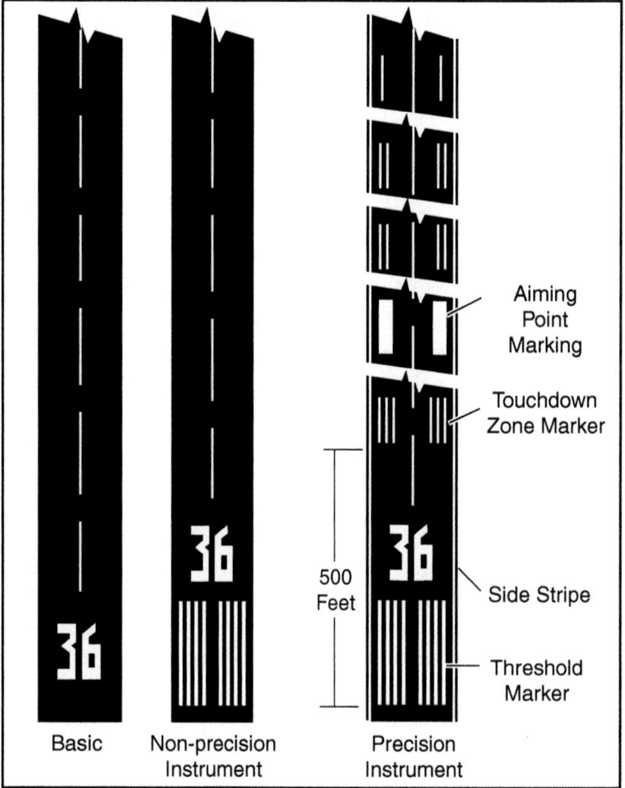

Figure 3-5. The common types of runway markings for VFR, nonprecision, and precision runways are shown here. The threshold marker, touchdown zone marker, aiming point marking, and side stripes on the precision instrument approach runways are there to aid pilots who are making instrument approaches.

At some airports, obstructions off the end of the runway may dictate the necessity for a runway with a **displaced threshold**. The beginning of the landing portion of the runway, or threshold, is marked by a solid white line with yellow arrows leading up to it. Even though the first few hundred feet of pavement cannot be used for landing, it may be available for taxiing, the landing rollout, and takeoffs.

Another extension found on the ends of some runways is a **blast pad/stopway area**. The blast pad is an area where propeller or jet blast can dissipate without creating a hazard to others. A blast pad is different from the area preceding a displaced threshold because it cannot be used for taxiing, takeoffs, or landings. The stopway area is paved so that, in the event of an aborted takeoff, an aircraft can use it to decelerate and come to a stop. Because of its reduced weight-bearing capabilities, no one is allowed to use a blast pad/stopway area for taxiing, landing, or departing. The beginning of the landing portion of the runway is marked with a solid white line, just as it is with the displaced threshold. [Figure 3-6]

Another airport marking you will need to become familiar with is the one associated with a closed runway or taxiway. When a runway or taxiway is unusable, a large " X"

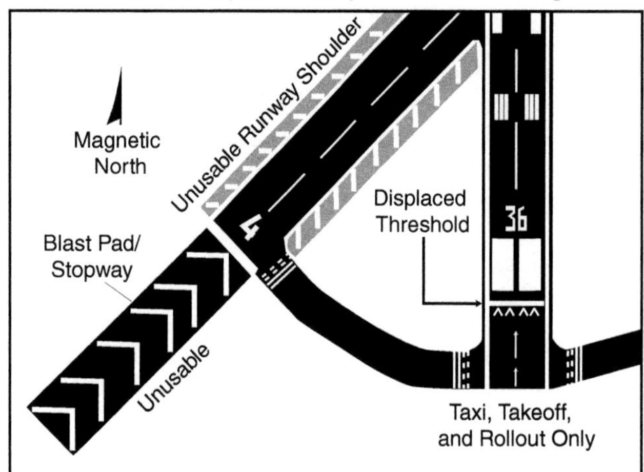

Figure 3-6. A displaced threshold is identified by the white arrows leading up to a solid white line. The blast pad/stopway area is painted with yellow chevrons, which indicate the structure of the pavement is unusable for normal operations. There also may be areas with yellow diagonal stripes on each side of the runway where the pavement strength is reduced.

is painted or displayed on both ends. Although the surface may appear to be usable, the runway or taxiway cannot be used safely.

TAXIWAYS

Taxiways are easily identified by a continuous yellow centerline stripe. Many times, taxiways are labeled " Taxiway A," " Taxiway B," and so on, to help you identify routes to and from runways. As you transition from the taxiway to the runway, you will see hold lines, which are generally 125 feet to 250 feet from the touchdown area of the runway in use. Normally, there is a sign nearby that identifies the associated runway. Larger airports may have additional taxiway/runway location signs, as well as direction, destination, and information signs. At a nontowered airport, you should stop and check for traffic and cross the hold lines only after ensuring that no one is on an approach to land. At a tower controlled airport, the controller may ask you to hold short of the runway for landing traffic. In this case, you should stop before the hold lines and proceed only after you are cleared to do so, and have checked for traffic.

At some airports the hold lines may be placed farther from the runway to prevent any interference from an instrument landing system (ILS). This means you may find two hold lines for some runways. The one closest to the runway is the normal hold line, while the one farthest away is the ILS hold line. At other locations only an ILS hold line may be used.

AIRPORT SIGNS

There are six types of airport signs which assist you while operating on the airport surface: mandatory instruction signs, location signs, direction signs, destination signs, information signs, and runway distance remaining signs.

1 **Mandatory Instruction Signs** denote an entrance to a runway, a critical area, or an area prohibited to aircraft. These signs are red with white letters or numbers.

2 **Location Signs** identify either the taxiway or runway where your aircraft is located. These signs are black with yellow inscriptions and a yellow border and do not have arrows. Location signs also identify the boundary of the runway or ILS critical area for aircraft exiting the runway. In this case, the signs are yellow with black markings.

3 **Direction Signs** indicate directions of taxiways and have black inscriptions on a yellow background. These signs always contain arrows which show the approximate direction of the turn.

4 **Destination Signs** also have a yellow background with a black inscription indicating a destination on the airport. These signs always have an arrow showing the direction of the taxiing route to that destination. When the arrow on the destination sign indicates a turn, the sign is located prior to the intersection.

5 **Information Signs** advise you of such things as areas that cannot be seen from the control tower, applicable radio frequencies, and noise abatement procedures. These signs also use a yellow background with black inscriptions.

6 **Runway Distance Remaining Signs** are used to provide distance remaining information to pilots during takeoff and landing. The signs are located along the sides of the runway, and consist of a white numeral on a black background. The signs indicate the distance remaining in thousands of feet. [Figure 3-7]

AERONAUTICAL LIGHTING

To help you better identify airports and runway layouts, all public use airports that are lighted for nighttime operations use FAA-approved lighting and colors.

AIRPORT BEACON

The combination of light colors from an airport beacon indicates the type of airport. Airport beacons at civilian land airports use alternating white and green lights. Beacons at military airports have two flashes of white that alternate with a single green light.

Most airport beacons are on from dusk until dawn. The beacon usually isn't on during the day unless the ceiling is

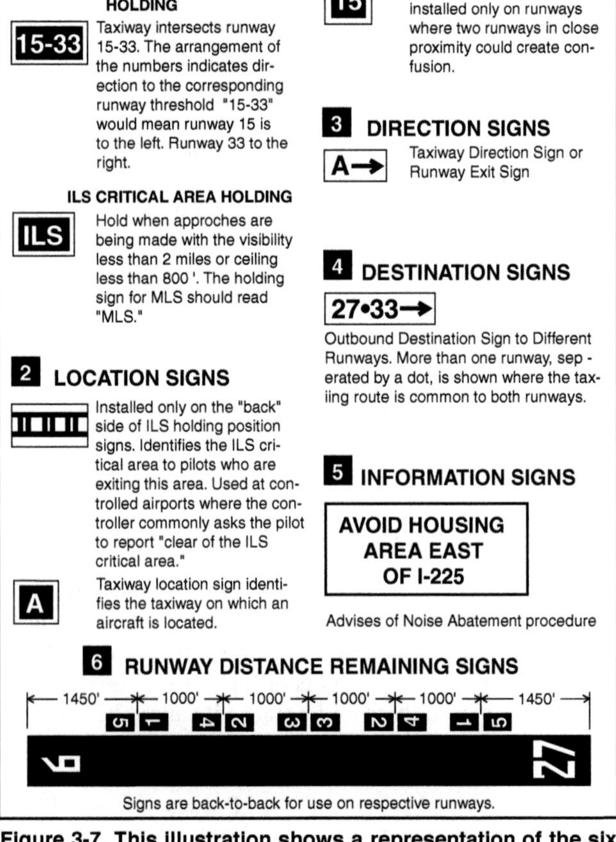

Figure 3-7. This illustration shows a representation of the six types of signs that can be found on an airport surface.

less than 1,000 feet and/or the ground visibility is less than three statute miles, the normal VFR minimums. You should not rely solely on the operation of the airport beacon to indicate if weather conditions are IFR or VFR. At many airports the beacon is turned on by a photoelectric cell or time clock and ATC personnel cannot control them. There is no regulatory requirement for daylight airport beacon operation, and it is your responsibility to comply with proper preflight planning as required by FAR 91.103.

APPROACH LIGHTING SYSTEMS

Some airports have complex lighting systems to help instrument pilots transition to visual references at the end of an instrument approach. These **approach lighting systems** can begin as far away as 3,000 feet from the threshold along the extended runway centerline, and can aid VFR pilots operating at night.

VISUAL GLIDESLOPE INDICATORS

To help you judge the aircraft's glidepath, many airports have visual glideslope indicators installed. The indicator lights are located on the side of the runway and are helpful for maintaining the approach glide path. One of the most common is the **visual approach slope indicator** (VASI).

VASI configurations vary and may have either two or three bars. Two-bar systems have near and far bars and may include 2, 4, or 12 light units. The VASI glide path provides safe obstruction clearance within 10° of the extended runway centerline out to 4 n.m. from the threshold. You should not begin a descent using VASI until your aircraft is aligned with the runway. When landing at a tower-controlled airport that has a VASI, regulations require you to remain on or above the glide path until a lower altitude is necessary for safe landing.

The lights associated with a VASI are either white or red, depending on the angle of your glide path. If both light bars are white, you are too high; if you see red over red, you are below the glide path. If the far bar is red and the near bar is white, you are on the glide path. The memory aid, " red over white, you're all right," is helpful in recalling the correct on-glide-path indication. The normal glide path angle is 3°.

Some larger airports utilize a three-bar VASI system that incorporates two different glide paths. If you encounter a three-bar VASI system, use the two lower bars as if it were a standard two-bar VASI.

Another system is the **precision approach path indicator** (PAPI). It has two or four lights installed in a single row. The PAPI is normally located on the left side of the runway and can be seen up to 20 miles at night. If all of the PAPI system lights are white, you are too high. If only the light unit on the far right is red and the other three are white, you are slightly high. When you are on the glide path, the two lights on the left will be white and the two lights on the right will be red. If you are slightly low, only the light on the far left will be white. If you are below the glide path, all four of the lights will be red.

THRESHOLD LIGHTS

If your destination airport has a visual glide slope system, it will lead you to the touchdown zone. At night, there are three ways to tell where the runway begins. If the runway has a displaced threshold, there will be a set of green lights on each side of the white threshold line to indicate the beginning of the landing portion of the runway. If the threshold is not displaced, the beginning of the runway pavement will have a row of green lights across it. Because threshold lights are a different color when viewed from the opposite direction, you will see green lights designating the approach end of the runway and red lights for the departure end.

Sometimes high intensity white strobe lights are placed on each side of the runway to mark the threshold. These are called **runway end identifier lights** (REILs) and are used in conjunction with the green threshold lights.

RUNWAY EDGE LIGHTS

Runway edge lights are classified according to three intensity levels: **high**, **medium**, and **low**. At some airports, you can adjust the intensity of the high and medium runway edge lights by using the radio transmitter. At others, the lights are preset or are adjusted by air traffic controllers. Runway edge lights are white, except on instrument runways where amber replaces white on the last 2,000 feet or one-half the runway length, whichever is less, to form a caution zone for landings.

IN-RUNWAY LIGHTING

Some runways incorporate flush **runway centerline lights**, and may include **runway-remaining lights** in the final 3,000 feet as viewed from the takeoff or approach position. Alternate red and white lights are seen from the 3,000-foot point to the 1,000-foot point, and all red lights are seen for the last 1,000 feet of the runway. From the opposite direction, these are seen as white lights.

TAXIWAY LIGHTING

Where installed, blue taxiway edge lights guide you from the runway to the ramp area. At some airports, green taxiway centerline lights may also be installed. These lights are located along the taxiway centerline in both straight and curved portions of the taxiway. They also may be located along designated taxiing paths in portions of runways, ramps, and apron areas.

PILOT-CONTROLLED LIGHTING

Pilot-controlled lighting is the term used to describe airport lighting systems that you can activate by keying the aircraft's microphone on a specified radio frequency. Typically, this type of system activates approach, runway, and taxiway lights at some unattended airports. Other types of airport lighting may also be pilot controlled, such as VASI and REIL lights.

To activate pilot-controlled lights, you should initially key your microphone seven times on the specified frequency to turn all the lights on at maximum intensity. If conditions dictate a lower intensity, adjustments can be made where a variable intensity capability is provided. At these locations, key your microphone five times for medium-intensity lighting and three times for the lowest intensity. For each adjustment, you must key the microphone the required number of times within a period of five seconds.

OBSTRUCTION LIGHTING

The purpose of obstruction lighting is to give you advanced warning of obstructions on and off the airport. For example, obstruction lights are installed on prominent structures such as towers, buildings and, sometimes, even powerlines. Bright red and high intensity white lights are typically used. Keep in mind that there may be guy-wires extending from the top of the tower to the ground.

2. Properly identifies and interprets airport, runway, and taxiway signs, markings, and lighting.

- You must understand the meaning of all airport signs, taxiway and runway markings, as well as all airport lighting.

EXERCISES

1. Runway numbers correlate to ______________ ________.
2. Taxiways are easily identified by a continuous ______ (yellow, white) centerline stripe.
3. When there are two sets of hold lines associated with an ILS runway, the one ______ (closest, farthest) to the runway is the normal hold line.
4. A mandatory instruction sign uses white lettering on a ________ background.
5. On a two-bar VASI, if you see red over red you are _____ the glide path.
6. High intensity strobe lights placed on each side of the runway to mark the threshold are called ______ ______ ______ lights.

SAMPLE ORAL QUESTIONS

1. Explain how a blast pad/stopway area is different from a displaced threshold.

____
____
____
____
____
____
____
____

2. What is the purpose of an ILS critical area and how is it marked?

____
____
____
____
____
____
____
____
____

1. A displaced threshold cannot be used for landing, but is available for taxiing, takeoffs, and rolling out after landing. A blast pad, on the other hand, is an area where propeller or jet blast can dissipate without creating a hazard to others and can not be used for any ground operations except in an emergency.

2. It is possible for aircraft near the runway to interfere with the ILS signal. A critical area keeps aircraft on the ground from interfering with the ILS signal. You may find two hold lines; the one closest to the runway is the normal hold line, while the one farthest away is the ILS hold line. At other locations only an ILS hold line may be used. In addition, there may be an ILS critical area sign to mark the area.

3. A civilian airport beacon uses alternating white and green lights. When the beacon is on during the day, it typically indicates that the airport is below normal VFR minimums, that is, the ceiling is less than 1,000 feet and/or the ground visibility is less than three statute miles.

3. What combination of light colors do civilian airport beacons use and what does it mean when a beacon is on during the day?

4. When an airport is equipped with pilot-controlled lighting, you can activate approach, runway, and taxiway lights by keying the aircraft's microphone on a specified radio frequency. Normally, you key the microphone seven times to turn all the lights on at maximum intensity. At locations where you can control the intensity, key your microphone five times for medium intensity, or three times for low intensity. For each adjustment, you must key the microphone the required number of times within a period of five seconds.

4. How do you operate pilot-controlled lighting?

ADDITIONAL QUESTIONS

5. Define the six types of signs found on airports and describe their appearance.
6. What distances are associated with threshold markers, fixed distance markers, and touchdown zone markers?

EXERCISE ANSWERS

1. magnetic north
2. yellow
3. closest
4. red
5. below
6. runway end identifier

REFERENCES

JEPPESEN:

Private Pilot Manual/Video – Chapter 4B

FAA:

Flight Training Handbook (AC 61-21)

Pilot's Handbook of Aeronautical Knowledge (AC 61-23/FAA-H-8083-25)

Aeronautical Information Manual

CHAPTER 4

TAKEOFFS, LANDINGS, AND GO-AROUNDS

A. TASK: NORMAL AND CROSSWIND TAKEOFF AND CLIMB (ASEL and ASES)

NOTE: If a crosswind condition does not exist, the applicant's knowledge of crosswind elements shall be evaluated through oral testing.

REFERENCES: FAA-H-8083-3; POH/AFM

Objective: To determine that the applicant:

1. Exhibits knowledge of the elements related to a normal and crosswind takeoff, climb operations, and rejected takeoff procedures.
2. Positions the flight controls for the existing wind conditions.
3. Clears the area, taxies into the takeoff position and aligns the airplane on the runway center/takeoff path.
4. Retracts the water rudders, as appropriate, (ASES) and advances the throttle smoothly to takeoff power.
5. Establishes and maintains the most efficient planing/lift-off attitude and corrects for porpoising and skipping. (ASES)
6. Lifts off at the recommended airspeed and accelerates to V_Y.
7. Establishes a pitch attitude that will maintain V_Y +10/-5 knots.
8. Retracts the landing gear, if appropriate, and flaps after a positive rate of climb is established.
9. Maintains takeoff power and V_Y +10/-5 knots to a safe maneuvering altitude.
10. Maintains directional control and proper wind drift correction throughout the takeoff and climb.
11. Complies with noise abatement procedures.
12. Completes the appropriate checklist.

Objective: To determine that the applicant:

1. **Exhibits knowledge of the elements related to a normal and crosswind takeoff, climb operations, and rejected takeoff procedures.**

NORMAL AND CROSSWIND TAKEOFF AND CLIMB

A thorough knowledge of takeoff and climb principles is an extremely important part of safe flight. In fact, statistics show that takeoff accidents, while slightly less frequent than landing accidents, are much more tragic. Although normal and crosswind takeoffs and climbs are one continuous maneuver, for the purpose of this discussion, we will divide them into three separate stages. The stages are: the takeoff roll, the lift-off, and the climb.

THE TAKEOFF ROLL

After taxiing onto the runway, the airplane should be carefully aligned with the runway centerline. After releasing the brakes, the throttle should be smoothly and continuously advanced to maximum allowable power. An abrupt application of power may cause the airplane to yaw sharply to the left because of the torque effects of the engine and propeller. With this in mind, the throttle should always be advanced smoothly and continuously to prevent any sudden swerving.

As you advance the throttle, monitor the engine instruments so as to note immediately any malfunction or indication of insufficient power. As the airplane starts forward, you should slide both feet down on the rudder pedals so that the toes or balls of your feet are off the brakes.

RUDDER APPLICATION

Before you add power, the rudder should be in a neutral position. Then as power is added, apply right rudder pressure to counteract engine torque. During the takeoff roll, maintain directional control with the rudder pedals. The steerable nosewheel or tailwheel is usually sufficient to maintain directional control until airspeed increases to the point where the rudder becomes more effective.

You must use whatever rudder pressure is needed to keep the airplane headed straight down the runway. The use of brakes for steering purposes should be avoided since it can result in slower acceleration, a longer takeoff distance, and possibly severe swerving.

When taking off in a crosswind, the wind striking the vertical stabilizer attempts to weathervane the airplane. In this situation, extra rudder pressure must be applied to counteract the weathervaning tendency.

AILERON APPLICATION

When conducting a normal takeoff, you should keep the ailerons neutral throughout the takeoff roll. However, if a crosswind is present, you must turn the ailerons into the wind, much the same as when taxiing in a crosswind. At the beginning of the takeoff roll, you should use full aileron deflection into the wind. This causes the airflow over the wing with the raised aileron to hold that wing down. As with the rudder, when the airplane accelerates, the ailerons become more effective; therefore, you must reduce the amount of aileron deflection gradually as airspeed increases.

ELEVATOR APPLICATION

During the takeoff roll, apply slight back pressure. As speed is gained, the elevator control will tend to assume a neutral position if the airplane is correctly trimmed. Once rotation speed is reached, increase back pressure to lift the nosewheel for takeoff.

Keep in mind that the takeoff attitude is a compromise between holding the nose on the ground and selecting an attitude which is too nose high. Holding the nosewheel on the ground too long increases the length of runway required for takeoff, whereas an excessively nose-high attitude may force the aircraft into the air prematurely resulting in the aircraft settling back to the runway. Also, a high angle of attack may create excessive drag and not allow the aircraft to accelerate to lift off speed.

THE LIFT-OFF

A good takeoff requires the proper takeoff attitude and requires only minimum pitch adjustments after the airplane lifts off. As the aircraft rotates and lifts off the runway, the position of the nose in relation to the horizon should be noted, then elevator pressure applied as necessary to hold this attitude. Furthermore, the wings must be kept level by applying aileron pressure as necessary. Even as the airplane leaves the ground, you must continue to maintain straight flight as well as hold the proper pitch attitude.

During takeoffs in strong, gusty winds, it is advisable that an extra margin of speed be obtained before the airplane is allowed to leave the ground. A takeoff at the normal liftoff speed may result in lack of positive control, or a stall, when the airplane encounters a sudden lull in wind, or other turbulent air currents. In this case you should hold the airplane on the ground longer to attain more speed, then make a smooth, positive rotation to leave the ground.

In crosswind conditions, as the nosewheel (or tailwheel) is lifted off the runway, holding aileron control into the wind results in the downwind wing rising and the downwind main wheel lifting off the runway first.

If a significant crosswind exists, the main wheels should be held on the ground slightly longer than in a normal takeoff so that a smooth but definite lift-off can be made. This procedure allows the airplane to leave the ground under positive control. More importantly, it avoids imposing excessive side loads on the landing gear and prevents possible damage resulting from the airplane settling back to the runway while drifting.

As both main wheels leave the runway, the airplane will drift sideways with the wind unless adequate wind correction is maintained. It is important, then, to establish and maintain the proper amount of crosswind correction prior to lift-off; that is, aileron pressure toward the wind to keep the upwind wing from rising and rudder pressure as needed to prevent weathervaning. [Figure 4-1]

THE CLIMB

Upon lift-off, the airplane should be flying at approximately the attitude which will allow it to accelerate to its best rate-of-climb airspeed. The best rate-of-climb speed (V_Y) is that speed at which the airplane will gain the most altitude over a period of time.

If the proper pitch attitude is maintained, the aircraft should accelerate rapidly after it becomes airborne. However, only after it is certain the airplane will remain airborne and a definite climb is established, should the flaps and landing gear be retracted (if the airplane is so equipped).

It is recommended that takeoff power be maintained until at least 500 feet above the surrounding terrain and obstacles. Normally, the combination of best rate-of-climb (V_Y) and maximum allowable power will give an additional margin

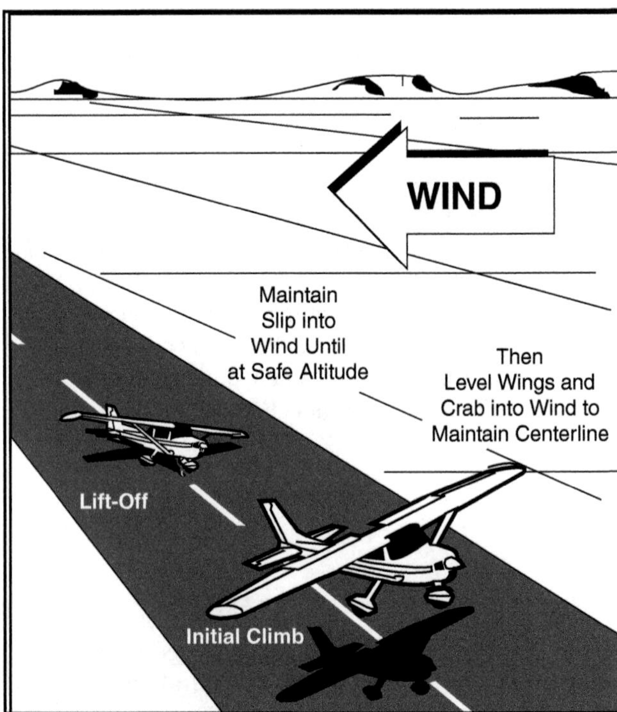

Figure 4-1. At lift-off in a crosswind, you should maintain a slip into the wind until safely above the ground. Then, establish a crab that will maintain the extended runway centerline.

of safety, in that sufficient altitude is attained in minimum time from which the airplane can be safely maneuvered in case of engine failure or other emergency.

Since the power on the initial climb is fixed at the takeoff power setting, the airspeed must be controlled by making slight pitch adjustments. When doing this, it is best to make the necessary pitch change using outside references and hold the new attitude momentarily while you glance at the airspeed indicator to verify the new attitude is correct.

Once you've established the recommended climbing airspeed and a safe maneuvering altitude is reached, the power should be adjusted to the recommended climb setting and the airplane trimmed to relieve any control pressures. During the initial climb, it is important that the takeoff path remain aligned with the runway to avoid the hazards of drifting into obstructions, or the path of another aircraft which may be taking off from a parallel runway.

During the climb in a crosswind, proper control inputs result in the airplane slipping into the wind sufficiently to counteract any drifting effect once you become airborne. Once you have climbed above the ground, establish a crab into the wind so as to follow a ground track aligned with the extended runway centerline. The remainder of the climb technique is the same as used for a normal takeoff and climb.

2. Positions the flight controls for the existing wind conditions.

- When taxiing, position the controls for the existing wind conditions.
- For additional information on taxiing in quartering headwinds and tailwinds, refer to Chapter 2, Task D on page 2-10.
- You should consult the POH for the flap setting recommended by the manufacturer.

3. Clears the area, taxies into the takeoff position and aligns the airplane on the runway center.

- Before entering the runway, you should position the aircraft so you have a clear view of the final approach path.
- Once you have cleared the area and have been cleared onto the runway, taxi onto the runway centerline.
- Once aligned with the centerline, select a point on the cowl through which the runway centerline passes and use it as a reference for directional control during the takeoff roll.

4. Advances the throttle smoothly to takeoff power.

- After releasing the brakes, the throttle should be smoothly and continuously advanced to maximum allowable power.
- As you advance the throttle, monitor the engine instruments so as to note immediately any malfunction or indication of insufficient power.
- Once the aircraft begins to move, you must apply right rudder to counteract engine torque.

6. Lifts off at the recommended airspeed and accelerates to V_Y.

- At the rotation airspeed established in the pilot's operating handbook, apply the back pressure necessary to lift off.
- Your aircraft's rotation speed is __________ kts.
- When taking off in a direct headwind, the ailerons and elevator should be held in the neutral position.
- If taking off in a crosswind, the ailerons should be held into the wind to prevent the upwind wing from rising.
- After liftoff, establish the approximate attitude that allows the aircraft to accelerate to V_Y.
- V_Y for your aircraft is __________ kts.

7. Establishes a pitch attitude that will maintain V_Y +10/-5 knots.

- Since full power is used for takeoff, airspeed is controlled by making slight pitch adjustments.
- When making pitch adjustments, make the necessary pitch change using outside references and glance at the airspeed indicator to verify the proper attitude.
- Once established at V_Y, trim to relieve any control pressures.

8. Retracts the landing gear, if appropriate, and flaps after a positive rate of climb is established.

- Before retracting the landing gear, apply the brakes to stop the rotation of the wheels.
- Retract the landing gear after a positive rate of climb is established and insufficient runway remains for landing.
- Retract the flaps only after a positive rate of climb is established and a safe altitude and airspeed is obtained.

9. Maintains takeoff power and V_Y +10/-5 knots to a safe maneuvering altitude.

- It is recommended that takeoff power be maintained until at least 500 feet above the surrounding terrain and obstacles.

- The recommended climb power setting for your aircraft is __________.

10. Maintains directional control and proper wind-drift correction throughout takeoff and climb.

- As the nosewheel (or tailwheel) is raised in a crosswind, hold aileron into the wind so the downwind main wheel lifts off the runway first.
- As both main wheels leave the runway in a crosswind, allow the airplane to slip sufficiently into the wind to maintain the runway centerline.
- At a safe altitude, establish a crab into the wind to maintain the extended runway centerline.

11. Complies with noise abatement procedures.

- During your preflight you should become familiar with any applicable noise abatement procedures.
- Sources for noise abatement procedures include the control tower, Airport/Facility Directory, or posted signs on the airport.
- You must comply with any applicable noise abatement procedures.

12. Completes the appropriate checklist.

- You must complete all applicable checklists.

PROCEDURE (Normal Takeoff)

1. Pretakeoff check — Complete
2. Takeoff clearance — As required
3. Full power — Advance smoothly
4. Rudder — As required to maintain centerline
5. Rotation speed __________
6. Climb speed __________
7. Rudder — As required to control yaw

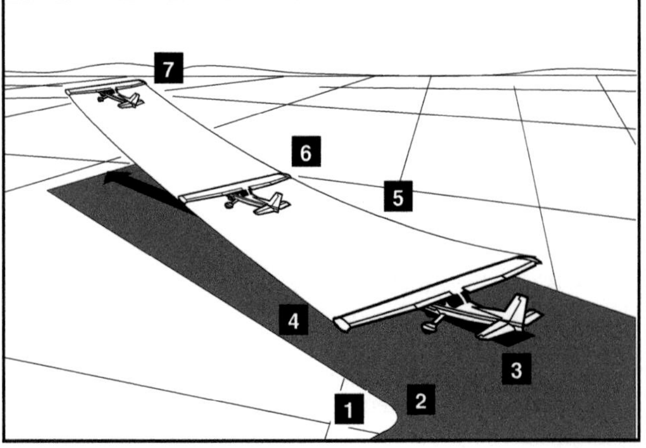

PROCEDURE (Crosswind Takeoff)

1. Pretakeoff check — Complete
2. Takeoff clearance — As required
3. Full power — Advance smoothly
4. Aileron — Into the wind
5. Rudder — As required to maintain centerline
6. Rotation speed __________
7. Climb speed __________
8. Rudder — As required to control yaw
9. Wind drift correction — Apply

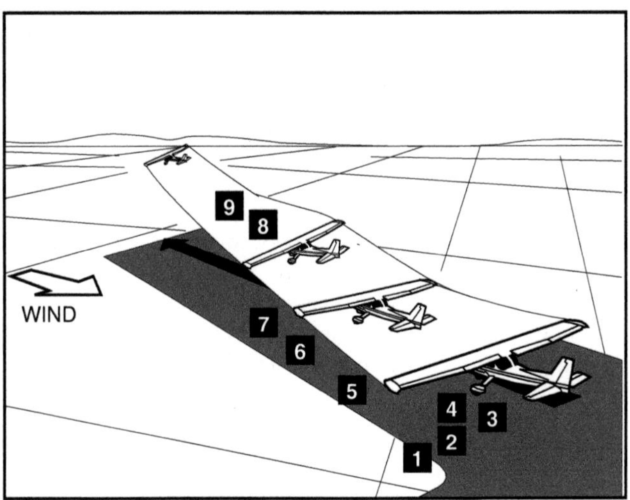

COMMON ERRORS

1. **Failing to maintain runway centerline during the initial takeoff roll.**

   Cause: Improper rudder application.

   Solution: You must anticipate the application of right rudder to overcome torque and the effects of any crosswind.

   Cause: Improper aileron application in a crosswind.

   Solution: In a crosswind, you should use full aileron deflection into the wind at slow speeds then gradually reduce the amount of deflection as speed increases.

2. **Excessive side loads as aircraft lifts off in a crosswind.**

   Cause: Inadequate crosswind correction during takeoff.

   Solution: You must establish the proper sideslip by allowing the downwind wing and main gear to lift off first while applying opposite rudder to keep the aircraft's longitudinal axis parallel with the extended runway centerline.

3. Failure to track the runway centerline after lift-off

Cause: Not visualizing the ground track and/or properly compensating for crosswind conditions.

Solution: Select a distant reference point that is on the extended centerline and fly to that point using the crab angle necessary.

4. Failure to maintain proper airspeed after lift-off.

Cause: Not maintaining the proper climb attitude.

Solution: Use outside references to establish the proper climb attitude and glance at the airspeed indicator to verify the appropriate airspeed is being maintained.

Cause: Improper use of trim.

Solution: Once V_Y is established, trim to relieve any control pressures.

EXERCISES

1. Before taxiing onto the runway, you should scan the final approach path for conflicting ____________.
2. During the takeoff roll, maintain directional control with the ____________.
3. It is recommended that you climb to at least __________ feet AGL before making any power reductions.
4. At the beginning of the crosswind takeoff roll, you should use full aileron deflection __________ (into, away from) the wind.
5. As power is added for takeoff you must apply __________ (left, right) rudder pressure to counteract engine torque.

SAMPLE ORAL QUESTIONS

1. Explain why an aircraft tends to weathervane during a crosswind takeoff.

____

____

____

____

____

____

____

1. The tendency to weathervane is a result of the wind striking the vertical stabilizer and rudder surfaces. The wind pushes on the tail, causing the nose of the airplane to turn into the wind. To counteract this tendency, you must apply rudder pressure in the opposite direction.

2. Explain aileron application throughout the takeoff roll in a crosswind.

____

____

____

____

____

____

____

____

____

____

2. At the beginning of the takeoff roll, you should use full aileron deflection into the wind. When doing this, the airflow over the wing with the raised aileron tends to hold that wing down, while airflow under the wing with the lowered aileron tends to push that wing up. As the airplane accelerates the ailerons become more effective. Therefore you must reduce the amount of deflection gradually, so it is just sufficient to counteract the crosswind.

3. How do you compensate for a crosswind after the airplane lifts off the runway?

3. During the initial liftoff in a crosswind, the aircraft should be slipping into the wind. In other words, the upwind wing should be lowered with the longitudinal axis aligned with the runway centerline. Once the aircraft is well above the ground you should crab the aircraft into the wind so that it tracks the extended runway centerline.

4. What does V_Y represent?

4. V_Y represents the aircraft's best rate of climb. At this speed, the aircraft will gain the most amount of altitude in a given period of time.

ADDITIONAL QUESTIONS

5. What are the significant differences between a normal and crosswind takeoff and climb?
6. Why is it advisable to obtain an extra margin of speed before the aircraft leaves the ground in gusty wind conditions?

EXERCISE ANSWERS

1. traffic
2. rudder
3. 500
4. into
5. right

REFERENCES

JEPPESEN:

Private Pilot Manual/Video – Chapter 8A

Private Pilot Maneuvers/Video – Maneuvers 7, 10, and 11

FAA:

Airplane Flying Handbook (FAA-H-8083-3)

Pilot's Operating Handbook and FAA-Approved Airplane Flight Manual

B. TASK: NORMAL AND CROSSWIND APPROACH AND LANDING (ASEL and ASES)

NOTE: If a crosswind condition does not exist, the applicant's knowledge of crosswind elements shall be evaluated through oral testing.

REFERENCES: FAA-H-8083-3; POH/AFM

Objective: To determine that the applicant:

1. Exhibits knowledge of the elements related to a normal and crosswind approach and landing.
2. Adequately surveys the intended landing area. (ASES)
3. Considers the wind conditions, landing surface, obstructions, and selects a suitable touchdown point.
4. Establishes the recommended approach and landing configuration and airspeed, and adjusts pitch attitude and power as required.
5. Maintains a stabilized approach and recommended airspeed, or in its absence, not more than 1.3 V_{SO}, +10/-5 knots, with wind gust factor applied.
6. Makes smooth, timely, and correct control application during the roundout and touchdown.
7. Contacts the water at the proper pitch attitude. (ASES)
8. Touches down smoothly at approximate stalling speed. (ASEL)
9. Touches down at or within 400 feet (120 meters) beyond a specified point, with no drift, and with the airplane's longitudinal axis aligned with and over the runway center/landing path.
10. Maintains crosswind correction and directional control throughout the approach and landing sequence.
11. Completes the appropriate checklist.

Objective: To determine that the applicant:

1. Exhibits knowledge of the elements related to a normal and crosswind approach and landing.

NORMAL AND CROSSWIND APPROACH AND LANDING

Normal and crosswind landings are made when the approach path has no obstacles and when the surface is firm, with ample length to stop the aircraft. When approaching to land with a wind present, even if it's directly down the runway, you must incorporate wind drift corrections in at least part of the normal approach phase.

During a landing, the touchdown and roll-out are influenced by factors and decisions made earlier in the traffic pattern. Normally, if you fly a stabilized downwind, base, and final, your touchdown and rollout is also smooth. When your traffic pattern is consistent and you fly a stabilized approach, you should only have to make minor adjustments for position and to compensate for wind.

DOWNWIND LEG

You should fly the downwind leg at a lateral distance from the runway appropriate to your airplane and local traffic requirements. Normally this distance ranges from about one-half to one mile from the runway. The airplane's downwind ground track should parallel the runway. Therefore, if a crosswind exists, you must crab into the wind to prevent drifting.

As you approach the 180° point, or the point opposite the intended landing area, you should be at the designated traffic pattern altitude near the aircraft's cruising speed. At the 180° point you should establish the descent power setting while maintaining altitude. This allows the airspeed to slow to approach speed.

When the airplane reaches approach airspeed, you normally maintain that speed and initiate a descent. However, you may need to delay the descent if the downwind leg must be extended to follow traffic.

The POH normally specifies the recommended approach speed. When an approach speed is recommended, you should maintain the speed as precisely as possible. If an approach speed is not recommended, use a final approach speed that is 1.3 times the power-off stall speed in the landing configuration (V_{SO}).

BASE LEG

After checking for other traffic, you normally begin the turn to base leg when the touchdown point is approximately 45° behind the wing. You may need to vary where you start the turn to base to compensate for variations in conditions. As you turn to base, the wind tends to push the airplane farther away from the runway. Therefore, it is usually necessary to turn more than 90° to apply the necessary crab angle.

As the airplane rolls out on base leg, you must assess your position and determine whether to make corrections in the approach pattern. This is often referred to as the key position. The significance of the key position is that it is an early decision point where you can easily make adjustments. This helps ensure a smooth approach and avoids large or abrupt last-minute corrections.

If the airplane is high at this point, you will land beyond the desired touchdown point. Therefore, you should either reduce power or extend additional flaps. If you are extremely high, you may need to make both adjustments. If the airplane is low or wide on base leg, or the wind is stronger than normal, you could land short of your desired point. Therefore, you should either begin the turn to final sooner, or add power. Retracting flaps is not considered an acceptable correction. Normally, once you extend the flaps, they are not retracted until you have landed or begin a go-around.

FINAL APPROACH

Before you turn to final, check the final approach path for conflicting traffic. The turn to final is usually completed at a distance of at least one-quarter mile from the runway threshold at an altitude of 300 to 400 feet AGL. Keep in mind that both distance and altitude vary due to differences in aircraft performance or adjustments for other traffic in the pattern. However, you should be able to continue a power-off approach to touchdown from any point on final.

Your objective when turning onto final should be to complete the turn on the extended runway centerline. To accomplish this, you must vary the point at which you initiate the turn to final to compensate for specific wind conditions. For example, when there is a tailwind on base, you must start the turn to final early.

As the airplane rolls out on final, it should be at the approach airspeed as specified in the POH, or 1.3 V_{SO}, as appropriate. At this point, you should frequently check the approach speed against outside references until you begin the landing transition. In gusty or turbulent conditions, you should conduct the approach at a slightly higher airspeed. This provides more positive control of the airplane when strong horizontal wind gusts, or up and down drafts, are experienced. These landing approaches are usually performed at the normal approach speed plus one-half of the wind gust factor. For example, if the normal speed is 65 knots and the wind gusts increase 20 knots, an airspeed of 75 knots is appropriate. To maintain positive control, an approach in turbulent air or gusty crosswinds may require the use of partial wing flaps. In any case, the airspeed and the amount of flaps should be as the airplane manufacturer recommends.

When established on the proper descent path and stabilized at the correct airspeed, the airplane's descent rate is usually controlled by power while the attitude is held constant. If the airplane looks as if it will land short of the desired touchdown spot, you cannot stretch a glide by raising the nose and slowing the airspeed; instead, you must add power. Conversely, if the approach is high, diving for the runway causes an increase in airspeed which must eventually be dissipated in the flare. This results in the airplane floating down the runway.

Your required rate of descent on final approach is directly affected by the headwind component. For example, as wind speed increases, your groundspeed decreases requiring a decrease in your rate of descent.

LANDING

The actual landing phase consists of three elements — the flare, the touchdown, and the roll-out. To land on a specified point, you must estimate the distance the aircraft will float. To do this, estimate the point where the glide path intersects the ground, commonly referred to as the aiming point, and add the approximate distance to be traveled in the flare. In most training aircraft you usually touch down several hundred feet beyond the aiming point.

FLARE

The flare begins at different altitudes for airplanes of varying weights and approach speeds. However, for most training airplanes, it begins at approximately 10 to 15 feet above the ground. Initiate the flare with a gradual increase in back pressure on the control wheel to reduce speed and decrease the rate of descent. Ideally, the airplane should reach a near zero descent rate approximately one foot above the runway at about 8 to 10 knots above the stall speed with the power at idle.

TOUCHDOWN

As you approach your touchdown point, you should attempt to hold the airplane off the runway by increasing back pressure. This results in the airplane settling slowly to the runway in a slightly nose-high attitude as it approaches the stall speed. The pitch attitude at touchdown should be very close to that used for takeoff, with the nosewheel held clear of the runway.

To flare and touch down smoothly, you must utilize both visual and kinesthetic cues. For example, if you concentrate on an area too close to the airplane, the airspeed blurs objects on the ground and causes your actions to be delayed or too abrupt. On the other hand, if you concentrate on an area that is too far down the runway, you will be unable to accurately judge your height above the ground. Consequently, your reactions will be slow. [Figure 4-2]

ROLL-OUT

After touchdown, allow the airspeed to diminish and lower the nosewheel gently. As the airplane touches down,

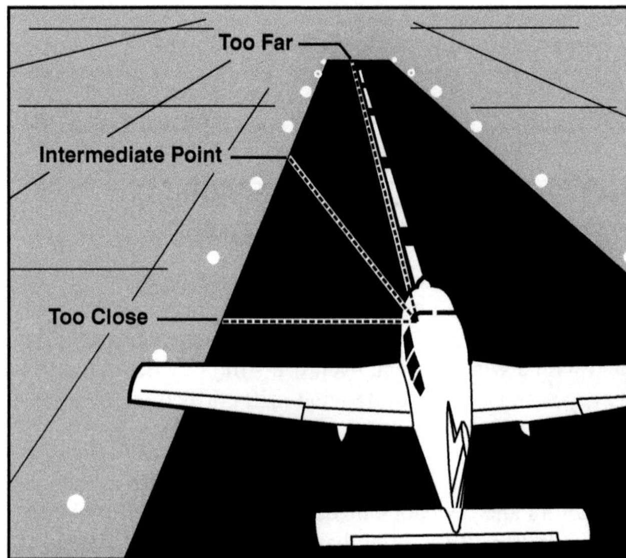

Figure 4-2. You must concentrate on an area that is at the correct distance ahead of the airplane to properly flare and touch down. In general, look ahead of the airplane about the same distance as when you are driving a car at the same speed.

your feet should be in the same position on the rudder pedals as they were during the flare. With your heels on the floor, there is no tendency to use the brakes inadvertently.

During the roll-out, maintain directional control with rudder pressure. If a crosswind is present, you should turn the aileron control slightly into the wind to counteract rolling tendencies. However, as the aircraft slows, you must increase aileron deflection to compensate for the decrease in control surface effectiveness.

CROSSWIND LANDINGS

Most aircraft, due to design, have a demonstrated crosswind capability. This can typically be found in the pilot's operating handbook and FAA-approved flight manual. You should note that this is not a limitation.

Any wind acting on an airplane during a crosswind landing can be divided into two components. One is a headwind component which acts along the airplane's ground track and the other is a crosswind component acting 90° to the ground track. The resultant or relative wind, then, is somewhere between the two components. The headwind component and the crosswind component can be determined by reference to a crosswind component chart. [Figure 4-3]

There are two usual methods of accomplishing a cross-wind approach and landing — the crab method, and the wing-low, or sideslip method. The crab method requires a high degree of judgment and timing; therefore, the wing-low method is recommended in most cases although a combination of both methods may be used.

The wing-low method compensates for a crosswind from any angle, but more important, it enables you to simultaneously keep the airplane's ground track and the longitudinal axis aligned with the runway centerline throughout the final approach, roundout, touchdown, and after-landing roll. This prevents the airplane from touching down sideways and imposing damaging side loads on the landing gear.

To use the wing-low method, align the airplane's heading with the runway centerline, note the rate and direction of drift, then promptly apply drift correction by lowering the upwind wing. The amount of wing which must be lowered depends on the rate of drift. You must simultaneously apply opposite rudder to prevent the aircraft from turning and keep the longitudinal axis aligned with the runway. In other words, the drift is controlled with aileron, and the heading with rudder. In this configuration, the airplane will be slipping into the wind just enough that both the resultant flight path and the ground track are aligned with the runway.

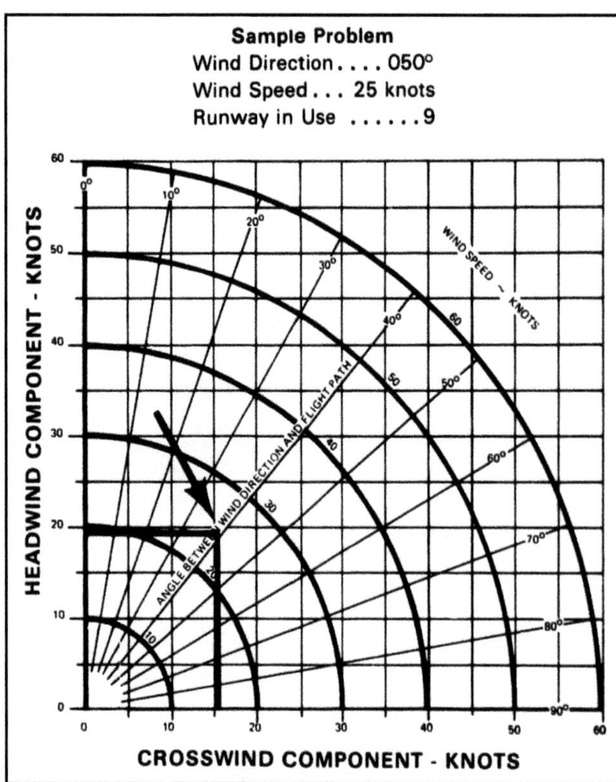

Figure 4-3. First, determine the angle between the wind and runway (090° – 050° = 40°). Enter the crosswind component chart at the point where the angle of 40° meets the wind speed of 25 knots. Proceed horizontally to the left and read the headwind component of 19 knots, or move vertically down and read the crosswind component of 16 knots.

Flaps can and should be used during most approaches since they tend to have a stabilizing effect on the airplane. However, the degree to which flaps should be extended will vary with the airplane's handling characteristics, as well as the wind velocity. Full flaps may be used so long as the crosswind component is not in excess of the airplane's capability or unless the manufacturer recommends otherwise.

CROSSWIND FLARE

Generally, the flare, or roundout, can be made as in a normal landing approach but the application of a crosswind correction must be continued as necessary to prevent drifting. Since airspeed decreases during the roundout, the flight controls gradually become less effective; as a result, it is necessary to gradually increase the deflection of the rudder and ailerons to maintain the proper amount of drift correction.

CROSSWIND TOUCHDOWN

The crosswind correction (aileron control into the wind and opposite rudder) should be maintained throughout the roundout, and the touchdown made on the upwind main wheel. As forward momentum decreases after initial contact, the weight of the airplane causes the downwind main wheel to gradually settle onto the runway. [Figure 4-4]

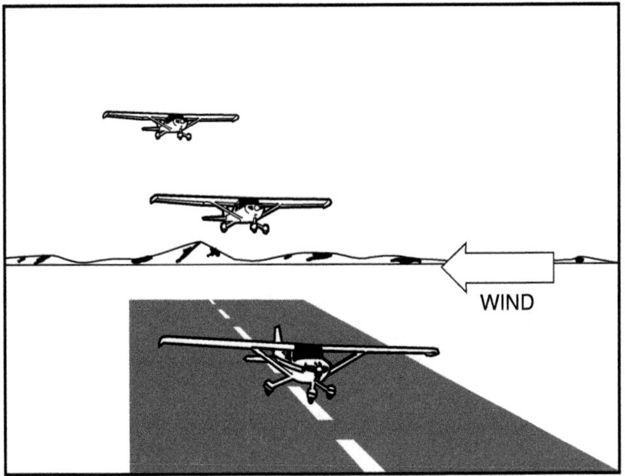

Figure 4-4. Start the flare at the normal altitude and hold the wing down throughout the flare and touchdown. This causes the airplane to touch down initially on one main wheel.

CROSSWIND AFTER-LANDING ROLL

While the airplane decelerates during the after-landing roll, more and more aileron must be applied to keep the upwind wing from rising. At the same time, the relative wind becomes more of a crosswind and exerts a greater lifting force on the upwind wing. Consequently, when the airplane slows to taxi speed, the aileron control must be held fully toward the wind.

3. Considers the wind conditions, landing surface, obstructions, and selects a suitable touchdown point.

- Typically, you should select a runway which best favors the wind.
- The runway surface and length must allow you to land safely given the existing conditions. This includes the type of surface, as well as factors such as rain, ice, or snow on the runway.
- If possible, select a runway which is free of tall obstacles which could interfere with a normal approach path.
- Select a touchdown point that provides adequate obstruction clearance and sufficient distance to safely complete the roll-out.

4. Establishes the recommended approach and landing configuration and airspeed, and adjusts pitch attitude and power as required.

- Prior to landing, consult the POH and/or landing checklist for the recommended flap settings and corresponding approach speeds.
- In the absence of a recommended approach speed use 1.3 V_{SO}.
- You should use outside references to maintain the proper pitch attitude throughout the approach.
- Use power to control the rate of descent while maintaining the appropriate airspeed. Additional power decreases the rate of descent while less power increases the rate of descent.

5. Maintains a stabilized approach and the recommended approach airspeed, or in its absence not more than 1.3 V_{SO}, +10/–5 knots, with gust factor applied.

- To maintain a stabilized approach, you must make small corrections in a timely fashion so as to avoid large or abrupt last-minute corrections.
- Once the aircraft is configured properly for landing, trim to relieve any control pressures.
- In gusty conditions you should increase your approach speed by 1/2 the gust factor.
- The approach speed for your aircraft is _________ kts.

6. Makes smooth, timely, and correct control application during the roundout and touchdown.

- Begin your flare at approximately 10 to 15 feet above the ground. Initiate the roundout by gradually increasing back pressure to reduce speed and decrease the rate of descent.
- An approach in a crosswind requires aileron to lower the upwind wing and opposite rudder to align the longitudinal axis of the aircraft with the runway.
- During the flare in a crosswind, the application of crosswind correction must be continued to prevent drifting.

8. Touches down smoothly at the approximate stalling speed.

- Continue to hold the aircraft off the ground until it settles at the approximate stall speed.
- The pitch attitude at touchdown should be similar to the pitch attitude used for takeoff.
- To flare and touch down smoothly, you must utilize both visual and kinesthetic cues.
- A good rule of thumb is to look ahead of the airplane about the same distance as when you drive a car at the same speed.

9. Touches down at or within 400 feet (120 meters) beyond a specified point, with no drift, and with the airplane's longitudinal axis aligned with and over the runway center/landing path.

- To land on a specified point, you must aim several hundred feet in front of the desired landing point.
- Prior to touchdown, use the rudder to align the longitudinal axis of the airplane with the runway centerline.
- The main wheels of the aircraft should touch down first. If in a crosswind, the upwind main wheel should make contact with the runway first.

10. Maintains crosswind correction and directional control throughout the approach and landing.

- When using the wing-low method during the approach, you must maintain a sideslip all the way to the runway.
- During the roll-out, maintain directional control with the rudder pedals, and turn the ailerons into the wind to keep the upwind wing from rising.

11. Completes the appropriate checklist.

- You must complete all required checklists prior to landing.
- It is recommended that the before-landing checklist be completed on downwind.
- The after-landing checklist should be completed once you have cleared the active runway.

PROCEDURE (Normal Landing)

Pattern Altitude __________

1. Prelanding check — Complete
2. Power — As required __________ RPM
3. Flaps (when airspeed permits) — As Required
4. Glidepath — Maintain with pitch and power
5. Flare — As required __________ feet above runway
6. Touchdown — Nose high, airspeed __________
7. Roll-out — Gradually lower nose, maintain centerline

PROCEDURE (Crosswind Landing)

Pattern Altitude __________

1. Prelanding check — Complete
2. Wind correction angle — Apply
3. Sideslip — Establish prior to threshold
4. Track the runway — Maintain
5. Flare — As required, maintain slip attitude
6. Touchdown — Nose high, airspeed __________ plus wind adjustment
7. Roll-out — Aileron into wind; use rudder to track centerline

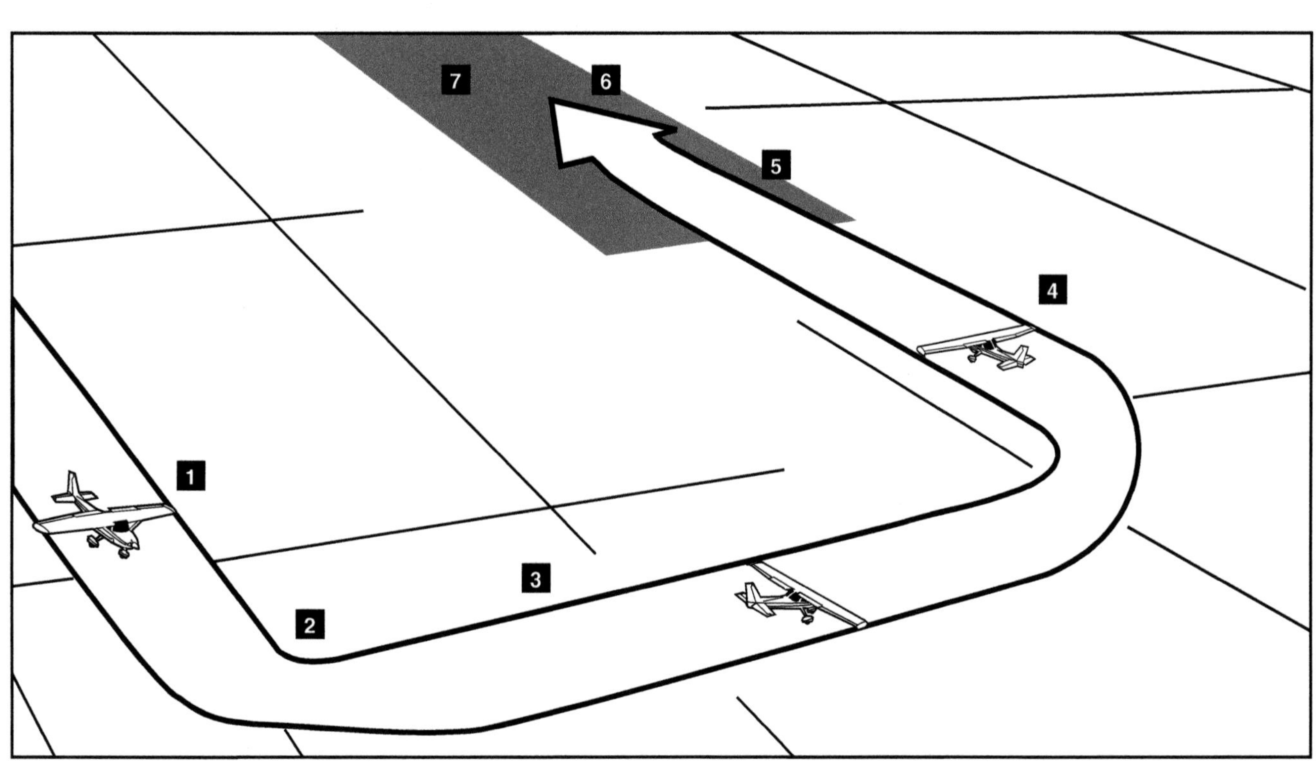

COMMON ERRORS

1. **Overcontrolling the airplane, not maintaining a stabilized approach.**

   Cause: Waiting too long, or not recognizing when it is necessary to make a correction.

   Solution: Make smooth, positive corrections early in the pattern, and trim the aircraft for the desired flight attitude.

2. **Overshooting or undershooting the turn to final.**

   Cause: Not properly compensating for wind on the base leg.

   Solution: When experiencing a tailwind on base, begin your turn to final early. When experiencing a headwind, delay the turn to final.

3. **Drifting off the extended runway centerline.**

   Cause: Not properly compensating for wind drift.

   Solution: Mentally extend the centerline through some recognizable landmarks and establish a crab that allows you to fly over them during final approach.

   Cause: Not compensating for the change in wind when you are near the surface.

   Solution: Use the rudder to align the longitudinal axis of the aircraft with the runway, and adjust the amount of wing dip to control drift.

4. **Floating during the roundout.**

   Cause: Excessive airspeed on approach.

   Solution: Maintain the appropriate approach speed all the way to the flare.

5. **Failure to maintain centerline during the rollout.**

   Cause: Improper crosswind control application after touchdown.

   Solution: Use rudder to maintain centerline while turning the aileron control into the wind to compensate for wind drift.

6. **Flaring too high or too low.**

   Cause: Selecting a reference point that is too close or too far from the airplane.

   Solution: Look ahead of the airplane about the same distance you would when driving a car at the same speed.

7. **Landing beyond the specified landing point.**

   Cause: Not selecting an aiming point on the runway, or using the touchdown point as the aiming point.

   Solution: Select an aiming point that allows for the distance to be traveled in the flare.

EXERCISES

1. The downwind leg should typically be flown between __________ to __________ mile from the runway.

2. ________ (True, False) If the airplane is low on final you can regain the proper glidepath by retracting the flaps.

3. You typically begin the turn to base leg when the touchdown point is approximately __________° behind the wing.

4. When on final approach, your descent rate is controlled by __________ (power, pitch).

5. When making an approach in turbulent conditions it is recommended that you add __________ the wind gust factor to the normal approach speed.

SAMPLE ORAL QUESTIONS

1. Why is the roll out on base leg a key position in the approach?

   ____
   ____
   ____
   ____
   ____
   ____
   ____

1. The significance of the key position is that it is an early decision point where you can easily make major adjustments. This helps ensure a smooth approach and avoids large or abrupt last-minute corrections.

2. You should either begin the turn to final sooner than normal, or add power. Retracting the flaps is not considered an acceptable correction. Normally, once you extend the flaps, they are not retracted until you have completed the landing or abandoned the landing approach.

2. When on base, what corrective options do you have if you determine that you are low?

3. There are two usual methods of accomplishing a crosswind approach and landing — the crab and the wing-low. The crab method requires a high degree of judgment and timing; therefore, the wing-low method is recommended in most cases although a combination of both methods may be used. To use the wing-low method, align the airplane's heading with the centerline of the runway, note the rate and direction of drift, then promptly apply drift correction by lowering the upwind wing. The amount the wing must be lowered depends on the rate of drift. You must simultaneously apply opposite rudder to prevent the aircraft from turning and keep the longitudinal axis aligned with the runway. In other words, the drift is controlled with aileron, and the heading with rudder.

3. Explain the recommended method for maintaining the extended runway centerline when approaching in a crosswind.

ADDITIONAL QUESTIONS

4. What are the significant differences between a normal and crosswind landing?

5. Know how to use a crosswind component chart.

EXERCISE ANSWERS

1. 1/2, 1

2. False

3. 45°

4. power

5. 1/2

REFERENCES

JEPPESEN:

Private Pilot Manual/Video – Chapter 8A

Private Pilot Maneuvers/Video – Maneuvers 8, 13, and 14

FAA:

Airplane Flying Handbook (FAA-H-8083-3)

Pilot's Operating Handbook and FAA-Approved Airplane Flight Manual

C. TASK: SOFT-FIELD TAKEOFF AND CLIMB (ASEL)

REFERENCES: FAA-H-8083-3; POH/AFM

Objective: To determine that the applicant:

1. Exhibits knowledge of the elements related to a soft-field takeoff and climb.
2. Positions the flight controls for existing wind conditions and to maximize lift as quickly as possible.
3. Clears the area; taxies onto the takeoff surface at a speed consistent with safety without stopping while advancing the throttle smoothly to takeoff power.
4. Establishes and maintains a pitch attitude that will transfer the weight of the airplane from the wheels to the wings as rapidly as possible.
5. Lifts off at the lowest possible airspeed and remains in ground effect while accelerating to V_X or V_Y, as appropriate.
6. Establishes a pitch attitude for V_X or V_Y, as appropriate, and maintains selected airspeed +10/-5 knots, during the climb.
7. Retracts the landing gear, if appropriate, and flaps after clear of any obstacles or as recommended by the manufacturer.
8. Maintains takeoff power and V_X or V_Y +10/-5 knots to a safe maneuvering altitude.
9. Maintains directional control and proper wind-drift correction throughout the takeoff and climb.
10. Completes the appropriate checklist.

Objective: To determine that the applicant:

1. Exhibits knowledge of the elements related to a soft-field takeoff and climb.

SOFT-FIELD TAKEOFF AND CLIMB

A soft-field takeoff should be conducted anytime you take off from a surface that substantially decreases aircraft acceleration. This includes runways that are covered with tall grass, sand, mud, or snow. The objective of the soft-field takeoff is to transfer the weight of the airplane from the landing gear to the wings and get airborne as quickly and smoothly as possible. This minimizes the drag caused by the soft surface and helps prevent debris from damaging the aircraft. If possible, you should go on at least one dual flight and practice soft-field takeoffs and landings from a grass or dirt runway.

The soft-field takeoff procedure requires you to accelerate the airplane in a nose-high attitude, keeping the nosewheel clear of the surface during most of the takeoff ground run. Ground effect is utilized to allow the aircraft to become airborne at an airspeed slower than normal. Then the airplane remains in ground effect while it accelerates to the proper climb speed.

GROUND EFFECT

During takeoff and landing, ground effect causes an increase in lift when the airplane is within one wingspan of the ground. This increase in lift allows the airplane to remain airborne at very low airspeeds. Ground effect is caused by the redirection of air between the wings of the airplane and the ground. The intensity of ground effect is strongest when just above the ground and decreases rapidly to near zero when higher than one wingspan above the surface.

PRETAKEOFF CONSIDERATIONS

You actually begin the soft-field takeoff procedure before entering the runway. During the taxi, as much weight as possible is transferred from the nosewheel to the main wheels by using full-up elevator (or stabilator) deflection with a slight amount of power. If possible, you should conduct the before-takeoff check on a hard surface. Furthermore, wing flaps, if recommended by the manufacturer, should be lowered prior to starting the takeoff. After you complete the pretakeoff checklist, you must clear the approach and departure areas as well as the traffic pattern prior to taxiing onto the soft surface.

TAKEOFF

As the airplane is aligned with the runway, full power must be applied smoothly and as rapidly as the powerplant will accept it. As the airplane accelerates, apply back pressure to establish a positive angle of attack and reduce the amount of weight on the nosewheel. In tailwheel aircraft, the tail should be kept low to maintain the inherent positive angle of attack and to avoid any tendency of the airplane to nose over as a result of soft spots, tall grass, or deep snow.

As the engine develops full power, right rudder pressure will be required to maintain directional control due to the effects of torque, P-factor, and spiraling slipstream. Also, be prepared for the nosewheel to quickly come off the runway shortly after the ground roll begins. When this happens, you must steer using only the rudder.

As speed increases, elevator effectiveness increases requiring you to release control wheel back pressure during the takeoff roll. If this isn't done, the aircraft could assume an excessively nose-high attitude resulting in complete loss of forward visibility. The attitude of the airplane during the ground roll is critical. If you allow the airplane to get in an extremely nose-high attitude, the tail skid could come in contact with the runway. Also, the drag created by an extremely nose-high attitude may be so significant that the aircraft will not accelerate adequately. Conversely, too low an attitude will slow the transfer weight from the main wheels to the wings, and could cause the nosewheel to settle back onto the runway.

As lift develops, more and more of the airplane's weight will be supported by the wings, thereby minimizing the drag caused by the surface. If this attitude is accurately maintained, the airplane will become airborne at an airspeed slower than a safe climb speed because of the action of ground effect.

LIFTOFF AND CLIMB OUT

After becoming airborne, the nose should be lowered very gently so the wheels remain clear of the surface. This allows the airplane to accelerate in ground effect to the best rate-of-climb speed (V_Y), or best angle-of-climb speed (V_X) if obstacles must be cleared. Exercise extreme care immediately after the airplane becomes airborne and while it accelerates, to avoid settling back onto the surface. An attempt to climb prematurely or too steeply may cause the airplane to settle back to the surface.

After a definite climb is established, and the airplane has accelerated to V_Y, retract the landing gear and flaps, if so equipped. In the event an obstacle must be cleared after a soft-field takeoff, the climb-out must be performed at the best angle-of-climb airspeed (V_X) until the obstacle has been cleared. After reaching this point you should accelerate to V_Y and retract the flaps and landing gear. The power may then be reduced to the normal climb setting. [Figure 4-5]

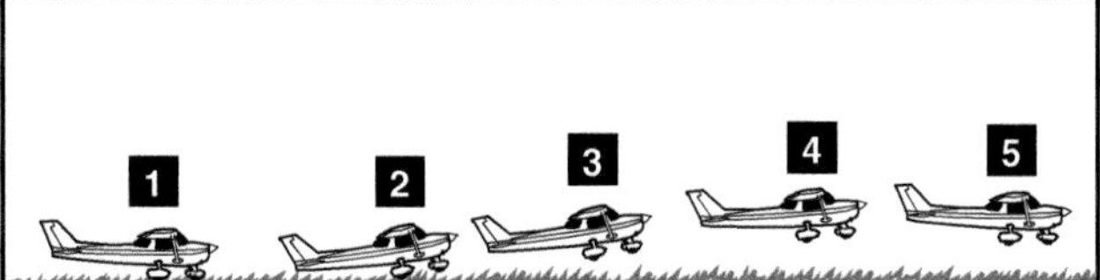

Figure 4-5. If you establish the proper pitch attitude during acceleration (position 1), the nosewheel will be clear of the surface during much of the ground roll (position 2), and the airplane will lift off at or slightly below the power-off stall speed (position 3). After liftoff, reduce the pitch attitude gradually to level flight (position 4), allowing the airplane to accelerate within ground effect to the normal climb airspeed (position 5).

2. Positions the flight controls for existing wind conditions and to maximize lift as quickly as possible.

- When taxiing, position the controls for the existing wind conditions.
- During taxi, you should apply full elevator back pressure when on a soft surface.
- Prior to takeoff, you should position the flaps to the manufacturer's recommended setting.

3. Clears the area; taxies onto the takeoff surface at a speed consistent with safety while advancing the throttle smoothly to takeoff power.

- Prior to taxiing onto the runway, clear the approach and departure ends of the runway, as well as the traffic pattern.
- Taxi onto the runway centerline without stopping at a safe speed and immediately transition into the takeoff roll by smoothly advancing the throttle.

4. Establishes and maintains a pitch attitude that will transfer the weight of the airplane from the wheels to the wings as rapidly as possible.

- At the start of the takeoff roll, the control wheel should be full back until the nosewheel leaves the ground.
- With the nosewheel off the ground, directional control must be maintained with the rudder only.
- To prevent an excessive nose-up attitude, be prepared to release elevator (or stabilator) back pressure as speed increases.

5. Lifts off at the lowest possible airspeed and remains in ground effect while accelerating to V_X or V_Y, as appropriate.

- As the airplane lifts off, reduce back pressure to stop the initial climb and maintain level flight just above the runway.
- If no obstacle is present, you must allow the airplane to accelerate to V_Y in ground effect.
- V_Y for your aircraft is ____________ kts.
- If an obstacle is present, accelerate to V_X and climb until the obstacle is cleared.
- V_X for your aircraft is ____________ kts.
- Once the obstacle is cleared, accelerate to V_Y.

6. Establishes a pitch attitude for V_X or V_Y, as appropriate, and maintains selected airspeed +10/-5 knots, during the climb.

- Use outside references to establish the approximate pitch attitude required to maintain V_Y while cross-checking the airspeed indicator.
- Once V_Y is established, trim to relieve any control pressures.

7. Retracts the landing gear, if appropriate, and flaps after clear of any obstacles or as recommended by the manufacturer.

- After a positive rate of climb is established, and the airplane has accelerated to V_Y, retract the landing gear, if equipped.
- Begin retracting flaps only if all obstacles are cleared and airspeed permits.
- Retract the flaps one increment at a time.

8. Maintains takeoff power and V_X or V_Y +10/-5 knots to a safe maneuvering altitude.

- It is recommended that takeoff power be maintained until reaching at least 500 feet above the surrounding terrain and obstacles.

9. Maintains directional control and proper wind-drift correction throughout the takeoff and climb.

- As the nosewheel (or tailwheel) is raised off the runway in a crosswind, hold aileron control into the wind allowing the downwind main wheel to lift off the runway first.
- As both main wheels leave the runway in a crosswind, allow the airplane to slip sufficiently into the wind to maintain the runway centerline while accelerating in ground effect.
- At a safe altitude, establish a crab into the wind to maintain the extended runway centerline.

10. Completes the appropriate checklist.

- You must complete all applicable checklists.

PROCEDURE

1 Pretakeoff check — Complete

2 Takeoff clearance — As required

3 Wing flap position __________

4 Full power — Advance smoothly as aircraft is aligned

5 Elevator pressure — Apply to lift nosewheel off surface

6 After liftoff — Accelerate in ground effect

7 Climb speed __________

8 Wing flaps (when speed and altitude permit) — Up

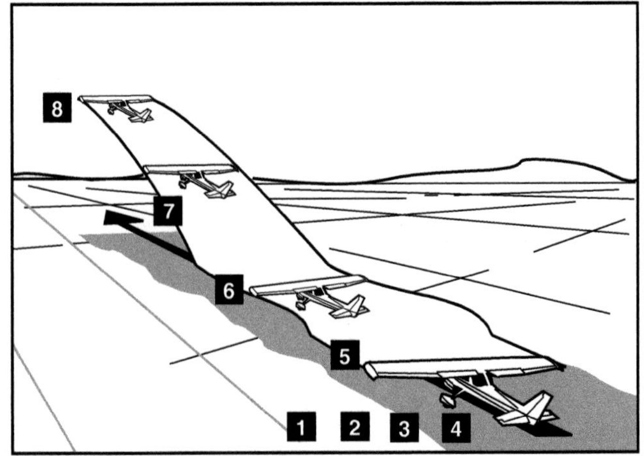

COMMON ERRORS

1. **Maintaining an excessively nose high attitude.**

   Cause: Trying to hold full elevator back pressure throughout the takeoff roll.

   Solution: As the aircraft accelerates, elevator effectiveness increases, requiring you to reduce back pressure.

2. **Allowing the nose wheel to settle back on the runway during the ground roll.**

   Cause: Improper attitude control during the ground roll.

   Solution: Use visual references out the front and side of the aircraft to maintain the proper pitch attitude.

3. **Settling back onto the runway after the aircraft lifts off.**

   Cause: Overcontrolling, releasing too much back pressure as the aircraft leaves the ground.

   Solution: Once the aircraft lifts off, you must gradually release back pressure without allowing the aircraft to settle back onto the runway.

4. **Climbing out of ground effect before reaching V_Y.**

   Cause: Not reducing the pitch attitude after liftoff.

   Solution: As the aircraft lifts off, you must reduce the pitch attitude enough to allow the aircraft to accelerate in ground effect.

5. **Failure to maintain proper airspeed after liftoff.**

   Cause: Not maintaining the proper climb attitude.

   Solution: Use visual references to establish the proper climb attitude and cross-check the airspeed indicator to verify the proper speed is maintained.

Cause: Excessive elevator pressures required to maintain proper aircraft attitude.

Solution: Use trim to relieve control pressures.

EXERCISES

1. _____ (True, False) the objective of the soft-field takeoff is to transfer the weight of the airplane from the landing gear to the wings as soon as possible.
2. __________ __________ allows an airplane to fly before the normal lift-off speed.
3. As the airplane lifts from the runway surface, you must __________ (reduce, maintain) the amount of back pressure .
4. You may need to apply additional right rudder pressure during the ground roll to offset the effects of torque, spiraling slipstream, and __________.
5. _____ (True, False) You should stop the aircraft at the end of the runway prior to takeoff.

SAMPLE ORAL QUESTIONS

1. What causes ground effect and where are its effects most noticeable?

____

____

____

____

____

2. Discuss the pretakeoff considerations associated with a takeoff from a soft field.

____

____

____

____

____

____

____

____

____

____

____

3. What are some of the consequences of having an excessively high nose-up attitude during the ground roll?

____

____

____

____

____

____

1. Ground effect is caused by the redirection of air between the wings and the ground. This redirection of air causes an increase in lift when an aircraft is within one wingspan of the ground.

2. While taxiing, as much weight as possible is transferred from the nosewheel to the main wheels by using full-up elevator (or stabilator) deflection with a slight amount of power. If possible, you should conduct the before-takeoff check on a hard surface. Furthermore, wing flaps, if recommended by the manufacturer, should be lowered prior to starting the takeoff. After you complete the pretakeoff checklist, you must clear the approach and departure areas as well as the traffic pattern prior to taxiing onto the soft surface.

3. If the airplane is in an extremely nose-high attitude, the tail skid could come in contact with the runway. Also, the drag created could be so significant that the aircraft would not accelerate adequately.

4. When would you conduct a soft-field takeoff?

4. It is best to conduct a soft-field takeoff whenever you are departing a grass or dirt runway, or a paved runway that is covered with snow or has several imperfections.

ADDITIONAL QUESTIONS

5. Explain how to conduct a soft-field takeoff.

6. When should the flaps be retracted when conducting a soft-field takeoff?

EXERCISE ANSWERS

1. True

2. Ground effect

3. reduce

4. P-factor

5. False

REFERENCES

JEPPESEN:

Private Pilot Manual/Video – Chapter 8A

Private Pilot Maneuvers/Video – Maneuver 27

FAA:

Airplane Flying Handbook (FAA-H-8083-3)

Pilot's Operating Handbook and FAA-Approved Airplane Flight Manual

D. TASK: SOFT-FIELD APPROACH AND LANDING (ASEL)

REFERENCES: FAA-H-8303-3; POH/AFM

Objective: To determine that the applicant:

1. Exhibits knowledge of the elements related to a soft-field approach and landing.
2. Considers the wind conditions, landing surface and obstructions, and selects the most suitable touchdown area.
3. Establishes the recommended approach and landing configuration, and airspeed; adjusts pitch attitude and power as required.
4. Maintains a stabilized approach and recommended airspeed, or in its absence not more man 1.3 V_{SO}, +10/–5 knots, with gust factor applied.
5. Makes smooth, timely, and correct control application during the roundout and touchdown.
6. Touches down softly with no drift, and with the airplane's longitudinal axis aligned with the runway/landing path.
7. Maintains crosswind correction and directional control throughout the approach and landing.
8. Maintains the proper position of the flight controls and sufficient speed to taxi on the soft surface.
9. Completes the appropriate checklist.

Objective: To determine that the applicant:

1. Exhibits knowledge of the elements related to a soft-field approach and landing.

SOFT-FIELD APPROACH AND LANDING

The objective of a soft-field landing is to control the airplane in a manner so the wings support the weight of the airplane as long as practical. This minimizes the drag and stresses imposed on the landing gear by rough or soft surfaces. After landing, you want to ease the weight of the airplane from the wings to the main wheels as gently and slowly as possible.

The approach to a soft field is similar to the normal approach used to a paved runway. The major difference between the two is that during the soft-field landing, the airplane is held 1 to 2 feet above the surface as long as possible to allow the wheels to touch down gently at minimum speed.

The use of flaps during soft-field landings aids in touching down at minimum speed and is recommended whenever practical. However, in low-wing aircraft the flaps may suffer damage from mud, stones, or slush that is thrown up by the wheels.

Proper pitch and power control are important during the entire approach and landing, but become most critical during the landing flare and touchdown segments. Normally, you maintain a small amount of power during the touchdown to facilitate a nose-high, soft touchdown. When you maintain power, the slipstream flow over the empennage makes the elevator (or stabilator) more effective. However, you must exercise caution not to maintain too much power or the airplane will float excessively. [Figure 4-6]

Touchdown on a soft or rough field should be made at the lowest possible airspeed with the airplane in a nose-high attitude. In tailwheel airplanes, the tailwheel should touch down at the same time or just before the main wheels, and then should be held down by maintaining firm back elevator pressure throughout the landing roll. This minimizes any tendency for the airplane to nose over and provides aerodynamic braking.

In aircraft with nosewheels, after the main wheels touch the surface, you should hold sufficient back elevator (or stabilator) pressure to keep the nosewheel off the ground as long as aerodynamically possible. Then you should gently lower the nosewheel to the surface. A slight addition of power during and immediately after touchdown usually aids in easing the nosewheel down.

The use of brakes on a soft field is typically not needed due to the drag created by the soft surface. Furthermore, braking could impose a heavy load on the nose gear causing it to dig

Figure 4-6. A small amount of power may be used during the flare and touchdown. Maintaining a slight amount of power facilitates a nose-high landing. Power also helps slow the rate at which the main wheels settle onto the runway.

into the surface. In fact, you may find that in some cases power needs to be increased to keep the aircraft moving or from becoming stuck in the soft surface.

2. Considers the wind conditions, landing surface and obstructions, and selects the most suitable touchdown area.

- Typically, you should select a runway which best favors the wind.
- The runway surface and length must allow you to land safely given the existing conditions. This includes the type of surface, as well as factors such as rain, ice, or snow on the runway.
- If possible, select a runway that is free of tall obstacles which could interfere with a normal approach path.
- Select a touchdown point that provides adequate obstruction clearance and sufficient distance to safely complete the roll-out.
- Be alert for hazards that may exist on soft fields such as standing water, wheel tracks, deep snow, or tall grass.

3. Establishes the recommended approach and landing configuration, and airspeed; adjusts pitch attitude and power as required.

- Prior to landing, you should consult the POH or landing checklist for the recommended flap settings and corresponding approach speeds.
- You should use outside references to maintain the proper pitch attitude.
- Power is your primary method to control the rate of descent while maintaining the appropriate airspeed.

4. Maintains a stabilized approach, and recommended approach airspeed, or in its absence, not more than 1.3 V_{S0}, +10/–5 knots, with gust factor applied.

- To maintain a stabilized approach, you must make small corrections in a timely fashion so as to avoid large or abrupt last-minute corrections.
- Once the aircraft is configured properly for landing, trim to relieve any control pressures.
- In the absence of a recommended approach speed use 1.3 V_{S0}.
- In gusty conditions you should increase your approach speed by 1/2 the gust factor.
- The approach speed for your aircraft is ________ kts.

5. Makes smooth, timely, and correct control application during the roundout and touchdown.

- Begin your flare at approximately 10 to 15 feet above the ground. Initiate the roundout by gradually increasing back pressure to reduce speed and decrease the rate of descent.
- Typically you should maintain a small amount of power during the touchdown to facilitate a nose-high, soft landing.

6. Touches down softly with no drift, and with the airplane's longitudinal axis aligned with, the runway/landing path.

- When approximately one foot above the runway, gradually increase back pressure to reduce speed and allow the aircraft to settle.
- Use rudder to align the nose of the aircraft with the runway centerline.
- The main wheels should touch down at a minimum sink rate.

7. Maintains crosswind correction and directional control throughout the approach and landing.

- When using the wing-low method during the approach, you must maintain a sideslip all the way to the runway.
- During the roll-out, maintain directional control with the rudder pedals, and turn the aileron control into the wind to prevent the upwind wing from rising.

8. Maintains the proper position of the flight controls and sufficient speed to taxi on the soft surface.

- After the main wheels touch down, maintain elevator (or stabilator) back pressure to keep the nosewheel off the ground as long as aerodynamically possible.
- Be prepared to add power to keep the aircraft moving until you reach a firm surface.
- Typically brakes are not needed because of the drag created by the soft surface.

9. Completes the appropriate checklist.

- You must complete all required checklists prior to landing.
- It is recommended that the before-landing checklist should be completed on downwind.
- The after-landing checklist should be completed once you have taxied onto a hard surface.

PROCEDURE

1 Prelanding check — Complete
2 Power — As required __________ RPM
3 Flaps (as airspeed permits) — Full
4 Glidepath and Airspeed — Maintain
5 Flare — Nose high with no excessive airspeed
6 Touchdown — Nose high, airspeed __________
7 Roll-out — Keep nosewheel off surface as long as possible

COMMON ERRORS

1. **Excessive floating or ballooning in the flare.**

   Cause: Maintaining too much power prior to touchdown.

   Solution: Use only a slight amount of power. The exact amount of power required varies with aircraft weight and atmospheric conditions.

2. **Allowing the nosewheel to touch down prematurely.**

   Cause: Failure to maintain full back pressure after touchdown.

   Solution: Once the aircraft touches down and begins to slow, full back pressure must be maintained.

3. **Hard touchdown after flare.**

   Cause: Improper judging of the aircraft's height above the ground.

   Solution: To judge your height above the runway, look ahead and slightly off to the side of the airplane about the same distance as when you are driving a car at the same speed. Also slight power will slow the rate the aircraft settles.

4. **Failure to maintain the runway centerline during the rollout.**

   Cause: Improper crosswind control application after the airplane touches down.

   Solution: Use rudder to maintain the centerline while turning the ailerons into the wind to counter any rolling tendency caused by a crosswind.

   Cause: Not being able to see over the cowling.

   Solution: Use the runway's edge as a reference to maintain the centerline.

   Cause: Increase in density altitude above the runway surface.

   Solution: On warm, sunny days, be prepared for an abrupt increase in density altitude and corresponding loss of lift within approximately 50 feet of the runway.

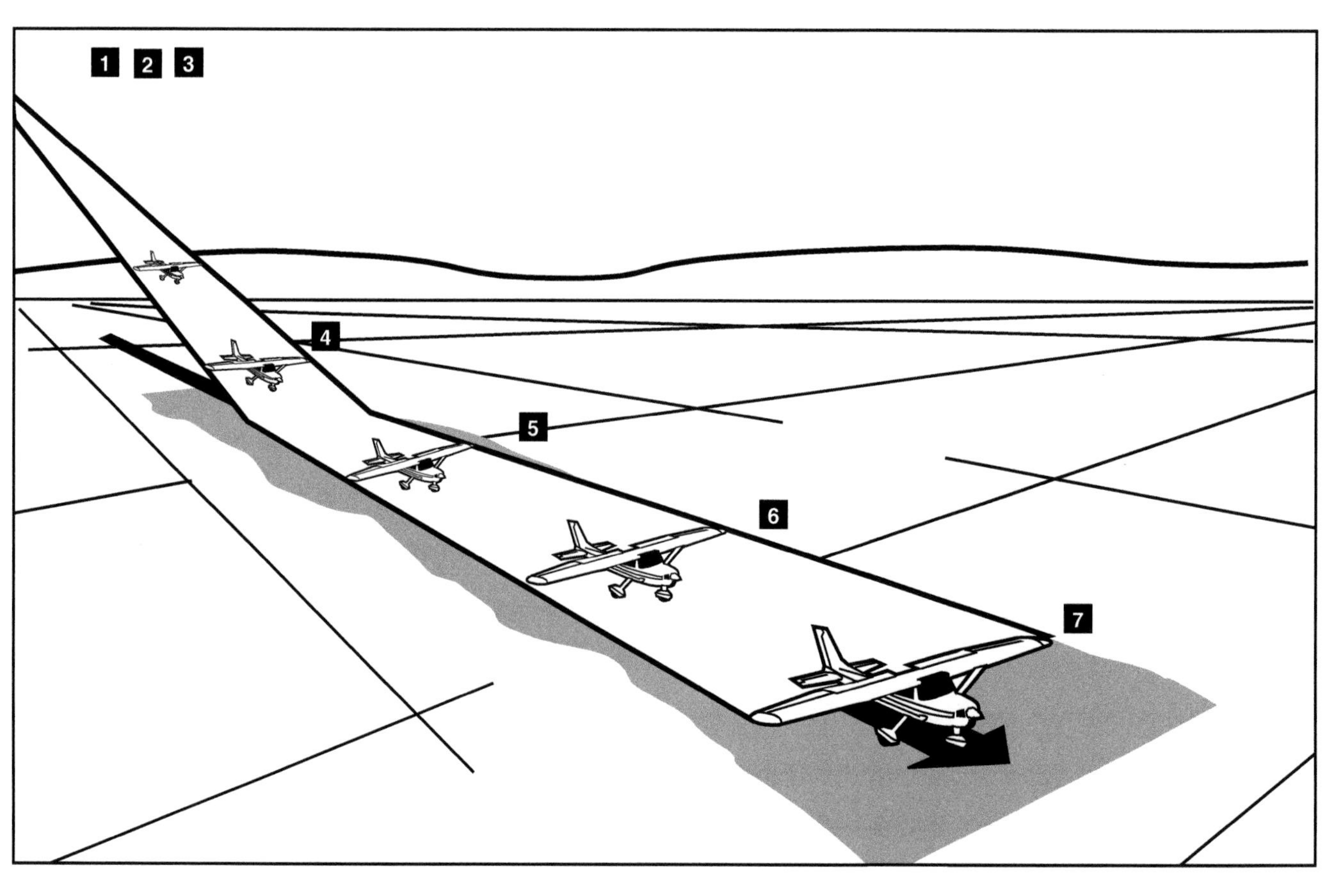

EXERCISES

1. The descent path to a soft-field is __________ (similar to, shallower than) that for a normal landing.
2. _____ (True, False) It is acceptable not to use full flaps if there is a strong probability that they may suffer damage from mud, stones, or slush thrown up by the wheels.
3. To help hold the nosewheel off the ground after touchdown, the addition of __________ helps make the elevator more effective.
4. When flaps are used for a soft-field landing you __________ (should, should not) retract them during the roll out.

SAMPLE ORAL QUESTIONS

1. What is your objective when making a soft-field landing?

1. The objective of a soft-field landing is to control the airplane in a manner so the wings support the weight of the airplane as long as practical. This minimizes the drag and stresses imposed on the landing gear by rough or soft surfaces.

2. What is the purpose of holding the nose off the ground after a soft-field touchdown?

2. By keeping the nosewheel off the soft surface during most of the landing roll, you prevent it from possibly sinking into the ground. This reduces the possibility of an abrupt stop during the landing roll.

3. Explain the main difference between a normal and soft-field landing.

3. The main difference between a normal and soft-field landing is that during the soft-field landing, the airplane is held approximately one to two feet above the surface as long as possible to dissipate forward speed and allow the main wheels to touch down gently.

4. What are some of the considerations when selecting a touchdown point for a soft-field landing?

4. When selecting a touchdown point, you should try to select a runway that is free of tall obstacles and that provides adequate distance to safely complete the rollout. Furthermore, you should always be alert for hazards such as standing water, wheel tracks, deep snow, or tall grass that are often associated with a soft field.

ADDITIONAL QUESTIONS

5. Explain why you should apply power as you touch down on a soft field.

6. Explain why you should avoid using the brakes when doing a soft-field landing.

EXERCISE ANSWERS

1. similar to
2. True
3. power
4. should not

REFERENCES

JEPPESEN:

Private Pilot Manual/Video – Chapter 8A
Private Pilot Maneuvers/Video – Maneuver 28

FAA:

Airplane Flying Handbook (FAA-H-8303-3)
Pilot's Operating Handbook and FAA-Approved Airplane Flight Manual

E. TASK: SHORT-FIELD TAKEOFF (CONFINED AREA - ASES) AND MAXIMUM PERFORMANCE CLIMB (ASEL and ASES)

REFERENCES: FAA-H-8303-3; POH/AFM

Objective: To determine that the applicant:

1. Exhibits knowledge of the elements related to a short-field (confined area ASES) takeoff and maximum performance climb.
2. Positions the flight controls for the existing wind conditions; sets the flaps as recommended.
3. Clears the area, taxies into takeoff position utilizing maximum available takeoff area and aligns the airplane on the runway center/takeoff path.
4. Selects an appropriate take off path for the existing conditions (ASES).
5. Applies brakes (if appropriate), while advancing the throttle smoothly to takeoff power.
6. Establishes and maintains the most efficient planing/lift-off attitude and corrects for porpoising and skipping (ASES).
7. Lifts off at the recommended airspeed, and accelerates to the recommended obstacle clearance airspeed or V_X.
8. Establishes a pitch attitude that will maintain the recommended obstacle clearance airspeed, or V_X, +10/-5 knots, until the obstacle is cleared, or until the airplane is 50 feet (20 meters) above the surface.
9. After clearing the obstacle, establishes the pitch attitude for V_Y, accelerates to V_Y, and maintains V_Y, +10/-5 knots, during the climb.
10. Retracts the landing gear, if appropriate, and flaps after clear of any obstacles or as recommended by the manufacturer.
11. Maintains takeoff power and V_Y, +10/-5 knots to a safe maneuvering altitude.
12. Maintains directional control and proper wind-drift correction throughout the takeoff and climb.
13. Completes the appropriate checklist.

Objective: To determine that the applicant:

1. **Exhibits knowledge of the elements related to a short-field takeoff and maximum performance climb.**

SHORT-FIELD TAKEOFF AND CLIMB

When practicing short-field takeoffs it is usually assumed that, in addition to a short runway, there is an obstruction that you must clear at the end of the runway. The obstruction is typically considered to be approximately 50 feet in height.

In order to accomplish a maximum performance takeoff safely, you must be familiar with the use and effectiveness of the best angle-of-climb speed (V_X) for your aircraft. V_X is the speed which results in the greatest gain in altitude for a given distance over the ground. It is usually slightly less than the best rate-of-climb speed (V_Y) which provides the greatest gain in altitude per unit of time. You can find both of these speeds in the Pilot's Operating Handbook and FAA-Approved Airplane Flight Manual.

The pretakeoff checklist for short-field takeoffs is the same as that used for normal takeoff procedures, except that you set the flaps as recommended by the manufacturer. The recommended flap setting varies between airplanes and can range from no flaps to approximately one-half flaps.

Initiate a short-field takeoff by taxiing into position as close as possible to the end of the runway's usable surface. Hold the brakes, apply full power, and then release the brakes. This procedure enables you to determine that the engine is functioning properly and is developing full power before you take off.

As you begin the takeoff roll, the airplane's pitch attitude and angle of attack should be adjusted for the minimum amount of drag and the quickest acceleration. In nosewheel aircraft this involves very little use of the elevator control, since the airplane is already in a low drag attitude. In tailwheel aircraft, the tail should be allowed to rise slightly, and then held in a tail-low attitude until rotation speed is attained.

For the steepest climb-out and best obstacle clearance, accelerate to liftoff speed with the aircraft's full weight on the landing gear. As you approach rotation speed the airplane should be firmly rotated, by applying back pressure on the elevator control. Do not try to rotate early. Attempting to pull the airplane off the ground prematurely, or to climb too steeply, may cause the airplane to settle back to the runway or into the obstacles.

Since most airplanes accelerate rapidly after lift-off, additional back pressure is typically required to hold a constant airspeed. After becoming airborne, maintain a straight climb at the reccomended obstacle clearance or V_X until all obstacles have been cleared or, if no obstacles are involved, until an altitude of at least 50 feet above the takeoff surface is attained. Thereafter the pitch attitude should be lowered slightly, and the climb continued at the best rate-of-climb speed (V_Y) until you reach a safe maneuvering altitude. Since the power setting is fixed, airspeed is controlled by adjusting the pitch attitude which in turn varies the climb angle. [Figure 4-7]

On short-field takeoffs, the flaps and landing gear should remain in the takeoff position until clear of all obstacles (or as recommended by the manufacturer) and V_Y has been established. It is generally unwise for you to be looking in the cockpit or reaching for flap and landing gear controls,

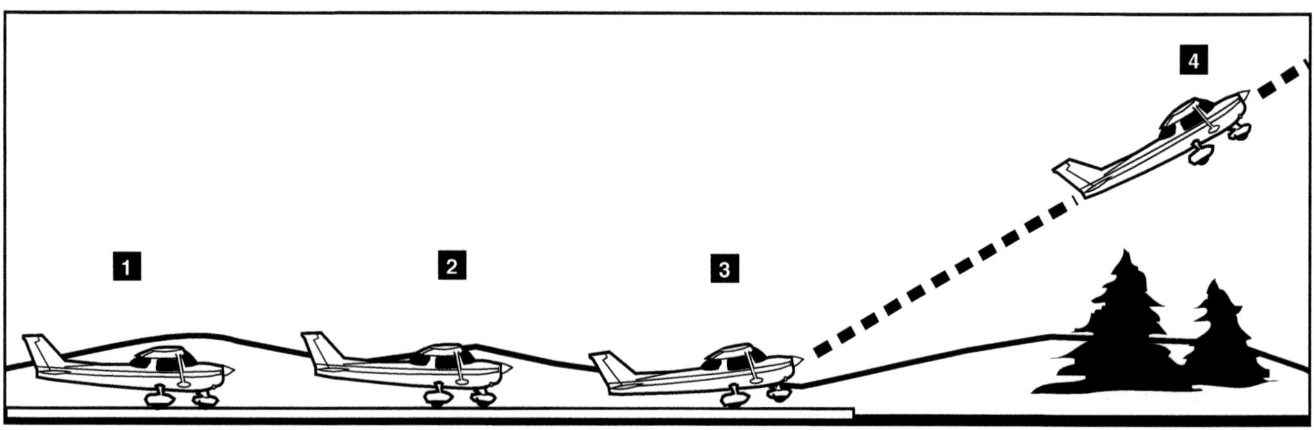

Figure 4-7. The initial takeoff roll involves little or no use of elevator (or stabilator) control beyond permitting it to assume a neutral position (position 1). As you reach the recommended rotation speed (position 2), apply prompt, positive back pressure to establish the proper takeoff attitude (position 3). Hold this attitude until the best angle-of-climb speed (obstacle clearance speed) is established, then maintain this speed until the obstacle is cleared (position 4).

until obstacle clearance is assured. When V_Y is established, begin retracting the landing gear and flaps as specified by the manufacturer. It is best to raise the flaps in increments to avoid a sudden loss of lift and settling of the airplane. After the flaps and landing gear are retracted the power should be reduced to the normal climb setting.

2. Positions the flight controls for the existing wind conditions; sets the flaps as recommended.

- When taxiing, position the controls for the existing wind conditions.
- You should consult the POH for the flap setting recommended by the manufacturer.

3. Clears the area, taxies into takeoff position utilizing maximum available takeoff area and aligns the airplane on the runway center.

- Before entering the runway, you should position the aircraft so you have a clear view of the final approach path.
- Once you have cleared the area, taxi to the very end of the runway's usable surface and align the aircraft with the centerline.
- Once aligned with the centerline, select a point on the cowl through which the runway centerline passes and use it as a reference for directional control during the takeoff roll.

5. Applies brakes while advancing the throttle smoothly to takeoff power.

- While holding the brakes, advance the throttle smoothly and continuously to maximum allowable power.
- As you advance the throttle, monitor the engine instruments so as to note immediately any malfunction or indication of insufficient power.
- Once the engine develops full power, release the brakes and begin the takeoff roll.
- As the aircraft begins to roll, apply right rudder to counteract engine torque.

7. Lifts off at the recommended airspeed, and accelerates to the recommended obstacle clearance airspeed or V_X

- At the rotation airspeed established in the pilot's operating handbook, apply the back pressure necessary to lift off.
- Your aircraft's liftoff speed is __________ kts.
- When taking off in a direct headwind, the ailerons and elevator should be held in the neutral position.
- When taking off in a crosswind, the yoke should be turned into the wind and the rudder used to keep the airplane on the runway centerline.
- After liftoff, establish the approximate attitude which allows the aircraft to accelerate to the reccomended obstacle clearance speed or V_X.
- The obstacle clearance speed or V_X for your aircraft is __________ kts.

8. Establishes a pitch attitude that will maintain the recommended obstacle clearance airspeed,or V_X, +10/ -5 knots, until the obstacle is cleared, or until the airplane is 50 feet (20 meters) above the surface.

- Immediately after takeoff, pitch for the aircraft obstacle clearance speed or V_X and maintain this speed until clear of obstacles or until you are 50 feet above the surface.
- Since full power is used for takeoff, airspeed is controlled by making slight pitch adjustments.

- When making pitch adjustments, make the necessary pitch change using outside references and glance at the airspeed indicator to verify the proper attitude and airspeed.

9. After clearing the obstacle, establishes the pitch attitude for V_Y, accelerates to V_Y, and maintains V_Y, +10/-5 knots during the climb.

- Once clear of obstacles, use outside references to reduce the aircraft's pitch to an attitude that allows you to accelerate to V_Y.
- Cross-check the airspeed indicator to verify the pro-per pitch attitude.
- V_Y for your aircraft is ___________ kts.

10. Retracts the landing gear, if appropriate, and flaps after clear of any obstacles or as recommended by the manufacturer.

- Landing gear and flaps should remain extended until clear of all obstructions, or after you've accelerated to V_Y.
- Retract landing gear and flaps when a positive rate of climb is indicated on the altimeter and VSI.
- Retract flaps incrementally to avoid a sudden loss of lift.

11. Maintains takeoff power and V_Y, +10/-5 knots to a safe maneuvering altitude.

- It is recommended that takeoff power be maintained until reaching at least 500 feet AGL.
- The recommended climb power setting for your aircraft is __________.

12. Maintains directional control and proper wind -drift correction throughout the takeoff and climb.

- As the nosewheel (or tailwheel) is raised off the runway in a crosswind, hold aileron control into the wind so the downwind main wheel lifts off the runway first.
- As both main wheels leave the runway in a crosswind, allow the airplane to slip sufficiently into the wind to maintain the runway centerline.
- At a safe altitude, establish a crab into the wind to maintain the extended runway centerline.

13. Completes the appropriate checklist.

- You must complete all applicable checklists.

PROCEDURE

1 Pretakeoff check — Complete
2 Takeoff clearance — As required
3 Wing flap position __________
4 Brakes — Hold
5 Full power — Apply smoothly
6 Brakes — Release
7 Rotation speed __________
8 Best angle-of-climb speed __________ (V_X)

AFTER OBSTACLE IS CLEARED:

9 Climb speed __________ (V_Y)
10 Wing flaps (when speed and altitude permit) — Up

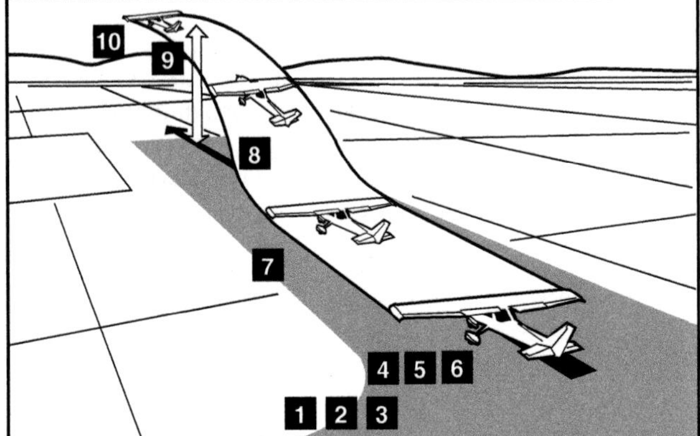

COMMON ERRORS

1. **Early rotation.**

   Cause: Fear of the approaching end of the runway.

   Solution: Rotate when you reach the appropriate airspeed, as shown in the POH. Attempting to rotate early may cause the airplane to settle back to the runway.

2. **Flying with excessive airspeed after lift-off; not holding V_X.**

   Cause: Improper pitch attitude.

   Solution: Once airborne, immediately establish the appropriate pitch attitude for V_X and cross-check the airspeed indicator to verify the proper speed.

3. **Failure to use the entire runway available.**

   Cause: Force of habit.

   Solution: When asked to perform a short-field takeoff, taxi to the very end of the runway's usable surface.

4. **Starting the ground roll too early.**

   Cause: Improper use of the brakes.

   Solution: Do not release the brakes until the engine is developing full power.

EXERCISES

1. _____ (True, False) When beginning a short-field takeoff, you should begin the ground roll as soon as you enter the runway.
2. V_X represents the aircraft's best __________ of climb.
3. _____ (True, False) When performing a short-field takeoff, you should retract the flaps almost immediately after takeoff.
4. _____ (True, False) Once you begin the ground roll for a short-field takeoff, you should hold the control wheel in the full back position.

SAMPLE ORAL QUESTIONS

1. What is the difference between V_X and V_Y?

____

____

____

____

____

____

1. The aircraft's best angle-of-climb (V_X) is the speed which results in the greatest gain in altitude for a given distance over the ground. It is usually slightly less than the best rate-of-climb speed (V_Y) which provides the greatest gain in altitude per unit of time. You can find both of these speeds in the FAA-Approved Airplane Flight Manual or the Pilot's Operating Handbook.

2. Why should you hold the brakes while power is being added for a short-field takeoff?

____

____

____

2. By holding the brakes while advancing the throttle, you can verify that the engine is functioning properly and developing full power prior to take off.

3. When should you retract the flaps during a short-field takeoff?

____

____

____

____

3. On short-field takeoffs, the flaps and landing gear (if applicable) should remain in the takeoff position until clear of all obstacles (or as recommended by the manufacturer) and V_Y has been established.

ADDITIONAL QUESTIONS

4. Why is it important to maintain the best angle of climb airspeed, rather than the best rate of climb airspeed, during short-field takeoffs?
5. Why should you attempt to keep the weight of the aircraft on the wheels, as opposed to the wings, during a short-field takeoff?

EXERCISE ANSWERS

1. False
2. angle
3. False
4. False

REFERENCES

JEPPESEN:

Private Pilot Manual/Video – Chapter 8A

Private Pilot Maneuvers/Video – Maneuver 25

FAA:

Airplane Flying Handbook (FAA-H-8303-3)

Pilot's Operating Handbook and FAA-Approved Airplane Flight Manual

F. TASK: SHORT-FIELD APPROACH (CONFINED AREA-ASES) AND LANDING (ASEL and ASES)

REFERENCES: FAA-H-8303-3; POH/AFM

Objective: To determine that the Applicant:

1. Exhibits knowledge of the elements related to a short-field (confined area ASES) approach and landing.
2. Adequately surveys the intended landing area. (ASES)
3. Considers the wind conditions, landing surface, obstructions, and selects the most suitable touchdown point.
4. Establishes the recommended approach and landing configuration and airspeed; adjusts pitch attitude and power as required.
5. Maintains a stabilized approach and recommended approach airspeed, or in its absence, not more than 1.3 V_{SO}, +10/-5 knots, with wind gust factor applied.
6. Makes smooth, timely, and correct control application during the roundout and touchdown.
7. Selects the proper landing path, contacts the water at the minimum safe airspeed with proper pitch attitude for the surface conditions (ASES).
8. Touches down smoothly at minimum control airspeed (ASEL).
9. Touches down at or within 200 feet (60 meters) beyond a specified point, with no side drift, minimum float and with the airplane's longitudinal axis aligned with and over the runway center/landing path.
10. Maintains crosswind correction and directional control throughout the approach and landing sequence.
11. Applies brakes (ASEL), or elevator control (ASES), as necessary, to stop in the shortest distance consistent with safety.
12. Completes the appropriate checklist.

Objective: To determine that the applicant:

1. Exhibits knowledge of the elements related to a short-field approach and landing.

SHORT-FIELD APPROACH AND LANDING

To land within a short field or a confined area, you must maintain precise control of the rate of descent and airspeed. This produces an approach that clears any obstacles, results in little or no floating during the roundout, and permits the airplane to be stopped in the shortest possible distance.

Whenever you conduct a short-field landing you should always use the procedures recommended in the Pilot's Operating Handbook and FAA-Approved Airplane Flight Manual. These procedures generally involve the use of full flaps, and the final approach started from an altitude of at least 500 feet higher than the touchdown area. In the absence of a manufacturer's approach speed, a speed of not more than 1.3 V_{SO} should be used. In gusty winds, no more than one-half the gust factor should be added. Remember, excessive airspeed could result in the aircraft touching down too far from the runway threshold or an after-landing roll that exceeds the available landing area.

Once full flaps have been extended, you should simultaneously adjust the power and the pitch attitude to establish and maintain the proper descent angle and airspeed. Since short-field approaches are power-on approaches, you must adjust the pitch attitude to establish and maintain the desired rate or angle of descent, and adjust power to maintain the desired airspeed. However, coordinated pitch and power adjustments are usually required.

If it appears during the approach that you will touch down well beyond your desired point, leaving insufficient room to stop, power may be reduced while lowering the pitch attitude to increase the rate of descent. On the other hand, if it appears that the descent angle will not ensure safe obstacle clearance, increase power while simultaneously raising the pitch attitude to decrease the rate of descent. However, care must be taken to avoid an excessively low airspeed. If the speed becomes too slow, an increase in pitch and application of full power may only result in an increased rate of descent. In this situation, the angle of attack is so great and so much drag is created that the maximum available power is insufficient to overcome it. This is generally referred to as operating in the " region of reverse command" or operating on the " back side of the power curve."

Touchdown should occur at the minimum controllable airspeed with a pitch attitude that results in a power-off stall when the throttle is closed. However, in this configuration, you must avoid closing the throttle rapidly before you are ready to touch down or an immediate increase in the rate of descent and a hard landing could result.

After touchdown, close the throttle and lower the nose. To stop the aircraft in the shortest possible distance, apply maximum braking while holding the control wheel full aft. This provides aerodynamic braking by the wings and places more weight on the main wheels for improved braking.

3. Considers the wind conditions, landing surface, obstructions, and selects the most suitable touchdown point.

- Typically, you should select a runway which best favors the wind.
- The runway surface and length must allow you to land safely given the existing conditions. This includes the type of surface, as well as factors such as rain, ice, or snow on the runway.
- You should select a touchdown point that provides adequate obstruction clearance and sufficient distance to safely complete the roll-out.

4. Establishes the recommended approach and landing configuration and airspeed; adjusts pitch attitude and power as required.

- Prior to landing, you should consult the POH or landing checklist for the recommended flap settings.
- You should use outside references to maintain the proper pitch attitude.
- You must use power to control the rate of descent while maintaining the appropriate airspeed. Additional power decreases the rate of descent while less power increases the rate of descent.
- The manufacturer's recommended flap setting when conducting a short-field approach and landing for your aircraft is __________ kts.

5. Maintains a stabilized approach and the recommended approach airspeed, or in its absence not more than 1.3 V_{SO}, +10/–5 knots, with wind gust factor applied.

- To maintain a stabilized approach, you must make small corrections in a timely fashion so as to avoid large or abrupt last-minute corrections.
- Once the aircraft is configured properly for landing, trim to relieve any control pressures.
- Consult the POH or landing checklist for the recommended approach speed.
- In the absence of a recommended approach speed, use 1.3 V_{SO}.
- In gusty conditions you should increase your approach speed by no more than 1/2 the gust factor.
- The approach speed to conduct a short-field approach and landing for your aircraft is __________ kts.

6. Makes smooth, timely, and correct control application during the roundout and touchdown.

- Maintain a positive pitch attitude to the flare (roundout) and touchdown.
- An approach in a crosswind requires you to lower the upwind wing using the ailerons and align the aircraft's longitudinal axis with the runway by using opposite rudder.
- During the flare in a crosswind, the application of crosswind correction must be continued to prevent drifting.

8. Touches down smoothly at minimum control airspeed.

- The touchdown should occur at the minimum controllable airspeed with a pitch attitude that results in a power-off stall when the throttle is closed.

9. Touches down at or within 200 feet (60 meters) beyond a specified point, with no side drift, minimum float and with the airplane's longitudinal axis aligned with and over the runway center.

- To land on a specified point, you must select an aiming point that is in front of the specified landing point.
- Just prior to touchdown, use the rudder to align the longitudinal axis of the airplane with the runway centerline.

10. Maintains crosswind correction and directional control throughout the approach and landing.

- When using the wing-low method during the approach, you must maintain a sideslip all the way to the runway.
- In a crosswind, the upwind main wheel will make contact with the runway first.
- During the roll-out, maintain directional control with the rudder pedals, and turn the aileron control into the wind to prevent the upwind wing from rising.

11. Applies brakes, as necessary, to stop in the shortest distance consistent with safety.

- After touchdown, lower the nose and begin braking firmly and evenly.
- For maximum braking effectiveness, apply elevator back pressure.
- Retract the flaps, if recommended, and continue braking until the aircraft is completely stopped.

12. Completes the appropriate checklist.

- You must complete all required checklists prior to landing.
- It is recommended that the before-landing checklist be completed on downwind.
- The after-landing checklist should be completed once you have cleared the active runway.

PROCEDURE

1. Prelanding check — Complete
2. Power — Idle, or __________ RPM
3. Flaps (as speed permits) — Full
4. Glidepath — Maintain at constant angle to clear obstacle
5. Flare — Nose high with no excessive airspeed
6. Touchdown — Just above stall, lower nose immediately
7. Roll-out — Apply brakes as required, maintain centerline

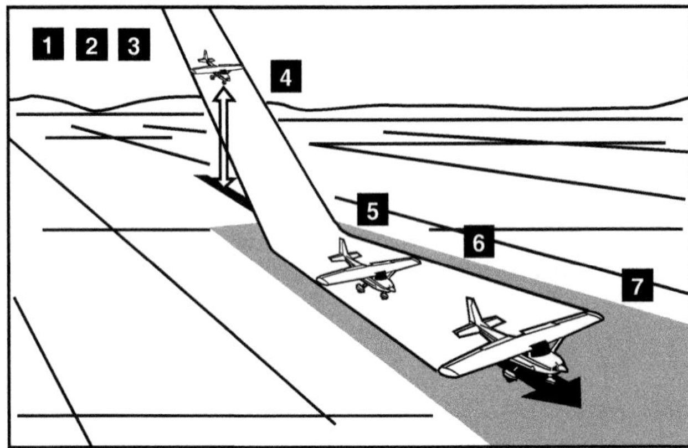

COMMON ERRORS

1. **Poor airspeed control during the approach.**

   Cause: Failing to establish and maintain a stabilized approach.

   Solution: Maintain the approach airspeed by making small, coordinated adjustments to pitch and power. Use trim as necessary.

2. **Losing directional control after touchdown.**

   Cause: Using poor braking techniques such as uneven application of brakes, or applying brakes before touching down.

   Solution: Use equal pressure on both brakes after the airplane has touched down.

   Cause: Relaxing the control inputs when the airplane touches down.

   Solution: Maintain proper control inputs until the airplane is completely stopped.

3. **Landing too far down the runway.**

   Cause: Floating due to excessive airspeed and/or power.

   Solution: Touch down at the minimum controllable airspeed in a pitch attitude that results in a stall when the throttle is closed.

EXERCISES

1. _____ (True, False) If no approach speed is specified in the POH for a short-field landing, use 1.3 V_{S0}.
2. When operating on the "back side of the power curve," maximum power may be __________ to decrease the rate of descent.
3. A good short-field approach and landing is characterized by a landing with little or no __________.
4. Once established on final approach, make _________ adjustments in pitch and power to maintain the proper descent angle and airspeed.

SAMPLE ORAL QUESTIONS

1. Why are full flaps typically used for short-field landings?

1. The use of full flaps results in a steep approach without gaining excessive airspeed. This better enables you to clear obstacles in the approach path and touch down on the runway with minimal forward speed.

2. Conducting a short-field approach and landing with excessive airspeed could result in a touch down that is too far from the runway threshold or an after-landing roll that exceeds the available landing area. Because of this, you must use the final approach speed recommended by the manufacturer. In the absence of a recommended speed, use no more than 1.3 V_{S0}.

2. Explain the consequences of making an approach to a short field with excessive airspeed.

3. Since short-field approaches are power-on approaches, you must adjust the pitch attitude to establish and maintain the desired rate or angle of descent, and adjust power to maintain the desired airspeed. However, a coordinated combination of both pitch and power adjustments is usually required.

3. How are pitch and airspeed controlled during a short-field approach?

ADDITIONAL QUESTIONS

4. How does elevator back pressure aid in braking?
5. Explain the short-field landing procedures for your airplane.

EXERCISE ANSWERS

1. True
2. insufficient
3. floating
4. small

REFERENCES

JEPPESEN:

Private Pilot Manual/Video – Chapter 8A

Private Pilot Maneuvers/Video – Maneuver 26

FAA:

Airplane Flying Manual (FAA-H-8303-3)

Pilot's Operating Handbook and FAA-Approved Airplane Flight Manual

K. TASK: FORWARD SLIP TO A LANDING (ASEL and ASES)

REFERENCES: FAA-H-8303-3; POH/AFM

Objective: To determine that the applicant:

1. Exhibits knowledge of the elements related to forward slip to a landing.
2. Considers the wind conditions, landing surface and obstructions, and selects the most suitable touchdown point.
3. Establishes the slipping attitude at the point from which a landing can be made using the recommended approach and landing configuration and airspeed; adjusts pitch attitude and power as required.
4. Maintains a ground track aligned with the runway center/landing path and an airspeed, which results in minimum float during the roundout.
5. Makes smooth, timely, and correct control application during the recovery from the slip, the roundout, and the touchdown.
6. Touches down smoothly at the approximate stalling speed, at or within 400 feet (120 meters) beyond a specified point, with no side drift, and with the airplane's longitudinal axis aligned with and over the runway center/landing path.
7. Maintains crosswind correction and directional control throughout the approach and landing sequence.
8. Completes the appropriate checklist.

Objective: To determine that the applicant:

1. Exhibits knowledge of the elements related to forward slip to a landing.

FORWARD SLIP TO A LANDING

Forward slips are a method of steepening an approach without increasing airspeed. Typically, a forward slip is used when landing on short runways with obstructions, or when making a forced landing. Airplanes equipped with flaps should not attempt a forward slip with the flaps extended, unless otherwise noted in the Pilot's Operating Handbook. Most aircraft that prohibit slips are placarded accordingly. However, in the absence of a placard, don't assume you can perform slips. Always be aware of the limitations of your airplane by reading the POH.

Forward slips differ from sideslips in terms of the direction of the longitudinal axis. In a forward slip, the longitudinal axis of the airplane is at an angle to the aircraft's flight path. In a sideslip, however, the longitudinal axis remains parallel with the aircraft's flight path. You use the sideslip maneuver when conducting a crosswind approach and landing.

Forward slips are accomplished with the throttle at idle, while one wing is lowered by use of the ailerons. Simultaneously, the airplane's nose must be yawed in the opposite direction by applying opposite rudder so that the airplane's longitudinal axis is at an angle to its original flight path. The degree to which the nose is yawed should be such that the original ground track is maintained. The nose should also be raised as necessary to prevent the airspeed from increasing. [Figure 4-8]

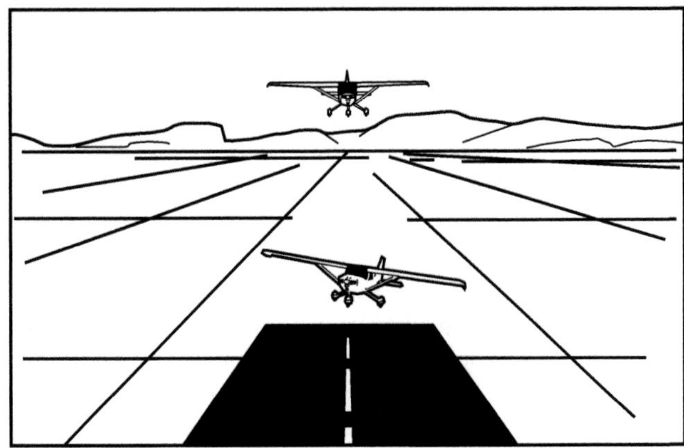

Figure 4-8. To initiate a forward slip, lower one wing by using aileron control. At the same time, apply opposite rudder to keep the airplane from turning in the direction of the lowered wing. This procedure keeps the airplane's ground track in alignment with the extended centerline of the runway, but allows the nose of the airplane to angle away from the runway. To prevent the airspeed from increasing, raise the nose slightly above the standard gliding position. In this attitude, the glide path steepens, even though the airspeed remains constant.

If a slip is used during the last portion of a final approach, the longitudinal axis of the airplane must be aligned with the runway prior to touchdown. Failure to accomplish this would impose severe sideloads on the landing gear.

Recovery from a slip is accomplished by leveling the wings and simultaneously releasing rudder pressure. At the same time you must readjust the pitch attitude to the normal glide attitude. If rudder pressure is released abruptly the nose will swing too quickly and cause the airplane to gain speed.

Because of the location of the pitot tube and static port on most aircraft, airspeed indications may have considerable error when the airplane is in a slip. You must be aware of this possibility and recognize a properly performed slip by the attitude and position of the airplane, the sound of the airflow, and the feel of the flight controls.

2. Considers the wind conditions, landing surface and obstructions, and selects the most suitable touchdown point.

- Typically, you should select a runway which best favors the wind.

- When conducting a forward slip to a landing in a crosswind, initiate the slip into the wind by lowering the upwind wing.
- The runway surface and length must allow you to land safely given the existing conditions. This includes the type of surface, as well as factors such as rain, ice, or snow on the runway.
- You should select a touchdown point that provides adequate obstruction clearance and sufficient distance to safely complete the roll-out.

3. Establishes the slipping attitude at the point from which a landing can be made using the recommended approach and landing configuration and airspeed; adjusts pitch attitude and power as required.

- Do not initiate a forward slip unless the landing is assured. Furthermore, the maneuver should never be continued below the normal glide path.
- Use idle power with the carburetor heat on (if applicable).
- To enter a forward slip, lower one wing and apply opposite rudder to the extent required to maintain your desired ground track.
- Adjust the pitch as necessary to maintain a normal approach speed.

4. Maintains a ground track aligned with the runway center and an airspeed, which results in minimum float during the roundout.

- Use the rudder to keep the aircraft aligned with the runway centerline.
- Maintain the recommended approach airspeed. In the absence of a recommended speed use 1.3 V_{S0}.

5. Makes smooth, timely, and correct control application during the recovery from the slip, the roundout, and the touchdown.

- Recovery from a forward slip is accomplished by simultaneously leveling the wings and releasing rudder pressure.
- If rudder pressure is released abruptly, the nose will quickly swing into line resulting in an increase in airspeed and floating during the flare.
- Once recovered from the slip, transition into the flare and touchdown.

6. Touches down smoothly at the approximate stalling speed, at or within 400 feet (120 meters) beyond a specified point, with no side drift, and with the airplane's longitudinal axis aligned with and over the runway center.

- Continue to hold the aircraft off the ground until it settles at the approximate stall speed.
- The pitch attitude at touchdown should be close to the pitch attitude used at takeoff.
- To flare and touch down smoothly, you must utilize both visual and kinesthetic cues.
- To land on a specified point, you must select an aiming point that is several hundred feet in front of the specified landing point.
- Just prior to touchdown, use the rudder to align the longitudinal axis of the airplane with the runway centerline.
- The main wheels of the aircraft should touch down first. When landing in a crosswind, the upwind main wheel should contact the runway first.

7. Maintains crosswind correction and directional control throughout the approach and landing sequence.

- When using the wing-low method during the approach, you must maintain a sideslip all the way to the runway.
- During the roll-out, maintain directional control with the rudder pedals, and turn the aileron control into the wind to prevent the upwind wing from rising.

8. Completes the appropriate checklist.

- You must complete all required checklists prior to landing.
- It is recommended that the before-landing checklist be completed on downwind.
- The after-landing checklist should be completed once you have cleared the active runway.

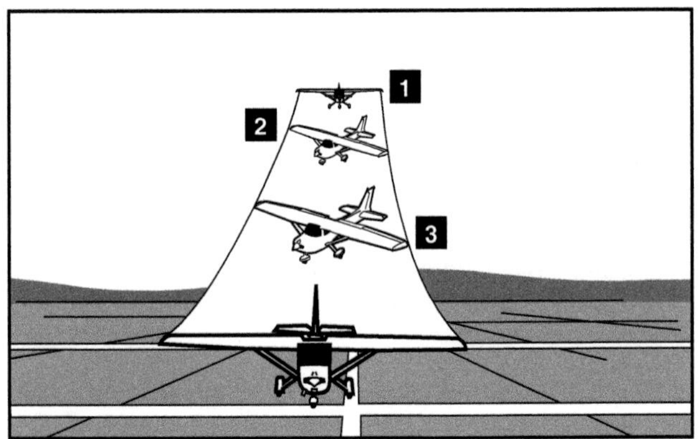

PROCEDURE

1. Aileron — As desired, wing low in direction of slip
2. Opposite Rudder — As required to maintain track
3. Airspeed — Maintain with pitch

Note: The airspeed indicator may be unreliable during slip.

COMMON ERRORS

1. **Making a flat slip.**

   Cause: Allowing the low wing to gradually rise with the nose still yawed.

   Solution: Use outside references to maintain the proper bank angle.

2. **Landing short of your touchdown point.**

   Cause: Failure to recognize the rapid loss of altitude.

   Solution: Decide on a recovery altitude and never allow the aircraft to descend below the normal glide path.

3. **Landing the airplane at an angle to the centerline.**

   Cause: Failure to realign the longitudinal axis with the runway centerline before touchdown.

   Solution: Recover from the forward slip sufficiently above the runway to allow time to align the longitudinal axis with the runway centerline.

5. **Not maintaining the desired approach airspeed.**

   Cause: Poor pitch control.

   Solution: When a slip is entered, the nose should be raised as necessary to prevent airspeed from increasing. Furthermore, during the recovery the nose should not be allowed to swing into position too abruptly.

EXERCISES

1. _____ (True, False) Full power should be used when performing slips to ensure a high margin of safety when operating near the ground.

2. If the aircraft is allowed to touchdown at an angle to the runway centerline, heavy __________ __________ may be imposed on the landing gear.

3. _____ (True, False) A forward slip to a landing is appropriate when trying to salvage a bad approach.

4. _____ (True, False) A forward slip to a landing places the longitudinal axis of the airplane parallel with the flight path.

5. When possible, you should execute a slip with the ____________________ wing lowered into the wind.

SAMPLE ORAL QUESTIONS

1. What is the difference between a forward slip and a sideslip?

   ____

   ____

   ____

   ____

   ____

   ____

   ____

1. Forward slips differ from sideslips in terms of the direction of the longitudinal axis. In a forward slip, the longitudinal axis of the airplane is at an angle to the aircraft's flight path. In a sideslip, however, the longitudinal axis remains parallel with the aircraft's flight path.

2. Prior to entering a slip, you should decide when to terminate the maneuver. This should be based on how much altitude is to be lost, the surrounding terrain, wind, and pilot experience level. When initiating the recovery, simultaneously level the wings and neutralize the rudder. Regardless of when the recovery is accomplished, always land with the longitudinal axis aligned with the runway centerline to minimize stress on the landing gear and to avoid side loads.

3. Slipping accelerates the descent beyond the normal descent rate. Unless the landing is assured prior to entering a slip, the increased descent rate caused by the slip could put the aircraft below the normal glide path.

2. Describe the recovery from a forward slip.

3. Why should a forward slip only be used when the landing is assured?

ADDITIONAL QUESTIONS

4. Explain the implications of using flaps during a slip.
5. What determines the amount of bank to be used in the forward slip?

EXERCISE ANSWERS

1. False
2. side loads
3. False
4. False
5. upwind

REFERENCES

JEPPESEN:

Private Pilot Maneuvers/Video – Maneuver 14

FAA:

Airplane Flying Handbook (FAA-H-8303-3)

Pilot's Operating Handbook and FAA-Approved Flight Manual

L. TASK: GO-AROUND / REJECTED LANDING (ASEL and ASES)

REFERENCES: FAA-H-8303-3; POH/AFM

Objective: To determine that the applicant:

1. Exhibits knowledge of the elements related to a go-around/rejected landing.
2. Makes a timely decision to discontinue the approach to landing.
3. Applies takeoff power immediately and transitions to climb pitch attitude for V_Y, and maintains V_Y +10/–5 knots.
4. Retracts the flaps as appropriate.
5. Retracts the landing gear, if appropriate, after a positive rate of climb is established.
6. Maneuvers to the side of the runway/landing area to clear and avoid conflicting traffic.
7. Maintains takeoff power V_Y +10/-5 to a safe maneuvering altitude.
8. Maintains directional control and proper wind-drift correction throughout the climb.
9. Completes the appropriate checklist.

Objective: To determine that the applicant:

1. Exhibits knowledge of the elements related to a go-around/rejected landing..

GO-AROUND

Since the purpose of making an approach is to land the aircraft, many pilots find the idea of a rejected landing difficult to accept. However, if for any reason the successful outcome of an approach is in question, safety dictates that you initiate a go-around.

DECISION MAKING

There are numerous reasons that justify discontinuing an approach and initiating a go-around. These include:

— overshooting the final approach course
— an extremely low base to final
— being excessively high or excessively low in the pattern
— an aircraft or other obstruction on the runway
— wake turbulence, wind shear, or an excessive crosswind component
— generally, if the aircraft has not touched down on the first one-third of the runway
— ATC instructing a go-around
— anytime you feel uncomfortable with the approach

One important aspect of the decision-making process involves timeliness. Do not wait until the last possible moment to make a decision to go-around. In fact, you should mentally prepare yourself for the possibility of having to initiate a go-around on every landing.

INITIATING A GO-AROUND

When the decision is made to discontinue an approach and perform a go-around, full power should be immediately and smoothly applied and the airplane's pitch attitude increased to slow or stop the descent. However, if the pitch attitude is increased excessively in an effort to prevent the airplane from mushing onto the runway, the airplane may stall.

After the descent has been stopped, the landing flaps may be partially retracted as recommended by the manufacturer. However, caution must be used in retracting the flaps. Typically it is recommended that the flaps be retracted in small increments to allow the airplane to accelerate as they are raised. A sudden and complete retraction of the flaps at a low airspeed could cause a dramatic loss of lift and cause the airplane to settle onto the runway.

If the aircraft is equipped with retractable landing gear it is generally recommended that the flaps be retracted (at least partially) before retracting the landing gear. The reason for this is that on most aircraft, full flaps produce more drag than the landing gear. Furthermore, the airplane could inadvertently touch down as the go-around is initiated.

When full power is applied, it is usually necessary to hold a considerable amount of forward pressure on the control wheel since the airplane was trimmed for the approach. In addition, right rudder pressure must be applied to counteract torque and P-factor. To help keep the aircraft in a safe climbing attitude, you should re-trim the airplane to relieve at least the heavy control pressures. Since airspeed typically builds rapidly with the application of full power, and the controls become more effective, this initial trim setting is to relieve the heavy control pressures until a more precise trim setting can be obtained.

After a positive rate of climb is established, the landing gear should be retracted and the airplane allowed to accelerate to the best rate-of-climb speed (V_Y) before the final flap retraction is accomplished. Make a gentle turn to the right side of the runway. [Figure 4-9]

2. Makes a timely decision to discontinue the approach to landing.

- The safest go-around is one that is initiated early in the approach. Never wait until the last moment.
- Waiting until the aircraft is low and slow to initiate a go-around wastes precious altitude and airspeed.

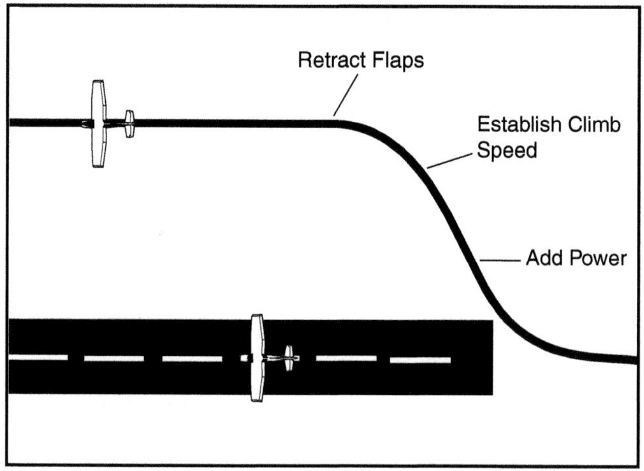

Figure 4-9. When you initiate a go-around, adjust your flight path to be far enough to the side of the runway that it does not interfere with an airplane taking off. In this position, you can see the runway clearly.

- The turn from base to final is referred to as the " key position." This is a good time to begin considering the possibility of a go-around, even if you are stabilized.
- If you have any doubt about making a safe approach and landing, execute a go-around immediately.

3. Applies takeoff power immediately and transitions to climb pitch attitude for V_Y, and maintains V_Y +10/–5 knots.

- When the decision is made to go-around, immediately add full power.
- Stop your descent by increasing the pitch attitude just above that required for level flight.
- As power is applied, be prepared to hold a considerable amount of forward pressure on the control wheel to maintain a safe climb attitude.
- Right rudder pressure will be necessary to counteract the effects of torque and P-factor.

4. Retracts the flaps as appropriate.

- Once full power is added, retract the first increment of flaps or as recommended by the manufacturer. Flaps should be raised one increment at a time to prevent a sudden loss of lift.
- The manufacturer's recommended go-around flap setting for your aircraft is __________.

5. Retracts the landing gear, if appropriate, after a positive rate of climb is established.

- Typically, the landing gear is retracted after the flaps are at least partially retracted.
- A positive rate of climb, as indicated on the altimeter and VSI, must be established before the landing gear is retracted.
- Once established at V_Y, retract the final increment of flaps and trim to relieve any control pressures.
- V_Y in your aircraft is __________ kts.

6. Maneuvers to the side of the runway to clear and avoid conflicting traffic.

- Make a gentle turn to the right, then straighten out to fly parallel to the runway as you climb. Go far enough from the runway so that you will not interfere with other traffic using the same runway. Be very careful and use good judgment if there is a parallel runway to the right of the one you are using.
- Maintains takeoff power VY +10/-5 to a safe maneuvering altitude.

7. Maintains takeoff power V_Y +10/-5 to a safe maneuvering altitude.

- It is recommended that takeoff power be maintained until reaching at least 500 feet AGL.
- The recommended climb power setting for your aircraft is __________ RPM.
- Once traffic pattern altitude is reached, you should accelerate to the appropriate speed and then make power adjustments as necessary.
- Since full power is used for a go-around, airspeed is controlled by making slight pitch adjustments.
- When making pitch adjustments, make the necessary pitch change using outside references and glance at the airspeed indicator to verify the proper airspeed.

8. Maintains directional control and proper wind-drift correction throughout the climb.

- Once you are climbing at V_Y, establish a crab into the wind to maintain your course.

9. Completes the appropriate checklist.

- You must complete all applicable checklists.

COMMON ERRORS

1. **Initiating the go-around at too low an altitude.**

   Cause: Making a late decision to go-around.

   Solution: Determine the likelihood of a safe landing, early in the approach. The turn from base to final, or the "key position," is a good time to assess the progress of the approach.

2. **Allowing the aircraft to get too slow once the go-around is initiated.**

   Cause: Not maintaining the proper pitch attitude.

   Solution: As power is added in a go-around, the aircraft typically pitches upward requiring a considerable amount of forward pressure to maintain a safe climb attitude.

3. **Aircraft yawing to the left.**

   Cause: Failing to compensate for torque and P-factor while adding power.

   Solution: As full power is added, you must apply right rudder to keep the aircraft from yawing to the left.

EXERCISES

1. _____ (True, False) If you initiate a go-around from a high approach, you should attempt to land the aircraft on the next approach without fail.
2. _____ (True, False) Once the decision to go-around has been made, "clean up" the aircraft to reduce drag, by retracting all of the flaps and the landing gear.
3. When initiating a go-around you should apply __________ power.
4. When climbing out after a go-around, pitch for __________.

SAMPLE ORAL QUESTIONS

1. Why shouldn't the flaps be retracted all at once when executing a go-around?

   ____
   ____
   ____
   ____
   ____
   ____
   ____
   ____

2. Why does the aircraft need to be re-trimmed after a rejected landing?

   ____
   ____
   ____
   ____
   ____
   ____
   ____
   ____
   ____
   ____

1. Although the flaps create additional drag, they also provide added lift. If all of the flaps are retracted at once, the aircraft would experience a dramatic loss of lift near the ground, and possibly cause the aircraft to settle onto the runway or even stall.

2. When preparing for a normal landing, the trim is adjusted for a relatively low power setting and low airspeed. Therefore, when a go-around is initiated the nose of the aircraft typically rises sharply. If the aircraft isn't re-trimmed, a considerable amount of forward pressure would have to be maintained.

3. Items that justify initiating a go-around include:

— overshooting the final approach course
— an extremely low base to final
— being excessively high or excessively low in the pattern
— an aircraft or other obstruction on the runway
— wake turbulence, wind shear, or an excessive cross-wind component
— ATC instructing a go-around
— anytime you feel uncomfortable with the approach

3. List several items that justify initiating a go-around.

____
____
____
____
____
____
____
____

ADDITIONAL QUESTIONS

4. Why should carburetor heat be turned off for a go-around?

5. How many times should you go-around before actually landing?

EXERCISE ANSWERS

1. False
2. False
3. full
4. V_Y

REFERENCES

JEPPESEN:

Private Pilot Maneuvers/Video – Maneuver 13

FAA:

Airplane Flying Handbook (FAA-H-8303-3)

Pilot's Operating Handbook and FAA-Approved Airplane Flight Manual

CHAPTER 5

PERFORMANCE MANEUVER

A. TASK: STEEP TURNS (ASEL and ASES)

REFERENCES: FAA-H-8083-3; POH/AFM

Objective: To determine that the applicant:

1. Exhibits knowledge of the elements related to steep turns.
2. Establishes the manufacturer's recommended airspeed or if one is not stated, a safe airspeed not to exceed V_A.
3. Rolls into a coordinated 360° turn; maintains a 45° bank.
4. Performs the task in the opposite direction, as specified by the examiner.
5. Divides attention between airplane control and orientation.
6. Maintains the entry altitude, ±100 feet (30 meters), and airspeed, ±10 knots, bank, ± 5°; and rolls out on the entry heading, ±10°

Objective: To determine that the applicant:

1. **Exhibits knowledge of the elements related to steep turns.**

FORCES ACTING ON A TURNING AIRPLANE

You create the necessary turning force by banking the airplane so that the direction of lift is inclined. In a turn, one component of lift acts vertically to oppose weight, just as it does in straight-and-level flight, while another acts horizontally. To maintain altitude, you increase lift by increasing back pressure and, therefore, the angle of attack, until the vertical component of lift equals weight. The horizontal component of lift, called **centripetal force**, is directed inward, toward the center of rotation. It is this center- seeking force which causes the airplane to turn. Centripetal force is opposed by **centrifugal force**, which acts outward from the center of rotation. When the opposing forces are balanced, the airplane maintains a constant rate of turn, without gaining or losing altitude.

LOAD FACTOR

When you are in a turn, the wings must support both the weight of the airplane and its contents, and the load imposed by centrifugal force. **Load factor** is the ratio of the load supported by the airplane's wings to the actual weight of the aircraft and its contents. If the wings are supporting twice as much weight as the weight of the airplane and its contents, the load factor is two. The term "G-forces" describes flight loads caused by the aircraft maneuvering. For example, a utility category airplane is certified to +4.4 G's and –1.76 G's. [Figure 5-1]

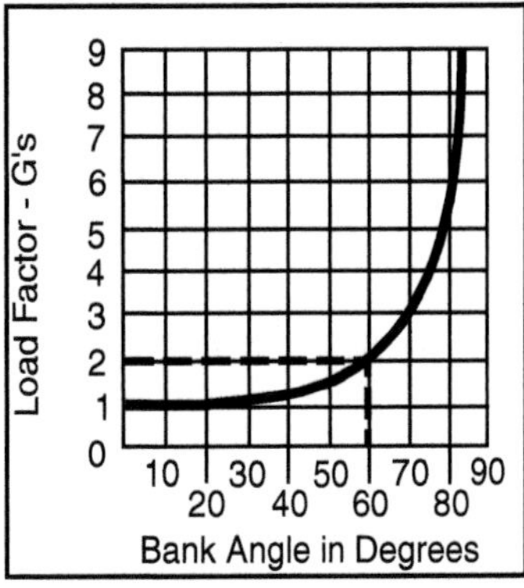

Figure 5-1. During constant altitude turns, the relationship between load factor, or G's, and bank angle is the same for all airplanes. For example, with a 60° bank, two G's are required to maintain level flight. This means the airplane's wings must support twice the weight of the airplane and its contents, although the actual weight of the airplane does not increase.

LOAD FACTOR AND STALL SPEED

You can easily stall an airplane in a turn at a higher-than-normal airspeed. As the angle of bank increases in level turns, you must increase the angle of attack to maintain altitude. As you increase the angle of bank, the stall speed also increases. [Figure 5-2]

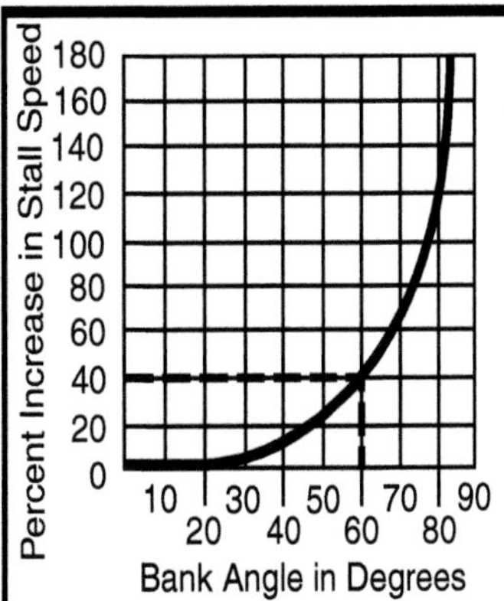

Figure 5-2. If you attempt to maintain altitude during a turn by increasing the angle of attack, the stall speed increases. The percent of increase is moderate with small bank angles. However, once you increase the bank angle beyond 45°, the percent of increase rises rapidly. For example, in a 60°, constant-altitude bank, the stall speed increases by 40%; a 75° bank increases stall speed by 100%.

OVERBANKING TENDENCY

As you enter a turn and increase the angle of bank, you may notice the tendency of the airplane to continue rolling into an even steeper bank, even though you neutralize the ailerons. The **overbanking tendency** is caused by the additional lift on the outside, or raised, wing. The outside wing is traveling faster than the inside wing. This increases lift on the outside wing and tends to roll the airplane beyond the desired bank angle.

USE OF POWER

Normally, you add power as the bank angle approaches 45°. Even when you apply power, the airspeed usually decreases and you must apply considerable back pressure to maintain altitude. You can use the trim to help relieve control wheel pressure in the turn, but you must remember to change the trim again as you complete the turn and rollout to straight-and-level flight.

2. Establishes the manufacturer's recommended airspeed or if one is not stated, a safe airspeed not to exceed V_A.

- Maneuvering speed, V_A, represents the maximum speed at which you can stall the airplane or apply full and abrupt control movement without causing structural damage.
- V_A typically changes with changes in gross weight. As gross weight increases, V_A increases, and as gross weight decreases, V_A decreases. The reason for this is that an aircraft operating at lighter weights is subject to more rapid acceleration from gusts and turbulence.
- To determine V_A for your aircraft, consult the aircraft's POH.
- V_A in your aircraft __________ kts at __________ lbs.

3. Rolls into a coordinated 360° turn; maintains a 45° bank.

- Prior to beginning the maneuver, you should align the aircraft with a section line or road. This will help you track your progress into the turn.
- Note your heading before entering the turn.
- Roll into a coordinated 45° banked turn; however, don't roll in too rapidly or you may have difficulty establishing the proper pitch attitude.
- To acheive the proper roll-in rate, begin counting as you enter the turn. It should take approximately seven seconds to reach 45°.
- Additional power may be required to maintain airspeed.

4. Performs the task in the opposite direction, as specified by the examiner.

- After completing a 360° turn, you should roll into a turn in the opposite direction as directed by the examiner.

5. Divides attention between airplane control and orientation.

- Use both visual and instrument references throughout the maneuver.
- Use visual references to establish the proper pitch attitude while periodically cross-checking the instruments.
- You must maintain a constant awareness of the aircraft's altitude, airspeed, bank angle, and location in the turn.

6. Maintains the entry altitude, ± 100 feet (30 meters), and airspeed, ± 10 knots, ± 5°; and rolls out on the entry heading, ±10°.

- Use a combination of bank and pitch adjustments to maintain altitude during the turn.
- Use power to maintain your desired airspeed.
- Once established in the turn, increase or decrease the bank as necessary to maintain altitude. Maintain a bank angle between 40° and 50° throughout the maneuver.
- As you roll out of the turn, you must decrease pitch and power as required to maintain your desired altitude and airspeed.
- The rollout should be timed so that you reach wings level at the same heading you began.
- As a rule of thumb, you should lead the rollout 20°.

PROCEDURE

Always clear the area by performing clearing turns before any maneuver.

Altitude __________ Airspeed __________

1 Roll-in — Moderate rate

2 Bank angle — Maintain __________°

3 Elevator pressure — As required to maintain altitude

4 Power — __________ (RPM, MAP)

5 Rollout — Lead the rollout point by __________°

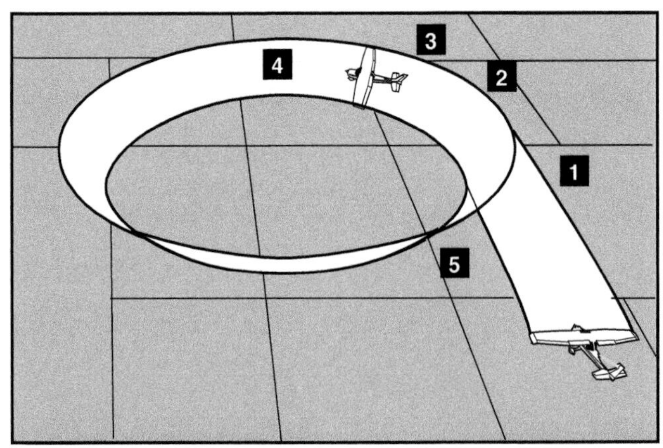

COMMON ERRORS

1. **Gain or loss of altitude during entry.**

   Cause: Back pressure applied improperly.

   Solution: Begin applying back pressure when you pass through 30° of bank.

2. **Gain or loss of altitude during the turn.**

   Cause: Not dividing your attention between outside and instrument references.

   Solution: Use outside references to establish the pitch attitude and cross-check the instruments to verify you are maintaining altitude.

3. **Loss of orientation.**

   Cause: Fixating on the nose of the aircraft.

   Solution: Beginning the manuver with the aircraft aligned with roads or section lines helps you maintain orientation.

4. **Gaining altitude when reversing the turn.**

   Cause: Not releasing back pressure when you roll out of one turn and into another.

   Solution: Release back pressure as you roll outof the first turn and increase back pressure as you approach 30° of bank on the second turn.

EXERCISES

1. The airplane turns because of the ____________ component of lift.

2. As you roll into a steep turn, drag ____________, requiring an ________in power to maintain airspeed.

3. If a fully loaded airplane weighs 2,100 pounds, what is the approximate weight the wings must support during a constant altitude turn with 60° of bank?

   a. 2,100 lbs.
   b. 3,150 lbs.
   c. 4,200 lbs.
   d. 5,250 lbs.

4. In a utility category airplane, _________ is the maximum number of positive G's the aircraft is stressed for.

5. Overbanking tendency is caused by the increased amont of lift being produced by the_________ wing as it moves through the air at a _________ speed.

SAMPLE ORAL QUESTIONS

1. As an airplane enters a turn, one component of lift acts vertically to oppose weight, while another acts horzontally, To maintain altitude, you increase lift by increasing back pressure until the vertical component of lift equals weight. The horizontal component of lift called centripetal force, is directed inward toward the center of rotation. It is this center-seeking force which causes the airplane to turn. Centripetal force is opposed by centrifugal force, which acts outward from the center of rotation. When the opposing forces are balanced, the airplane maintains a constant rate of turn, without gaining or losing altitude.

1. Describe the forces acting on an airplane in a turn.

____

____

____

____

____

____

2. Explain what causes overbanking tendency.

2. As you enter a turn, the airplane tends to continue rolling into a steeper bank, even though you neutralize the ailerons. This overbanking tendency is caused by the additional lift on the outside, or raised, wing. The outside wing is traveling faster than the inside wing. This increase lift on the outside wing and tends to roll the airplane beyond the desired bank angle.

3. Explain the relationship between V_A and aircraft weight.

3. As aircraft weight increases, V_A increaases. Likewise, when aircraft weight decreases, V_A also decreases.

4. What is the relationship between angle of bank and stall speed?

4. As the angle of bank increases in level turns, you must increase the angle of attack to maintain altitude. As you increase the angle of bank the stall speed also increases. The percent of increase in stall speed is fairly moderate with shallow bank angles — less than 45°. However, once you increase the bank angle beyond 45°, the percent of increse in the stall speed rises rapidly. For example, in a 60° constant-altitude bank, the stall speed increses by 40%; a 75° bank increases stall speed by 100%.

ADDITIONAL QUESTIONS

5. Why is power required when making a turn?
6. What is the definition of maneuvering speed (V_A)?

EXERCISE ANSWERS

1. horizontal
2. increases, increase
3. c
4. 4.4G's
5. outside, higher

REFERENCES

JEPPESEN:

Private Pilot Manual/Video – Chapter 3C

Private Pilot Maneuvers/Video – Maneuvers 9 and 21

FAA:

Airplane Flying Handbook (FAA-H-8083-3)

Pilot's Operating Handbook and FAA-Approved Airplane Flight Manual

CHAPTER 6

GROUND REFERENCE MANEUVERS

A. TASK: RECTANGULAR COURSE (ASEL and ASES)

REFERENCE: FAA-H-8083-3

Objective: To determine that the applicant:

1. Exhibits knowledge of the elements related to a rectangular course.
2. Selects a suitable reference area.
3. Plans the maneuver so as to enter a left or right pattern, 600 to 1,000 feet AGL (180 to 300 meters) at an appropriate distance from the selected reference area, 45° to the downwind leg.
4. Applies adequate wind-drift correction during straight-and-turning flight to maintain a constant ground track around the rectangular reference area.
5. Divides attention between airplane control and the ground track and while maintaining coordinated flight.
6. Maintains altitude, ±100 feet (30 meters); maintains airspeed, ±10 knots.

Objective: To determine that the applicant:

1. Exhibits knowledge of the elements related to a rectangular course.

RECTANGULAR COURSE

A rectangular course simulates a traffic pattern and helps you develop the skills needed to fly a uniform traffic pattern. This maneuver requires you to combine several factors, including dividing your attention between flying the airplane and following a prescribed flight path, and compensating for the effects of wind.

The first step in flying any ground reference maneuver is to determine the wind direction and speed. There are several ways you can do this. For example, prior to departure, you should obtain the wind direction and speed on the surface as well as aloft. Then, as you approach the practice area, verify the direction and velocity of the wind by looking for visual cues such as blowing smoke or dust, advancing wave patterns on water and grain fields, or blowing rows of trees. You should also notice your airplane's drift and crab angle. Another method is to fly a 360° constant airspeed, constant bank turn. Your path over the ground will provide valuable information about the wind. [Figure 6-1]

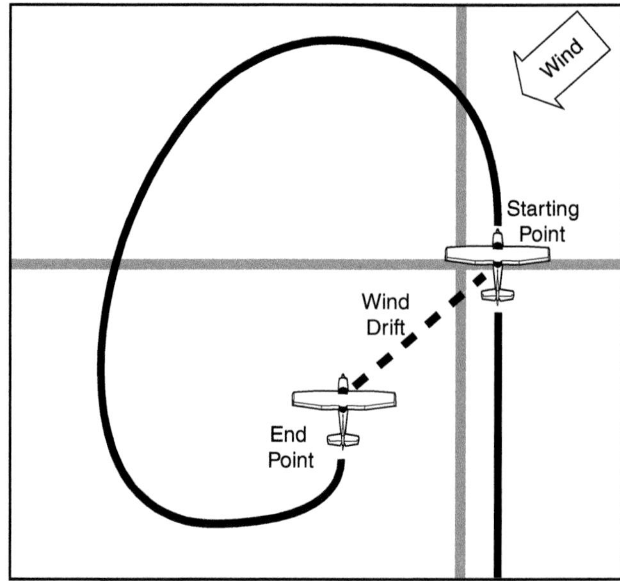

Figure 6-1. The difference between the starting point and the ending point (the wind drift) of a 360° constant airspeed, constant bank turn will indicate the direction and strength of the wind.

2. Selects a suitable reference area.

SELECTING A FIELD

When selecting a field to fly a rectangular course, you should pick one that is clear of other traffic and populated areas as well as have a suitable emergency landing site within power-off gliding distance. The field should have sides between one-half and one mile in length. These dimensions are rough guidelines, but the shape should be square or rectangular within the approximate limits given.

3. Plans the maneuver so as to enter a left or right pattern, 600 to 1,000 feet AGL (180 to 300 meters) at an appropriate distance from the selected reference area, 45° to the downwind leg.

BEGINNING THE MANEUVER

Prior to beginning the maneuver, you should establish the aircraft at an altitude between 600 and 1,000 feet AGL. You begin the maneuver on a 45° angle to the downwind leg. Once established on the downwind leg, the airplane should follow a ground track that is parallel to the side of the field. Typically, the distance from the field boundary is approximately one-quarter to one-half mile.

4. Applies adequate wind-drift correction during straight-and-turning flight to maintain a constant ground track around the rectangular reference area.

CORRECTING FOR WIND

Once established on course, you must apply the proper wind correction (crab) on each leg so your ground track remains rectangular. However, when flying directly downwind, no crab is necessary. You also must compensate for varying groundspeeds. For example, upon completion of the downwind leg, your groundspeed is highest, requiring a greater angle of bank on the turn to crosswind. As you proceed through the first turn, the crosswind component changes and you must adjust the amount of crab used to compensate. Your greatest heading change and steepest bank will occur when transitioning from downwind to crosswind leg.

As you roll out of the turn on the crosswind leg, the aircraft must be crabbed into the wind. If this isn't done, the aircraft will drift away from the field. Since the aircraft is in a crab on crosswind, the amount of heading change required to make the turn to upwind is less than 90°.

When on the upwind leg, and flying directly into the wind, no crab is required. Upon completion of the upwind leg, your groundspeed is lowest, requiring a shallow angle of bank to the second crosswind leg.

Since the aircraft must be established in a crab immediately on the second crosswind leg, less than 90° of turn is required. As you approach the turn to downwind, you will have to turn more than 90°. Furthermore, your groundspeed will increase in the turn requiring you to increase the angle of bank throughout the turn.

As you gain experience flying a rectangular course, you will practice the maneuver in differing wind conditions. [Figure 6-2]

5. Divides attention between airplane control and the ground track and while maintaining coordinated flight.

- You must effectively divide your attention between the aircraft and outside references. Do not focus on one item.
- To aid in aircraft control, set the power and trim the aircraft for level flight prior to beginning the maneuver.
- You must maintain a constant awareness of the aircraft's altitude, airspeed, bank angle, coordination, and location throughout the maneuver.

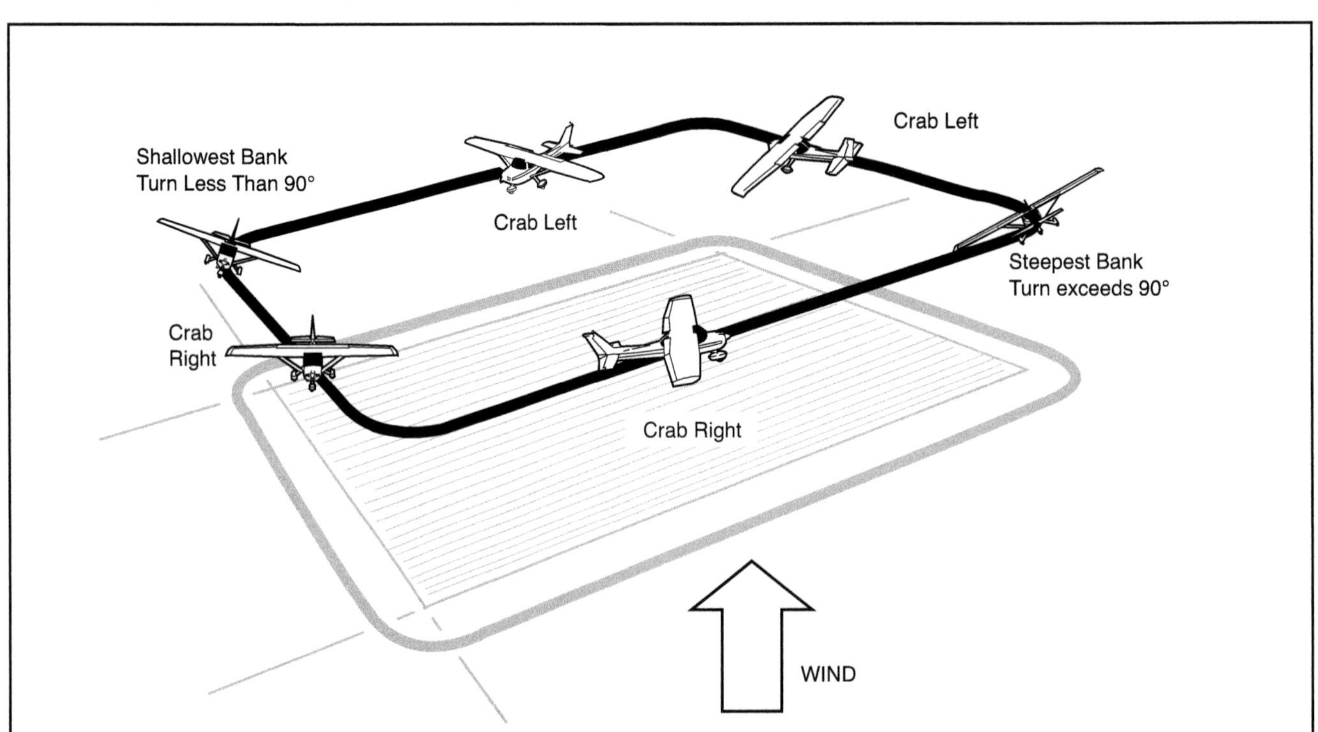

Figure 6-2. The complexity of the rectangular course maneuver is increased when the wind blows diagonally across the rectangular course. In this situation, your greatest heading change and steepest bank occur when transitioning from the two legs on which a quartering tailwind exists.

6. Maintains altitude, ± 100 feet (30 meters); maintains airspeed, ± 10 knots.

- You must divide your attention between looking outside and scanning the instrument panel.
- Use outside references to establish the appropriate pitch altitude and periodically check the altimeter to verify you are maintaining altitude.
- Set the power prior to entering the maneuver so airspeed remains constant.

PROCEDURE

Always clear the area by performing clearing turns before any maneuver.

Altitude _____ Airspeed _____

Power _____ (RPM, MAP)

1 First track — Establish wind correction angle, if required

2 Downwind to crosswind — Maximum bank ___°, more than 90° of turn

3 Crosswind to upwind — Normal bank, less than 90° of turn

4 Upwind to crosswind — Shallow bank, less than 90° of turn

5 Crosswind to downwind — Increase to maximum bank, more than 90° of turn

COMMON ERRORS

1. Turning Errors.

Cause: Undershooting a leg when turning into a headwind, or overshooting when turning to a tailwind.

Solution: You must take into consideration the groundspeed as well as the amount of heading change required when transitioning from one leg to another.

2. Insufficient or excessive wind correction angles.

Cause: Failure to compensate properly for wind drift.

Solution: After you establish a crab angle, check the ground track and modify the aircraft's crab angle as necessary.

3. Poor Coordination.

Cause: Improper use of ailerons and rudder during turns, and attempting to crab by use of the rudder only.

Solution: Use a combination of aileron and rudder during turns and when establishing the appropriate crab angle. You should also check the inclinometer once established.

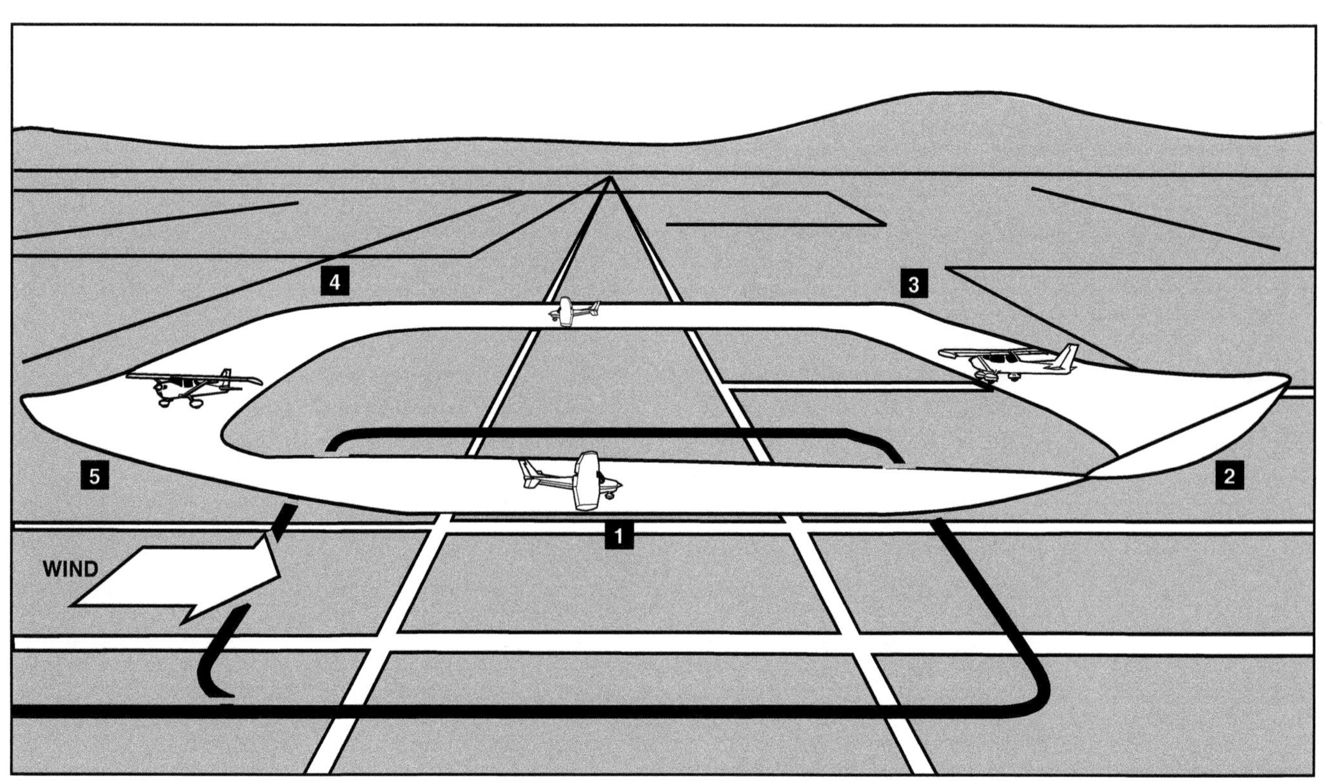

4. Gain or Loss of Altitude.

Cause: Failure to use visual references and set a correct pitch attitude.

Solution: Use outside references to set the correct pitch attitude, and periodically check the altimeter to verify your altitude.

Cause: Improper use of trim.

Solution: Relieve excessive control wheel pressures by trimming the aircraft prior to beginning the maneuver.

EXERCISES

1. A rectangular course simulates a ________________.
2. The rectangular pattern should be flown at an altitude between _____ and _____ feet AGL.
3. When flying a rectangular course, your angle of bank should not exceed _____°.
4. The amount of bank used to turn from one leg to the next depends on the aircraft's __________.
5. You should enter the rectangular pattern mid-field on the __________ leg at a ____° angle.
6. The turn from the downwind leg to the crosswind leg requires the _______ (steepest, shallowest) bank angle.

SAMPLE ORAL QUESTIONS

1. When choosing a suitable field to fly a rectangular pattern, what are some things you should look for?

1. The field should be well away from other traffic and populated areas. The sides of the field should be between one-half mile and one mile in length. These dimensions are rough guidelines, but the shape should be square or rectangular. You should also select an area that affords the opportunity for a safe emergency landing.

2. Explain the relationship between the aircraft groundspeed and the angle of bank required to transition from one leg of the rectangular course to the next.

2. The higher the groundspeed, the greater the bank angle required to make the turn to the next leg. Furthermore, as groundspeed decreases, the bank angle decreases.

ADDITIONAL QUESTIONS

3. What is the purpose of flying a rectangular pattern?
4. Explain how your desired ground track is maintained.

EXERCISE ANSWERS

1. traffic pattern
2. 600, 1,000
3. 45
4. groundspeed
5. downwind, 45
6. steepest

REFERENCES

JEPPESEN:

Private Pilot Manual/Video – Chapter 3C
Private Pilot Maneuvers/Video – Maneuver 22

FAA:

Airplane Fkying Handbook (FAA-H-8083-3)

B. TASK: S-TURNS (ASEL and ASES)

REFERENCE: FAA-H-8083-3

Objective: To determine that the applicant:

1. Exhibits knowledge of the elements related to S-turns.
2. Selects a suitable ground reference line.
3. Plans the maneuver so as to enter at 600 to 1000 feet (180 to 300 meters) AGL, perpendicular to the selected reference line.
4. Applies adequate wind-drift correction to track a constant radius turn on each side of the selected reference line.
5. Reverses the direction of turn directly over the selected reference line.
6. Divides attention between airplane control and the ground track and while maintaining coordinated flight.
7. Maintains altitude, ±100 feet (30 meters); maintains airspeed, ±10 knots.

Objective: To determine that the applicant:

1. Exhibits knowledge of the elements related to S-turns.

S-TURNS

The S-turn is a useful tool for teaching you proper coordination and altitude control while dividing your attention between your ground track and airplane control. S-turns also require you to develop the skills necessary to follow an assigned ground track and arrive at specified points on assigned headings, much like turns in the traffic pattern.

The objective of S-turns is to fly two half circles of equal size on opposite sides of a selected reference line. To do this you must vary the bank angle in each turn to compensate for wind drift and changing groundspeed. The first step in flying any ground reference maneuver is to determine the wind direction and speed. For additional information on how to determine wind direction and speed, refer to Chapter 6, Task A on page 6-1.

2. Selects a suitable ground reference line.

SELECTING A REFERENCE LINE

The most common reference lines used for conducting S-turns are roads and section lines. When choosing a reference line, it should be well away from other traffic and populated areas. Furthermore, the reference line should lie perpendicular to the wind. The terrain surrounding the reference line should be suitable for executing an emergency landing.

3. Plans the maneuver so as to enter at 600 to 1000 feet (180 to 300 meters) AGL, perpendicular to the selected reference line.

- Begin the maneuver at an altitude between 600 and 1,000 feet AGL. It is helpful to select an altitude that is easily read on the altimeter, such as 2,000 feet or 3,500 feet.
- Enter the maneuver perpendicular to the selected reference line on a downwind heading.
- The first 180° turn in the maneuver is to the left, followed by a 180° turn to the right.

4. Applies adequate wind-drift correction to track a constant radius turn on each side of the selected reference line.

CORRECTING FOR WIND

The key to successfully completing S-turns is being able to visualize the maneuver and compensate for wind. For the example, as you approach the reference line, visualize the half circle ground track you will be making. Then, when you cross the reference line, immediately roll into a bank and follow your visualized ground track. Since your groundspeed is highest at the beginning of the maneuver, a steep bank angle is required. As you turn past the 90° point the aircraft's groundspeed begins to decrease, requiring you to gradually reduce the bank angle to track a symmetrical half circle.

5. Reverses the direction of turn directly over the selected reference line.

- As you approach the 180° point, time your roll-out so the airplane reaches wings level when crossing the reference line. As you begin to turn in the opposite direction, glance at the instruments to verify that you are maintaining the desired altitude and airspeed.

As you cross the reference line a second time, the aircraft is flying into the wind. To compensate for the slower groundspeed, you must use a shallow bank to maintain your desired turn radius. As you pass the 90° point upwind of the reference line the aircraft's groundspeed begins to increase, requiring you to gradually increase the bank angle until you roll-out to wings level over the reference line. [Figure 6-3]

6. Divides attention between airplane control and the ground track and while maintaining coordinated flight.

- You must effectively divide your attention between aircraft control and outside references.

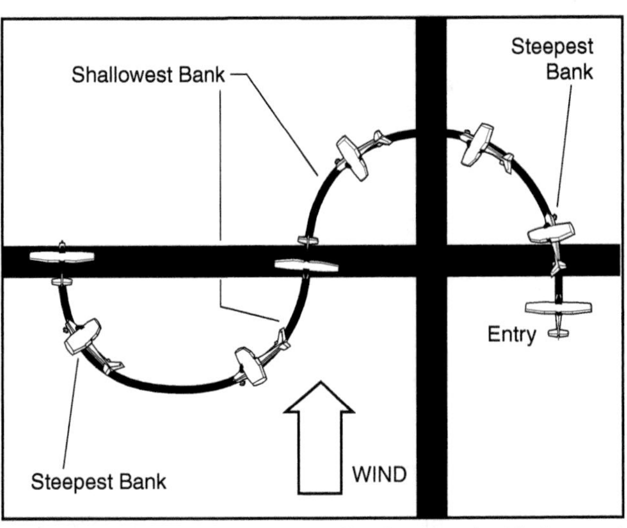

Figure 6-3. The shallowest angle of bank occurs just before and after the airplane crosses the road into the wind. The steepest bank occurs just before and after the airplane crosses the road downwind.

- To aid in aircraft control, set the power and trim the aircraft for level flight prior to beginning the maneuver.
- You must maintain a constant awareness of the air-craft's altitude, airspeed, bank angle, coordination, and location throughout the maneuver.

7. Maintains altitude, ± 100 feet (30 meters); maintains airspeed, ± 10 knots.

- You must divide your attention between looking outside and scanning the instrument panel.
- Use outside references to establish the appropriate pitch altitude and periodically check the altimeter to verify you are maintaining altitude.
- Set power prior to entering the maneuver so airspeed remains constant.

PROCEDURE

Always clear the area by performing clearing turns before any maneuver.

Altitude _____ Airspeed _____
Power _____ (RPM, MAP)

1 Initial bank — Brisk rate to _____° maximum
2 Downwind to crosswind — Decrease bank slowly
3 Crosswind to upwind — Decrease bank to wings level crossing reference line.
4 Upwind to crosswind — Increase bank slowly in opposite direction
5 Crosswind to downwind — Increase bank slowly to maximum
6 Roll-out — Wings level crossing reference line

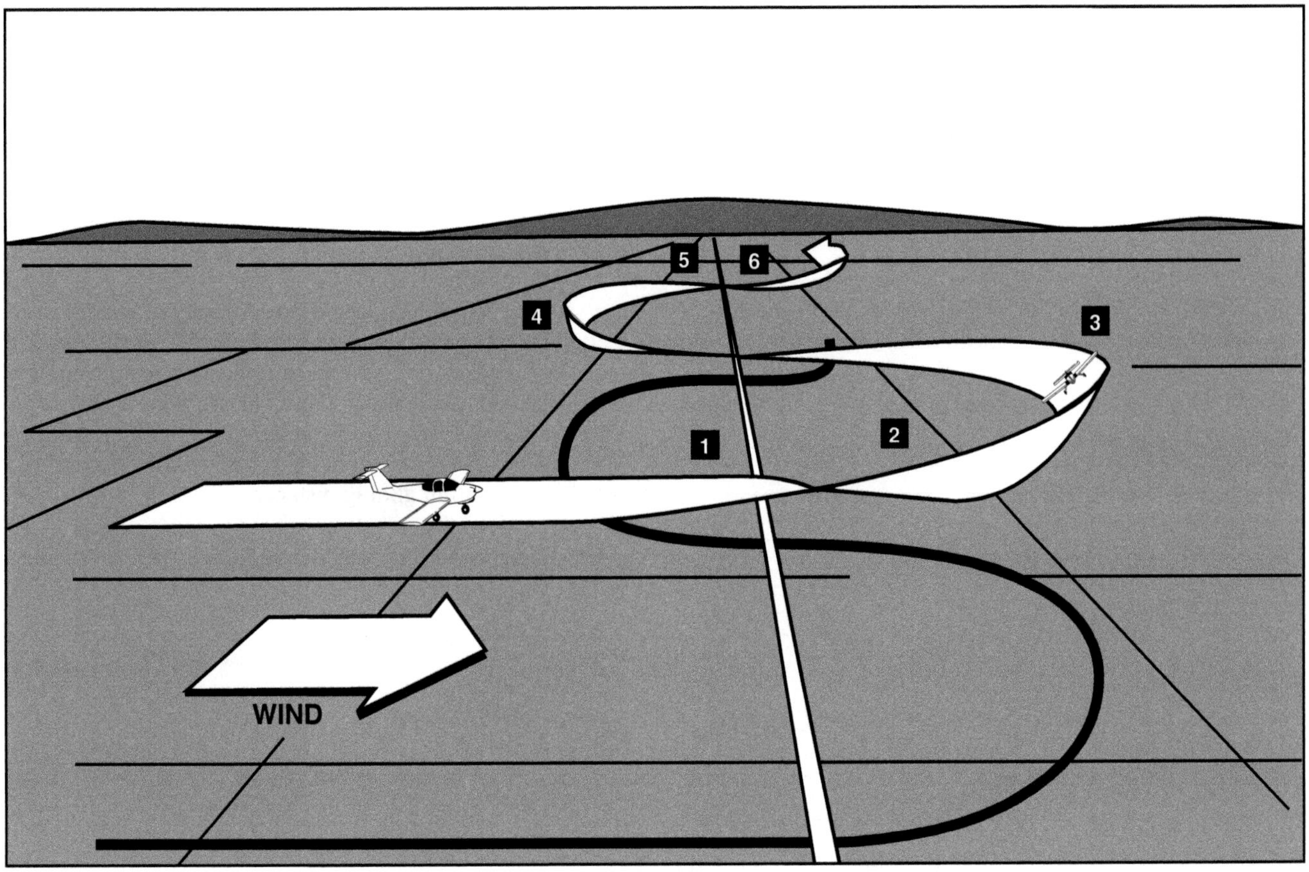

COMMON ERRORS

1. **Turns not symmetrical.**

   Cause: Not compensating properly for wind drift.

   Solution: Visualize your desired ground track, and compensate for varying groundspeeds by adjusting the aircraft's bank angle.

2. **Gain or loss of altitude and/or airspeed.**

   Cause: Not dividing your attention between aircraft control and looking outside.

   Solution: Set the pitch attitude to maintain level flight using visual references and establish points along the S-turns to remind you to scan the instruments.

   Cause: Improper use of trim.

   Solution: Relieve excessive control wheel pressures by trimming the aircraft prior to beginning the maneuver.

3. **Improper bank application.**

   Cause: Not understanding where to use a steep or shallow bank.

   Solution: Remember: high groundspeed — steep bank, slow groundspeed — shallow bank.

EXERCISE

1. The reference line selected for S-turns should be _____ (parallel, perpendicular) to the wind.
2. ____ (True,False) You should begin S-turns while flying downwind.
3. The first in the series of S-turns should be done to the _____ (left, right).
4. The maximum amount of bank you may use is ____°.
5. The steepest bank occurs immediately ____ (upwind, downwind) of the reference line.

SAMPLE ORAL QUESTIONS

1. Explain the relationship between groundspeed and the bank angle required to maintain a constant radius turn.

____

____

____

____

____

____

2. What factors should be considered when picking a reference line for conducting S-turns?

____

____

____

____

____

____

____

____

____

____

____

1. As groundspeed increases, the bank angle required to maintain a constant radius turn also increases. Furthermore, as groundspeed decreases, the bank angle required to maintain a constant radius decreases.

2. Three main factors should be considered when selecting a reference line. These include: air traffic, ground population, and suitable terrain. You should always select a reference line that is clear of local air traffic, congested areas, and obstructions. The reference line should also have suitable terrain for an emergency landing within gliding distance.

ADDITIONAL QUESTIONS

3. What is the purpose of practicing S-turns?

EXERCISE ANSWERS

1. perpendicular
2. True
3. left
4. 45
5. downwind

REFERENCES

JEPPESEN:

Private Pilot Manual/Video – Chapter 3C
Private Pilot Maneuvers/Video – Maneuver 23

FAA:

Airplane Flying Handbook (FAA-H-8083-3)

C. TASK: TURNS AROUND A POINT (ASEL and ASES)

REFERENCE: FAA-H-8083-3

Objective: To determine that the applicant:

1. Exhibits knowledge of the elements related to turns around a point.
2. Selects a suitable ground reference point.
3. Plans the maneuver so as to enter at 600 to 1000 feet (180 to 300 meters) AGL, at an appropriate distance from the reference point.
4. Applies adequate wind drift correction to track a constant radius turn around the selected reference point.
5. Divides attention between airplane control and the ground track and while maintaining coordinated flight.
6. Maintains altitude, ±100 feet (30 meters); maintains airspeed, ±10 knots.

Objective: To determine that the applicant:

1. Exhibits knowledge of the elements related to turns around a point.

TURNS AROUND A POINT

Turns around a point further refine your skills in making constant radius turns around an object on the ground while maintaining a constant altitude. The objective is to help develop your ability to divide your attention between controlling the airplane and following a predetermined ground track, all the while compensating for the effects of wind.

2. Selects a suitable ground reference point.

SELECTING A REFERENCE POINT

Always select an area that affords the opportunity for a safe emergency landing within gliding distance of the maneuver. The reference point should be prominent and easily distinguished, yet small enough to establish a definite location. The point should be in the center of an area away from livestock, buildings, or concentrations of people on the ground. Trees, isolated haystacks, or other small landmarks can be used as reference points; however, they are not as effective as intersections of roads or fence lines. By selecting a road or fence line, you can mentally project these lines to their logical intersection should the wing momentarily block your view during the maneuver. However, you should be able to perform this maneuver around any object, as designated by the examiner.

3. Plans the maneuver so as to enter at 600 to 1000 feet (180 to 300 meters) AGL, at an appropriate distance from the reference point.

- Begin the maneuver at an altitude between 600 and 1,000 feet AGL. It is helpful to select an altitude that is easily read on the altimeter, such as 3,500 feet or, 4,000 feet.
- Enter the maneuver downwind at a distance equal to radius of desired turn.
- The first turn in the maneuver is to the left.

4. Applies adequate wind-drift correction to track a constant radius turn around the selected reference point.

CORRECTING FOR WIND

As you arrive abeam the selected point on downwind to begin the maneuver, the aircraft's groundspeed is high, requiring you to roll into a 45° bank to the left. Then, carefully plan your track over the ground and vary the bank, as necessary, to maintain that track. [Figure 6-4]

As you gain experience, you should practice turns around a point in both directions. Remember, the angle of bank at any given point is dependent on the radius of the circle being flown, the wind velocity, and the groundspeed.

5. Divides attention between airplane control and the ground track and while maintaining coordinated flight.

- You must effectively divide your attention between aircraft control and outside references.
- To aid in aircraft control, set the power and trim the aircraft for level flight prior to beginning the maneuver.

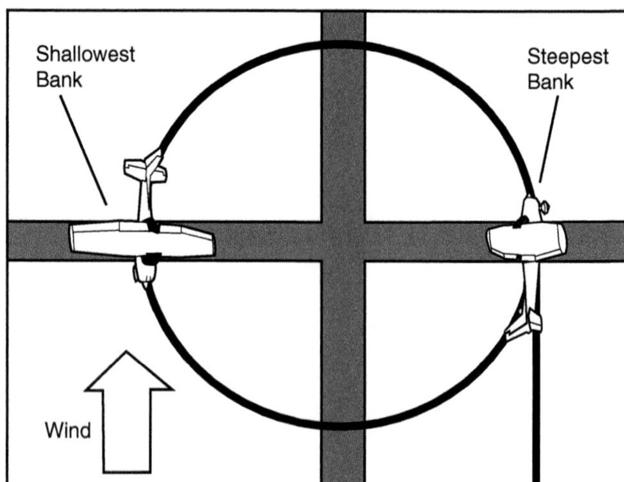

Figure 6-4. When entering this maneuver downwind, the aircraft's groundspeed is highest, requiring you to roll into the maximum bank when abeam the reference point. As you continue the turn, groundspeed decreases requiring you to decrease the angle of bank as necessary until the aircraft crosses the road into the wind. Throughout the second 180° of turn, steadily increase the angle of bank until directly downwind.

- You must maintain a constant awareness of the aircraft's altitude, airspeed, bank angle, coordination, and location throughout the maneuver.

6. Maintains altitude, ± 100 feet (30 meters); maintains airspeed, ± 10 knots.

- You must divide your attention between looking outside and scanning the instrument panel.
- Use outside references to establish the appropriate pitch attitude and periodically check the altimeter to verify you are maintaining altitude.
- Set power prior to entering the maneuver so airspeed remains constant.

PROCEDURE

Always clear the area by performing clearing turns before any maneuver.

Altitude ______, Airspeed ______
Power ______ (RPM, MAP)

1 Initial bank — Smooth roll-in rate to _____° maximum
Downwind to crosswind — Decrease bank slowly
2 Crosswind to upwind — Continue decreasing bank to
3 shallowest point
Upwind to crosswind — Increase bank slowly
4 Crosswind to downwind — Increase bank slowly to
5 maximum

COMMON ERRORS

1. **The ground track is not symmetrical.**

   Cause: Not compensating properly for changes in groundspeed.

   Solution: Visualize your desired ground track around the point and compensate for varying groundspeeds by adjusting the aircraft bank.

2. **Not maintaining assigned altitude and airspeed.**

   Cause: Not properly dividing your attention between flying the aircraft and looking outside.

   Solution: Set the pitch attitude using outside references, while monitoring ground track and cross-checking instruments.

   Cause: Improper use of trim.

   Solution: Relieve excessive control wheel pressures by trimming the aircraft prior to beginning the maneuver.

3. **Improper bank application.**

   Cause: Not understanding where to apply the steepest bank.

   Solution: Remember: high groundspeed — steep bank, slow groundspeed — shallow bank.

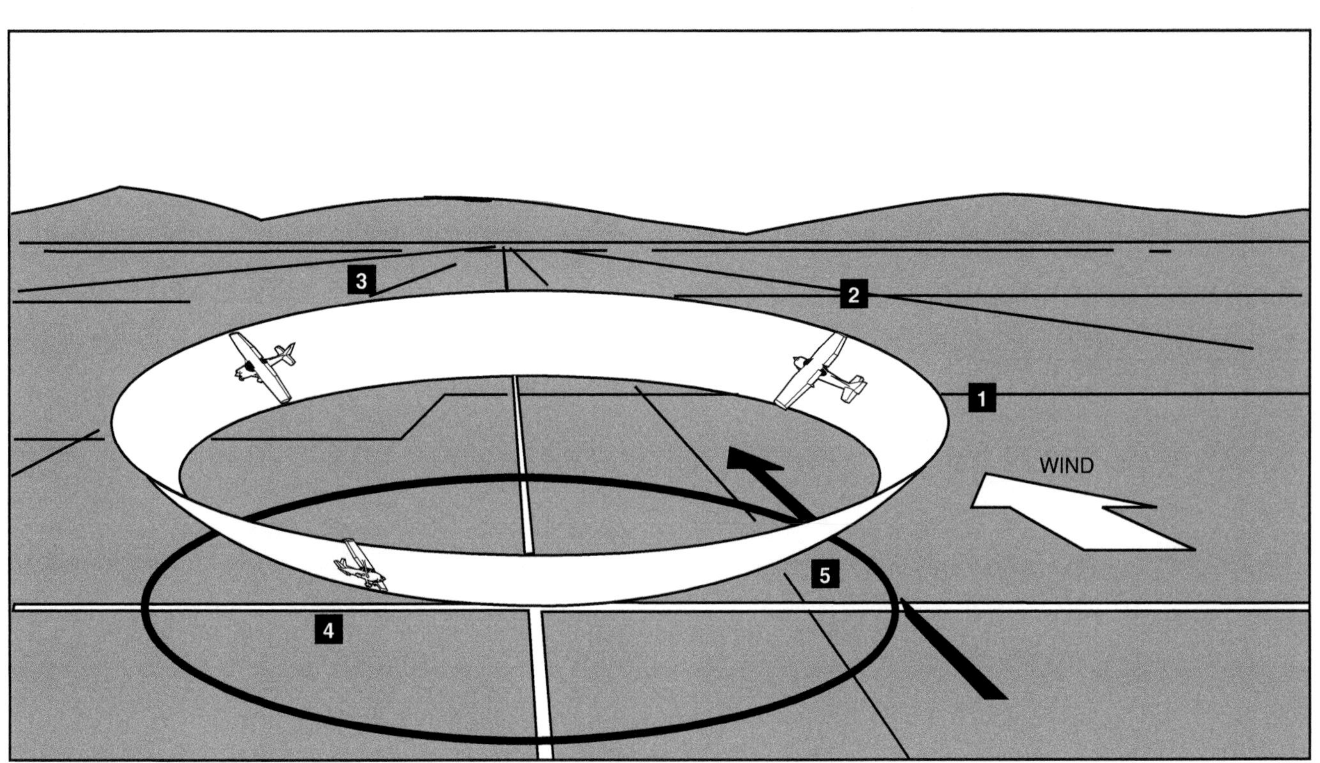

EXERCISES

1. You should begin a turn around a point from a _____ (upwind, downwind) heading.
2. The maximum angle of bank used for this maneuver is _____°.
3. The steepest bank occurs abeam the reference point when heading ___________ (upwind, downwind).
4. Turns around a point should be flown at an altitude between _____ and _____ feet AGL.

SAMPLE ORAL QUESTIONS

1. Explain the relationship between groundspeed and the bank angle required to maintain a constant radius circle around a point.

1. As groundspeed increases, the bank angle required to maintain a constant radius turn increases. As groundspeed decreases, the bank angle required to maintain a constant radius decreases.

2. What are the advantages of using a fence or road intersection as a reference point for conducting turns around a point?

2. Road or fence lines leading to an intersection allow you to mentally picture the reference point should the wing momentarily block your view.

ADDITIONAL QUESTIONS

3. What is the purpose of practicing turns around a point?

EXERCISE ANSWERS

1. downwind
2. 45
3. downwind
4. 600, 1,000

REFERENCES

JEPPESEN:

Private Pilot Manual/Video – Chapter 3C

Private Pilot Maneuvers/Video – Maneuver 24

FAA:

Airplane Flying Handbook (FAA-H-8083-3)

NAVIGATION

A. TASK: PILOTAGE AND DEAD RECKONING (ASEL and ASES)

REFERENCES: AC 61-23/FAA-H-8083-25.

Objective: To determine that the applicant:

1. Exhibits knowledge of the elements related to pilotage and dead reckoning.
2. Follows the preplanned course by reference to landmarks.
3. Identifies landmarks by relating surface features to chart symbols.
4. Navigates by means of precomputed headings, groundspeeds, and elapsed time.
5. Corrects for and records the differences between preflight groundspeed and heading calculations and those determined en route.
6. Verifies the airplane's position within three (3) nautical miles of the flight-planned route.
7. Arrives at the en route checkpoints within five (5) minutes of the initial or revised ETA and provides a destination estimate.
8. Maintains the appropriate altitude, ± 200 feet (60 meters) and headings, ±15°.

Objective: To determine that the applicant:

1. Exhibits knowledge of the elements related to pilotage and dead reckoning.

PILOTAGE

Pilotage is a form of navigation by visual reference to surface landmarks such as rivers, roads, or railroads. You compare symbols on aeronautical charts with their corresponding features on the ground. Sectional charts are designed for pilotage; they contain a detailed portrayal of terrain and man-made obstructions. Remember to always fly with current aeronautical charts, even when flying over familiar territory. Man-made obstructions are constantly changing, and an out-of-date chart could be a liability when you are trying to identify your position.

One of the advantages of pilotage is that it is relatively easy to perform and does not require special equipment. Even with the most basic airplane you can navigate by pilotage. On the other hand, pilotage has a number of disadvantages. In areas where few prominent landmarks are present, pilotage can be difficult. A direct course may be impractical if there are few good landmarks. You also may be limited by visibility. If haze, smoke, or fog reduces visibility, your ability to navigate by pilotage diminishes.

Flying by pilotage requires you to select an altitude that allows you to identify the key landmarks, or checkpoints, on your route of flight. Obviously, if you fly at too high an altitude, the selected references may be so small that you can't identify them. Conversely, flying too low also presents problems. Aside from the dangers of high terrain and tall obstructions, flying too low gives you a poor perspective for identifying landmarks except those with vertical development. In addition to weather considerations, selection of a cruising altitude depends on the terrain you are flying over, as well as the types of checkpoints available. Of course, above 3,000 feet AGL, you must comply with VFR cruising altitudes.

SELECTING CHECKPOINTS

The checkpoints used to determine your position along a route of flight are useful only if they can be positively identified. When selecting checkpoints, you must attempt to pick those with distinctive features that will be easily recognizable from the air.

There are few rules to follow when selecting checkpoints, since each route you travel is different. However, one general guideline is to avoid using any single landmark as a sole reference. For example, you should not rely solely on a water tower to identify a small town, since other small towns in the area may have water towers, too. When flying by pilotage, it is important to take a look at the "whole picture." Whenever possible, compare your selected checkpoint against a combination of ground features so you can identify your position positively.

Intersecting lines, such as highways, railroad tracks, powerlines, or rivers normally provide good references for position identification. However, it is important to compare them with the surrounding terrain and landmarks.

Although primary roads are usually good checkpoints, secondary roads can be deceiving. Aeronautical charts do not include every road. Also, keep in mind that roads frequently require repair or alteration, and may change their appearance.

Rivers often provide excellent landmarks, especially when they have significant bends or curves; however, they may be somewhat deceptive. Some rivers have numerous tributaries, and the main body may be difficult to follow. During a flood stage, the appearance from the air may be significantly different from the chart pattern. During a drought, on the other hand, the body of water shown on a sectional chart may actually be a dried-up riverbed. Lakes usually provide good references for determining your position. However, as with rivers, you should be aware of seasonal variations. In many parts of the country, hundreds of small lakes exist within close proximity, and identifying a particular one can be extremely difficult.

Cities can have excellent landmark value. The yellow pattern printed on charts provides you with a good representation of the actual size and shape of the city when viewed from the air. You should be careful when using small towns and villages as checkpoints, though, because they often resemble one another from aloft.

FOLLOWING A ROUTE

There are two basic approaches to flying by pilotage. The first is to follow a major topographical feature, such as a river or highway. As the direction of the landmark changes, you simply alter your course to fly along its route. Although this is an easy means of navigating, a primary disadvantage is that a direct flight is usually impossible, so the length of your flight is increased. An alternative to an indirect route is to draw a straight line on your chart between the departure and destination airports and select the best available checkpoints along that route. A straight-line course not only decreases your time enroute, but also allows you to perform more accurate time, speed, and distance calculations.

ORIENTATION

Because pilotage is a visual means of navigation, maintaining an accurate orientation between your intended and actual route of flight is fundamental. If you become disoriented over unfamiliar or featureless terrain, determining your position can be difficult. The key to preventing disorientation is taking the time to plan your flight adequately.

Preparation for a cross-country flight by pilotage begins by studying the charts for the area you will be flying over. Use a straightedge to lay out a direct course between your departure and destination airports. With the course line drawn, you can select suitable checkpoints along your route. As you select a checkpoint, mark it on the chart so it will be usable when airborne. This is important even for short routes. [Figure 7-1]

After laying out your course and marking your checkpoints, carefully study the entire route. One of the most significant items in the example is the Class D airspace at Mansfield Lahm Airport that is outlined by the dashed line on the chart. If you intend to fly through the Class D airspace you must contact the tower and request permission to transit the area. However, if you choose to avoid the Class D airspace you can either climb above its vertical limit or alter your planned route. To overfly the airspace, you must climb above 3,800 feet MSL, the charted vertical limit. In addition, if you fly higher than 4,297 feet MSL you must comply with VFR cruising altitude rules.

DEAD RECKONING

Although pilotage can be used as a sole means of navigation, it's often used in combination with another form of navigation known as dead reckoning. **Dead reckoning** is a technique of navigation based on calculations of time, speed, distance, and direction. The four variables required

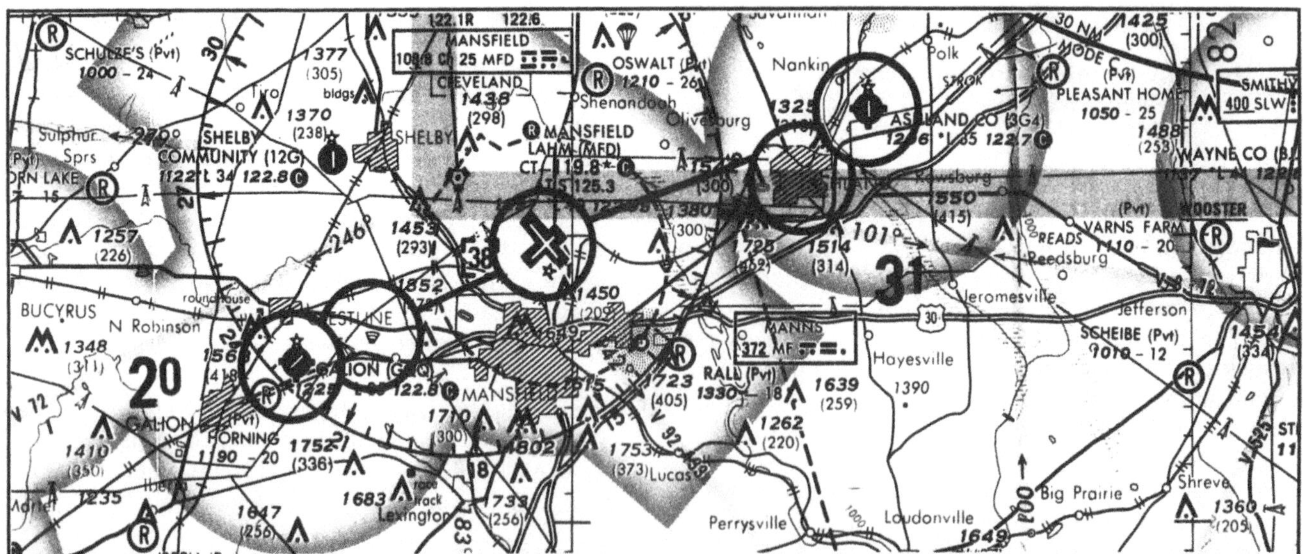

Figure 7-1. The outdoor theater northeast of Galion Airport between the two primary roads is a good selection for the first checkpoint. The Mansfield Lahm Airport is also a good checkpoint. The airport symbology alerts you to the fact that Class D airspace exists when the tower is in operation. The city of Ashland is the final checkpoint before you land.

to solve for heading and groundspeed are true airspeed, course, wind direction, and wind speed. These values allow you to predict the movement of your airplane along the intended route of flight.

FLIGHT PLANNING

The first step in dead reckoning is to draw a line on the chart between your departure and destination airports. Then, use a plotter to measure the distance. Your next step is to measure the true course. When doing this, select a line of longitude that is near the midpoint of the route. However, sometimes you will draw a course line that does not cross a meridian. Instead of extending the line until it finally crosses a line of longitude, you can use a line of latitude.

Another problem occurs when your departure and destination airports are on opposite sides of the same chart. Since the north and south sides depict adjacent areas, occasionally you will have to draw your course line from one side to the other. In order to help you extend this line accurately, an instruction guide is printed in the chart margin. To familiarize yourself with this procedure, you should practice it on a regular basis.

TRUE AND MAGNETIC VALUES

Because the course line drawn on a chart is in relation to true north and you normally fly by magnetic reference, you will need to correct for the variation between the two. You can do this by adjusting true course for variation to get magnetic course, or by adjusting true heading for variation to get magnetic heading. Typically, you solve for true heading first, since winds aloft are given in true direction and you know the true course. Then, you apply variation to true heading to get magnetic heading.

After plotting your true course, determine the effects of wind at your planned flight altitude. You'll need the winds aloft forecast from your preflight planning to estimate your true heading and groundspeed. As an example, assume you are making a flight between Kimball Airport and Sidney Airport. Use the following values for calculating your true heading and groundspeed:

True airspeed .... 105 kts.
True course .... 099°
True wind direction .... 310°
Wind speed .... 15 kts.

Solving the wind problem with a flight computer results in a true heading of 095° for your trip. This is the true course minus the wind correction angle. Your groundspeed is 118 knots.

NAVIGATION LOG

To help with your flight planning and enroute calculations, use a navigation log to record data pertaining to your trip. The **navigation log** allows you to list information in a systematic fashion and also helps you keep track of the progress of your flight.

For example, you can use the navigation log for determining your time enroute. By knowing the distance between checkpoints, along with your anticipated groundspeed, you can calculate the estimated time enroute (ETE) between them. While airborne, you can calculate your actual time enroute (ATE) and compare it to your estimated time to keep track of your flight's progress. If the actual winds aloft are substantially different than forecast, you can use your flight computer to recalculate your estimated time enroute and the fuel needed to reach your destination.

The key to computing ETE and fuel required during flight is an accurate groundspeed check. You can do this anywhere along a direct route. All you have to do is accurately record how long it takes to fly a known distance. For instance, if you fly 10 nautical miles in six minutes while maintaining a constant heading and indicated airspeed, your groundspeed is 100 knots. [Figure 7-2 on page 7- 4]

2. Follows the preplanned course by reference to landmarks.

- Once airborne, you will be expected to remain on course by referencing the course plotted on your sectional.
- This requires you to divide your attention between aircraft control and navigating.

3. Identifies landmarks by relating surface features to chart symbols.

- During the flight test, the examiner will periodically ask you to identify your position on the sectional.
- When doing this, point out symbols on the sectional chart that correspond to visible landmarks.

4. Navigates by means of precomputed headings, groundspeeds, and elapsed time.

- In addition to referencing your sectional, you will be expected to navigate by utilizing the heading, groundspeed, and elapsed time information contained in your flight log.

5. Corrects for and records the differences between preflight groundspeed and heading calculations and those determined en route.

- If your calculated fuel usage, groundspeed, or heading differ from actual, you must record the difference.
- Once a difference is noted, you must recalculate fuel usage, groundspeed, and heading information.

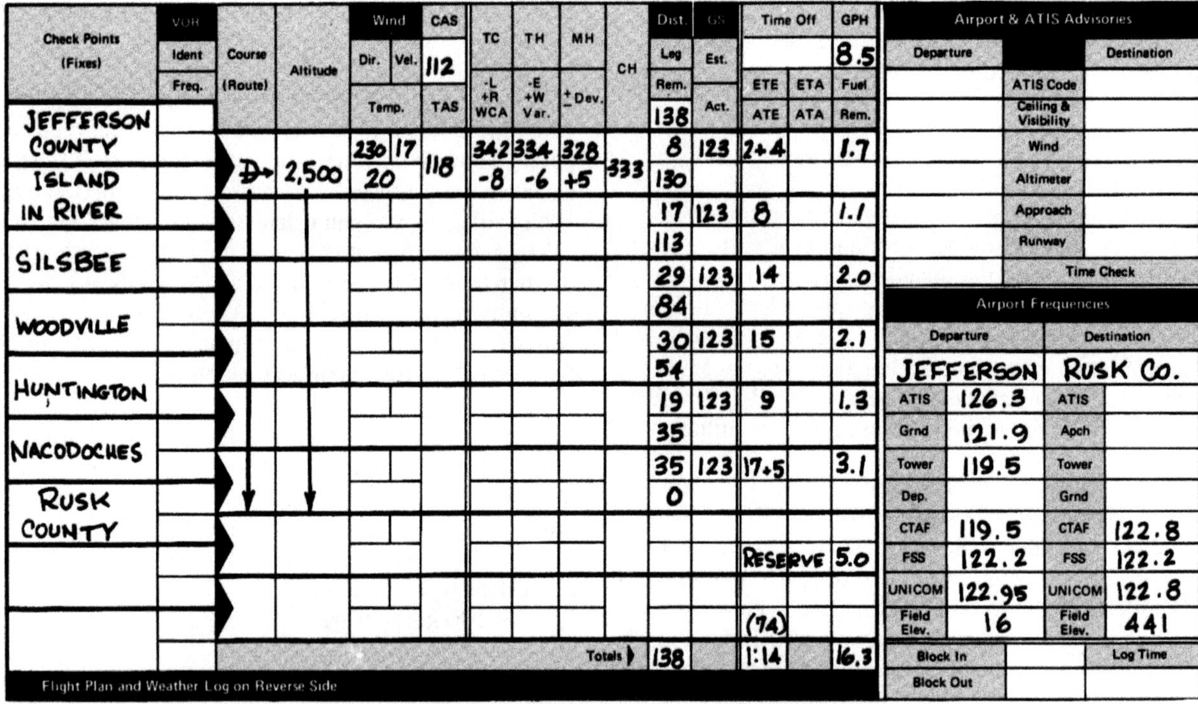

Check Points (Fixes)	VOR Ident / Freq.	Course (Route)	Altitude	Wind Dir. / Vel. / Temp.	CAS / TAS	TC / -L +R WCA	TH / -E +W Var.	MH / ±Dev.	CH	Dist. Leg / Rem.	GS Est. / Act.	Time Off ETE / ATE	ETA / ATA	GPH / Fuel / Rem.
JEFFERSON COUNTY					112					138				8.5
ISLAND IN RIVER		D→	2,500	230 / 17 / 20	118	342 / -8	334 / -6	328 / +5	333	8 / 130	123	2+4		1.7
SILSBEE										17 / 113	123	8		1.1
WOODVILLE										29 / 84	123	14		2.0
HUNTINGTON										30 / 54	123	15		2.1
NACODOCHES										19 / 35	123	9		1.3
RUSK COUNTY										35 / 0	123	17.5		3.1
												RESERVE		5.0
												(74)		
									Totals ▶	138		1:14		16.3

Flight Plan and Weather Log on Reverse Side

Airport & ATIS Advisories	Departure	Destination
ATIS Code		
Ceiling & Visibility		
Wind		
Altimeter		
Approach		
Runway		
Time Check		

Airport Frequencies	Departure: JEFFERSON		Destination: RUSK CO.
ATIS	126.3	ATIS	
Grnd	121.9	Apch	
Tower	119.5	Tower	
Dep.		Grnd	
CTAF	119.5	CTAF	122.8
FSS	122.2	FSS	122.2
UNICOM	122.95	UNICOM	122.8
Field Elev.	16	Field Elev.	441
Block In		Log Time	
Block Out			

Figure 7-2. This is a completed navigation log for a direct flight. Notice the trip distance of 138 n.m. will require 1 hour, 14 minutes, at a groundspeed of 123 knots. Also note that the frequency box has been completed to provide easy access to this information during the flight.

6. Verifies the airplane's position within three (3) nautical miles of the flight-planned route.

- During the cross-country portion of the flight test, you must remain within 3 nautical miles of your flight planned route.
- You must also be able to identify your current position at all times.

7. Arrives at the en route checkpoints within five (5) minutes of the initial or revised ETA and provides a destination estimate.

- You must carefully track your actual time enroute (ATE) so you can accurately calculate your actual time of arrival (ATA) at each checkpoint.
- Your actual time of arrival (ATA) and your estimated time of arrival (ETA) must be within 5 minutes for all checkpoints and your final destination.

8. Maintains the appropriate altitude, ± 200 feet (60 meters) and headings, ±15°.

- You must adequately divide your attention between navigating and flying to maintain your desired enroute altitude and heading.

EXERCISES

1. Navigating by visual reference to landmarks is known as ______________.
2. Because man-made structures change, you should always fly with __________ sectional charts.
3. Calculating time, speed, distance, and direction is a form of navigation called ___________ ___________.
4. Isogonic lines printed on sectional charts show degrees of ______________.
5. What four variables are required to determine the aircraft heading and groundspeed?

   ____________________, ____________________,
   ____________________, ____________________.

6. Assume you are making a flight between Akron Airport and Meadowlake Airport. Use the following values for calculating your true heading and groundspeed:

   True airspeed .... 120 kts.
   True course .... 190°
   True wind direction .... 270°
   Wind speed .... 12 kts.

   Determine your:

   True heading __________.
   Groundspeed __________.

SAMPLE ORAL QUESTIONS

1. What is pilotage?

1. Pilotage is a form of navigation by reference to landmarks. Flying by pilotage is accomplished by comparing symbols on aeronautical charts with their corresponding features on the ground. One advantage of pilotage is that it is relatively easy to perform and does not require special instruments. On the other hand, pilotage does have some disadvantages. For example, in areas where few prominent landmarks are present, pilotage can be difficult. Also, if haze, smoke, or fog reduces visibility, your ability to navigate by pilotage diminishes.

2. Describe the characteristics of a good visual checkpoint.

2. When selecting checkpoints, you must attempt to pick those with distinctive features recognizable from the air. Although there are few specific rules to follow when selecting checkpoints, one general guideline is to avoid using any single landmark as a sole reference. For example, you should not rely solely on a water tower to identify a small town, since other small towns in the area may also have water towers. When using pilotage, it is important to take a look at the "whole picture." Whenever possible, compare your selected checkpoints against a combination of ground features so you can identify your position positively.

3. What is dead reckoning?

3. Dead reckoning is a technique of navigation based on calculations of time, speed, distance, and direction. These values allow you to predict the movement of your airplane along your intended route of flight.

4. Given the following information:

   True airspeed ....120 kts.
   True course ....090°
   True wind direction ....320°
   Wind speed ....9 kts.

   Determine your true heading and groundspeed.

4. Both true heading and groundspeed can be calculated using the variables given. Solving the wind problem with a flight computer results in a true heading of 087°. This represents the true course minus the wind correction angle. Your groundspeed is 126 knots.

ADDITIONAL QUESTIONS

5. During the oral portion of the test you may be asked to explain why you chose the checkpoints you did.
6. You also may be asked to explain the calculations made on your flight plan.
7. Are pilotage or dead reckoning often used as a sole means of navigation? Why?

EXERCISE ANSWERS

1. pilotage
2. current
3. dead reckoning
4. variation
5. True airspeed, true course, wind direction, and wind speed
6. 196°, 117 kts.

REFERENCES

JEPPESEN:

Private Pilot Manual/Video – Chapters 9A, 11A and 11B

FAA:

Airplane Flying Handbook (FAA-H-8083-3)

Pilot's Handbook of Aeronautical Knowledge (AC 61-23/FAA-H-8083-25)

AC 61-84 Role of Preflight Preparation

B. TASK: NAVIGATION SYSTEMS AND RADAR SERVICES (ASEL and ASES)

REFERENCES: FAA-H-8083-3, AC 61-23/FAA-H-8083-25; Navigation Equipment Operation Manuals, AIM.

Objective: To determine that the applicant:

1. Exhibits knowledge of the elements related to navigation systems and radar services.
2. Demonstrates the ability to use an airborne electronic navigation system.
3. Locates the airplane's position using the navigation system.
4. Intercepts and tracks a given course, radial or bearing, as appropriate.
5. Recognizes and describes the indication of station passage, if appropriate.
6. Recognizes signal loss and takes appropriate action.
7. Uses proper communication procedures when utilizing radar services.
8. Maintains the appropriate altitude, ± 200 feet (60 meters) and headings ±15°.

Objective: To determine that the applicant:

1. **Exhibits knowledge of the elements related to navigation systems and radar services.**

VHF OMNIDIRECTIONAL RANGE (VOR)

Of the many types of navigation systems available, the **very high frequency omnidirectional range** (VOR) system is the one you will probably use the most. A basic VOR system provides course guidance and approximate magnetic headings. The VOR system actually uses three different types of ground facilities. The basic VOR station provides course guidance, while VOR/DME and VORTAC facilities provide both course and distance information.

PRINCIPLES OF OPERATION

A VOR station transmits radio beams, called radials, outward in every direction. Actually, there are an infinite number of radials, but you are primarily concerned with the 360 that are numbered clockwise from magnetic north. Many VOR stations are connected by specific radials, which form Victor airways. When navigating between two stations you typically change from one station to the next at the midpoint.

VOR signals are transmitted in the very high frequency range and travel on a line-of-sight basis. Obstacles such as mountains or the curvature of the earth, can reduce the reception distance of the signal. In certain situations, terrain features can render the signals unusable for navigation purposes. You can find these exceptions published in the *Airport/Facility Directory* under the individual VOR listings. The reception range also varies with altitude. At low altitudes you must be close to the station to receive a reliable signal. As your altitude increases, you can use the VOR at greater distances from the station.

CLASSES OF VOR FACILITIES

There are three classes of VOR facilities: the **terminal VOR** (TVOR), the **low altitude VOR** (LVOR), and **high altitude VOR** (HVOR). The TVOR provides terminal guidance and should not be used farther than 25 n.m. from the station at altitudes below 1,000 feet AGL or above 12,000 feet AGL. You may use an LVOR reliably up to 40 n.m. from the station at altitudes between 1,000 and 18,000 feet AGL. HVOR is effective to various ranges and most airways are defined by HVORs that have a maximum reception range of 130 n.m. The class designation of a VOR facility can be found in the *Airport/Facility Directory*.

VOR AIRBORNE EQUIPMENT

Your airborne equipment consists of an antenna, a receiver, and an indicator. Although most airborne VOR equipment is similar in appearance and operation, you should familiarize yourself with the particular make and model you are using. Information is normally available in the POH or in separate publications from the radio manufacturer.

VOR NAVIGATION

VOR navigation is simple to use once you understand its basic principles. To navigate effectively, you must complete certain preliminary steps. The first is to obtain the VOR frequency from the appropriate aeronautical chart and enter it into the VOR receiver. Next, identify the station to ensure that you have entered the correct frequency. A station is identified by a three-letter Morse code signal or by a combination of code and a repetitive voice transmission that gives the name of the VOR. If you don't hear the identifier, it may mean that the station is not operating or that you are out of range of the facility. When a station is shut down for maintenance, it may radiate a T-E-S-T code (— • ··· —), or the identifier may be removed.

COURSE INFORMATION

It's important to remember that radials travel outward from the VOR station. When flying away from a VOR on a given radial, your heading and the VOR course read at the top of the indicator will be approximately the same. When going to the station, however, your heading is the reciprocal of the radial you are following. Of course, wind can cause some heading variation. [Figure 7-3]

TO-FROM INDICATIONS

The TO-FROM indicator helps you maintain your sense of orientation with respect to the station. With the course selector properly set, a FROM indication shows you are flying away from the station. When flying toward the station, it shows TO.

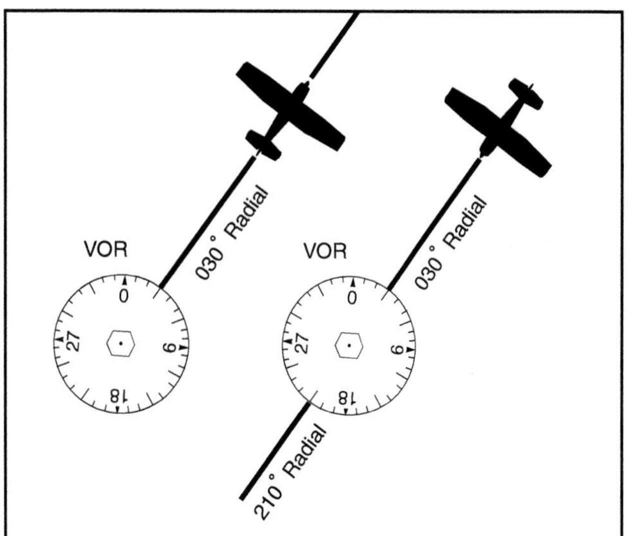

Figure 7-3. When you are flying away from a VOR station on the 030° radial (in a no-wind condition), your heading indicator will read 030°. On the other hand, if you fly inbound to the station on the 030° radial, your heading will be 210°.

The TO-FROM indicator also helps you determine which course will provide the most direct route to a VOR station. For example, after you tune and identify the station, simply turn the course selector until the TO-FROM indicator shows TO. Continue turning the selector until the CDI centers. The reading under the index is your magnetic course to the station when no wind exists. As you fly over the station, the TO indication disappears, and is replaced briefly by an OFF or NAV indication. On some equipment, a red flag is displayed momentarily. If these indications appear at times other than station passage, it means the VOR signal is too weak for reliable navigation. As you pass the station, the FROM appears indicating you are traveling away from the station.

It's important to remember that the aircraft's heading has no direct relationship to the course selected in the VOR indicator. The VOR indicator reflects your position relative to the station, regardless of the direction you are flying. However, when you actually navigate with VOR, the headings you fly must be in general agreement with the selected course.

USING VOR NAVIGATION

The most common VOR navigation performed is flying from one station to another during cross-country flights. You will use a process called tracking to accomplish this. Tracking involves entering a course in the course selector and maintaining that course by keeping the CDI centered. In a crosswind situation, the wind causes you to drift off course, so you need to make a series of corrections to regain the desired course and maintain it. This technique is called bracketing.

VOR ORIENTATION

Determining your position with respect to VOR navaids is called **VOR orientation**. To do this, turn the course selector until the TO-FROM indicator shows FROM. Continue turning the selector until the CDI centers. The reading under the index represents the radial you are on. Once you determine the magnetic course to a station using the VOR indicator, you can determine your distance from the station by cross-checking it with a second VOR. When doing this, you should select two radials that are nearly perpendicular to each other. That way you can locate your position more accurately.

INTERCEPTING RADIALS

In some situations, you may want to navigate on a different radial than the one you're on. Essentially, you must fly from one radial to another. This is called **intercepting**. To use an intercept, you must visualize where you are from the station, and where you want to go. The intercept angle you use may range from 20° to 90°, depending on your position and distance from the station. [Figure 7-4]

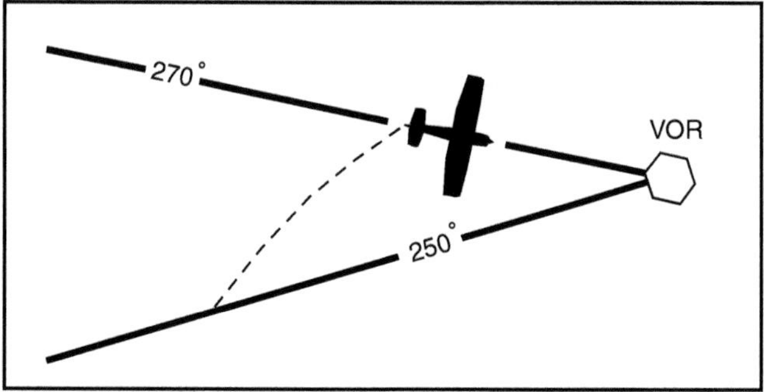

Figure 7-4. While tracking inbound on the 250° radial with a course of 070°, you decide to intercept the 270° radial inbound. After turning left to establish an intercept angle, enter the new inbound course (090°) into the course selector. When the CDI begins to center, turn right and track inbound.

VOR CAUTIONS

There are two aspects of VOR navigation with which you should exercise caution. The first concerns unusual CDI fluctuations. Certain propeller r.p.m. settings can cause the CDI to fluctuate as much as six degrees. By varying the propeller r.p.m. slightly, you normally will eliminate this problem. The second aspect is a situation called reverse sensing.

Reverse Sensing

If you mistakenly set the course selector to the reciprocal of your desired course, the CDI will deflect away from the course you want to follow. This situation is known as **reverse sensing**. It can be very confusing, because following the normal procedure of correcting toward the needle will actually take you farther off course. To remedy this, you must set the VOR course selector to the reciprocal (180° opposite) of the radial.

To illustrate this point, assume you want to track inbound on the 090° radial. In the course selector, you mistakenly enter a course of 090° and fly a magnetic heading of 270° to the station. Your heading indicator now differs from the course selected by 180°. In addition, you have a FROM

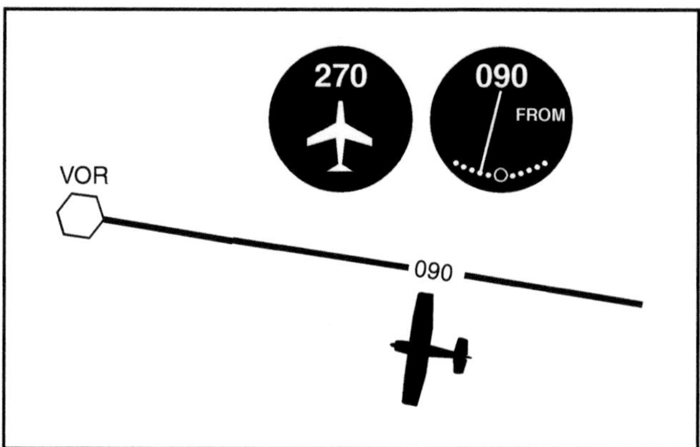

Figure 7-5. Your CDI is deflected toward the left, indicating that a turn to the left will bring you on course. However, with reverse sensing, this will take you farther from course. In this situation, you should enter the desired course of 270° into the course selector so you will have a TO indication and correct sensing.

indication while flying inbound to the station. This is a reverse sensing situation. [Figure 7-5]

AUTOMATIC DIRECTION FINDER

Another navigation system, and one that you could use as a backup to VOR, is the **automatic direction finder** (ADF). Unlike VOR, ADF does not rely on line-of-sight transmissions. This allows reliable navigation at lower altitudes than VOR and, depending on the facility, may also provide greater reception range. Your airborne ADF equipment is capable of receiving radio signals from ground facilities called **nondirectional radio beacons** (NDBs), as well as commercial broadcast stations.

ADF EQUIPMENT

ADF equipment in the aircraft permits low/medium frequency (L/MF) signals to be received through the antenna, relayed to the ADF receiver where they are processed, and then sent to the ADF indicator. Although most automatic direction finders have similarities in appearance and operation, you should familiarize yourself with the make and model installed in the airplane you plan to use. Consult the POH or other publication provided by the radio manufacturer.

NDBs are shown on aeronautical charts and can be used for either VFR or IFR operations. They transmit signals that travel both as ground waves that penetrate obstacles and as sky waves that are refracted by the ionosphere. Selected commercial broadcast stations of the AM class are also shown on aeronautical charts. However, their use is restricted to VFR operations, since they are required to identify themselves only once each hour.

Once you have tuned and identified the station, the needle on the bearing indicator will point to that station. At this time, you should use the ADF test function to ensure the signal is reliable. Check your operator's handbook to see how this function works on the ADF you're using.

ADF BEARING INDICATORS

With L/MF facilities, bearings are used to describe your position rather than radials. A **bearing** is the horizontal direction to or from any point, which is measured clockwise through 360°, from magnetic north. A bearing indicator gives you the horizontal direction, or angle, between your aircraft and the station. Actually, there are two types of bearing indicators — the fixed card and the movable card. We will discuss the fixed-card indicator only. For information on movable card ADFs, consult your Private Pilot Manual.

The fixed-card bearing indicator measures **relative bearing** — the angular difference between the airplane's longitudinal axis and a straight line drawn from the airplane to the station. This value is measured clockwise from the airplane's nose. To fly directly to a station, you must add your magnetic heading to your relative bearing. This value, called **magnetic bearing**, takes you directly to the station. Stated as a formula, magnetic heading (MH) + relative bearing (RB) = magnetic bearing (MB). If the total is more than 360°, you will need to subtract 360° to find the magnetic bearing to the station. [Figure 7-6]

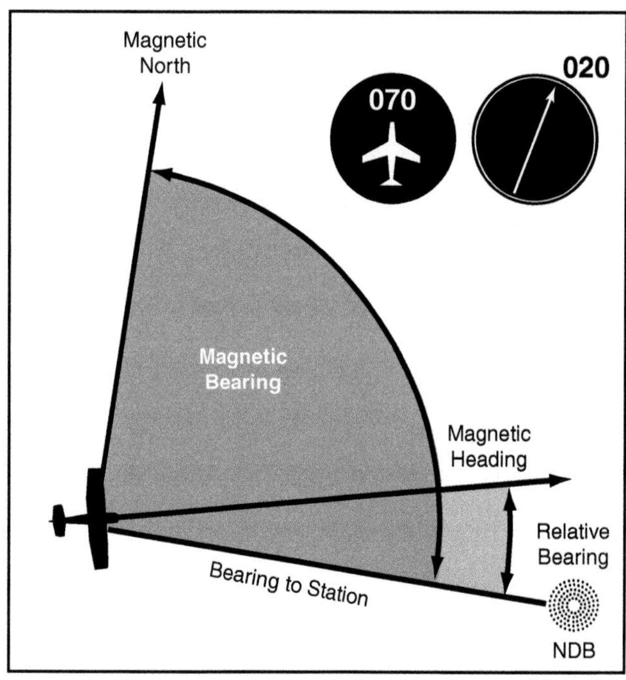

Figure 7-6. In this sample problem, the ADF bearing indicator is pointing 020° to the right of the aircraft's nose. This is a 020° relative bearing. To find the magnetic bearing to the station, read the magnetic heading of 070° from the heading indicator, then use the formula to determine the magnetic bearing: MH (070°) + RB (020°) = MB (090°). This means you should turn to a course of 90° to get to the station.

HOMING

A procedure where you always keep the nose of the aircraft pointing directly at the station is called **homing**. You do this by keeping the fixed-card bearing pointer on the aircraft's nose, or at 0°. In a no-wind situation, the magnetic heading will remain constant as you fly inbound to the station. However, in a crosswind situation, the wind will push you off course, so you must adjust the magnetic heading to keep the nose of the aircraft pointing at the station.

ORIENTATION

To locate your position using an ADF, you need to determine the **reciprocal bearing**, which is the bearing from the station. First, add your magnetic heading and your relative bearing to determine your magnetic bearing to the station. Next, find the reciprocal bearing by adding or subtracting 180° from the magnetic bearing. If the magnetic bearing is less than 180°, add 180°; if it is more than 180°, subtract 180° to get the reciprocal.

TRACKING

The tracking procedure you learned for VOR navigation is similar to the procedure used for ADF navigation. It involves flying a heading that will maintain a desired bearing to the station. If the wind is blowing, bracketing is required to determine the wind correction angle (WCA), and then a corresponding bearing is used to maintain a steady track. When on course, the wind correction angle should be exactly equal to the number of degrees the bearing indicator points left or right of the aircraft's nose. For example, if your WCA is 10° left, the station will be 10° to the right, and the bearing pointer will also indicate 10°.

As you pass over the station, the needle tends to fluctuate. You are cautioned not to "chase" the needle, since many of the indications are erroneous close to the station. When the needle stabilizes at or near the 180° position, you have passed the station. If you do not pass directly over the facility, station passage occurs when the needle is steady and points to either wingtip position.

ADF INTERCEPTS

ADF intercepts are accomplished in a manner similar to those required for bracketing procedures, but the angles used are much greater. Use the ADF formula to help you with this procedure. Assume you are located southwest of an NDB on the 250° bearing and want to track inbound to the station on the 270° bearing. [Figure 7-7]

ADF CAUTIONS

You should be aware of the limitations concerning L/MF navigation. The VFR reception range for L/MF facilities can vary greatly, depending on transmitter power, atmospheric conditions, and time of day. The ADF indicator does not have an OFF flag, so the tendency may be to use it when the signals are unreliable. A proper identification and test will counter this problem. You also should continuously monitor the station's ident feature, keeping in mind that commercial broadcast st ations may not identify themselves regularly. The ident information for NDBs can be found in the associated frequency box on sectional charts. You also can find NDBs within the airport listings in the *Airport/Facility Directory*.

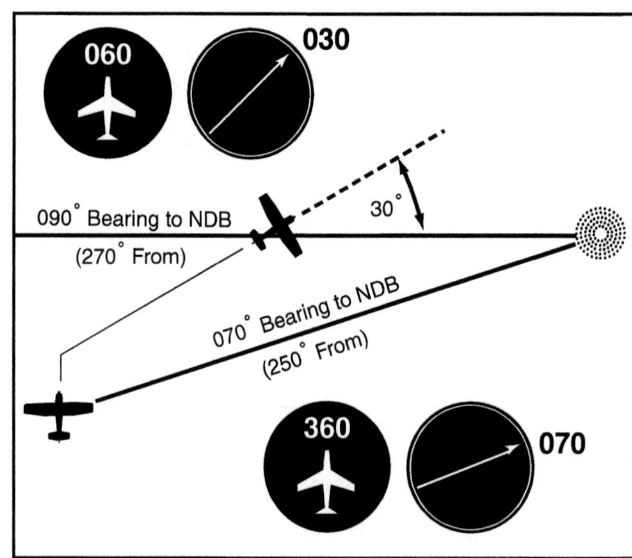

Figure 7-7. A heading of 060° will give you an intercept angle of 30° to the 090° bearing to the station (270° From). When the bearing pointer indicates 30°, you will know you have intercepted the 90° bearing to the station (270° From), and you can turn inbound.

ADVANCED NAVIGATION

Some of the aircraft you fly during your training may have more advanced navigation systems and equipment. This discussion is designed to give you an overall view of the capabilities of some of these navigation systems; it is not intended to make you operationally proficient. If you need detailed information, refer to the POH or manufacturer's description for the particular equipment in question.

VORTAC-BASED RNAV

So far, you have become familiar with VOR and ADF, which are the systems you will probably use most frequently in the beginning. The next step for many pilots is area navigation. **Area navigation** (RNAV) allows you more lateral freedom in navigation, because it does not require you to track directly TO or FROM navigation facilities. RNAV systems which utilize VOR/DME or VORTAC sites are referred to as VORTAC-based. **VORTAC-based area navigation** provides you with both course and distance information and allows you to fly to a predetermined point without overflying VOR/DME or VORTAC facilities. [Figure 7-8]

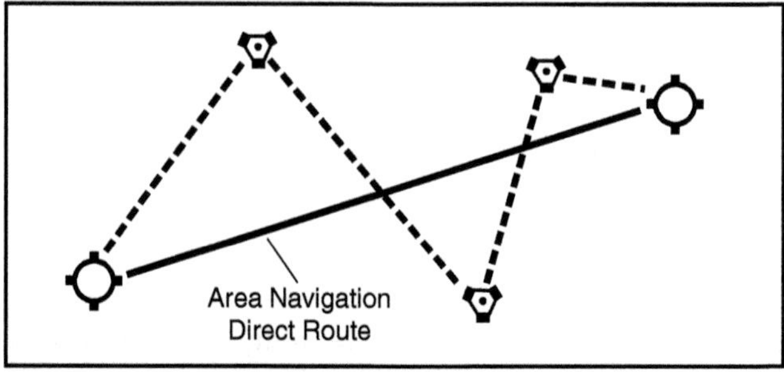

Figure 7-8. With VOR routes, you typically travel from facility to facility. With RNAV capability, you can eliminate the zigzag flight path and fly in a straight line.

RNAV OPERATION

VORTAC-based RNAV uses a **courseline computer** (CLC) which permits you to create "phantom stations" for use in navigation. Basically, the computer relocates, or offsets, the navigation aid to the desired radial and distance from the original location. The computer uses this information to create the phantom stations, or **waypoints**. For a long cross-country flight, you will have a series of waypoints that collectively define an RNAV route.

Another desirable RNAV feature is that you navigate using the VOR indicator. With RNAV, the needle deflections still indicate course displacement, but the deviation scale is in nautical miles and not degrees. Each dot on the horizontal scale represents a given value, such as .5 n.m. or 10 n.m., depending on what the manufacturer has set. When you are using RNAV, the DME will show the correct distance from you to the waypoint, but the groundspeed information also depends on the manufacturer. Some groundspeed readouts indicate the groundspeed in relation to the original facility, not the waypoint. Be sure to study the information supplied by the manufacturer for the RNAV equipment you are using.

LONG RANGE NAVIGATION

Long range navigation or LORAN is another popular navigation system. A LORAN receiver gets position information in the form of latitude and longitude coordinates from a chain of low frequency (LF) transmitters. The chain transmits a synchronized signal on a frequency of 100 kHz in the form of ground and sky waves. [Figure 7-9]

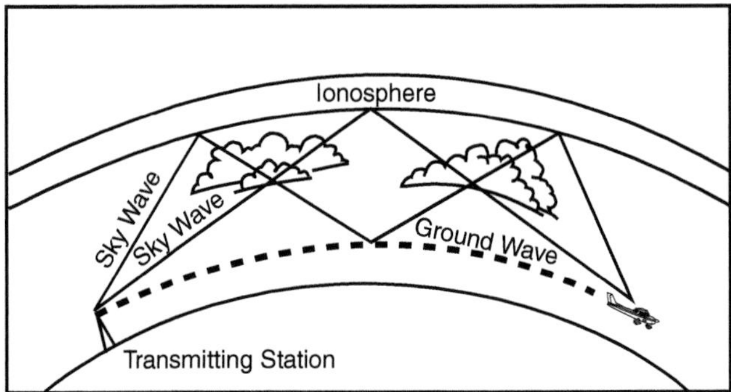

Figure 7-9. Since low frequency ground waves follow the contour of the earth, the reception range of LORAN signals is great (often 600 to 1,200 n.m. over land), and the transmitters can be located several hundred miles apart. Sky waves are also formed by LORAN signals but are not considered as reliable for navigation as ground waves.

You will find there are many types of LORAN receivers on the market with very different capabilities and operating requirements. The various receivers are differentiated primarily by the software programs or data bases they use. A typical LORAN receiver can compute bearing and distance from your present position to your intended destination. However, some data bases can give you navigation information, such as wind direction and velocity, fuel consumption, nearest airports in case of an in-flight emergency, audible warnings before you enter special use airspace, radio frequencies, and phone numbers. This is why it is so important to study the manufacturer's handbook to determine the capabilities of the particular LORAN you are using.

LORAN CAUTIONS

Although LORAN is a popular navigation system, it does have some drawbacks. Since LORAN uses low frequency AM radio signals, electrical disturbances such as thunderstorms and precipitation static can cause interference. It is not unusual to experience signal loss when you are flying in areas of electrical activity or heavy precipitation. An aircraft passing through rain, ice, or snow builds up a static charge that degrades signal reception. Static discharge wicks on airfoil trailing edges, fuselage grounding, and special antenna coatings are used to combat precipitation static.

A major limitation of LORAN deals with characteristics of the radio signals themselves. Even though they are very accurate (especially over water), they have a tendency to travel over land at different speeds. Surface type, foliage, seasonal changes, and weather can affect the speed of the radio waves and, consequently, their accuracy.

GLOBAL POSITIONING SYSTEM

The **global positioning system** or GPS is another type of radio aid that is well suited for aviation. GPS is a space based radio positioning, navigation, and time-transfer system developed by the Department of Defense. It provides highly accurate position, velocity, and time information on a global basis to an unlimited number of properly equipped users. The system is functional 24 hours a day, and is unaffected by weather. GPS is based on accurate and continuous knowledge of the spatial position of each satellite in the system with respect to the user. The GPS receiver automatically selects appropriate signals from the satellites in view and, through triangulation, translates these signals into a two- or three-dimensional position fix with speed information. System accuracy for civil users is approximately 328 feet (100 meters) horizontally.

VFR RADAR SERVICES

Radar traffic information service, also called VFR radar advisory service, is intended to alert you to air traffic that is relevant to your route of flight. When controllers call out a possible conflict, they will reference the traffic's position relative to yours. For instance, if a controller says, *"traffic at 11 o'clock,"* it means the traffic appears to the controller to be about 30° left of your nose. You should look for the traffic anywhere between the nose (12 o'clock) and left wing (9 o'clock). After you locate the traffic, tell the controller you have the traffic *"in sight."* If you do not see the traffic, acknowledge the advisory by telling the controller *"negative contact."*

Radar traffic information service is usually available from any ATC radar facility. However, keep in mind that many factors, such as limitations of radar, volume of traffic, controller workload, or frequency congestion, may prevent the controller from providing this service. Even when it is available, it is not intended to relieve you of your responsibility for collision avoidance.

TRANSPONDER

The transponder is an integral part of the ATC radar system. Since transponder returns are the basis for radar separation, regulations require they be tested and inspected every 24 calendar months for operations in controlled airspace. Regulations further require that, if transponder equipped, you must operate the transponder when you are in controlled airspace, including the Mode C feature (if installed). If you fly at and above 10,000 feet MSL (except for the airspace at and below 2,500 feet AGL) or within 30 nautical miles of any designated Class B airspace primary airport from the surface to 10,000 feet MSL, you must have and operate a transponder with Mode C capability.

The function selector of a typical transponder has several positions: OFF, STY (STANDBY), ON, ALT (ALTITUDE), and TST (TEST). In the **STANDBY** position, the transponder is warmed up and ready for operation but does not reply to interrogations. As a general rule, you should switch the transponder from STANDBY to ON as late as practical on takeoff. Switch to ALTITUDE if your transponder has Mode C automatic altitude reporting equipment. The ON position selects Mode A and is appropriate when your transponder doesn't have Mode C automatic altitude equipment.

Before using the Mode C information from your transponder, the controller must verify your altitude readout is valid. To do this, the controller typically asks, "*verify at 7,500*," (or other appropriate altitude). If you respond "*affirmative*," the altitude readout can be used for separation. ATC may also ask you to "*squawk ident*." If so, you should press the IDENT button momentarily and release it.

Of course, your transponder must be set to the correct code for the IDENT feature to work. For VFR operations, you normally use code 1200 unless a different code is assigned by a controller. You should be careful to avoid codes 7500, 7600, and 7700 when you are making routine code changes on your transponder. Inadvertent selection of these codes may cause momentary false alarms at radar facilities. Code 7500 alerts ATC that an aircraft has been hijacked; 7600 is used after the failure of two-way radio communications; and 7700 is used for emergencies.

TERMINAL VFR RADAR SERVICE

This is a national program which has four types of service: basic radar, terminal radar service area (TRSA), Class C, and Class B. The type of service provided at a given airport is published in the *Airport/Facility Directory*.

Basic radar service includes safety alerts, traffic advisories, limited radar vectoring when requested, and sequencing at locations with established procedures. The objective of this service is to monitor the flow of arriving IFR and VFR aircraft into the traffic pattern and provide traffic advisories to departing VFR aircraft. Departing VFR pilots should request the service through ground control on initial contact.

TRSA service provides basic radar service, as well as sequencing of all IFR and participating VFR aircraft and separation between all participating VFR aircraft within the TRSA.

Class C service provides, in addition to basic radar service, approved separation between IFR and VFR aircraft, and sequencing of VFR aircraft, including sequencing of VFR arrivals to the primary airport.

Class B service provides basic radar service, approved separation of aircraft based on IFR, VFR, and/or weight, and sequencing of VFR arrivals to the primary airport, or surrounding airports.

Pilots operating under VFR are required to participate in Class B and C services. However, participation in basic and TRSA service, although encouraged, is voluntary for VFR pilots.

ENROUTE VFR RADAR SERVICE

Enroute VFR radar service, commonly referred to as VFR Flight Following, is offered by most Air Route Traffic Control Centers (ARTCCs) and provides you with traffic advisories when flying outside the terminal area. When utilizing this service, ATC will assign you a transponder code so they can track your progress and advise you of any observed radar targets in your vicinity. However, this service is not intended to relieve you of your responsibility for continual vigilance to see and avoid other traffic.

When receiving VFR Flight Following, you should monitor the assigned ATC frequency at all times. This helps enable ATC in identifying a possible radio failure or in providing assistance should an emergency arise. If you no longer wish to participate in the Flight Following service, advise the controller before changing frequencies.

There are several factors that can prevent ATC from providing VFR Flight Following service. These include: limitations in radar coverage, volume of traffic, and controller workload. Controllers possess complete discretion for determining whether they can provide or continue to provide this service in a specific case. However, most controllers typically provide service when requested.

When contacting an ATC facility to request VFR Flight Following, your initial transmission should sound like this, "*Minneapolis Center, Skyhawk 19620 request*." The word "*request*" alerts ATC that an aircraft has a request for services that does not require their immediate attention.

Typically, ATC will reply by stating, "*Skyhawk 19620 go ahead with your request.*" When stating your request, you should provide your aircraft type, N-number, cruising altitude, approximate position, route of flight, and request for services. For example, "*Skyhawk 19620 is level at 6,500 feet, approximately 20 miles northwest of Mankato, VFR to St. Cloud, request VFR Flight Following.*" If ATC can provide service they will give you a squawk code to enter into your transponder: "*Skyhawk 19620 squawk 3725.*"

Once you are radar identified, ATC will verify your altitude and provide you with traffic advisories as long as you remain within radar coverage.

2. Demonstrates the ability to use an airborne electronic navigation system.

- The examiner will ask you to navigate TO and FROM one or more facility.
- You must be able to obtain frequencies for navigational facilities from a sectional chart.
- Prior to using a facility you must listen to the Morse code identifier to ensure positive signal reception.

3. Locates the airplane's position using the navigation system.

- Once you have identified a facility, you will be asked to determine your position in relation to the facility.
- For a VOR, turn the OBS until you get a FROM indication with the needle centered. The number indicated on the course selector is the radial FROM the station that you are on.
- For LORAN or GPS based navigation systems, your position is defined in terms of latitude/longitude coordinates.
- For an NDB, the head of the needle always points TO the station.

4. Intercepts and tracks a given course, radial or bearing, as appropriate.

- During the flight portion of the practical exam, you may be asked to intercept both VOR radials and NDB bearings.
- You also will be expected to track a radial and/or bearing TO and FROM the navigation facility.

5. Recognizes and describes the indication of station passage, if appropriate.

- Station passage on a VOR indicator is identified by a "flip" of the TO/FROM flag.
- Station passage on an ADF is indicated when the bearing pointer swings beyond 90° either side of the aircraft's nose.

6. Recognizes signal loss and takes appropriate action.

- Signal loss on an OBS is identified by an OFF or NAV flag appearing, or loss of the Morse code identifier.
- Signal loss on an ADF is identified by the loss of the Morse code and/or voice identifier.

7. Uses proper communication procedures when utilizing radar services.

- When talking to ATC, always utilize proper phraseology.
- For additional information on communication phraseology, refer to Chapter 3, Task A on page 3-1.

8. Maintains the appropriate altitude, ± 200 feet (60 meters) and headings ±15°.

- You must divide your attention between navigating and flying the airplane to maintain your desired enroute altitude.
- Use outside references to keep the aircraft in a straight-and-level flight attitude and cross-check the flight instruments to verify the proper heading and altitude.
- Use trim to relieve any control pressures.

EXERCISES

1. As you fly to a VOR station, you should first tune the VOR receiver to the proper frequency and ________ the station.

2. _____ (True, False) The heading of the airplane has a direct relationship to the radial selected on the VOR indicator.

3. When the CDI deflects away from the course you want to follow, you are experiencing ________________ ________________.

4. When tracking to an NDB on a heading of 180° in a no-wind condition, the ADF needle of a fixed-card indicator will show _________°.

5. _____ (True, False) An ADF is limited to line of sight, similar to a VOR.

6. The standard transponder code for VFR operations is ______________.

SAMPLE ORAL QUESTIONS

1. List, respectively, the transponder code you should use for an emergency, lost communications, and hijacking?

____

____

____

____

1. The transponder codes for an emergency, lost communications, and hijacking are 7700, 7600, and 7500 respectively.

2. If you are flying on a magnetic heading of 020° and your bearing pointer is 30° right of the nose, what is your magnetic bearing to the station?

____

____

____

____

____

2. By using the formula Magnetic Heading (MH) + Relative Bearing (RB) = Magnetic Bearing (MB), you can determine your magnetic bearing to the station. The answer is 050° (020° + 030° = 050°).

3. List the steps in determining your position relative to a VOR facility.

____

____

____

____

____

____

3. Once you have tuned and identified a station you should turn the course selector until a FROM indication appears. Continue turning the selector until the CDI centers. The reading under the top index represents the radial FROM the station you are on.

4. Discuss the reception limitations of VOR facilities.

____

____

____

____

____

____

____

____

____

____

____

____

4. VOR signals are transmitted in the very high frequency range and travel on a line-of-sight basis. This means obstructions such as mountains, buildings, or the curvature of the earth can reduce the reception range of VOR signals. Although you typically change frequencies at the midpoint between VOR facilities, certain terrain features may make this impractical. For information on the reception ranges for a particular VOR, consult the Airport/Facility Directory.

ADDITIONAL QUESTIONS

5. Identify both VOR and NDB facilities on a sectional chart and interpret all the information in the associated facility box.

6. Briefly describe the services available with each type of radar service.

EXERCISE ANSWERS

1. identify
2. False
3. reverse sensing
4. 0°
5. False
6. 1200

REFERENCES

JEPPESEN:

Private Pilot Manual/Video – Chapters 5A, 9B, 9C, and 9D

FAA:

Airplane Flying Handbook (FAA-H-8083-3)

Pilot's Handbook of Aeronautical Knowledge (AC 61-23/FAA-H-8083-25)

Aeronautical Information Manual

C. TASK: DIVERSION (ASEL and ASES)

REFERENCES: AC 61-23/FAA-H-8083-25; AIM.

Objective: To determine that the applicant:

1. Exhibits knowledge of the elements related to diversion.
2. Selects an appropriate alternate airport and route.
3. Makes an accurate estimate of heading, groundspeed, arrival time, and fuel consumption to the alternate airport.
4. Maintains the appropriate altitude, ± 200 feet (60 meters) and heading, ±15°.

Objective: To determine that the applicant:

1. Exhibits knowledge of the elements related to diversion.

DIVERSION

Among the aeronautical skills you must have is the ability to plot a course, in flight, to an alternate airport when continuation to your original destination is impractical.

Situations that may justify diverting to an alternate include unforecast weather at the original destination, runway closures, fuel exhaustion, or unavailability of fuel at your original destination. The latter two indicate miscalculations and omissions during the preflight planning. Another possible reason for diverting is if you arrive at your destination and discover the crosswind component exceeds the capability of the aircraft. In this situation, you should not hesitate to divert to an alternate airport.

As you know, computing course, time, speed, and distance information in flight requires the same computations used when preflight planning. However, because of the limitations in cockpit space, available equipment, and because you must divide your attention between making calculations, operating the airplane, and scanning for other aircraft, you should take advantage of all possible shortcuts and rule-of-thumb computations.

When in flight, it is rarely practical to actually plot a course on a sectional chart and mark checkpoints and distances. Furthermore, because an alternate airport is usually not very far from your original course, actual plotting is seldom necessary.

A course to an alternate can be measured accurately with a protractor or plotter, but can also be measured with reasonable accuracy using a straightedge and the compass rose depicted around VOR stations. This approximation can be made on the basis of a radial from a nearby VOR or an airway that closely parallels the course to your alternate. However, you must remember that the magnetic heading associated with a VOR radial or printed airway is outbound from the station. To find the course TO the station, it may be necessary to determine the reciprocal of the heading indicated.

Distances can be determined by using a plotter, or by placing a finger or piece of paper between the two and then measuring the approximate distance on the mileage scale at the bottom of the chart.

If radio aids are used to divert to an alternate, you must select the appropriate facility, properly identify the station by listening to the Morse code identifier, and determine the course or radial to intercept or follow.

Before changing course to proceed to an alternate, you must consider the relative distance to all suitable alternates, select the one most appropriate, and then determine the magnetic course to the alternate selected. Once you determine the aircraft's new heading, you should turn to establish this new course immediately, and then calculate wind correction, actual distance, and estimated time and fuel required while proceeding toward the alternate.

To complete all plotting, measuring, and computation involved before diverting to the alternate airport may only aggravate an actual emergency. Therefore, it is important to develop the ability to orient yourself immediately with a chart and to make rapid and reasonably accurate computations of headings and arrival time estimates.

2. Selects an appropriate alternate airport and route.

- Before changing course, you should first consider the relative distance and route of flight to all suitable alternates.
- In addition, you should consider the type of terrain along the route.
- If the circumstances warrant, it is typically easier to navigate to an alternate airport that has a VOR or NDB facility on the field.

3. Makes an accurate estimate of heading, groundspeed, arrival time, and fuel consumption to the alternate airport.

- Once established on course, use the winds aloft nearest to your diversion point to calculate a heading and groundspeed.
- Once you've calculated your groundspeed, determine a new arrival time and fuel consumption.

4. Maintains the appropriate altitude, ± 200 feet (60 meters) and heading, ± 15°.

- You must give priority to operating the aircraft while dividing your attention between flying and planning.
- When determining an altitude to use when diverting, you should consider cloud heights, winds, terrain, and radio reception.
- Once established at altitude, use trim to relieve any control pressures.
- Use outside references to maintain straight-and-level flight when cross-checking the altimeter and heading indicator to verify your altitude and heading.

EXERCISES

1. _____ (True, False) When diverting to an alternate, it is appropriate to use estimates and rules-of-thumb to determine heading, groundspeed, time enroute, and fuel requirements.

2. _____ (True, False) A course to an alternate can be determined with reasonable accuracy using a straightedge and a compass rose depicted on a sectional chart.

3. _____ (True, False) The only accurate way to navigate to an alternate is to use radio navigation.

4. _____ (True, False) When navigating to an alternate using a VOR, you don't have to identify the facility by listening to the morse code identifier.

SAMPLE ORAL QUESTIONS

1. Some of the constraints of planning in the aircraft include limited cockpit space and available equipment as well as dividing your attention between making calculations, flying the aircraft, and scanning for other traffic.

2. Distances can be determined by using a plotter, or by placing a finger or piece of paper between the two points and then measuring the approximate distance on the mileage scale at the bottom of the chart.

1. What are some of the constraints of planning in the cockpit while enroute?

____

____

____

____

____

2. How can you quickly determine distances when diverting to an alternate airport?

____

____

____

____

ADDITIONAL QUESTIONS

3. What are the factors that should be considered when selecting a course to an alternate airport?

4. What are some realistic situations where you would divert to another airport?

EXERCISE ANSWERS

1. True
2. True
3. False
4. False

REFERENCES

JEPPESEN:

Private Pilot Manual/Video – Chapter 11B

FAA:

Airplane Flying Handbook (FAA-H-8083-3)

Pilot's Handbook of Aeronautical Knowledge (AC 61-23/FAA-H-8083-25)

D. TASK: LOST PROCEDURES (ASEL and ASES)

REFERENCES: AC 61-23/FAA-H-8083-25; AIM.

Objective: To determine that the applicant:

1. Exhibits knowledge of the elements related to lost procedures.
2. Selects an appropriate course of action.
3. Maintains an appropriate heading and climbs, if necessary.
4. Identifies prominent landmarks.
5. Uses navigation systems/facilities and/or contacts an ATC facility for assistance, as appropriate.

Objective: To determine that the applicant:

1. **Exhibits knowledge of the elements related to lost procedures.**

LOST PROCEDURES

At one time or another every pilot will become lost or at least "temporarily" disoriented. When this happens, the natural reaction is to panic and fly to where you assume you are supposed to be. As a result, you will typically become completely disoriented and end up flying further away from your desired course. To prevent this you must exercise good judgment, and, above all, don't panic.

There are several different actions you can take when you are unsure of the airplane's position. The best choice depends upon the specific circumstances, but usually they should be applied in the following sequence.

When unsure of your position, you should continue to fly your original heading and watch for recognizable landmarks, while rechecking the calculated position on your flight plan. By plotting a point based on the estimated distance and compass direction flown from your last noted checkpoint as though there were no wind, you can determine the aircraft's position within a given area. This area is commonly referred to as the "circle of error." If you are certain that the wind is no more than 30 knots, and it has been 30 minutes since your last known checkpoint, the radius of the circle should be about 15 nautical miles. It is then a matter of continuing straight ahead, and checking the landmarks within this circle. The most likely position will be downwind from the desired course. [Figure 7-10]

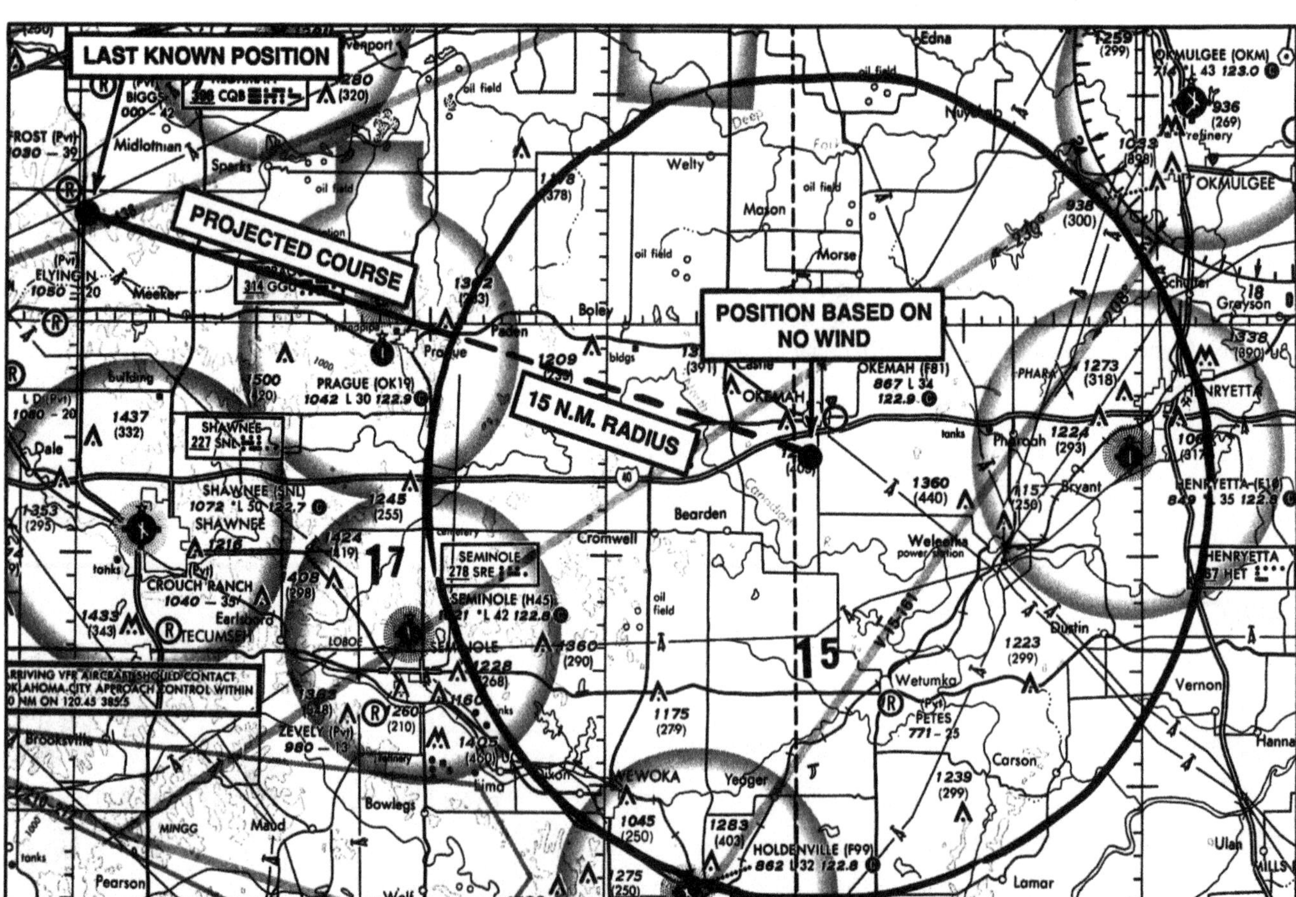

Figure 7-10. Plot a circle of error to establish an area where you are located. The size of this area is based on your estimated distance and heading from your last noted checkpoint as though there is no wind. If you are certain the wind is no more than 30 knots, and it has been 30 minutes since your last known checkpoint, the radius of the circle should be about 15 nautical miles.

If this procedure fails to identify your position, you should change course toward the nearest concentration of prominent landmarks shown on the chart. If some town or developed area is sighted, you can circle to observe identifiable features or markings. However, you must comply with the minimum safe altitudes prescribed in the FARs.

RADIO NAVIGATION AIDS

Another method available for determining your position is through the use of radio navigation aids. If you are unable to determine your exact position through the use of pilotage and dead reckoning, you may be able to do it by utilizing one or more navigation facilities. For example, once you have determined your approximate location using the procedure described earlier, you can examine your sectional chart for VOR or NDB facilities that may be within range. To verify that a facility is usable, you must tune in the facility and listen for the Morse code identifier.

When using a VOR facility, turn the OBS until you get a FROM indication and the needle is centered. Then draw a line from the VOR facility on the radial indicated. Your position is somewhere on that line.

If an NDB facility is used, ensure your heading indicator corresponds with the magnetic compass and determine your magnetic bearing to the station (MH + RB = MB). Then, add or subtract 180° to determine the magnetic bearing from the station and draw a line on your sectional chart. As described above, your position is somewhere on that line.

At this point you can navigate to the identified facility, use your sectional chart to identify your position and proceed, or use a second navigational facility, if available, to more accurately determine your position.

ATC SERVICES

Anytime you feel you are in an undesirable situation, you should immediately ask for assistance from an ATC or FSS facility. These facilities can usually identify your position through radar or direction finding (DF) equipment. When contacting either of these facilities you should follow what is referred to as the "Four C's." The four C's stand for **Climb**, **Communicate**, **Confess**, and **Comply**.

Climb reminds you to climb, if possible, for better radar and DF detection. In addition, climbing typically increases the range of both communication and navigation radios.

Communication means you should try communicating with any available facility. The appropriate frequencies can be found in the *Airport/Facility Directory*. If you are unable to determine the exact frequency you should use the emergency frequency of 121.5.

Confess means that when contacting ATC or any other ground based facility, tell them your situation. If you are in need of immediate assistance, you should begin the transmission with the phrase "MAYDAY, MAYDAY, MAYDAY" followed by the emergency message.

Comply reminds you to comply with the instructions received. Remember, immediately ask questions or request clarification if you do not understand any instruction, or if you cannot comply with clearance.

VHF DIRECTION FINDING (DF)

If an ATC facility cannot be reached or if radar services are not available, an FSS specialist may be able to assist you with a **VHF direction finder** (VHF/DF). Direction finding equipment requires two-way radio communications with the FSS.

The FSS specialist will ask you to key your microphone while the direction finding equipment "homes" in on your radio signal. The specialist can determine your location from the FSS and then give you headings to guide you to an airport or provide other assistance.

Unlike radar, DF determines only your direction from the FSS. It does not reveal how far away you are. However, the specialist can calculate your distance from the station by having you fly at a 90° angle to the station and determine the time between bearing changes. In addition, an FSS specialist can notify additional locations with DF equipment as well as ATC and possibly use a second DF bearing or radar to determine your exact position. Towers and FSSs with DF service are listed in the *Airport/Facility Directory*.

2. Selects an appropriate course of action.

- The most important thing to remember when lost is to remain calm and do not panic.
- When lost you have several options. They include plotting a circle of error, using a radio navigation facility, contacting ATC, or utilizing a ground based facility that has DF equipment.

3. Maintains an appropriate heading and climbs, if necessary.

- When unsure of your position you should continue to fly the original heading, if possible, and watch for recognizable landmarks.
- If deteriorating weather or rising terrain dictate, you should make an appropriate heading change.
- Weather permitting, you should climb for better radio and navigation reception.
- Climbing can also enhance your ability to see identifiable landmarks and features.

4. Identifies prominent landmarks.

- If you spot a prominent landmark, such as a good-sized town or prominent body of water, you should fly toward it and attempt to identify it on your sectional.
- To verify your position, you should attempt to identify other nearby landmarks.

5. Uses navigation systems/facilities and/or contacts an ATC facility for assistance, as appropriate.

- If you are near a navigation facility, you can use it to identify your direction from the station.
- If more than one facility is used, you can identify your position through cross-fixing.
- Anytime you are unsure of your position or feel that the safety of the flight is in jeopardy, it is wise to try to contact ATC.

EXERCISES

1. _____ (True, False) When unsure of your position you should continue to fly your original heading, if possible.
2. The greatest hazard to discovering that you have not arrived at a given checkpoint is __________.
3. Identify the four C's. ____________, ____________, ____________, and ____________.
4. If winds are no more than 30 knots, and it has been 30 minutes since the last known check point, the radius for the circle of error should be approximately_________ nautical miles.

SAMPLE ORAL QUESTIONS

1. When unsure of your position, why shouldn't you change your heading immediately in the direction you think your course is?

____

____

____

____

2. When should you ask for DF assistance?

____

____

____

____

____

3. List several methods you can use to determine your position when you are unsure of your position.

____

____

____

____

____

1. A natural reaction when you are unsure of your position is to panic and fly to where you assume you are supposed to be. As a result, you will typically become disoriented and end up flying further from your desired course.

2. You can ask for DF services at anytime. Most flight service specialists will provide assistance whenever requested. In fact, most will conduct practice DF operations if requested. If an emergency arises you should ask for assistance immediately.

3. When lost, you can determine your position by plotting a circle of error, using navigation facilities, establishing radar contact with ATC, or by contacting a ground based facility that can offer direction finding services.

4. Direction finding equipment requires two-way radio communications with the FSS. The FSS specialist will ask you to key your microphone while the direction finding equipment "homes" in on your radio signal. The specialist can determine your location from the FSS and give you headings to guide you to an airport or provide other assistance. Unlike radar, DF determines only your direction from the FSS. It does not reveal your actual distance from the FSS.

4. Explain the procedures for using VHF direction finding (DF) services.

ADDITIONAL QUESTIONS

5. Explain why it is better to make a precautionary landing rather than run out of fuel.

EXERCISE ANSWERS

1. True
2. panic
3. climb, communicate, confess, comply
4. 15

REFERENCES

JEPPESEN:

Private Pilot Manual/Video – Chapters 5A, 5B, 9A, 9B, 9C

FAA:

Airplane Flying Handbook (FAA-H-8083-3)

Pilot's Handbook of Aeronautical Knowledge (AC 61-23/FAA-H-8083-25)

SLOW FLIGHT AND STALLS

A. TASK: MANEUVERING DURING SLOW FLIGHT (ASEL and ASES)

REFERENCES: FAA-H-8083-3; POH/AFM

Objective: To determine that the applicant:

1. Exhibits knowledge of the elements related to maneuvering during slow flight.
2. Selects an entry altitude that will allow the task to be completed no lower than 1,500 feet (460 meters) AGL.
3. Establishes and maintains an airspeed at which any further increase in angle of attack, increase in load factor, or reduction in power, would result in an immediate stall.
4. Accomplishes coordinated straight-and-level flight, turns, climbs, and descents with landing gear and flap configurations specified by the examiner.
5. Divides attention between airplane control and orientation.
6. Maintains the specified altitude, ±100 feet (30 meters); specified heading, ±10°; airspeed, +10/-0 knots and specified angle of bank, ±10°.

Objective: To determine that the applicant:

1. **Exhibits knowledge of the elements related to maneuvering during slow flight.**

MANEUVERING DURING SLOW FLIGHT

The purpose of maneuvering during slow flight is to help you develop a feel for the airplane's controls at slow airspeeds, as well as gain an understanding of how load factor, pitch attitude, airspeed, and altitude control relate to each other. Maneuvering during slow flight simulates how the airplane responds in an approach-to-land configuration. The speed used for slow flight should be slow enough to induce stall indications with any significant reduction in airspeed or power, or an increase in load factor or pitch.

LOAD FACTOR

As discussed in Chapter 5, load factor is the ratio of weight supported by the wings to the actual weight of the aircraft. During stabilized flight, an aircraft experiences a load factor of 1 G. However, any change in flight attitude, such as a level turn or increase in pitch attitude, increases the aircraft's load factor as well as its stall speed. Because the airspeed is just above a stall during slow flight, any maneuvering during slow flight is done with a corresponding change in power to prevent the aircraft from stalling.

PITCH ATTITUDE

To maintain the proper pitch attitude during slow flight, you should divide your attention between outside references and instrument indications. Primarily, you want to keep your eyes outside the cockpit to keep the nose in a stable attitude, and glance at the panel to monitor airspeed and altitude.

AIRSPEED AND ALTITUDE CONTROL

After the aircraft is established in slow flight, airspeed is controlled by pitch, and altitude by power. If you attempt to climb by applying back pressure, airspeed decreases and the aircraft stalls. To climb, increase power to the appropriate climb setting and slightly increase pitch to maintain your desired airspeed. Once established in the climb, use trim to reduce control pressure. To descend, reduce power and adjust pitch attitude slightly to maintain airspeed.

TURNS

While turning, part of the total lift force is diverted to make the airplane turn. During a turn at normal cruise speed, you must apply slight back pressure to gain the vertical lift needed to maintain level flight. To perform turns in slow flight, you must use a slightly different technique. Shallow turns are accomplished by adding power to maintain sufficient airspeed. In some cases, full power may be required. To maintain coordination, use right rudder to offset P-factor and torque.

2. Selects an entry altitude that will allow the task to be completed no lower than 1,500 feet (460 meters) AGL.

- Select an entry altitude that satisfies the 1,500-foot AGL safety requirement.
- It is best to select an altitude that is easily read on the altimeter such as 3,000 feet or 3,500 feet.
- Your entry altitude ________.

3. Establishes and maintains an airspeed at which any further increase in angle of attack, increase in load factor, or reduction in power, would result in an immediate stall.

- Determine these speeds during training with your instructor before the practical test. Don't wait to go through this for the first time with the examiner. This will take some practice to become proficient and confident.
- In order to determine an approximate speed for your airplane begin by establishing 1.2 V_{S1}. Reduce the speed slowly until the stall warning horn comes on. Continue until any further reductions will result in a stall.
- To determine V_{S1}, refer to the pilot's operating handbook for your aircraft.
- V_{S1} in your aircraft ________. 1.2 V_{S1} ________.

4. Accomplishes coordinated straight-and-level flight, turns, climbs, and descents with landing gear and flap configurations specified by the examiner.

- The examiner will specify the configurations to use.
- As you enter a turn, add power as needed to maintain altitude.
- As power is added, increase right rudder pressure to offset P-factor and torque.
- Adjust power to initiate a climb or descent. Add power to climb and reduce power to descend.
- If no turn is required, use visual references to maintain a wings level attitude and cross-check the heading indicator to maintain a specific heading.
- When turning, use both visual and instrument references to maintain the specified bank angle.
- Slowly roll into coordinated turns as specified by the examiner.
- Always be aware of your position in the turn and anticipate the rollout.
- The rollout should be timed so that you reach wings level on the specified heading.
- A rule of thumb is to lead the rollout by one-half the bank angle.
- While climbing and descending, maintain an awareness of instrument indications in order to level off at the proper altitude.

5. Divides attention between airplane control and orientation.

- Use both visual and instrument references throughout the maneuver.
- Monitor the instrument panel to the extent required to identify inadvertent climbs, descents, and airspeed changes.
- Use outside references to maintain the appropriate pitch and wings level attitude.
- You must maintain a constant awareness of the aircraft's altitude, airspeed, and heading throughout the maneuver.

6. Maintains the specified altitude, ±100 feet (30 meters); specified heading, ±10°; airspeed, +10/-0 knots and specified angle of bank, ±10°.

- Use power to maintain your desired altitude, and anticipate power changes.
- Use visual references to maintain level flight, and cross-check for the desired heading.
- If necessary, use shallow banks to return to your desired heading.
- Use pitch to maintain your desired airspeed.

PROCEDURE

Always clear the area by performing clearing turns before any maneuver.

ENTRY

Altitude ________, Airspeed ________

1. Power — Reduce
2. Pitch — As required
3. Flaps (as speed permits) — Extend
4. Airspeed ________ — Maintain

5 Trim — As required
6 Turns — As specified by the examiner

RECOVERY

7 Power — Maximum
8 Pitch — As required to maintain altitude
9 Flaps — (as speed permits) - Retract

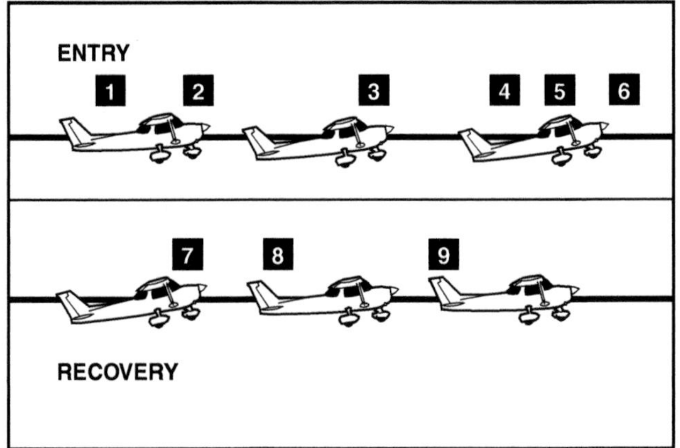

COMMON ERRORS

1. **Gain or loss of altitude during entry.**

   Cause: Raising the nose too quickly or too slowly when transitioning.

   Solution: Reference the altimeter to maintain level flight and use trim as necessary.

2. **Gain or loss of altitude during maneuver.**

   Cause: Not using power appropriately.

   Solution: Don't hesitate to increase or decrease power to maintain level flight.

   Cause: Improper use of trim.

   Solution: Trim the airplane as necessary.

3. **Poor heading control.**

   Cause: Not compensating for torque and P-factor.

   Solution: Add necessary rudder inputs to maintain heading.

EXERCISES

1. When maneuvering during slow flight, use ________ to initiate a climb, and ____________ to change airspeed.
2. When maneuvering during slow flight, what left turning tendencies are most pronounced when power is added?

   ____________ and ____________
3. When recovering from slow flight, what dictates when you can retract the flaps?

   ____
4. ______ (True, False) Load factor and "G" forces have a direct relationship.

SAMPLE ORAL QUESTIONS

1. At slow airspeeds, less air flows over the control surfaces resulting in reduced control effectiveness. At airspeeds near V_{S0}, the loss of effectiveness is typically more apparent.
2. The goal of training in slow flight is to simulate airplane response in an approach-to-land configuration. This allows the pilot to become familiar with aircraft responses at slow speeds for safer traffic pattern operations.

1. Why are the airplane's control surfaces less effective at slow airspeeds?

   ____
   ____
   ____
   ____
2. How does slow flight apply to normal flight operations?

   ____
   ____
   ____
   ____
   ____
   ____

3. Explain how climbs and descents are accomplished during slow flight.

____

____

____

____

____

____

3. Throttle is used to make changes in altitude. If a climb is desired, power is increased; if a descent is desired, power is decreased. Rudder should be used while adding power to compensate for left turning tendencies. Elevator or pitch inputs are used to control airspeed.

ADDITIONAL QUESTIONS

4. Why should bank be limited in this maneuver?

5. During recovery, why is full power added before retracting flaps?

EXERCISE ANSWERS

1. power, pitch

2. P-factor, torque

3. airspeed

4. True

REFERENCES

JEPPESEN:

Private Pilot Manual/Video – Chapters 3A and 3C

Private Pilot Maneuvers/Video – Maneuver 17

FAA:

Airplane Flying Handbook (FAA-H-8083-3)

Pilot's Operating Handbook and FAA-Approved Airplane Flight Manual

B. TASK: POWER-OFF STALLS (ASEL and ASES)

REFERENCES: FAA-H-8083-3, AC 61-67; POH/AHM.

Objective: To determine that the applicant:

1. Exhibits knowledge of the elements related to power-off stalls.
2. Selects an entry altitude that allows the task to be completed no lower than 1,500 feet (460 meters) AGL.
3. Establishes a stabilized descent in the approach or landing configuration, as specified by the examiner.
4. Transitions smoothly from the approach or landing attitude to a pitch attitude that will induce a stall.
5. Maintains a specified heading, ±10°, in straight flight; maintains a specified angle of bank not to exceed 20°, ±10°; in turning flight, while inducing the stall.
6. Recognizes and recovers promptly after the stall occurs by simultaneously reducing the angle of attack, increasing power to maximum allowable, and leveling the wings to return to a straight-and-level flight attitude with a minimum loss of altitude appropriate for the airplane.
7. Retracts the flaps to the recommended setting; retracts the landing gear, if retractable, after a positive rate of climb is established.
8. Accelerates to V_X or V_Y before the final flap retraction; returns to the altitude, heading, and airspeed specified by the examiner.

Objective: To determine that the applicant:

1. **Exhibits knowledge of the elements related to power-off stalls.**

AERODYNAMICS

Before you can fully understand the aerodynamics of stalls, you must have a good understanding of basic aerodynamic concepts and terminology. With this in mind, let's briefly review the four forces.

There are four forces acting on the airplane during flight. They are: lift, weight, thrust, and drag. **Lift** is the upward force created by the wings. **Weight** opposes lift and is caused by the pull of gravity. **Thrust** is the forward force, and it varies with the amount of engine power being produced. Opposing thrust is **drag**, which is a retarding force that limits the speed of the airplane. [Figure 8-1]

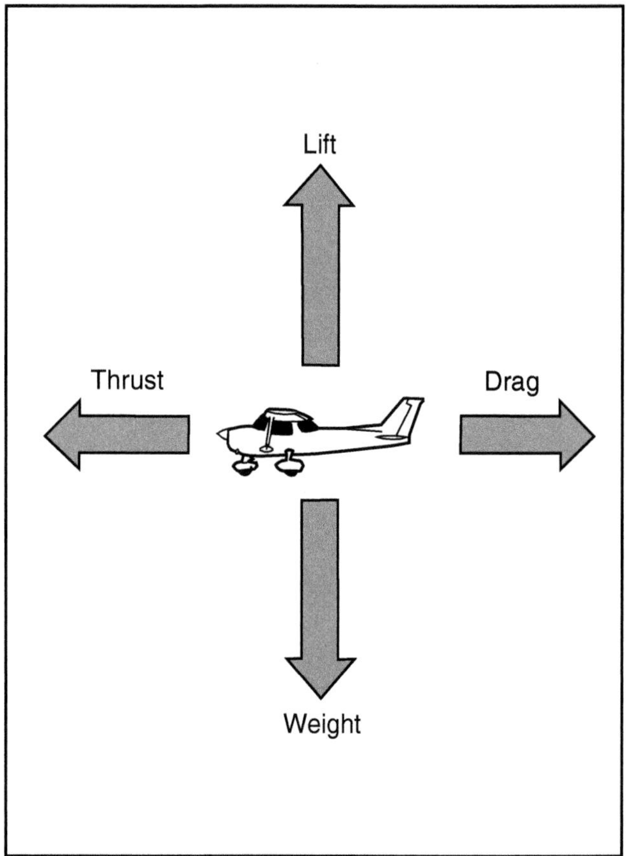

Figure 8-1. In straight-and-level, unaccelerated flight, the four forces are in equilibrium. Weight is equal to and directly opposite lift; thrust is equal to and directly opposite drag.

LIFT

Lift is the aerodynamic force that opposes weight. In straight-and-level, unaccelerated flight, weight and lift are equal, and the airplane is in a state of equilibrium. If the other aerodynamic factors remain constant, the airplane remains at a constant altitude and airspeed.

The wing is designed to divide the airflow into areas of high pressure below the wing and comparatively lower pressure above the wing. This pressure differential is the primary source of lift.

BERNOULLI'S PRINCIPLE

The basic principle of airflow pressure differential was discovered by Daniel Bernoulli, a Swiss physicist. **Bernoulli's Principle** says, "as the velocity of a fluid (air) increases, its internal pressure decreases."

A wing is shaped to take advantage of this principle. The curvature on the upper camber causes air to accelerate as it passes over the wing. This reduces the pressure above the wing while the pressure under the wing remains constant. This pressure differential creates lift.

NEWTON'S THIRD LAW OF MOTION

Another way of explaining lift is provided by Newton's Third Law of Motion, which states that "for every action there is an equal and opposite reaction." The forward motion of the wing and the shape of the airfoil create a downwash of air behind the wing. This action of the airflow over and under the wing accelerates air downward, and the resulting reaction exerts an upward lifting force on the wing.

AIRFOILS

An airfoil is any surface which provides lift when it interacts with air. Some of the terms used to describe the wing, and the interaction of the airflow about it, are listed here. Match the listed terms to the diagram below.

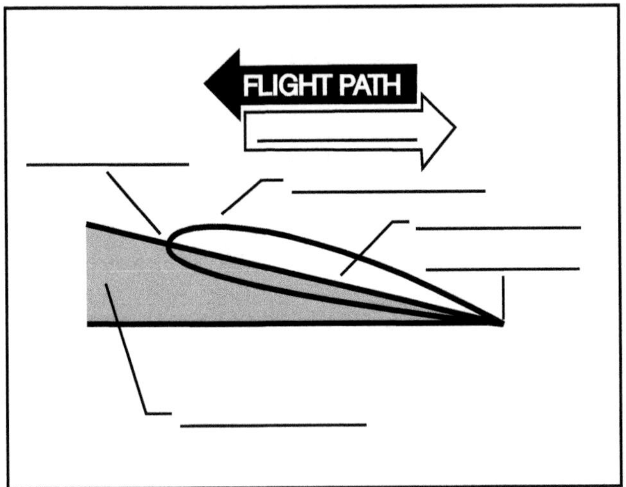

1. **Leading edge** — This part of the airfoil meets the airflow first.

2. **Trailing edge** — This is the portion of the airfoil where the airflow over the upper surface rejoins the lower surface airflow.

3. **Chord line** — The chord line is an imaginary straight line drawn through an airfoil from the leading edge to the trailing edge.

4. **Camber** — The camber of an airfoil is the characteristic curve of its upper and lower surfaces. The upper camber is more pronounced, while the lower camber is comparatively flat.

5. **Angle of attack** — This is the angle between the chord line of the airfoil and the relative wind.

6. **Relative wind** — This is the direction of the airflow with respect to the wing. If a wing moves forward horizontally, the relative wind moves backward horizontally. Relative wind is parallel to and opposite the flight path of the airplane.

CHANGING ANGLE OF ATTACK

You have direct control over angle of attack. During flight at normal operating speeds, if you increase the angle of attack by pulling back on the yoke, you increase lift. Likewise, if you decrease the angle of attack, you decrease lift.

CHANGING AIRSPEED

Another way to control lift is with airspeed. For a given angle of attack, the faster a wing travels, the greater the lift produced. The amount of lift produced is proportional to the square of the airplane's speed. In other words, if airspeed is doubled, lift is increased by a factor of four. On the other hand, if the speed is reduced by one-half, lift decreases to one-quarter of its previous value.

ANGLE OF ATTACK AND AIRSPEED

Total lift depends on the combined effects of airspeed and angle of attack. Since you control both angle of attack and airspeed, you can control lift. When speed decreases, you must increase the angle of attack to maintain the same amount of lift. Conversely, if you want to maintain the same amount of lift at a higher speed, you must decrease the angle of attack.

WEIGHT

Weight always acts straight down, toward the center of the earth. The weight of the airplane varies with the equipment installed, passengers, cargo, and fuel load. During a flight, total weight of an airplane decreases as fuel is burned.

THRUST

Thrust propels an aircraft forward and opposes drag. In propeller-driven airplanes, thrust is provided by the propeller. Each propeller blade is cambered like an airfoil. This shape, plus the angle of attack of the blades, creates reduced pressure in front of the propeller which, essentially produces lift in a forward direction.

When you increase power, thrust also increases, causing the airplane to accelerate. However, as speed increases, drag also increases. The airplane accelerates only when thrust exceeds drag. When drag again equals thrust, the airplane stops accelerating and maintains a constant airspeed.

When you reduce thrust in level flight, drag becomes greater than thrust and causes the airplane to decelerate. But as the airplane slows, drag diminishes. When drag decreases enough to equal thrust, the airplane no longer decelerates.

DRAG

Drag acts in opposition of thrust and is broadly classified as either parasite or induced.

PARASITE DRAG

Parasite drag is caused by any aircraft surface that interferes with the smooth airflow around the airplane. Parasite drag normally is divided into three types: form drag, skin friction drag, and interference drag.

Form drag is created by any structure which protrudes into the relative wind. The amount of drag created is related to both the size and shape of the structure. For example, a square strut will create more drag than a rounded strut.

Skin friction drag is caused by the roughness of the airplane's surfaces. Even though these surfaces may appear smooth, they may be quite rough when viewed through a microscope. A thin layer of air clings to these rough surfaces and creates small eddies which contribute to drag.

Interference drag occurs when varied currents of air over an airplane meet and interact. This interaction creates additional drag. One example of this type of drag is the mixing of air where the wing and fuselage join.

Each type of parasite drag varies with the speed of the airplane. The combined effect generally is proportional to the square of the airplane's speed. In other words, if airspeed doubles, parasite drag increases fourfold. This is the same formula that applies to lift. Because it increases rapidly with airspeed, parasite drag is predominant at high speeds. On the other hand, at low speeds, parasite drag decreases significantly.

INDUCED DRAG

Induced drag is the main by-product of the production of lift and is directly related to the angle of attack of the wing. The greater the angle of attack, the greater the induced drag. Unlike parasite drag, induced drag is inversely proportional to the square of the speed. This means that when speed is decreased by half, induced drag increases fourfold.

TOTAL DRAG

Total drag is the sum of parasite and induced drag. The total drag curve represents these combined forces and is plotted against airspeed. [Figure 8-2]

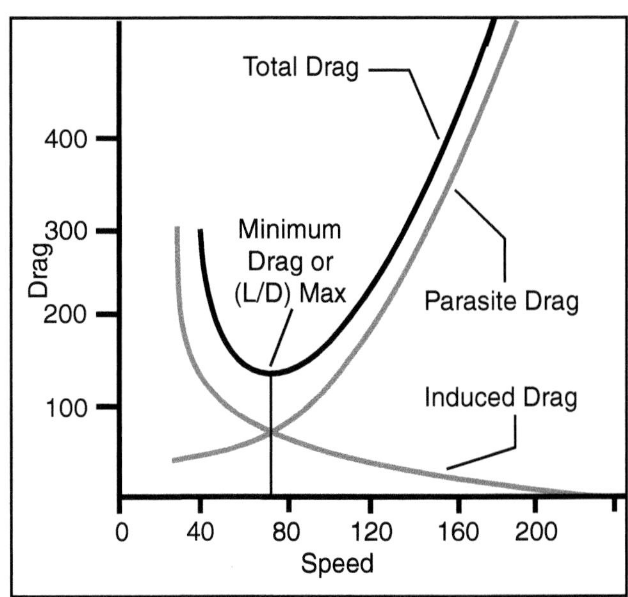

Figure 8-2. The low point on the total drag curve shows the airspeed at which drag is minimized. This is the point where the lift-to-drag ratio is greatest. It is referred to as L/D_{max}.

STALLS

A **stall** is caused by the separation of airflow from the wing's upper surface as it exceeds its critical angle of attack. This is due to the loss of sufficient airflow over the wings. For a given airplane, a stall occurs at the same angle of attack, regardless of airspeed, flight attitude, or weight. However, it's important to remember that an airplane can stall at any airspeed and any attitude. Stall characteristics vary from airplane to airplane. In most training airplanes, the onset of a stall from a level flight attitude is gradual. The first indications are typically provided by a stall warning horn or a slight buffeting of the airplane. To recover from a stall, you must restore the smooth airflow over the wing. This is accomplished by decreasing the angle of attack to a point below the critical angle of attack.

Although the critical angle of attack does not vary with weight, the stalling speed does. It increases slightly as weight increases and decreases as weight decreases. This means you need slightly more airspeed to stay above the stalling speed in a heavily loaded airplane.

AIRFOIL DESIGN FACTORS

In an effort to make training aircraft safer, manufacturers employ several design characteristics that help provide adequate warning before the stall moves to the ailerons. For example, **wing twist** lowers the angle of incidence at the wingtip, resulting in the tip having a lower angle of attack as it approaches the stall. Thus, you get stall indications and still have positive control of the ailerons. Other design features include **stall strips** and **stall fences**. Stall strips are small metal strips near the root on the leading edge of the wings. They disrupt the flow of air near the root in order to induce a stall before it proceeds to the tips. **Stall fences** are placed farther outboard on the wing and create a barrier or fence to prevent rough air from passing over the ailerons. This preserves aileron effectiveness.

POWER-OFF STALLS

Stalls are practiced with two goals in mind. They allow you to gain familiarity with the stall characteristics of your airplane; and secondly, you become conditioned to recover from an inadvertent stall quickly and with a minimal loss in altitude.

Power-off stalls are performed in the landing configuration and are used to simulate an accidental stall during approach. The speed used to practice a power-off stall should be the aircraft's approach speed. If higher speeds are used during the stall entry, an abnormally nose-high attitude could result.

To enter a stall, apply carburetor heat (if required), reduce power to idle, apply flaps as specified by your instructor or examiner (once a safe flap extension speed has been attained), establish a normal glide, and trim the airplane. To allow you to get a better feel for the aircraft, it is recommended that you practice power-off stalls with different flap settings. Next, start to slow the airplane by applying back pressure on the control wheel. Directional control should be maintained with the rudder, the wings held level by the ailerons, and a constant pitch attitude maintained with the elevator until the full stall occurs.

As part of your stall/spin awareness training, you will be required to recognize the signs of an impending stall. For example, while the stall warning horn acts as a good aural warning, buffeting and decay of control effectiveness are good aerodynamic indications of an approaching stall.

RECOVERY AND SECONDARY STALLS

As stall recovery is initiated, your first action is to add power while simultaneously relaxing back pressure to reduce the angle of attack. The amount of back pressure that must be relaxed should be enough to break the stall with minimal loss of altitude. You must also use rudder pressure to maintain coordination. Normally, flaps are then retracted to an intermediate setting; however, the retraction procedures for stall recovery vary widely from one airplane to another. Once the wing begins flying again and airspeed approaches V_X, raise the nose to return to level or climbing flight. However, if the nose is raised too fast, additional G-loading is exerted on the wings which in turn increases the stall speed. If the stall speed increases beyond the current airspeed, the aircraft will enter a secondary stall. [Figure 8-3]

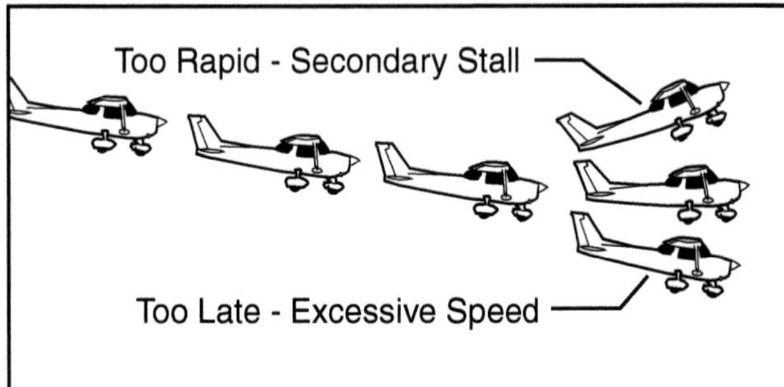

Figure 8-3. Applying back pressure too abruptly will result in a secondary stall. Applying back pressure too late will cause an excessive loss of altitude.

IMMINENT STALLS

During stall training, you will do both full stalls and imminent stalls. Sometimes referred to as an incipient stall, an imminent stall is characterized by buffeting and a decay in control effectiveness. If you react promptly with the correct control response, the aircraft will not completely stall.

TURNING FLIGHT STALLS

Recovery from power-off stalls should also be practiced from turns to simulate an accidental stall during a turn from base leg to final approach. When practicing these stalls, use section lines or roads as references to line up the aircraft on a base to final. As you begin the maneuver, the turn should continue at a uniform rate until the complete stall occurs. However, the stall should occur no later than the imaginary "line-up" on final. If the turn is not properly coordinated when approaching the stall, one wing may stall before the other. For example, if the airplane is in a slip, the outer wing may stall first and drop abruptly.

After the full stall occurs, the recovery should be made straight ahead with the wings leveled through coordinated use of the controls.

2. Selects an entry altitude that will allow the task to be completed no lower than 1,500 feet (460 meters) AGL.

- Since you must recover from a stall no lower than 1,500 feet AGL, you should begin the maneuver at an altitude of at least 2,000 feet AGL.
- It is best to select an altitude that is easily read on the altimeter, such as 3,000 or 3,500 ft.
- Your entry altitude __________.

3. Establishes a stabilized descent in the approach or landing configuration, as specified by the examiner.

- Establish the landing configuration by applying carb heat (if necessary) and reducing power.
- Begin extending flaps as specified when a safe flap extension speed (V_{FE}) is attained.
- V_{FE} for your aircraft__________ kts.
- Use a combination of pitch and power adjustments to obtain the appropriate approach speed.

4. Transitions smoothly from the approach or landing attitude to a pitch attitude that will induce a stall.

- As airspeed decreases, apply back pressure to maintain a pitch attitude that will induce a stall.
- Maintain this attitude until the wings stall.

5. Maintains a specified heading, ±10°, in straight flight; maintains a specified angle of bank not to exceed 20°, ±10°; in turning flight, while inducing the stall.

- Use outside references such as section lines and the horizon to maintain a wings level attitude and glance at the heading indicator to hold a specific heading.

- When practicing turning stalls, use both outside references and the attitude indicator to maintain the angle of bank specified by the examiner.

6. Recognizes and recovers promptly after the stall occurs by simultaneously reducing the angle of attack, increasing power to maximum allowable, and leveling the wings to return to a straight-and-level flight attitude with a minimum loss of altitude appropriate for the airplane.

- Buffeting or lack of control effectiveness signals the onset of a stall.
- Recover from a stall by simultaneously decreasing pitch, applying power, and leveling the wings.
- As the speed approaches V_X, return to level flight.
- Do not raise the nose too abruptly after recovering, or you could induce a secondary stall

7. Retracts the flaps to the recommended setting; retracts the landing gear, if retractable, after a positive rate of climb is established.

- Retract the flaps using the procedures recommended by the manufacturer.
- Retract the landing gear, if retractable, when a positive rate of climb is established.

8. Accelerates to V_x or V_y before the final flap retraction; returns to the altitude, heading, and airspeed specified by the examiner.

- After accelerating to V_Y, retract the final increment of flaps.
- V_Y for your aircraft ___________.

PROCEDURE

Always clear the area by performing clearing turns before any maneuver.

ENTRY

Altitude _________, Airspeed _________

1 Carburetor heat — As required
2 Power — Idle, or _________ RPM
3 Wing flaps _________
4 Bank — As desired (do not exceed 30°)
5 Pitch attitude — Maintain until stall occurs

RECOVERY

6 Elevator pressure — Release
7 Power — Maximum
8 Carburetor heat — As required
9 Wings — Level
10 Flying speed — Maintain
11 Altitude — Maintain
12 Wing flaps — As desired

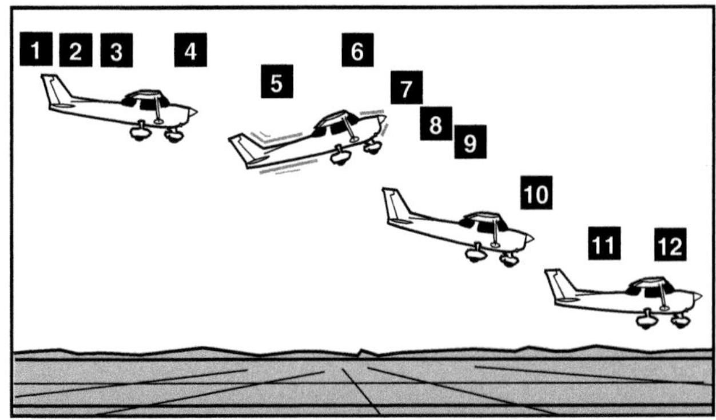

COMMON ERRORS

1. **Aircraft mushes rather than stalling.**

   Cause: Nose not high enough to induce a full stall.

   Solution: As speed decreases, add back pressure until indications of a stall occur.

2. **Not maintaining the bank angle specified.**

   Cause: Not scanning visual and/or instrument references (fixation).

   Solution: Maintain your desired bank angle by scanning the horizon and attitude indicator.

3. **Excessive loss of altitude during the recovery.**

   Cause: Lowering the nose too far during the recovery.

   Solution: Push the nose forward just to the extent required to break the stall. Then, as V_X is reached, raise the nose to a climb attitude.

EXERCISES

1. What are the four aerodynamic forces?

   _________________ _________________

   _________________ _________________

2. A stall occurs at the same _________ _________ _________ regardless of airspeed, flight attitude, or weight.

3. When wing twist is used in the design of a wing, it creates a _________ (higher, lower) angle of incidence at the tip.

4. _____ (True, False) The airplane will stall at a lower angle of attack with flaps extended.

5. Secondary stalls are caused by using ____________ (excessive, insufficient) back pressure during recovery.

SAMPLE ORAL QUESTIONS

1. Explain how wing twist, stall strips, and stall fences affect the wing's stall characteristics?

2. Explain Newton's Third Law.

3. What is the difference between parasite and induced drag?

1. When designing a wing, manufacturers use several design techniques to provide adequate warning to an impending stall. One such technique is the use of wing twist, which decreases the angle of incidence near the tip. This causes the wing root to stall first, resulting in positive aileron control in the stall. Stall strips are small metal strips on the leading edge of the wing, near the root. They serve to disrupt the airflow at the wing root as you approach the stall. Stall fences are on top of the wing. These also help prevent burbling air from flowing over the ailerons.

2. As an airplane flies through the air, the airfoil forces air downward. Newton's Third Law states that for every action, there is an equal and opposite reaction. Downwash behind the wing is the action, and the equal and opposite reaction is lift.

3. Parasite drag is caused by any aircraft surface that interferes with the smooth airflow around the airplane. Parasite drag normally is divided into three types: form drag, skin friction drag, and interference drag. The combined effect of these three types of parasite drag is proportional to the square of the airplane's speed. In other words, if airspeed doubles, parasite drag increases fourfold. Induced drag is the main by-product of the production of lift and is directly related to the angle of attack of the wing. The greater the angle of attack, the greater the induced drag. Unlike parasite drag, induced drag is inversely proportional to the square of the speed. This means that when speed is decreased by half, induced drag increases fourfold.

4. A wing stalls whenever its critical angle of attack is exceeded. As a wing approaches its critical angle of attack, the airflow over the wing begins to separate and become turbulent. The disrupted airflow separates from the wing surface, and stalls.

4. Why does a wing stall?

____

____

____

____

____

____

____

ADDITIONAL QUESTIONS

5. Why might one wing drop when doing full stalls?
6. Why should you practice power-off stalls?
7. Explain Bernoulli's Principle.
8. How does airspeed affect lift and drag?
9. What defines a wing's angle of attack?

EXERCISE ANSWERS

1. lift, weight, thrust, and drag
2. angle of attack
3. lower
4. True
5. excessive

REFERENCES

JEPPESEN:

Private Pilot Manual/Video – Chapters 3 and 8A

Private Pilot Maneuvers/Video – Maneuver 18

FAA:

Airplane Flying Handbook (FAA-H-8083-3)

Stall and Spin Awareness Training (AC 61-67)

Pilot's Operating Handbook and FAA-Approved Airplane Flight Manual

C. TASK: POWER-ON STALLS (ASEL and ASES)

NOTE: In some high performance airplanes, the power setting may have to be reduced below the practical test standards guideline power setting to prevent excessively high pitch attitudes (greater than 30° nose up).

REFERENCES: FAA-H-8083-3, AC 61-67; POH/AFM

Objective: To determine that the applicant:

1. Exhibits knowledge of the elements related to power-on stalls.
2. Selects an entry altitude that will allow the task to be completed no lower than 1,500 feet (460 meters) AGL.
3. Establishes the takeoff or departure configuration. Sets power to no less than 65 percent available power.
4. Transitions smoothly from the takeoff or departure attitude to the pitch attitude that will induce a stall.
5. Maintains a specified heading, ±10°, in straight flight; maintains a specified angle of bank not to exceed 20°, ±10°, in turning flight, while inducing the stall.
6. Recognizes and recovers promptly after the stall occurs by simultaneously reducing the angle of attack, increasing power as appropriate, and leveling the wings to return to a straight-and-level flight attitude with a minimum loss of altitude appropriate for the airplane.
7. Retracts the flaps to the recommended setting; retracts the landing gear if retractable, after a positive rate of climb is established.
8. Accelerates to V_X or V_Y before the final flap retraction; returns to the altitude, heading, and airspeed specified by the examiner.

Objective: To determine that the applicant:

1. Exhibits knowledge of the elements related to power-on stalls.

POWER-ON STALLS

Power-on stalls are practiced in the takeoff configuration from straight climbs and climbing turns to simulate an inadvertent stall during takeoff and/or departure. This type of stall can occur if you attempt to take off at too slow an airspeed and apply excessive back pressure to the control wheel. This produces an extreme nose-high attitude and high angle of attack. The power-on, turning stall normally occurs during the departure turn following takeoff and generally results from distractions that divert your attention from flying the airplane.

Aerodynamically, power-on stalls are similar to power-off stalls. To enter the stall, establish a takeoff or departure configuration, and slow the airplane to a normal liftoff speed. The purpose of reducing the speed to liftoff speed before advancing the throttle is to avoid an excessively steep nose-up attitude for a long period before the airplane stalls. When the desired speed is attained, the throttle should be set at takeoff power for the takeoff stall or the recommended climb power for the departure stall while establishing a climb attitude.

In most airplanes, once the stalling attitude is attained, elevator back pressure must be increased as airspeed decreases until the stall occurs. In order to maintain directional control and coordination, increase right rudder pressure as you increase the power and pitch attitude. Throughout the approach to the stall and the recovery, you should maintain coordinated flight. If this is not done, one wing could stall before the other and cause the aircraft to enter a spin.

Recovery from the stall is accomplished by immediately reducing the angle of attack and advancing the throttle to maximum power. Once you have regained flying speed, the airplane is returned to straight-and-level flight or a climb, as appropriate. When in normal level flight, the throttle is returned to a cruise power setting.

TURNING STALLS

The power-on turning stall is a variation of the power-on, straight-ahead stall. Enter a power-on turning stall in the same way you enter a straight-ahead stall, but with a bank of up to 30° to the left or right.

As you approach the stall, the angle of bank tends to steepen in a left turn and become shallower in a right turn. This occurs because torque and P-factor tend to roll the airplane to the left. When you practice stalls in each of these variations, you should try to identify the indications of the approaching stall and use coordinated aileron and rudder application throughout the entire maneuver.

The recovery is the same as for the power-on, straight-ahead stall. Lower the nose while simultaneously applying full power, then use coordinated aileron and rudder pressures to return the airplane to straight-and-level flight or a climb, as appropriate.

2. Selects an entry altitude that will allow the task to be completed no lower than 1,500 feet (460 meters) AGL.

- Since you must recover from a stall no lower than 1,500 feet AGL, you should begin the maneuver at an altitude of at least 2,000 feet AGL.
- It is best to select an altitude that is easily read on the altimeter, such as 3,000 ft or 3,500 ft.
- Your entry altitude __________ .

3. Establishes the takeoff or departure configuration. Sets power to no less than 65 percent available power.

- To begin the maneuver, slow the airspeed to take-off speed to avoid an excessively high pitch attitude.
- On high performance aircraft, a reduced power setting may be used to avoid an excessive pitch attitude.

4. Transitions smoothly from the takeoff or departure attitude to the pitch attitude that will induce a stall.

- As airspeed decreases, you must increase back pressure until a stall occurs.
- When doing this maneuver, apply back pressure smoothly.

5. Maintains a specified heading, ±10°, in straight flight; maintains a specified angle of bank not to exceed 20°, ±10°, in turning flight, while inducing the stall.

- Use outside references, such as section lines, to maintain a wings level altitude and cross-check the heading indicator to hold a specific heading.
- When conducting turning stalls, use outside references and the attitude indicator to maintain the angle of bank specified by the examiner.

6. Recognizes and recovers promptly after the stall occurs by simultaneously reducing the angle of attack, increasing power as appropriate, and leveling the wings to return to a straight-and-level flight attitude with a minimum loss of altitude appropriate for the airplane.

- Buffeting or lack of control effectiveness signals the onset of a stall.
- Recover from a stall by simultaneously decreasing pitch and applying full power. Then level the wings.
- When speed permits, return to level flight.
- Do not raise the nose too abruptly after recovering, or you could induce a secondary stall.

7. Retracts the flaps to the recommended setting; retracts the landing gear if retractable, after a positive rate of climb is established.

- Retract the flaps using the procedures recommended by the manufacturer.
- Retract the landing gear, if retractable, when a positive rate of climb is established.

8. Accelerates to V_X or V_Y before the final flap retraction; returns to the altitude, heading, and airspeed specified by the examiner.

- After accelerating to V_Y, retract the final increment of flaps.
- V_Y for your aircraft __________.

PROCEDURE

Always clear the area by performing clearing turns before every maneuver.

ENTRY

Altitude __________ , Airspeed __________

1. Wing flaps (when speed permits) — As required
2. Power — Maximum or __________ RPM
3. Bank Angle — As required
4. Nose-high pitch attitude — Maintain until stall occurs

RECOVERY

5. Elevator pressure — Release
6. Power — Maximum
7. Wings — Level
8. Altitude — Maintain when airspeed permits
9. Power — As required
10. Wing flaps — As required

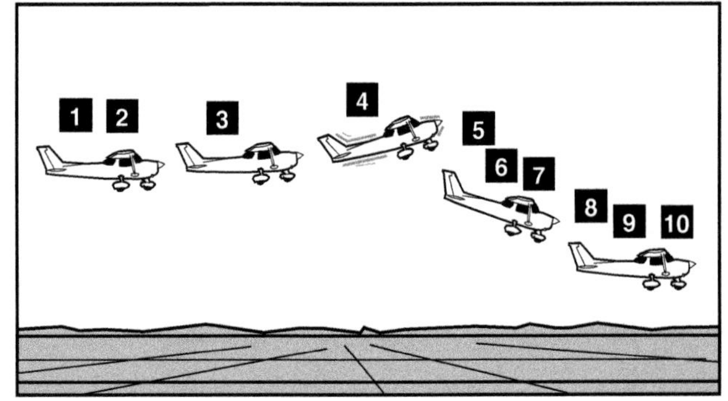

COMMON ERRORS

1. **Excessive nose high attitude prior to stalling.**

   Cause: Not reducing airspeed to take-off speed before starting the maneuver.

   Solution: Prior to beginning maneuver, reduce power and slow to liftoff speed.

2. **Not maintaining the bank angle specified.**

   Cause: Not scanning visual and/or instrument references (fixation).

   Solution: Maintain your desired bank angle by scanning the horizon and attitude indicator.

3. **Excessive loss of altitude during the recovery.**

   Cause: Lowering the nose too far during the recovery.

   Solution: During the recovery, pitch the aircraft's nose down just below the horizon. Then, raise the nose to level flight as soon as V_X is obtained.

4. **Not maintaining coordinated flight.**

   Cause: Not compensating for the effects of torque and P-factor.

   Solution: As pitch attitude increases and airspeed decreases, you must increase right rudder pressure to counter torque and P-factor.

5. **Entering a secondary stall.**

   Cause: Pulling the nose up too abruptly during the recovery.

   Solution: Allow airspeed to build sufficiently before returning to level flight.

EXERCISES

1. To recover from a power-on stall, apply full power and simultaneously __________ (increase, decrease) the angle of attack.
2. As airspeed __________, you must __________ back pressure to achieve the pitch required to stall the airplane.
3. The maximum bank angle permitted when practicing power-on, turning stalls is __________°.

SAMPLE ORAL QUESTIONS

1. Why must you hold right rudder pressure when executing power-on stalls?

   ____

   ____

   ____

   ____

2. Explain why you should slow to liftoff speed prior to executing a power-on stall.

   ____

   ____

   ____

   ____

3. Where are power-on stalls most frequently encountered?

   ____

   ____

   ____

   ____

   ____

   ____

1. As the pitch attitude and power are increased, and airspeed decreases, the effects of P-factor and torque become more pronounced. To offset this, additional right rudder pressure must be used.

2. The purpose of reducing the aircraft's speed to liftoff speed before the throttle is advanced is to avoid an excessively steep nose-up attitude for a long period before the airplane stalls.

3. Power-on stalls typically occur when you attempt to takeoff at too slow an airspeed and apply excessive back pressure. The power-on, turning stall normally occurs during the departure turn following takeoff. This type of stall generally results from distractions that divert your attention from flying the airplane.

ADDITIONAL QUESTIONS

4. Explain the procedure for recovering from a power-on stall.

5. How does slipstream affect the flight controls in a power-on stall?

EXERCISE ANSWERS

1. decrease

2. decreases, increase

3. 30°

REFERENCES

JEPPESEN:

Private Pilot Manual/Video – Chapters 3 and 8A

Private Pilot Maneuvers/Video – Maneuver 19

FAA:

Airplane Flying Handbook (FAA-H-8083-3)

Pilot's Operating Handbook and FAA-Approved Airplane Flight Manual

D. TASK: SPIN AWARENESS (ASEL and ASES)

REFERENCES: FAA-H-8083-3, AC 61-67; POH/AFM

Objective: To determine that the applicant exhibits knowledge of the elements related to spin awareness by explaining :

1. Aerodynamic factors related to spins.
2. Flight situations where unintentional spins may occur.
3. Procedures for recovery from unintentional spins.

Objective: To determine that the applicant exhibits knowledge of the elements related to spin awareness by explaining:

1. Aerodynamic factors related to spins.

SPIN AWARENESS

As a private pilot applicant, you are not required to perform spins on the practical test, however, you must have an understanding of the flight situations that may cause a spin, as well as the proper recovery techniques. Private pilot spin training emphasizes **awareness**, **prevention**, and **recovery** from an inadvertent spin, rather than performing the maneuver. Throughout your flying career, you should concentrate your efforts on **avoiding** the conditions that could lead to an unintentional spin. However, should you inadvertently enter a spin, you must have an understanding of how to recover quickly with a minimal loss of altitude.

AERODYNAMICS

A spin is often referred to as an aggravated stall which results in autorotation. In order for a spin to develop, a stall must occur first. However, a stall is essentially a coordinated maneuver where both wings are equally or almost equally stalled. In contrast, a spin is an uncoordinated maneuver with the wings unequally stalled. In this case, the wing that is more completely stalled will often drop before the other, and the nose of the aircraft will yaw in the direction of the low wing.

PHASES OF A SPIN

In light, training airplanes, a complete spin maneuver consists of three phases — incipient, developed, and recovery. The **incipient spin** is that portion of a spin from the time the airplane stalls and rotation starts until the spin is fully developed. A **fully developed** spin means the angular rotation rates, airspeed, and vertical speed are stabilized from turn to turn and the flight path is close to vertical. The **recovery** phase is characterized by the rotation rate slowing and the angle of attack on both wings decreasing below the critical angle. [Figure 8-4]

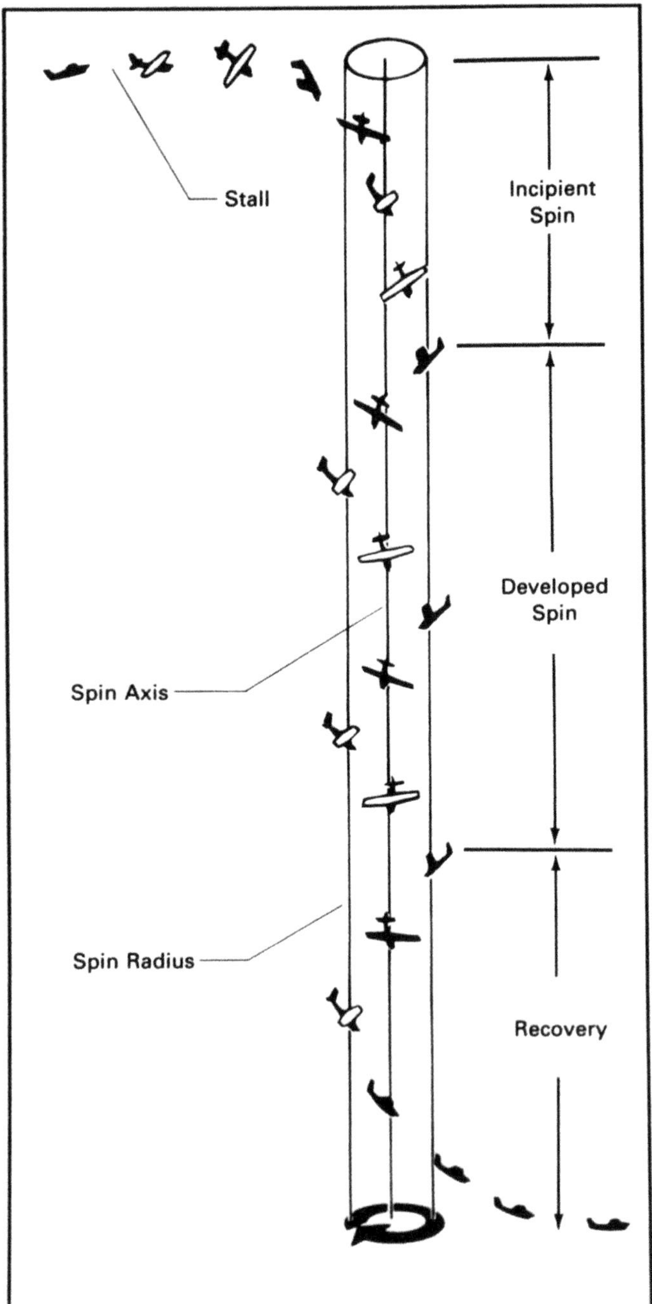

Figure 8-4. The incipient spin usually occurs rapidly in light airplanes (about 4 to 6 seconds) and consists of approximately the first two turns. At about the half-turn point, the airplane is pointed almost straight down, but the angle of attack is usually above that of the stall because of the inclined flight path. As the one-turn point approaches, the nose may come back up and the angle of attack continues to increase. As the airplane continues to rotate into the second turn, the flight path becomes more nearly vertical, and the pitching, rolling, and yawing motions become more repeatable. This is the beginning of the fully developed spin. The last phase, recovery, occurs when anti-spin forces overcome pro-spin forces. During recovery, the angle of attack on both wings decreases below the critical angle and the rotation rate slows. This phase can range from one quarter of a turn to several turns.

2. Flight situations where unintentional spins may occur.

FLIGHT CONDITIONS LEADING TO SPINS

Typically, the cause of an inadvertent spin is exceeding the critical angle of attack while performing an uncoordinated maneuver. The lack of coordination is normally caused by either too much or not enough rudder control for the amount of aileron being used. The result is a cross-controlled condition. If you do not initiate the stall recovery promptly, the airplane is more likely to enter a full stall that may develop into a spin. The spin that occurs from cross controlling usually results in rotation in the direction of the rudder being applied, regardless of which wing is raised. Coordinated use of the flight controls is important, especially when you are maneuvering at low airspeeds near the ground. This is emphasized by the fact that stall/spin accidents account for approximately 25% of all fatal general aviation accidents. On takeoff, the common cause of a stall/spin include preoccupation with situations inside or outside the cockpit, maneuvering to avoid other aircraft, maneuvering to clear obstacles, power failure, and incorrect flap setting. During the landing phase, the common causes include overshooting the turn from base to final, not flying a stabilized approach, pilot distraction, and power failure.

WEIGHT AND BALANCE

Even minor weight and balance changes can affect an aircraft's spin characteristics. For example, a forward center of gravity usually inhibits the high angles of attack necessary for a stall. Thus, an airplane with a forward CG tends to be more stall and spin resistant than an aircraft with an aft CG. In addition, spins with aft CG positions are flatter than ordinary spins. A **flat spin** is characterized by a near level pitch and roll attitude with the spin axis near the CG of the airplane. Recovery from a flat spin may be extremely difficult or even impossible.

In a training airplane, a back seat passenger or a suitcase in an aft baggage compartment can affect the CG enough to change the characteristics of a spin. Instead of an ordinary spin, a flat spin could easily occur.

3. Procedures for recovery from unintentional spins.

SPIN RECOVERY

It should be clear, as an applicant for a private pilot certificate, that you are not required to demonstrate flight proficiency in spin entries or spin recovery techniques. As already mentioned, the emphasis in stall/spin awareness training for private pilots is awareness of conditions that could lead to an unintentional stall or spin. You also need to have a basic understanding of how to recover from a spin.

Spin recovery techniques vary for different aircraft; therefore, you must follow the recovery procedures outlined in the POH for your airplane. The following is a general recovery procedure, but it should not be applied arbitrarily without regard for the manufacturer's recommendations.

Since an airplane must be in a stalled condition before it will spin, the first thing you should do is try to recover from the stall before the spin develops. However, if a spin develops, move the throttle to idle, neutralize the ailerons, and raise the flaps. Next, apply full rudder deflection opposite to the direction of the turn. When the rotation rate slows, briskly position the elevator forward to approximately the neutral position to decrease the angle of attack. As the rotation stops, neutralize the rudder and smoothly apply back pressure to recover from the steep nose-down pitch attitude. During recovery from the dive, make sure you avoid excessive airspeed and high G-forces. This could cause an accelerated stall, or even result in structural failure.

- List the specific spin recovery procedures for your airplane, as recommended by the manufacturer:

EXERCISES

1. _____ (True, False) Spins are a required maneuver for private pilot applicants.

2. A spin is a(n) ______________ (coordinated, uncoordinated) maneuver.

3. An aircraft must ______________ before it can spin.

4. _____ (True, False) The aircraft's center of gravity has no effect on spin characteristics.

SAMPLE ORAL QUESTIONS

1. Explain the purpose of stall/spin awareness training.

1. The purpose of stall/spin awareness training is to give you an understanding of the flight situations that can result in a spin. Private pilot spin training emphasizes awareness, prevention, and recovery from an unintentional spin. This training should get you to concentrate your efforts on avoiding the conditions that can lead to an unintentional spin.

2. What is an incipient spin?

2. In most light general aviation aircraft, the first two turns in the spin are incipient. Beyond that, it is usually a developed spin. It is the point in the maneuver that the movements about each axis — pitch, roll, and yaw — are accelerating.

3. How does G-loading affect the airplane during a spin?

3. During the initiation of a spin, **no** additional G- loading is present. In fact, only during recovery, when the nose is raised, is additional G-loading exerted on the aircraft. This is because airspeed remains very slow throughout a spin.

ADDITIONAL QUESTIONS

4. What causes an aircraft to enter a flat spin?
5. Why is spinning with flaps more hazardous than without flaps?

EXERCISE ANSWERS

1. False
2. uncoordinated
3. stall
4. False

REFERENCES

JEPPESEN:

Private Pilot Manual/Video – Chapters 3B and 8B
Private Pilot Maneuvers/Video – Maneuver 20

FAA:

Airplane Flying Handbook (FAA-H-8083-3)
Pilot's Operating Handbook and FAA-Approved Airplane Flight Manual
Stall and Spin Awareness Training (AC 61-67)

BASIC INSTRUMENT MANEUVERS

A. TASK: STRAIGHT-AND-LEVEL FLIGHT (ASEL and ASES)

REFERENCES: FAA-H-8083-3, FAA-H-8083-15.

Objective: To determine that the applicant:

1. Exhibits knowledge of the elements related to attitude instrument flying during straight-and-level flight.
2. Maintains straight-and-level flight solely by reference to instruments using proper instrument cross-check and interpretation, and coordinated control application.
3. Maintains altitude, ± 200 feet (60 meters); heading, ± 20°; and airspeed, ± 10 knots.

Objective: To determine that the applicant:

1. **Exhibits knowledge of the elements related to attitude instrument flying during straight-and-level flight.**

ATTITUDE INSTRUMENT FLYING

In order to fly solely by reference to instruments, you need to integrate three fundamental skills. They are the instrument cross-check, instrument interpretation, and aircraft control. Instrument cross-check requires you to logically and systematically observe, or scan, the instrument panel. Instrument interpretation begins with the knowledge of how each instrument indication relates to the aircraft's flight attitude. The last skill, aircraft control, requires smooth coordination of pitch, bank, power, and trim.

Although instrument training is required for private pilot certification, the purpose of this training is to allow you to get out of instrument conditions quickly and safely in case of an unintentional encounter. Even after you attain reasonable skill in performing the basic attitude instrument maneuvers and recoveries from unusual flight attitudes, you should never undertake flight in instrument conditions until you are appropriately rated.

During most of your private pilot training, you maintained straight-and-level flight with visual references. However, when flying this way, you typically cross-check your visual references with the altimeter, airspeed indicator, and heading indicator. During flight by instrument references, the natural horizon is replaced by the attitude indicator, and the remaining instruments have the same function as during visual flight. The general information provided by the attitude indicator is correlated with the specific information gained from the altimeter, airspeed indicator, heading indicator, vertical speed indicator, and turn coordinator.

SCANNING

The continuous and systematic cross-check of the flight instruments is known as scanning. The actual technique used to scan varies somewhat, depending on individual differences, the type of maneuver being conducted, and variations in airplane equipment. When scanning, the instruments are classified as primary and supporting. Primary instruments provide the most essential information, while the supporting instruments verify the information indicated on the primary instruments.

A problem many pilots have at first is scanning too rapidly and looking directly at the instruments without knowing exactly what information they're looking for. However, with familiarity and practice, definite scanning patterns begin to develop during specific flight conditions. These patterns help you control the airplane as it makes a transition from one flight condition to another.

When scanning, there are three common errors that will cause poor aircraft control. They are fixation, emphasis, and omission. **Fixation** occurs when you concentrate on a single instrument. You should look at each instrument only long enough to understand the information it presents, then continue on to the next one.

Similarly, you may find yourself placing too much **emphasis** on a single instrument, instead of relying on a combination of instruments necessary for airplane performance information. This differs from fixation in that you are using other instruments, but are giving too much attention to a particular one.

Omission occurs when you forget to include an instrument in your scan pattern. For example, during leveloff from a climb or descent, you may concentrate on pitch control, while forgetting about heading or roll information.

2. Maintains straight-and-level flight solely by reference to instruments using proper instrument cross-check and interpretation, and coordinated control application.

STRAIGHT-AND-LEVEL FLIGHT

To maintain straight-and-level flight by instrument reference, you must control the pitch and bank of the airplane through interpretation of the flight instruments.

PITCH CONTROL

The instruments used to interpret pitch are the attitude indicator, airspeed indicator, altimeter, and vertical speed indicator. Any change in the pitch registers on these instruments in direct proportion to the magnitude of the change.

PITCH INSTRUMENTS

During straight-and-level flight, the altimeter is considered the primary pitch instrument. Since your altitude should remain constant when the airplane is in level flight, any deviation in altitude indicates the need for a pitch change. The rate of change and direction of movement of the altimeter needle are both important indicators for maintaining level flight. Large pitch attitude deviations from level flight result in rapid altitude changes whereas slight pitch deviations produce much slower changes in the altimeter.

The instruments that support the altimeter include the attitude indicator, airspeed indicator, and vertical speed indicator (VSI), and should be used as a cross-check to verify what the altimeter is displaying. [Figure 9-1]

Altitude Correction Rules

When making changes in pitch, it's best to make small corrections to prevent overcontrolling. A good rule of thumb for altitude corrections of 100 feet or less is to adjust pitch by one-half bar width on the attitude indicator. When altitude corrections are this small, a power change is not required. For corrections in excess of 100 feet, use a full bar width correction initially and adjust the power and trim as necessary. As you establish these corrections, observe the rate of altitude change on the vertical speed indicator and the altimeter.

BANK CONTROL

To maintain a straight flight path, you must keep the aircraft's wings level with the horizon. The instruments used to interpret bank are the heading indicator, attitude indicator, and turn coordinator.

Figure 9-1. The instruments used for pitch control include the airspeed indicator, attitude indicator, altimeter, and the vertical speed indicator.

BANK INSTRUMENTS

In straight-and-level flight, the principal instrument used for bank control is the attitude indicator. As long as the wing bars in the indicator are level with the artificial horizon, straight flight will be maintained. This also applies to the miniature airplane on the turn coordinator. As long as the wings of the miniature airplane remain level and the ball centered, the aircraft is in level flight.

When in straight flight, the heading indicator should be checked frequently to determine whether a straight flight path is actually being maintained. This is particularly true when flying in turbulent air, as even a slight gust may bank the airplane and make it turn. [Figure 9-2]

Heading Correction Rule

A common rule for correcting to your heading is to use a bank angle equal to one-half the deviation. For example, if you are 20° off your desired heading, use the attitude indicator to enter a 10° bank angle. However, do not exceed the bank required for a standard-rate turn.

3. Maintains altitude, ± 200 feet (60 meters); heading, ± 20°; and airspeed, ± 10 knots.

- To maintain altitude, scan the altimeter, attitude indicator, vertical speed indicator, and airspeed indicator.
- To correct for deviations in altitude, make small corrections using the attitude indicator.
- For altitude corrections of 100 feet or less adjust pitch by one-half the bar width on the attitude indicator. For corrections in excess of 100 feet, use a full bar width correction.
- Maintain a heading by keeping the wings of the miniature airplane in the attitude indicator level with the horizon and cross-checking the heading indicator.
- To make heading corrections, make small corrections using the attitude indicator.
- If altitude is maintained, airspeed will remain within the ±10 knot requirement.

COMMON ERRORS

1. **Gain or loss of altitude.**

   Cause: Improper scan, fixating on, or emphasizing a single instrument.

Figure 9-2. The instruments used for bank control include the attitude indicator, heading indicator or directional gyro, and the turn coordinator.

Solution: Scan the altimeter, attitude indicator, VSI, and airspeed indicator to maintain altitude.

Cause: Improper trim.

Solution: Set the pitch attitude, and use trim to relieve control wheel pressure.

2. **Not maintaining an assigned heading.**

Cause: Improper scan, fixating on, or emphasizing a single instrument.

Solution: Use the attitude indicator and turn coordinator to maintain a wings level attitude and cross-check the heading indicator to verify your heading.

3. **Overcontrolling the aircraft.**

Cause: Applying excessive control wheel pressure and corrections.

Solution: Once established in level flight, use trim to remove any control pressures. If corrections are necessary, use small control inputs.

EXERCISES

1. The three fundamental skills used in attitude instrument flying are the instrument _____________, instrument ____________, and aircraft ___________.
2. The instrument which replaces the horizon during instrument flight is the ___________ indicator.
3. During straight-and-level flight, the four instruments providing pitch information are the airspeed indicator, the attitude indicator, the _________________, and the ___________ ___________ indicator.
4. During straight-and-level flight, the three instruments providing bank information are the attitude indicator, the _______________________ indicator, and the ____________ ____________.
5. ______ (True, False) A good tight grip on the control wheel ensures smooth and precise attitude control.

SAMPLE ORAL QUESTIONS

1. Explain how you would use the attitude indicator to make altitude corrections during straight-and-level flight.

____
____
____
____
____
____
____

2. How would you use the attitude indicator, turn coordinator, and heading indicator to maintain straight-and-level flight?

____
____
____
____
____
____
____
____
____

1. A rule of thumb for making altitude corrections of less than 100 feet is to use a one-half bar width adjustment on the attitude indicator. For corrections in excess of 100 feet, use a full bar width correction and adjust power.

2. To maintain your desired heading, keep the wings of the miniature aircraft level with the artificial horizon in the attitude indicator. This also applies to the miniature airplane on the turn coordinator. As long as the wings of the miniature airplane remain level and the ball centered, the aircraft is in level flight. To verify a straight flight path is being maintained, the heading indicator should be checked frequently.

3. Fixation, emphasis, and omission are the three most common errors in scanning. Fixation occurs when you focus all of your attention on one instrument. Similarly, when you emphasize one instrument you are not relying on a combination of instruments to control the aircraft. Omission occurs when you forget to include an instrument in your scan pattern.

3. Explain the three common errors related to scanning.

____

____

____

____

____

____

____

____

ADDITIONAL QUESTIONS

4. Explain the three fundamental skills for instrument flying and how they are related.

5. What is the purpose of doing instrument training?

EXERCISE ANSWERS

1. cross-check (or scan), interpretation, control
2. attitude
3. altimeter, vertical speed
4. heading, turn coordinator.
5. False

REFERENCES

JEPPESEN:

Private Pilot Manual/Video – Chapter 2C
Private Pilot Maneuvers/Video – Maneuver 29

FAA:

Airplane Flying Handbook (FAA-H-8083-3)
Instrument Flying Handbook (FAA-H-8083-15)

B. TASK: CONSTANT AIRSPEED CLIMBS (ASEL and ASES)

REFERENCES: FAA-H-8083-3, FAA-H-8083-15.

Objective: To determine that the applicant:

1. Exhibits knowledge of the elements related to attitude instrument flying during constant airspeed climbs.
2. Establishes the climb configuration specified by the examiner.
3. Transitions to the climb pitch attitude and power setting on an assigned heading using proper instrument cross-check and interpretation, and coordinated control application.
4. Demonstrates climbs solely by reference to instruments at a constant airspeed to specific altitudes in straight flight and turns.
5. Levels off at the assigned altitude and maintains that altitude, ± 200 feet (60 meters); maintains heading, ± 20°; maintains airspeed, ± 10 knots.

Objective: To determine that the applicant:

1. Exhibits knowledge of the elements related to attitude instrument flying during constant airspeed climbs.

CONSTANT AIRSPEED CLIMBS

In an emergency, when adverse weather is encountered, a climb solely by reference to flight instruments may be the only course of action to ensure clearance of obstructions and terrain, or to reach an area clear of weather above a layer of fog, haze, or low clouds. When performing this maneuver, you must maintain a constant airspeed. Typically, V_Y is used since it is well above a stall and allows for a nominal rate of climb; however, the power setting and pitch attitude determine the specific airspeed.

2. Establishes the climb configuration specified by the examiner.

- Select the flap and gear (if applicable) configuration specified by the examiner.
- Establishing the desired configuration before starting the climb will permit a more stabilized climb and requires less division of attention once the climb is started.

3. Transitions to the climb pitch attitude and power setting on an assigned heading using proper instrument cross-check and interpretation, and coordinated control application.

TRANSITIONING TO CLIMB

When establishing a constant airspeed climb using instrument references, it is important that you do not overcontrol the airplane. It is much easier to achieve a desired climb airspeed and maintain a desired heading if the transition to a climb is done smoothly using small pitch changes.

Since the attitude indicator provides a visual representation of changes in pitch, it is considered the primary instrument for transitioning to a climb attitude. For example, to initiate a climb from cruise flight, raise the nose approximately two-bar widths in relation to the artificial horizon. You may advance power to the climb power setting at the same time you change pitch, provided you do not exceed maximum r.p.m. limits. Because of inertia, speed will not decrease immediately to the desired climb speed. Instead, you must give the airspeed time to stabilize, then increase or decrease elevator pressure as necessary to attain the desired airspeed. Once you have established a stabilized climb, trim away any control pressures. During the climb, the power should remain at a fixed setting and any deviations in airspeed should be corrected by making pitch adjustments.

During the climb entry, maintain wings level by referring to the attitude indicator and turn coordinator. To verify straight flight, refer to the heading indicator. If you deviate from your desired heading, use the attitude indicator to initiate a shallow bank in the desired direction.

To maintain the desired heading during the transition to climb, additional right rudder pressure will be required in order to compensate for P-factor torque. The rudder pressure required is directly dependent upon the airspeed. Therefore, right rudder pressure will be light at first, then as the aircraft slows, pressure must be increased.

INSTRUMENT CROSS-CHECK

As mentioned earlier, the attitude indicator is the primary instrument when transitioning to a climb. However, the altimeter and vertical speed indicator (VSI) must be cross-checked to verify the climb. For example, when a climb is initiated, the VSI displays the aircraft's immediate trend upward, while the altimeter shows an increase in altitude. [Figure 9-3]

THE LEVELOFF

You should begin the leveloff before reaching your assigned altitude. An effective guideline is to lead the altitude by 10% of the vertical speed indication. To begin the leveloff, apply smooth, forward elevator pressure until the miniature aircraft is level with the artificial horizon. Then cross-check the altimeter and VSI to verify the aircraft is in level flight. As you make the transition to level flight, airspeed will increase, and you will need to adjust the power as necessary to maintain your desired airspeed. Once the aircraft has stabilized, use trim to relieve all control pressures.

Figure 9-3. During the initial transition to a constant airspeed climb, the primary instrument for pitch is the attitude indicator while the altimeter and vertical speed indicator verify the climb.

4. Demonstrates climbs solely by reference to instruments at a constant airspeed to specific altitudes in straight flight and turns.

- All climbs performed for this task are conducted solely by reference to the flight instruments on a specified heading.
- The examiner will specify the airspeed to be used in the climb, as well as the leveloff altitude.

5. Levels off at the assigned altitude and maintains that altitude, ± 200 feet (60 meters); maintains heading ± 20°; maintains airspeed, ± 10 knots.

- When leveling off, lead your leveloff altitude by 10% of the vertical speed indication.
- If you deviate from your assigned altitude use the attitude indicator to make small pitch changes and cross-check the altimeter to verify when you reach your target altitude.
- Maintain wings level by referencing the attitude indicator and cross-checking the heading indicator.
- If a constant altitude is maintained, airspeed will remain within the ±10-knot requirement.

COMMON ERRORS

1. Not maintaining an assigned airspeed and/or heading during the climb.

Cause: Improper scan, fixating on, or emphasizing a single instrument.

Solution: Reference the airspeed and heading indicators during your scan. Corrections to either airspeed or heading indications should be accomplished with small pitch and bank adjustments while referencing the attitude indicator.

Cause: Improper use of trim.

Solution: Once the proper climb airspeed is obtained, trim to relieve all control pressures.

Cause: Overcontrolling the aircraft when transitioning from cruise flight to a climb.

Solution: Slow your transition to the climb attitude and use light control inputs. This allows the airspeed to stabilize.

2. Exceeding the assigned altitude during the leveloff.

Cause: Failure to properly lead the leveloff altitude.

Solution: Lead the leveloff altitude by 10% of the vertical speed indication.

Cause: Breakdown in scanning technique.

Solution: Scan the VSI for the climb rate, and scan the altimeter for the appropriate leveloff lead point.

EXERCISES

1. During a constant airspeed climb you should adjust __________ to maintain a specific airspeed.
2. Your primary pitch instrument during a transition to a constant airspeed climb is the _______________ indicator.
3. In addition to the attitude indicator and turn coordinator, you must utilize the__________ indicator to maintain heading.
4. You should lead the leveloff by __________% of the vertical speed indication.

SAMPLE ORAL QUESTIONS

1. Explain why it is important to make a smooth transition to a constant airspeed climb.

____

____

____

____

____

2. How should you use the elevator trim when transitioning from level flight to a constant airspeed climb?

____

____

____

____

____

____

____

____

____

3. Describe the leveloff process from a constant airspeed climb.

____

____

____

____

____

____

____

____

1. A smooth transition allows the airspeed to stabilize while you trim the aircraft. This also helps you avoid overcontrolling.

2. Once the aircraft is established in a climb and the airspeed stabilizes, use trim to remove any control pressures. If the airspeed should deviate in the climb, use small pitch changes to correct the deviations and retrim once the airspeed stabilizes. To leveloff from a climb, apply forward pressure to the yoke until a level attitude is obtained. As airspeed increases in level flight, reduce the power to a cruise setting and trim once airspeed stabilizes.

3. You should lead your leveloff by 10% of the vertical speed indication. When leveling off, apply smooth, forward elevator pressure until the miniature aircraft on the attitude indicator is level with the artificial horizon. Then cross-check the altimeter and VSI to verify level flight. Adjust the power to maintain airspeed, and relax rudder pressure to maintain heading.

ADDITIONAL QUESTIONS

4. Explain the proper way to use power when entering a constant airspeed climb.

5. List the pitch and bank instruments used throughout a constant airspeed climb.

EXERCISE ANSWERS

1. pitch
2. attitude
3. heading
4. 10

REFERENCES

JEPPESEN:

Private Pilot Manual/Video – Chapter 2C
Private Pilot Maneuvers/Video – Maneuver 29

FAA:

Airplane Flying Handbook (FAA-H-8083-3)
Instrument Flying Handbook (FAA-H-8083-15)

C. TASK: CONSTANT AIRSPEED DESCENTS (ASEL and ASES)

REFERENCES: FAA-H-8083-3, FAA-H-8083-15.

Objective: To determine that the applicant:

1. Exhibits knowledge of the elements related to attitude instrument flying during constant airspeed descents.
2. Establishes the descent configuration specified by the examiner.
3. Transitions to the descent pitch attitude and power setting on an assigned heading using proper instrument cross-check and interpretation, and coordinated control application.
4. Demonstrates descents solely by reference to instruments at a constant airspeed to specific altitudes in straight flight and turns.
5. Levels off at the assigned altitude and maintains that altitude, ± 200 feet (60 meters); maintains heading, ± 20°; maintains airspeed, ±10 knots.

Objective: To determine that the applicant:

1. Exhibits knowledge of the elements related to attitude instrument flying during constant airspeed descents.

CONSTANT AIRSPEED DESCENTS

A constant airspeed descent solely by reference to instruments is used in an emergency situation when a VFR pilot unintentionally gets trapped above a layer of clouds or haze. In this situation, a descent to an altitude where visual reference to the ground can be re-established may be required. Generally, the descent should be made in straight flight. When performing this maneuver, you must maintain an airspeed specified by the examiner. Typically, the airspeed used should be well above a stall but no greater than the aircraft's design maneuvering speed.

2. Establishes the descent configuration specified by the examiner.

- Select the flap and gear (if applicable) configuration specified by the examiner.
- Establishing the desired configuration before starting the descent permits a more stabilized descent and requires less division of attention once the descent is started.

3. Transitions to the descent pitch attitude and power setting on an assigned heading using proper instrument cross-check and interpretation, and coordinated control application.

TRANSITIONING TO A DESCENT

When initiating a constant airspeed descent, it is much easier to maintain a desired airspeed and heading if the transition is done smoothly using small pitch and bank changes. The following method for entering a descent is effective either with or without an attitude indicator.

First, reduce power smoothly to obtain the desired descent airspeed while maintaining straight-and-level flight. Once the descent airspeed is established, power is further reduced and the nose is simultaneously lowered to maintain the desired airspeed. The power should remain at a fixed (constant) setting and deviations in airspeed corrected by making pitch changes. Using the throttle to control airspeed only adds to the workload. If the airspeed is too high or too low, you should apply only sufficient elevator pressure to start the airspeed indicator moving toward the desired airspeed.

The attitude indicator can be used to initiate the descent by placing the representative airplane at the appropriate pitch attitude below the artificial horizon and then checking the airspeed indicator to determine if the pitch attitude is correct. Deviations from the desired airspeed are corrected by again adjusting the pitch attitude. Once the pitch attitude and descent rate stabilize, you should trim the airplane to reduce control wheel pressure. During the stabilized descent, cross-check the airspeed indicator, attitude indicator, altimeter, and vertical speed indicator for pitch information. Since the airspeed must remain constant, the airspeed indicator is the primary pitch instrument.

As you enter a descent, maintain wings level by referring to the attitude indicator and turn coordinator. To verify straight flight, refer to the heading indicator. If you deviate from your desired heading, use the attitude indicator to initiate a shallow bank in the desired direction.

THE LEVEL OFF

An effective guideline you can use when leveling off is to lead the leveloff altitude by 10% of the vertical speed indication. As you reach the lead point, slowly add power to the appropriate level flight cruise setting, and smoothly adjust the pitch until the miniature airplane is level with the artificial horizon. Then cross-check the altimeter and VSI to verify the aircraft is in level flight. After the pitch attitude and airspeed are stabilized in straight-and-level flight, trim the aircraft to remove any control pressures. In level flight, the altimeter becomes the primary pitch instrument and the attitude indicator, airspeed indicator, and VSI verify pitch information.

4. Demonstrates descents solely by reference to instruments at a constant airspeed to specific altitudes in straight flight and turns.

- All descents performed for this task are conducted solely by reference to the flight instruments on a specified heading.

- The examiner will specify the airspeed to be used during the descent as well as the leveloff altitude.

5. Levels off at the assigned altitude and maintains that altitude, ± 200 feet (60 meters); maintains heading, ± 20°; maintains airspeed, ± 10 knots.

- When leveling off, lead your leveloff altitude by 10% of the vertical speed indication.
- If you should deviate from your assigned altitude use the attitude indicator to make small pitch changes and cross-check the altimeter to verify when you reach your target altitude.
- Maintain a heading by referencing the attitude indicator to keep the wings level and cross-checking the heading indicator.
- If a constant altitude is maintained, airspeed will remain within the ±10 knots required.

COMMON ERRORS

1. **Not maintaining an assigned airspeed and/or heading during the descent.**

   Cause: Improper scan, fixating on, or emphasizing a single instrument.

   Solution: Reference the airspeed and heading indicator during your scan. Corrections to either airspeed or heading indications should be accomplished with small pitch and bank adjustments when referencing the attitude indicator.

   Cause: Improper use of trim.

   Solution: Once the proper descent airspeed is obtained, trim to relieve all control pressures.

   Cause: Overcontrolling the aircraft when transitioning from cruise flight to a descent.

   Solution: Slow your transition to the descent attitude using light control inputs. This allows the airspeed to stabilize.

2. **Exceeding the assigned altitude during the leveloff.**

   Cause: Failure to properly lead the leveloff altitude.

   Solution: Lead the leveloff altitude by 10% of the vertical speed indication.

   Cause: Breakdown in scanning technique.

   Solution: Scan the VSI for the descent rate, and scan the altimeter for the appropriate leveloff lead point.

EXERCISES

1. During a constant airspeed descent you should adjust __________ to maintain a specific airspeed.
2. When transitioning from cruise flight to a descent, you should first reduce ________________ to obtain the desired descent airspeed.
3. When stabilized in a descent, your _____________ indicator and the _______________ _____________ support the attitude indicator for bank information.
4. The ______________ indicator is the primary pitch instrument when in a stabilized descent.

SAMPLE ORAL QUESTIONS

1. The attitude indicator is used to initiate a descent by placing the miniature airplane at an appropriate pitch attitude below the artificial horizon. The airspeed indicator is then cross-checked to determine if the pitch attitude is correct. Once stabilized in the descent, the airspeed indicator is the primary pitch instrument while the attitude indicator provides supporting pitch information.

1. Explain the role of the attitude indicator throughout a constant airspeed descent.

____

____

____

____

____

____

____

____

____

2. What instruments provide bank information during a stabilized descent?

____

____

____

2. The attitude indicator, turn coordinator, and heading indicator.

3. Explain how power is used to initiate a constant airspeed descent.

____

____

____

____

____

____

____

____

3. To begin a constant airspeed descent, power is smoothly reduced to obtain the desired descent airspeed. Once the descent airspeed is established, power is further reduced while the aircraft's nose is simultaneously lowered to maintain the desired airspeed.

ADDITIONAL QUESTIONS

4. What is the purpose of practicing constant airspeed descents?

5. Know what instruments provide bank and pitch information when conducting constant airspeed descents.

EXERCISE ANSWERS

1. pitch
2. power
3. heading, turn coordinator
4. airspeed

REFERENCES

JEPPESEN:

Private Pilot Manual/Video – Chapters 2C and 3A
Private Pilot Maneuvers/Video – Maneuver 29

FAA:

Airplane Flying Handbook (FAA-H-8083-3)
Instrument Flying Handbook (FAA-H-8083-15)

D. TASK: TURNS TO HEADINGS (ASEL and ASES)

REFERENCES: FAA-H-8083-3, FAA-H-8083-15.

Objective: To determine that the applicant:

1. Exhibits knowledge of the elements related to attitude instrument flying during turns to headings.
2. Transitions to the level-turn attitude using proper instrument cross-check and interpretation, and coordinated control application.
3. Demonstrates turns to headings solely by reference to instruments; maintains altitude, ± 200 feet (60 meters); maintains a standard rate turn and rolls out on the assigned heading, ± 10°; maintains airspeed, ± 10 knots.

Objective: To determine that the applicant:

1. **Exhibits knowledge of the elements related to attitude instrument flying during turns to headings.**

TURNS TO HEADINGS

As a private pilot, if you encounter adverse weather conditions, it is advisable for you to obtain directional guidance from ATC or initiate a 180° turn by instrument references to get back to VFR conditions.

When making turns in adverse weather conditions, there is nothing to be gained by maneuvering the airplane faster than your ability to keep up with the changes that occur on the flight instruments. It is advisable, then, to limit the angle of bank in all turns. A good guideline to follow when making turns is to use a bank angle equal to one-half of the difference between the present heading and the desired heading. However, the angle you use should not exceed that necessary for a standard-rate turn. A standard-rate turn is one during which the heading changes three degrees per second. On turn coordinators, this is shown when the wing tip of the representative airplane is lined up with the standard rate marker.

2. **Transitions to the level-turn attitude using proper instrument cross-check and interpretation, and coordinated control application.**

TRANSITIONING TO A TURN

Before starting a turn to any new heading, you should hold the airplane straight and level and determine the direction the turn is to be made. Then, based upon the amount of turn needed to reach the new heading, you should determine the rate or angle of bank to use.

To enter a turn, smoothly apply coordinated aileron and rudder pressure in the direction of the turn. At the same time, raise the pitch attitude slightly. The higher pitch is required to produce the additional lift needed to offset that portion of the vertical component of lift that is diverted to the horizontal component of lift during the turn.

For small heading changes, make small bank adjustments using the attitude indicator while cross-checking the heading indicator to monitor your progress. For a large heading change, use the attitude indicator to establish the approximate angle of bank required for a standard-rate turn while simultaneously adjusting the nose of the miniature airplane slightly above the artificial horizon. When the bank is stabilized, check the turn coordinator to verify you are maintaining a standard-rate turn. If you are not, use the attitude indicator to adjust the angle of bank accordingly. Once the bank and pitch are set, you may use trim to eliminate control wheel pressures.

Include the heading indicator in your scan to determine progress toward the desired heading. Also, check the altimeter to determine that a constant altitude is being maintained throughout the turn. [Figure 9-4]

ROLL-OUT

You will need to begin the rollout before reaching the desired heading. One guideline is to lead the rollout by one-half the bank angle. However, in light training airplanes, leading the rollout by 10° typically works well. Use coordinated aileron and rudder pressures to roll the wings level and stop the turn. The principal instrument reference for the rollout is the attitude indicator. Since you have held a slightly nose-high attitude throughout the turn, relax back pressure or apply nose-down trim, if needed, to prevent gaining altitude as you roll wings level.

3. **Demonstrates turns to headings solely by reference to instruments; maintains altitude, ± 200 feet (60 meters); maintains a standard-rate turn and rolls out on the assigned heading, ± 10°; maintains airspeed, ± 10 knots.**

- After transitioning into a turn, cross-check the attitude indicator with the altimeter to verify you are maintaining altitude.
- If the aircraft is climbing or descending, make slight pitch corrections using the attitude indicator.
- If you maintain altitude throughout the turn, airspeed will remain within the ±10 knot requirement.
- After transitioning into a turn, cross-check the attitude indicator with the turn coordinator to verify a standard-rate turn.
- You must include the heading indicator in your scan to monitor your progress in the turn.
- Begin your roll out approximately 10° prior to your assigned heading.

Figure 9-4. These instruments show a level, standard-rate turn to the right. The bank index at the top of the attitude indicator displays the bank angle as 15°. Notice, too, how the nose of the miniature airplane is slightly above the horizon bar.

COMMON ERRORS

1. **Not maintaining your assigned altitude or airspeed during the maneuver.**

   Cause: Improper scan, fixating on, or emphasizing a single instrument.

   Solution: Cross-check the attitude indicator with the altimeter to maintain altitude. If altitude is maintained, airspeed will vary only slightly.

   Cause: Improper use of trim.

   Solution: Once the turn is established, trim to relieve all control pressure.

2. **Exceeding your assigned heading during the roll-out.**

   Cause: Failure to lead the rollout.

   Solution: Lead the rollout by 10° or one-half the bank angle.

3. **Not maintaining your assigned altitude after the rollout.**

   Cause: Not reducing the pitch attitude as you roll out.

   Solution: As you roll out, you must relax back pressure. Reference the attitude indicator to reduce pitch to level flight.

   Cause: Improper use of trim.

   Solution: If trim was used in the turn, use nose-down pressure as you roll out, and use trim to relieve any control pressures.

EXERCISES

1. The ____________ ____________ is the primary instrument used when transitioning into a turn.

2. The ____________ ____________ is the primary instrument for maintaining a standard-rate turn.

3. Lead your desired heading by ______________ to rollout on your assigned heading.

4. The __________ __________ is the principle instrument for the determining when to begin your roll out.

SAMPLE ORAL QUESTIONS

1. When making turns in adverse weather conditions, there is nothing to be gained by maneuvering the airplane faster than your ability to keep up with the changes that occur on the flight instruments. It is advisable then, to limit all turns to no more than a standard rate.

1. Why should you limit all turns to a standard rate in adverse weather?

2. The higher pitch is required to produce the additional lift required to offset that portion of the vertical component of lift that is diverted to the horizontal component of lift during the turn.

2. Why must you increase pitch to maintain level flight when rolling into a standard-rate turn?

3. As you transition into the turn, use the attitude indicator to establish the approximate angle of bank required for a standard-rate turn and adjust the nose of the miniature airplane slightly above the artificial horizon. When the bank is stabilized, check the turn coordinator to verify you are maintaining a standard-rate turn. Also check the altimeter to verify you are maintaining altitude. If you notice deviations, use the attitude indicator to adjust the angle of bank and/or pitch accordingly.

3. Explain the role of the attitude indicator when making turns solely by instrument reference.

ADDITIONAL QUESTIONS

4. Describe how you would make a level 180° turn solely by instrument reference.

5. Know what instruments provide bank and pitch information when conducting turns to headings.

EXERCISE ANSWERS

1. attitude indicator
2. turn coordinator
3. 10°
4. heading indicator

REFERENCES

JEPPESEN:

Private Pilot Manual/Video – Chapter 2C
Private Pilot Maneuvers/Video – Maneuver 29

FAA:

Airplane Flying Handbook (FAA-H-8083-3)
Instrument Flying Handbook (FAA-H-8083-15)

E. TASK: RECOVERY FROM UNUSUAL FLIGHT ATTITUDES (ASEL and ASES)

REFERENCES: FAA-H-8083-3, FAA-H-8083-15.

Objective: To determine that the applicant:

1. Exhibits knowledge of the elements related to attitude instrument flying during unusual attitudes.
2. Recognizes unusual flight attitudes solely by reference to instruments; recovers promptly to a stabilized level flight attitude using proper instrument cross-check and interpretation and smooth, coordinated control application in the correct sequence.

Objective: To determine that the applicant:

1. **Exhibits knowledge of the elements related to attitude instrument flying during unusual attitudes.**

UNUSUAL ATTITUDES

When outside visual references are inadequate or lost, the VFR pilot is apt to unintentionally place the airplane in an unusual flight attitude. An unusual attitude is any unintentional attitude, such as an excessively nose-high attitude or extremely steep bank. Anytime an unusual attitude is entered, you should immediately initiate a recovery to bring the aircraft back to straight-and-level flight. Unlike the control inputs used for normal maneuvers, recovery from an unusual attitude may require large control movements. Nevertheless, such control applications must be smooth, positive, and prompt. To avoid aggravating the critical attitude with a control application in the wrong direction, the initial interpretation of the instruments must be accurate.

When in an unusual attitude, the attitude indicator provides you with both pitch and bank information. However, the attitude indicator can fail, or the pitch and bank limits of the instrument can be exceeded, resulting in false information. Therefore, you must cross-check the other instruments to confirm your flight attitude.

2. **Recognizes unusual flight attitudes solely by reference to instruments; recovers promptly to a stabilized level flight attitude using proper instrument cross-check and interpretation and smooth, coordinated control application in the correct sequence.**

INSTRUMENT INDICATIONS

When an unusual attitude is recognized on the flight instruments, your first objective is to identify what the airplane is doing and decide how to return to straight-and-level flight. There are two basic types of unusual attitudes: nose-high and nose-low.

A nose-high unusual attitude is identified by a nose-high pitch attitude, decreasing airspeed, and increasing altitude. [Figure 9-5]

In addition to the instruments, there are several outside cues that indicate a nose-high attitude. For example, as airspeed decreases the sound of the airflow outside the cabin also decreases and the controls become less effective.

RECOVERY

To prevent a stall from occurring, it is important to lower the nose quickly using positive forward control pressures, while simultaneously increasing power to help prevent further loss of airspeed. If the aircraft is in a bank the wings should be leveled after the nose is lowered and power added. After the airplane has been returned to straight-and-level flight and the airspeed returns to normal, the power can be reduced to a cruise setting.

NOSE-LOW ATTITUDE

The indications of a nose-low unusual attitude are: a nose-low pitch attitude, increasing airspeed, rapid loss of altitude, and a high rate of descent. Your primary objective in a nose-low unusual attitude recovery is to avoid an excessively high airspeed or load factor. [Figure 9-6]

As with nose-high attitudes, there are several outside cues that indicate a nose-low attitude. For example, as airspeed increases, so does the sound of the airflow outside the cabin. Furthermore, engine r.p.m. increases and the controls feel more solid.

RECOVERY

Recovery from a nose-low attitude must be initiated immediately to prevent the aircraft from exceeding its airspeed limits. Begin the recovery by reducing power to slow acceleration while simultaneously leveling the wings. Then, gently raise the nose to the level flight attitude. If you attempt to raise the nose before you roll the wings level, the increased load factor can result in an accelerated stall, a spin, or a force exceeding the airplane's design load factor.

COMMON ERRORS

1. **Failure to properly identify an unusual flight attitude.**

   Cause: Not correctly interpreting the flight instruments.

   Solution: You must carefully scan all the flight instruments and verify what the attitude indicator is displaying. Resist the temptation to fixate on a single instrument.

Figure 9-5. Here are the instrument indications of a typical nose-high unusual attitude. The primary objective for recovery from this situation is to prevent a stall.

Figure 9-6. This airplane is in a nose-low unusual attitude, as indicated by low pitch attitude, increasing airspeed, decreasing altimeter, and descent on the VSI.

2. Incorrect control application during recovery.

Cause: Trying to recover by "feel" rather than by interpreting the flight instruments.

Solution: Trust your flight instruments and resist the temptation to respond to your autokinetic senses.

Cause: Improperly interpreting the flight instruments.

Solution: Identify the unusual attitude by reference to the attitude indicator, and verify by reference to the other instruments.

3. Experiencing high load factors during the recovery from a nose-low unusual attitude.

Cause: Allowing the airspeed to build too much before recovering.

Solution: Initiate the recovery immediately after you identify the unusual attitude.

Cause: Use of excessive back pressure during recovery.

Solution: Apply moderate back pressure that allows recovery before exceeding airspeed limits and keeps the aircraft within load factor limits.

EXERCISES

1. The instrument that provides you with the most information when in an unusual attitude is the ________ ____________ indicator.

2. The turn coordinator and ______________ indicator confirm the bank information depicted on the attitude indicator.

3. The altimeter, ______________ indicator, and vertical speed indicator confirm the attitude depicted on the attitude indicator.

SAMPLE ORAL QUESTIONS

1. Explain what could happen if the wings are not rolled level before applying back pressure when recovering from a nose-low unusual attitude.

____

____

____

____

____

____

2. What could result if recovery from a nose-high or nose-low unusual attitude is not initiated immediately?

____

____

____

____

____

____

____

____

____

____

1. Increasing elevator back pressure before the wings are leveled tends to tighten the turn and cause excessive load factors to be placed on the aircraft.

2. If recovery from a nose-high unusual attitude is not initiated immediately, the aircraft may stall and possibly enter a spin. On the other hand, failure to recover immediately from a nose-low unusual attitude can lead to excessive G loading and/or exceed the aircraft's airspeed limits.

3. It is important to lower the nose quickly using positive forward control pressures, while simultaneously increasing power to help prevent further loss of airspeed. If the aircraft is in a bank the wings should be leveled after the nose is lowered and power added. After the airplane has been returned to straight-and-level flight and the airspeed returns to normal, the power can be reduced to a cruise setting.

3. Explain the steps for recovering from a nose-high unusual attitude.

____

____

____

____

____

____

____

____

____

____

ADDITIONAL QUESTIONS

4. Explain how the other cockpit instruments support the attitude indicator.

5. Explain the steps for recovering from a nose-low unusual attitude.

EXERCISE ANSWERS

1. attitude
2. heading
3. airspeed

REFERENCES

JEPPESEN:

Private Pilot Manual/Video – Chapter 2C

Private Pilot Maneuvers/Video – Maneuver 29

FAA:

Airplane Flying Handbook (FAA-H-8083-3)

Instrument Flying Handbook (FAA-H-8083-15)

F. TASK: RADIO COMMUNICATIONS, NAVIGATION SYSTEMS/FACILITIES, AND RADAR SERVICES (ASEL and ASES)

REFERENCES: FAA-H-8083-3, FAA-H-8083-15, AC 61-23/FAA-H-8083-25.

Objective: To determine that the applicant:

1. Exhibits knowledge of the elements related to radio communications, navigation systems/facilities, and radar services available for use during flight solely by reference to instruments.
2. Selects the proper frequency and identifies the appropriate facility.
3. Follows verbal instructions and/or navigation systems/facilities for guidance.
4. Determines the minimum safe altitude.
5. Maintains altitude, ± 200 feet (60 meters); maintains heading, ± 20°; maintains airspeed, ± 10 knots.

Objective: To determine that the applicant:

1. **Exhibits knowledge of the elements related to radio communications, navigation systems/facilities, and radar services available for use during flight solely by reference to instruments.**

RADIO COMMUNICATIONS, NAVIGATION SYSTEMS/FACILITIES AND RADAR SERVICES

If you, as a private pilot, should unintentionally encounter adverse weather conditions, it is recommended that you execute a 180° turn and head back to VFR conditions. When doing this, it is important that you utilize all available resources and services. This includes communicating with ATC or a flight service station, and using electronic navigation and radar services.

RADIO COMMUNICATIONS

Since most aircraft are equipped with a transponder, and ATC radar coverage spans the vast majority of the National Airspace System, you should utilize ATC services whenever possible. However, to obtain assistance and apply it effectively, you must be familiar with the appropriate procedures. The first thing you must understand is that anytime you are in doubt of the aircraft's position, or feel apprehensive about the safety of a flight, you should not hesitate to ask for help.

When contacting an ATC facility, begin the transmission with the name of the facility you are calling, followed by your aircraft's N-number, and the word "Request." If you are in need of immediate assistance, you should begin the transmission with the phrase "MAYDAY, MAYDAY, MAYDAY" followed by the emergency message. [Figure 9-7]

a. Transmit MAYDAY, MAYDAY,MAYDAY for distress, or PAN-PAN, PAN-PAN, PAN-PAN for urgency.
b. Name of station addressed
c. Aircraft identification and type
d. Nature of distress or urgency
e. Weather
f. Your intentions and request
g. Present position and heading
h. Altitude
i. Fuel remaining in minutes
j. Number of people on board
k. Any other useful information

Figure 9-7. When transmitting a distress or urgency message, you should transmit as many of the necessary elements above, preferably in the order listed.

If you have already established contact with an appropriate facility, you should transmit the emergency message on that frequency. If you do not know the frequency of either an ATC or FSS facility, you should use the designated emergency frequency of 121.5 MHz. Almost all flight service stations, radar facilities, and many aircraft monitor this frequency. You also may want to climb, if possible, for improved radio reception and radar coverage.

Regardless of the frequency used to obtain assistance, it is essential that you do not change frequencies unless instructed to do so, or unless absolutely necessary. If you do, advise the ground station of the new frequency and station name prior to the change. Furthermore, when talking to ATC do not hesitate to ask questions or clarify instructions when you do not understand or if you cannot comply with a clearance.

TRANSPONDER OPERATION

After establishing radio contact, ATC will ask you to squawk a specific transponder code. If you are unable to immediately establish communications with an ATC facility, and you are encountering an emergency, squawk 7700. If you are in an area of radar coverage, this will alert ATC of the emergency situation.

RADAR SERVICES

The most common service provided by ATC is the radar vector to a nearby airport or an area of good weather. When being vectored, you only need to communicate and follow instructions while devoting most of your attention to flying the airplane. However, to take full advantage of this service, there must be a strong link between you and the controller. Good phraseology and proper radio techniques are essential to maintaining this link. For example, when receiving radar vectors, you should acknowledge receiving the vector by repeating the vector and your aircraft call sign.

NAVIGATION FACILITIES

If radar services are not available and you encounter adverse weather, you can use a radio navigation facility to navigate back to VFR conditions. When doing this you should determine the location and frequency of a VOR or NDB that can be used for guiding you back to an area of better weather. Once determined, tune to the navaid frequency and listen carefully for the Morse code identifier. Once the station is identified, you should determine the appropriate VOR radial or NDB bearing that will take you back to VFR weather.

When using radio navigation, including GPS and LORAN, be aware that you will need to divide your attention between navigating and maintaining aircraft control. Your main concern, of course, must be airplane control.

2. Selects the proper frequency and identifies the appropriate facility.

- Use your aeronautical chart to select an appropriate navigational facility, and tune to the listed frequency.
- Listen to the Morse code identification to identify the facility and to ensure its operation.

3. Follows verbal instructions and/or navigation systems/facilities for guidance.

- When being radar vectored, you should turn to the headings specified, then climb or descend as directed by the controller.
- Remember to read back headings and altitudes given by the controller.
- If at any time you do not understand an instruction, ask for clarification.
- Receiving radar services does not permit you to violate Federal Aviation Regulations.
- When using a navigational facility, you should follow the selected VOR radial or NDB bearing and remain on course.
- When using a VOR, you should turn the OBS until the TO-FROM flag indicates TO and the CDI centers. Then, turn to the heading indicated and track to the station.
- When using an ADF, turn the airplane until the ADF needle points to 0°. Then, keep the needle in that position and home to the station.

4. Determines the minimum safe altitude.

- To maintain a safe altitude, you must refer to your aeronautical chart and the maximum elevation figures (MEF) for each quadrangle.
- When over mountainous terrain, add 2,000 feet to the MEF to determine the minimum safe altitude.
- When over nonmountainous terrain, add 1,000 feet to the MEF to determine the minimum safe altitude.
- When using radar services, the controller can tell you what the minimum safe altitude is for your location.

5. Maintains altitude, ± 200 feet (60 meters); maintains heading, ± 20°; maintains airspeed, ± 10 knots.

- To maintain altitude, align the miniature airplane with the artificial horizon and cross-check the altimeter to verify level flight.
- To maintain a heading, keep the miniature airplane level with the artificial horizon and cross-check the heading indicator to verify the heading is maintained.
- If you maintain an altitude and heading, the aircraft's airspeed should remain within ±10 knots.

COMMON ERRORS

1. Gain or loss of altitude.

Cause: Improper scan, fixating on, or emphasizing a single instrument.

Solution: Use the attitude indicator to maintain the appropriate pitch attitude and cross-check the altimeter to verify altitude in maintained.

Cause: Improper use of trim.

Solution: Use trim to relieve control wheel pressures.

Cause: Distraction with radios and navigation.

Solution: Divide attention between aircraft control and other tasks.

2. Not maintaining an assigned heading.

Cause: Improper scan, fixating on, or emphasizing a single instrument.

Solution: Use the attitude indicator or turn coordinator to maintain wings level, and cross-check the heading indicator to verify a heading is maintained.

3. Waiting too long before asking for assistance from ATC.

Cause: Having the attitude that nothing could happen to you, or the belief that you can work it out yourself.

Solution: As soon as a potentially dangerous situation arises, immediately ask for assistance.

EXERCISES

1. When you are in a distress situation, you should use the word _______________ when seeking assistance.
2. If an FSS or ATC facility cannot be contacted on a known frequency, you should use the designated emergency VHF frequency of __________ MHz.
3. The transponder code designating an emergency is ___________.
4. Before using a navigational facility, you should listen carefully for the __________ __________ identifer.
5. You should acknowledge all ATC instructions by restating the instruction given followed by your aircraft's __________ __________.

SAMPLE ORAL QUESTIONS

1. When should you ask for radar assistance?

1. You can ask for radar assistance at anytime. Most air traffic controllers will provide assistance whenever requested. If an emergency arises you should ask for assistance immediately. In this situation, you should begin your initial transmission with the phrase MAYDAY, MAYDAY, MAYDAY.

2. Why is it so important to utilize good phraseology and radio techniques when communicating ATC?

2. To take full advantage of radar services in an emergency situation, there must be a strong link between you and the controller. Good phraseology maintains this link and enhances understanding as well as safety.

3. What is the recommended procedure when encountering adverse weather conditions?

3. If you, as a private pilot, should unintentionally encounter adverse weather conditions, it is recommended that you execute a 180° turn and head back to VFR conditions. When doing this, it is important that you utilize all available resources and services. This includes communicating with ATC or a flight service station, and using electronic navigation and radar services.

ADDITIONAL QUESTIONS

4. Describe how you would utilize radio communications, available navigation facilities, and radar services to get out of unintentional instrument conditions.

5. Describe how you would utilize the aircraft's transponder in an emergency situation.

EXERCISE ANSWERS

1. MAYDAY
2. 121.5
3. 7700
4. Morse code
5. call sign

REFERENCES

JEPPESEN:

Private Pilot Manual/Video – Chapters 5A, 5B, 9B 9C and 9D

FAA:

Airplane Flying Handbook (FAA-H-8083-3)
Instrument Flying Handbook (FAA-H-8083-15

EMERGENCY OPERATIONS

A. TASK: EMERGENCY APPROACH AND LANDING (SIMULATED) (ASEL and ASES)

REFERENCES: FAA-H-8083-3; POH/AFM

Objective: To determine that the applicant:

1. Exhibits knowledge of the elements related to emergency approach and landing procedures.
2. Analyzes the situation and selects an appropriate course of action.
3. Establishes and maintains the recommended best-glide airspeed, ±10 knots.
4. Selects a suitable landing area.
5. Plans and follows a flight pattern to the selected landing area considering altitude, wind, terrain, and obstructions.
6. Prepares for landing, or go-around, as specified by the examiner.
7. Follows the appropriate checklist.

Objective: To determine that the applicant:

1. Exhibits knowledge of the elements related to emergency approach and landing procedures.

EMERGENCY APPROACH AND LANDING

In spite of the reliability of present-day aircraft engines, you must always be prepared to cope with situations which may require a forced landing caused by a partial or complete engine failure. In either of these situations, there are five general steps you should typically follow.

1. Maintain control of the airplane and establish the best glide speed.
2. Scan the immediate area for a suitable field.
3. Turn to a heading that will take you to that field.
4. Attempt to determine the cause of the power failure and restart the engine, if possible. Follow an appropriate emergency checklist and declare an emergency.
5. Set up a landing approach to your selected field.

2. Analyzes the situation and selects an appropriate course of action.

In emergency situations, you must analyze your immediate situation quickly and decide on an appropriate course of action. Although you don't have much time, it is still important to determine the course of action most likely to get you on the ground safely. The specific situation you find yourself in dictates the most appropriate course of action. For example, flying over open pastureland presents different options for emergency landings than flight over mountainous or tree-covered terrain. It is important to quickly assess your situation and take the best course of action depending on your specific circumstances.

3. Establishes and maintains the recommended best-glide airspeed, ±10 knots.

ESTABLISHING GLIDE SPEED

If the engine fails while in cruise flight, you should apply back pressure as you slow the airplane to the appropriate gliding airspeed. This speed is specified in the POH and provides the greatest horizontal travel for a given altitude. As you reach the best glide speed, trim the airplane to relieve any control pressures. This also aids in maintaining your appropriate gliding airspeed. If the airspeed is below the best glide speed when the engine fails, lower the nose immediately to accelerate to the gliding airspeed. Once the appropriate speed is obtained, trim the aircraft to maintain that speed.

Glide speed in your aircraft is __________ kts.

4. Selects a suitable landing area.

SELECTING A FIELD

There are many variables to consider in selecting a suitable field, including the wind direction and speed, length of the field, obstructions, and the surface condition. Naturally the perfect forced-landing field is an established airport, or a hard-packed, long smooth field with no high obstacles on the approach end; however, these ideal conditions may not be readily available, so the best available field must be selected. Cultivated fields are usually satisfactory and plowed fields are acceptable if the landing is made parallel to the furrows. Fields that have large boulders, ditches, or other features which present a hazard during the landing should be avoided.

Whenever possible, you should try to make an emergency landing into the wind. This allows for a slower touchdown speed and shorter ground roll. However, on occasion, it may be better to accept a crosswind landing on a long field, rather than attempt to land into the wind on a very short field. On another occasion, a downwind landing with light winds and no obstructions may be preferable to a landing into the wind with numerous obstructions.

Roads are another option when making an emergency landing. However, when considering a road, you must be alert for powerlines, signs, and automobile traffic. If you have any doubt as to whether you can avoid the obstructions associated with a road, it is probably better to land on an obstruction free field.

5. Plans and follows a flight pattern to the selected landing area considering altitude, wind, terrain, and obstructions.

MANEUVERING TO A LANDING

Once you have selected a place to land, you should head directly toward that point and any excess altitude should be dissipated near the intended landing area. From that vantage point, you are in a good position to scan the area for obstructions such as wires, fences, holes, tree stumps, and ditches.

It is inadvisable to circle away from the landing area and then try to make a long straight-in approach. The estimation of glide distance from a faraway point is difficult, even for experienced pilots. A circling approach over the landing area allows you to make adjustments for altitude and keeps you in a position from which you can reach your desired landing point. If you plan correctly, the airplane should be at the 180° point when you reach a normal traffic pattern altitude. From that point, the approach is like a normal power-off approach. [Figure 10-1]

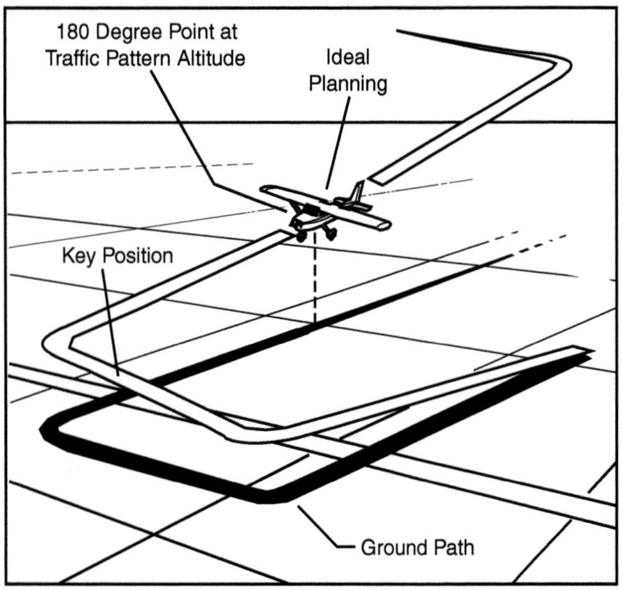

Figure 10-1. If you are able to maneuver the airplane to a normal downwind position, you should be able to use all of the normal cues to turn base leg, judge position, and turn to final.

Use flaps as required during the approach. Full flaps should be used only after the turn to final is completed and you are assured of reaching your intended touchdown point.

In many ways, the controlling factor in the successful accomplishment of a forced landing is the amount of altitude that is available. For example, if an actual engine failure should occur immediately after takeoff and before a safe altitude is reached, it is typically safer to establish the proper glide speed and land directly ahead or slightly to either side of your takeoff path. Attempting to turn back to the runway requires a considerable amount of altitude considering the fact that you must make a turn in excess of 180°.

6. Prepares for landing, or go-around, as specified by the examiner.

- Your first priority during a forced landing is to fly the airplane.
- The examiner will specify how the simulated emergency landing will terminate. Continue to prepare for an actual landing until the examiner instructs you to perform a go-around or to abort the forced landing.
- The examiner is attempting to determine how you would handle an emergency in a real situation, but it is not his intention to create a real emergency.

7. Follows the appropriate checklist.

- Once you have established the appropriate glide speed and located the best landing area, begin thinking about completing an appropriate emergency checklist.
- Items such as establishing the appropriate glide speed and checking the fuel and mixture should be committed to memory.
- If time permits, you must accomplish the appropriate checklist to ensure you have checked each item that can cause an engine failure.
- Attempt to follow an appropriate checklist but don't become pre-occupied with this task and forget to plan for the forced landing.

EXERCISES

1. Your first priority during a forced landing is to maintain positive ______________ of the aircraft.

2. _____ (True, False) You should always make a forced landing into the wind.

3. _____ (True, False) During an engine failure immediately after takeoff, it is best to land straight ahead rather than to try to turn back to the runway.

4. _____ (True, False) Full flaps should be used early in the emergency approach to ensure the slowest possible touchdown speed.

SAMPLE ORAL QUESTIONS

1. When considering a road for an emergency landing, you must be alert for powerlines, signs, and automobile traffic. If you have any doubt as to whether you can avoid the obstructions associated with a road, it is probably better to land on an obstruction free field.

1. What are some of the things you need to consider when landing on a road?

2. Whenever possible, you should try to make an emergency landing into the wind. This allows for a slower touchdown speed and shorter ground roll. However, on occasion, it may be better to accept a crosswind landing on a long field, rather than attempt to land into the wind on a very short field. On another occasion, a downwind landing with light winds and no obstructions may be preferable to a landing into the wind with numerous obstructions.

2. During the emergency approach and landing, when is it appropriate to make a crosswind or downwind landing?

3. It is inadvisable to circle away from the landing area and try to make a long straight-in approach because the estimation of glide distance from a faraway point is difficult. A circling approach over the landing area allows you to make adjustments for altitude and keeps you in a position from which you can reach your desired landing point.

3. Why is it inadvisable to circle away from your intended landing area and make a long straight-in approach to an emergency landing area?

4. 1. Maintain control of the airplane and establish the best glide speed.
   2. Scan the immediate area for a suitable field.
   3. Turn to a heading that will take you to that field.
   4. Attempt to determine the cause of the power failure and restart the engine, if possible. Follow an appropriate emergency checklist and declare an emergency.
   5. Set up a landing approach to your selected field.

4. What are the five broad steps you should typically follow when experiencing a partial or complete engine failure?

ADDITIONAL QUESTIONS

5. What are the procedures for landing without power in your airplane?

6. When should flaps and landing gear be extended during an emergency approach to landing?

EXERCISE ANSWERS

1. control
2. False
3. True
4. False

REFERENCES

JEPPESEN:

Private Pilot Manual/Video – Chapter 2B

Private Pilot Maneuvers/Video – Maneuver 16

FAA:

Airplane Flying Handbook (FAA-H-8083-3); POH/AIM.

Pilot's Operating Handbook and FAA-Approved Airplane Flight Manual

B. TASK: SYSTEMS AND EQUIPMENT MALFUNCTIONS (ASEL and ASES)

REFERENCES: FAA-H-8083-3; POH/AFM.

Objective: To determine that the applicant:

1. Exhibits knowledge of the elements related to system and equipment malfunctions appropriate to the airplane provided for the practical test.
2. Analyzes the situation and takes appropriate action for simulated emergencies appropriate to the airplane provided for the practical test for at least three (3) of the following:
   a. partial or complete power loss.
   b. engine roughness or overheat.
   c. carburetor or induction icing.
   d. loss of oil pressure.
   e. fuel starvation.
   f. electrical malfunction.
   g. vacuum/pressure, and associated flight instruments malfunction.
   h. pitot/static.
   i. landing gear or flap malfunction.
   j. inoperative trim.
   k. inadvertent door or window opening.
   l. structural icing.
   m. smoke/fire/engine compartment fire.
   n. any other emergency appropriate to the airplane.
3. Follows the appropriate checklist or procedure.

Objective: To determine that the applicant:

1. Exhibits knowledge of the elements related to system and equipment malfunctions appropriate to the airplane provided for the practical test.

SYSTEMS AND EQUIPMENT MALFUNCTIONS

This task discusses systems and equipment malfunctions that could occur in a light training aircraft. During the practical test, the examiner will ask you to explain the items pertaining to various systems and equipment failures. You are expected to know what could cause a malfunction, what the indications of a malfunction are, and what your response should be to correct any system or equipment failure. A key element in completing this task is your knowledge of the specific systems contained in your aircraft, as well as your knowledge of section three, Emergency Procedures, in your pilot's operating handbook.

2. Analyzes the situation and takes the appropriate action for simulated emergencies appropriate to the airplane provided for the practical test for at least three (3) of the following:

a. partial or complete power loss.

A common cause of a partial loss of power is carburetor or induction icing. In addition to the obvious drop in the noise level caused by the engine, a partial loss of power is also indicated by an immediate drop in r.p.m. If this happens, your first reaction should be to apply carburetor heat. Typically this causes an additional loss of r.p.m. until the ice begins to melt. If the ice build up is substantial it could take several minutes to melt it completely.

Another common cause of partial loss of power is a fuel/air mixture that is too lean. This typically happens when you forget to enrich the mixture during a descent. If you suspect this is the problem, you should adjust the mixture until full power is obtained.

b. engine roughness or overheat.

A rough running engine can be caused by contaminated fuel, an excessively rich or lean mixture, bad magneto, or plugged fuel injector. Conducting a thorough fuel contamination preflight inspection, and pretakeoff check are the best methods of avoiding these situations.

Identifying the exact cause of why an engine is running rough can be difficult. For example, if the fuel is contaminated there will be no obvious indication of it in flight. However, if you switch fuel tanks and engine roughness is eliminated, you have to assume that contaminated fuel exists in the opposite tank.

As mentioned earlier, engine roughness or partial loss of power can be caused by an excessively lean mixture. In addition, a lean mixture can also lead to high engine temperatures. An excessively rich mixture, on the other hand, has a cooling effect on the engine and can foul spark plugs. In either case, the mixture should be adjusted as necessary to eliminate engine roughness.

Sudden engine roughness is often the result of a bad magneto. You can identify a bad magneto by turning the ignition switch from BOTH to either the Left or Right position. The position that results in the largest r.p.m. drop is the bad magneto. If possible try different power settings to see if you can use both magnetos. If no improvement is apparent, switch to the good mag and proceed to the nearest airport.

c. carburetor or induction icing.

- As the fuel/air mixture passes through the carburetor the vaporization of fuel and drop in pressure causes the mixture to cool and release moisture.
- If the temperature in the carburetor is at or below freezing, ice can begin to form.
- Carburetor ice is identified by a drop in r.p.m. with a fixed-pitch propeller.
- Apply carburetor heat to remove any ice build up.

- Be alert for carburetor ice whenever the temperature is between 20°F and 70°F with visible moisture or high humidity.
- For additional information on carburetor icing refer to Chapter 1, Task G on page 1-49.

d. loss of oil pressure.

The best time to detect a problem in the oil system is during the preflight inspection. Any fresh oil on the underside of the aircraft or on the ground can indicate a probable leak. Also, check for any oil dripping from the crank case. An oil leak while in flight can be identified by a loss of oil pressure and a corresponding increase in engine temperature. If no increase in temperature is observed, the oil pressure gauge may be faulty.

e. fuel starvation.

Fuel starvation can be caused by an obstruction in a fuel line, fuel pump failure, or by running the fuel tanks empty. The first indication of fuel starvation is a drop in fuel pressure and corresponding loss of engine power. When either of these indications occur, you should push the mixture to full rich and turn on the boost pump, if installed, to try and regain fuel pressure. You should also switch the fuel selector to the fullest or opposite tank.

Most fuel starvation incidents and accidents are the direct result of poor planning and inadequate fuel management. To help prevent this from happening, you should visually inspect the amount of fuel in the tanks while the aircraft is on a firm, level surface. Furthermore, you should check the filler ports for leaks, and the fuel caps for security. If a fuel cap is not properly closed, the slip stream over the airplane will siphon a tank completely dry. Another thing you should do is ensure that the fuel vents are not obstructed. Their purpose is to equalize pressure in the tanks, as fuel is consumed, so the fuel flow to the engine is not interrupted by vacuum pressure.

To help prevent the fuel lines from becoming obstructed, take a sample of fuel from each tank and the fuel strainer. The condensation of moisture in partially filled fuel tanks can result in water entering fuel lines and restricting engine operation. If the water freezes in flight, the fuel will be blocked and the engine will quit. Filling tanks after the last flight of the day will minimize this.

f. electrical malfunction.

Your only means of monitoring the electrical system is through the ammeter. A charging ammeter (needle on the plus side) is normal following an engine start, since the battery power lost in starting is being replaced. After the battery is charged, the ammeter should stabilize near zero and the alternator will supply the electrical needs of the system. A discharging ammeter means the electrical load is exceeding the output of the alternator, and the battery is helping to supply system power. This may mean the alternator is malfunctioning, or the electrical load is excessive. In any event, you should reduce your electrical load.

Once the electrical load is reduced, check the circuit breaker for the alternator. Once you've confirmed the circuit breaker is in, turn both sides of the master switch off and then back on. If the ammeter indicates a change, the alternator is back on line. In this situation, the electrical equipment should be turned back on. If the discharge persists, you should continue flying with a reduced electrical load and land as soon as practicable.

g. vacuum/pressure, and associated flight instruments malfunction.

GYROSCOPIC INSTRUMENTS

The gyroscopic instruments include the turn coordinator, attitude indicator, and heading indicator. In most light training aircraft, the gyroscope in the attitude and heading indicators are driven by suction provided by an engine driven vacuum. The amount of suction being created is displayed on a suction gauge. If the vacuum system fails, a corresponding low suction indication will be displayed and the attitude and heading indicators will be unreliable. In some cases, however, the vacuum system may be functioning normally and a single instrument fails. This type of failure is identified by cross-checking all of the instruments to determine which instrument has failed.

The turn coordinator is the third gyroscopic instrument and is typically driven by electricity. If an electrical failure occurs or if the turn coordinator fails, a small red indicator will appear on the face of the instrument.

h. pitot/static.

PITOT-STATIC INSTRUMENTS

As discussed in Chapter 1, Task F, the pitot-static instruments utilize a pitot tube and a static port. Blockage of the pitot tube affects only the airspeed indicator, but a clogged static system affects the airspeed indicator, vertical speed indicator, and altimeter. For information on the specific instrument indications associated with a plugged pitot-tube or static port, refer to Chapter 1, Task G on page 1-53.

i. landing gear or flap malfunction.

A landing gear failure typically indicates a problem with the hydraulic or electrical system. A landing gear malfunction is usually identified by an indicator light or lack of indication. For example, you may select gear down but get no indication that the gear is down and locked. The first thing you should do in this situation is usually check to see if the gear is down and verify the bulbs in the indicator lights are functioning. Next, check the circuit breaker for the hydraulic pump.

If the landing gear fails to extend automatically, there is typically a method available to manually extend the gear or release the hydraulic pressure so the gear can fall. For additional information on how you can manually extend the landing gear on your aircraft, consult the airplane flight manual or pilot's operating handbook (POH).

A wing flap malfunction is usually caused by a broken control arm or an electrical failure. The flaps can fail in either the up or down position. If the flaps fail to extend, follow the procedures in the POH and make a no-flap landing. If the flaps should fail in the down position, maintain an airspeed below V_{FE} and land as soon as possible.

j. inoperative trim.

An inoperative trim is normally caused by a broken control arm or cable. If the trim should fail, you will not be able to relieve control wheel pressures. In this situation, you may want to try flying the aircraft at altitude using different speeds and configurations. This should give you an idea of what to expect when on approach to land.

k. inadvertent door or window opening.

The first thing you should do when a door or window comes open is to continue flying the airplane. Do not allow yourself to get so distracted with trying to close the door or window that aircraft control is compromised. If needed you should land the aircraft and then close the window or door.

In most cases a door or window opening in flight is not a serious emergency if handled properly. Most light training airplanes are not significantly affected by a door or window coming open. A door or window inadvertently coming open in flight is usually easy to identify due to the increase in noise and airflow in the cabin.

l. structural icing.

Most light training aircraft prohibit flight into known icing conditions. Should you encounter inadvertent icing conditions, most POHs recommend executing a 180° turn or changing altitude to obtain a warmer outside air temperature. Additional items that should be done include turning on any anti-ice or de-icing equipment, including pitot heat and interior defrosters to keep the pitot tube and windscreen clear.

m. smoke/fire/engine compartment fire.

Materials used in modern aircraft, and the installation techniques, make in-flight fires rare. However, if you do have smoke or fire, you need to determine its source. Refer to the POH for the specific immediate actions required. In some cases, you will find it useful to open vents and windows in the cabin. However, depending on the location of the fire, this action may fan the flames and make the situation worse. If cabin visibility is obstructed by smoke, try opening the vents and windows to determine if visibility improves. Be prepared to close them immediately if the smoke gets worse.

In nearly all cases of engine fire, your first action will likely be to shut off the fuel selector to reduce total pressure on the fuel system. This would result in an emergency landing without power. At this point, land and evacuate the aircraft as quickly as possible. In most cases, do not open aircraft vents or windows since this will create a lower pressure in the cabin where the flames will be drawn.

An electrical fire is usually evidenced by smoke behind the instrument panel, and usually has a distinctive smell. If you believe you have an electrical fire, immediately reduce the electrical load by turning off the master switch. If fire is present, close all the vents and use an extinguisher. After discharging the fire extinguisher you should ventilate the cabin and land as soon as possible.

n. any other emergency appropriate to the airplane.

- You must be familiar with all of the emergency procedures associated with your aircraft.
- In preparation for the practical test you should review the POH for your aircraft.

3. Follows the appropriate checklist or procedure.

- Always keep the checklist accessible with the Emergency Procedures tabbed.
- Initial items should be memorized so you can set up for the emergency in the shortest possible time.
- Once you have completed the items necessary to meet the needs of the emergency, obtain the appropriate checklist.

EXERCISES

1. Loss of __________ is a good indicator of carburetor ice on a fixed-pitch propeller airplane.

2. Loss of oil pressure is typically accompanied by an increase in engine __________.

3. The __________ is the only means of monitoring the electrical system.

4. If you experience a loss of vacuum pressure, typically the ____________ and ____________ indicators are affected.

5. In nearly all cases, your first reaction to an engine fire will be to shut off the __________ __________.

SAMPLE ORAL QUESTIONS

1. If water freezes at 32°F, how can you get carburetor ice when it's 70°F?

1. As the fuel/air mixture passes through the carburetor, the vaporization of fuel and drop in pressure causes the mixture to cool and release moisture. In some instances the temperature in the carburetor can drop 40°F. Because of this, carburetor icing can occur when it is 70°F and humid.

2. Why should you fill the fuel tanks after the last flight of the day?

2. The condensation of moisture in partially filled fuel tanks can result in water entering the fuel lines and restricting engine operation. If the water freezes in flight, the fuel will be blocked and the engine will quit. Filling tanks after the last flight of the day will minimize this.

3. What should you do if you notice a discharge on the ammeter?

3. A discharging ammeter means the electrical load is exceeding the output of the alternator, and the battery is helping to supply system power. In this situation, you should reduce the electrical load and check the circuit breaker for the alternator. Once you've confirmed the circuit breaker is in, turn both sides of the master switch off and then back on. If the ammeter indicates a charge, the alternator is back on line and the electrical equipment should be turned back on. If the discharge persists, you should continue flying with a reduced electrical load and land as soon as practicable.

4. The first thing you should do when a door or window comes open is to continue flying the airplane. Do not allow yourself to get so distracted with trying to close the door or window that aircraft control is compromised. If needed, you should land the aircraft and then close the window or door.

4. What is your primary task if a window or door should come open in flight?

ADDITIONAL QUESTIONS

5. Is your airplane certified for flight into known icing conditions? How would you determine this?
6. Describe the procedures for handling an engine fire.
7. What are the indications of an excessive rate of charge? What actions would you take?
8. Be familiar with all of the emergency procedures outlined in the POH for your aircraft.

EXERCISE ANSWERS

1. r.p.m.
2. temperature
3. ammeter
4. attitude, heading
5. fuel selector

REFERENCES

JEPPESEN:

Private Pilot Manual/Video – Chapters 2B, 2C, and 3B

FAA:

Airplane Flying Handbook (FAA-H-8083-3); POH/AFM.

C. TASK: EMERGENCY EQUIPMENT AND SURVIVAL GEAR (ASEL and ASES)

REFERENCES: FAA-H-8083-3; POH/AFM

Objective: To determine that the applicant:

1. Exhibits knowledge of the elements related to emergency equipment and survival gear appropriate to the airplane and environment encountered during flight. Identifies appropriate equipment that should be aboard the airplane.

Objective: To determine that the applicant:

1. **Exhibits knowledge of the elements related to emergency equipment and survival gear appropriate to the airplane and environment encountered during flight. Identifies appropriate equipment that should be aboard the airplane.**

EMERGENCY EQUIPMENT AND SURVIVAL GEAR

For flight over uninhabited land areas, it is wise to take and know how to use survival equipment for the type of climate and terrain. In addition, appropriate survival gear should be taken on all over water flights. If a forced landing occurs at sea, chances for survival are governed by the degree of crew proficiency in emergency procedures and by the availability and effectiveness of water survival equipment.

Survival gear and related equipment should be stowed in a location that can be accessed in the event of an emergency landing. Furthermore all survival gear should be secured so it is not tossed about the cabin in turbulence or in a rough off-airport or water landing. Typically, most emergency equipment is stowed in the aft portion of the aircraft. In the case of a forward crash, this placement helps keep the equipment intact.

Remember to always brief your passengers on the location and use of all survival equipment. In the event you should become incapacitated, your passengers must know where to find and how to use all emergency equipment.

Written instructions should be kept with the survival equipment. This includes instructions for the operation of flares, handheld radios, and preparation of food rations. If a raft is included, inflation instructions should be placed in a conspicuous place on the outside of the raft. Items such as medications and food should be clearly labeled, as well as their method of consumption.

Some survival equipment require periodic servicing. For example, the ELT batteries must be replaced or recharged after half of their useful life has expired or one hour of cumulative use. Additional equipment that must be serviced on a regular basis includes life rafts, flashlights, and emergency beacons. Food supplies should also be checked and replenished periodically.

- Weapons and flares should be stowed according to the manufacturer's recommendations. Do not stow these items in a place where they may be inadvertently set off by moving objects.
- Liquids, such as water and medications, should be kept in sealed containers and protected from punctures.
- Batteries and matches should be stored in a water tight container.
- For overwater operations, personal flotation devices should be available to each passenger and pilot.
- In mountainous areas, each occupant should have protective, warm clothing.
- In hot desert conditions, protection from the sand and sun should be considered. Items that provide cover as well as sun block may be included.
- In every environment, pack plenty of food and water for each person.
- Commercially available survival kits are available at pilot supply shops, camping and sporting goods stores, and through mail order suppliers.
- Consider the following items when assembling your own survival kit:

  1. Metal container with lid
  2. Knife (Swiss Army, Boy Scout)
  3. Candle
  4. Waterproof matches
  5. Garbage bag (for a rain coat)
  6. Flares
  7. Plastic tape and nylon rope
  8. Whistle
  9. First Aid kit containing aspirin, bandages, antibiotic oiment, scissors, snakebite kit, antiseptic wipes, needle and thread.
  10. Non-perishable food, water, sugar cubes.
  11. Protective dry clothing
  12. Mirror or reflective device
  13. Flashlight
  14. Collapsible lightweight shelter
  15. Handheld communication radio
  16. Spare batteries for flashlight and radio
  17. Personal medications
  18. Survival guide pamphlet

- Before the flight, consider emergencies that could arise that are not included in the checklists, and plan a course of action.
- Keep in mind that the POH will have a checklist for some flight emergencies. These checklists should be used for every emergency.

EXERCISES

1. _____ (True, False) It is not necessary to bring warm clothing for mountain flights during warm summer months.
2. As the pilot, you should brief your passengers on the __________ and ____________ of all survival gear.
3. _____ (True, False) Batteries and matches should be stored in a water-proof container.

SAMPLE ORAL QUESTIONS

1. When is the ELT battery required to be replaced?

____

____

____

____

____

____

____

____

____

____

____

____

1. According to FAR 91.207, the ELT battery must be replaced or recharged when the transmitter has been in use for more than one cumulative hour; or when 50% of its useful life has expired. The expiration date for replacing or recharging batteries must be marked on the outside of the transmitter and noted in the aircraft maintenance records.

2. Why is it necessary to brief passengers on the operation and location of survival equipment?

____

____

____

____

____

____

____

2. In the event of a forced landing, you may be injured, unconscious, or otherwise incapacitated. In this type of situation, others need to know where to find and how to use all emergency equipment.

ADDITIONAL QUESTIONS

3. How should essentials such as water and food be stored?

4. What survival items are pertinent to the areas you fly?

EXERCISE ANSWERS

1. False

2. location, use

3. True

REFERENCES

JEPPESEN:

Private Pilot Manual/Video – Chapter 5B

FAA:

FAA-H-8083-3; POH/AFM

CHAPTER 11

NIGHT OPERATIONS

A. TASK: NIGHT PREPARATION (ASEL and ASES)

REFERENCES: FAA-H-8083-3, AC 61-23/FAA-H-8083-25, AC 67-2; AIM, POH/AFM

Objective: To determine that the applicant exhibits knowledge of the elements related to night operations by explaining :

1. Physiological aspects of night flying as it relates to vision.
2. Lighting systems identifying airports, runways, taxiways and obstructions, and pilot controlled lighting.
3. Airplane lighting systems.
4. Personal equipment essential for night flight.
5. Night orientation, navigation, and chart reading techniques.
6. Safety precautions and emergencies unique to night flying.

Objective: To determine that the applicant exhibits knowledge of the elements related to night operations by explaining:

1. Physiological aspects of night flying as it relates to vision.

THE EYE

The eye works in much the same way as a camera. Both have an adjustable opening, or iris, to allow light in and the lens to focus on an image. The receptor in a camera is film; in the eye the receptor is the retina. Within the retina there are two types of cells called rods and cones. The small center area of the retina is called the fovea and it sends sharply focused messages to the brain through the optic nerve.

CONES

Cones are concentrated around the center of the retina and gradually diminish in number as the distance from the center increases. Cones allow you to perceive color by sensing red, blue, and green light. The cones, however, do not function well in darkness, which explains why we cannot see color as vividly at night as we can during the day.

RODS

The rods are your main night receptors and are concentrated outside the center of the retina. The number of rods increases as you move toward the edge of the retina. Rods "see" only in black and white. Because the rods are not located directly behind the pupil, they are responsible for much of our peripheral vision. Images that move are perceived more easily by rods than by cones. [Figure 11-1]

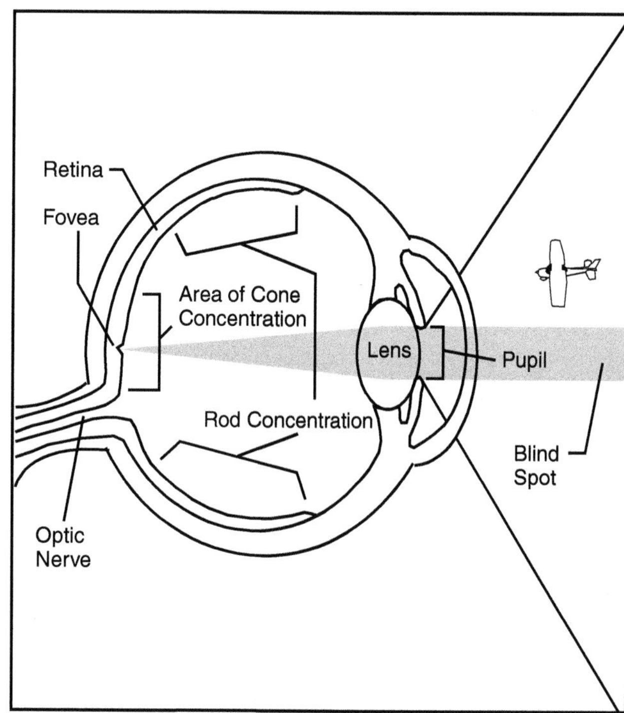

Figure 11-1. In low light, the cones lose much of their visual acuity, while rods become more receptive. The eye sacrifices sharpness for sensitivity. Your ability to see an object directly in front of you is reduced, and you lose much of your depth perception, as well as your judgment of size.

NIGHT VISION

When light conditions change from day to night, many physiological aspects must be considered. For example, your cones adapt quite rapidly to changes in light intensities, but your rods do not. Rods can take up to 30 minutes to fully adapt to the dark. However, a bright light can destroy your night vision almost immediately. If this happens your rods will need another 30 minutes to adapt again.

There are several things you can do to keep your eyes adapted to the dark. First, avoid bright lights before and during a flight. For 30 minutes before a night flight, avoid bright light sources such as headlights, landing lights, strobe lights, or flashlights. If you encounter a bright light, close one eye. This allows you to maintain your light sensitivity in one eye once the light is gone. When flying from daylight into an area of increasing darkness, sunglasses can be used to gain light sensitivity.

Red cockpit lighting also helps preserve your night vision; but, it severely distorts some colors, especially those found on aeronautical charts. On the other hand, white light impairs your night adaptation. However, a dim white light or carefully directed flashlight can enhance your night reading ability. When flying at night, keep the instrument panel and interior lights turned down as low as practical. This helps you see outside visual references more easily. If your eyes become blurry, blinking more frequently often helps.

Your diet and general physical health also have an impact on how well you can see in the dark. Deficiencies in vitamin A have been shown to reduce night visual acuity. Other factors, such as carbon monoxide poisoning, smoking, alcohol, certain drugs, and a lack of oxygen also can greatly decrease your night vision.

NIGHT SCANNING

Since the cones do not see well in the dark, you may not be able to see an object if you look directly at it. The concentration of cones in the center retina can create a night blindspot in the center of your vision. To see an object clearly, you must expose the rods to the image. This is accomplished by off-center viewing —looking 5° to 10° off center of the object you want to see.

When you look at an object, avoid staring at it too long. If you stare at an object without moving your eyes, the retina becomes accustomed to the light intensity and the image begins to fade. To keep it clearly visible, new areas in the retina must be exposed to the image. Small, circular eye movements help eliminate the fading. You also need to move your eyes more slowly from sector to sector than during the day to prevent blurring.

Another problem associated with night flying is **night myopia,** or night-induced nearsightedness. This is similar to empty field myopia in that when the eye has little to focus on, it tends to focus a few feet in front of the aircraft. This is more pronounced at night because of the lack of visual references. Focusing on distant light sources, no matter how dim, helps prevent the onset of night myopia.

A review of spatial disorientation and spatial illusions is also helpful for night flight preparation. For example, the illusion of a **false horizon** occurs when the natural horizon is obscured. It can result from confusing bright stars and city lights. A false horizon can occur while flying toward the shore of a large body of water. Because of the relative darkness of the water, the lights along the shoreline can be mistaken for stars. [Figure 11-2]

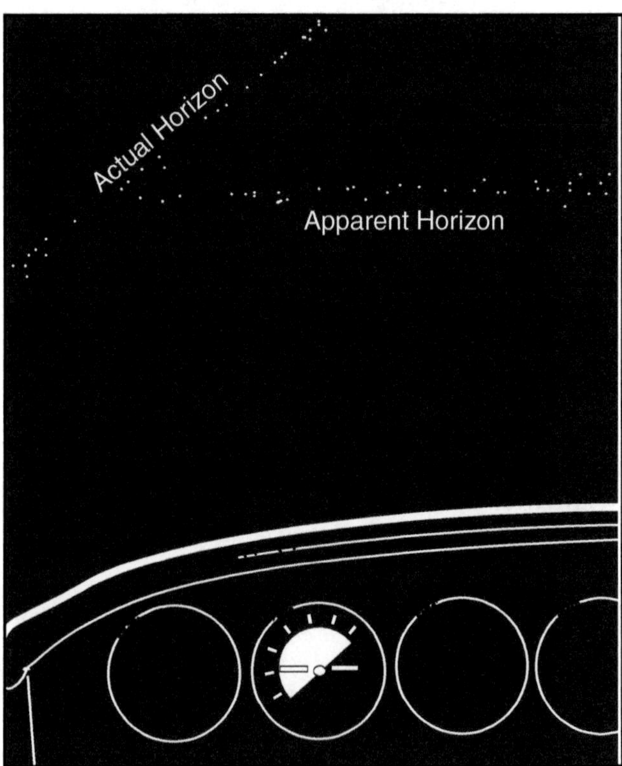

Figure 11-2. You can place your aircraft in an extremely dangerous flight attitude if you align the aircraft with the wrong lights. Here, the aircraft is aligned with a road and not the horizon.

VISUAL ILLUSIONS

You can experience visual illusions at any time, day or night. The next few paragraphs cover some of the illusions that commonly occur at night and some that you may encounter during the approach and landing.

Autokinesis is caused by staring at a single point of light against a dark background, such as a ground light or bright star. After a few moments, the light will appear to move on its own. If you attempt to align the aircraft in relation to the light, you may lose control of the airplane. You can guard against this illusion by maintaining a normal visual scan and by frequently referring to the instruments.

Landing illusions occur in many forms. Above featureless terrain or at night, there is a natural tendency to fly a lower-than-normal approach. Bright runway lights, steep surrounding terrain, and a wide runway can produce the illusion of being too low, and there is the tendency to fly a higher-than-normal approach. When you encounter these situations, you must be able to recognize and counteract them. When available, take advantage of visual glide slope indicators to verify your landing approach. In addition, look for other clues, such as steep or featureless surrounding terrain. If you suspect an illusion, fly a normal traffic pattern and avoid long, straight-in approaches.

2. Lighting systems identifying airports, runways, taxiways and obstructions, and pilot controlled lighting.

- For information on airport lighting see Chapter 3, Task C on page 3-13.

3. Airplane lighting systems.

AIRCRAFT LIGHTING

Regulations require all aircraft operated from sunset to sunrise to have special lights and equipment. The requirements for operating at night are found in FAR Part 91.

Position lights enable you to see where an aircraft is, as well as its direction of flight. The approved aircraft lights for night operations are a green light on the right wingtip, a red light on the left wingtip, and a white position light on the tail. In addition, a flashing aviation red or white **anti-collision light** is required for night flights. These flashing lights can be in a number of locations, but are most commonly found on the wingtips or tail. [Figure 11-3]

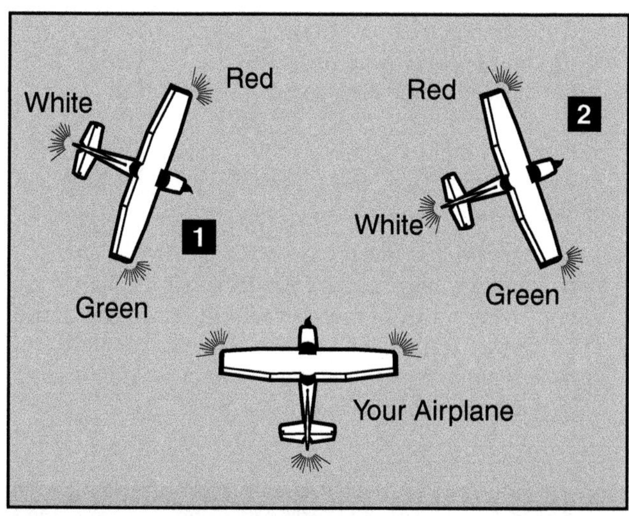

Figure 11-3. By interpreting the position lights on other aircraft, you can determine whether the aircraft is flying away from you or is on a collision course. If you see a red position light to the right of a green light, such as shown by aircraft number 1, it is flying toward you. You should watch this aircraft closely and be ready to change course. Aircraft number 2, on the other hand, is flying away from you, as indicated by the white position light.

Most airplanes have a **landing light**, and some have a **taxi light** to illuminate the runway and taxiway. Although you must visually check both the landing light and the taxi light for correct operation during the preflight inspection, do not allow these lights to operate for any length of time with the engine shut down, because of the high electrical drain on the battery.

Modern airplanes are equipped with a system for lighting the instrument panel and instruments. Prior to any night flight, check the panel lighting system to determine that it is operating satisfactorily. The light intensity should be adjusted just bright enough so you are able to read the instrument indications. If the lighting is too bright, a glare results and your night vision suffers.

4. Personal equipment essential for night flight.

EQUIPMENT

For any night flight, you should have at least one appropriate working flashlight, with adequate battery power. Some pilots prefer two flashlights, one with white light and one with red light, or a combination flashlight with white and red light options.

A sectional and other appropriate aeronautical charts are a necessity, as well as a navigation log and plotter, pens and/or pencils, a flight computer, kneeboard, and a clock. Most pilots prefer headsets or ear protection and a first aid kit and clothing appropriate to the season. Carry emergency equipment and survival gear appropriate for the planned flight. It's also a good idea to carry a handheld aviation radio as a backup.

5. Night orientation, navigation, and chart reading techniques.

NIGHT OPERATIONS

You can minimize the differences between day and night flight by scheduling a night checkout which begins at twilight. When doing this, your takeoffs, landings, and traffic pattern work begin in the more familiar daylight environment and, as darkness increases, you transition to night operation gradually.

For flight planning purposes, FARs dictate that you carry enough fuel to complete your planned flight and fly thereafter for 45 minutes at normal cruising speed. In addition, when plotting a route you should select a course that keeps you within reach of airports as much as possible. You should also fly at higher cruising altitudes so you can see lighted landmarks at greater distances. At higher altitudes, reception range of navigation aids is greater. Higher cruising altitudes also provide an improved margin of safety, especially for night flights. This is because range usually increases at higher altitudes, and gliding distance is greater in the event of engine failure.

On clear nights, the outlines of major cities and towns are clearly discernible at night. Major metropolitan areas are visible during favorable weather for distances up to 100 miles or more, depending upon the flight altitude. Major highways tend to stand out at night because of the presence of headlights. Less traveled roads are usually not so easy to see at night unless you are flying in bright moonlit conditions.

On clear, moonlit nights, outlines of the terrain and other surface features are dimly visible. For example, you can often identify the outlines of bodies of water by noting the reflection of the moonlight. However, on extremely dark nights, unlighted terrain features are nearly invisible.

For reading charts, you should use subdued white light. Considerable information on charts is printed in red and it sometimes disappears under red cabin lighting. If a map reading light is not available use your flashlight. Place special emphasis on the terrain elevations provided on the charts to ensure adequate obstruction clearance.

6. Safety precautions and emergencies unique to night flying.

SAFETY PRECAUTIONS

Use caution during engine startup at night, since it's difficult for other persons to determine that you intend to start the engine. In the daytime you shout, "Clear!" At night, in addition to this, turning on the position lights or momentarily flashing other aircraft lights helps warn others that the propeller is about to rotate.

Collision avoidance procedures are important at night. Since there is a reduction in outside references, you may have a tendency to spend too much time looking at the flight instruments. Therefore, you must make a special effort to devote enough time to scan for traffic.

If you need to make a forced landing at night, use the same procedures as those recommended for daytime emergency landings. If a landing light is available, turn it on during the final approach to assist you in avoiding obstacles in the approach path. Highways may be used as emergency landing strips at night, but you must exercise extreme caution to avoid any vehicular traffic, powerlines, or other obstructions crossing the highway.

EXERCISES

1. A red position light is located on the __________ wing, a __________ position light on the tail, and a green position light on the __________ wing.

2. In addition to calling, "Clear!" to warn others you are starting the engine, you can turn on the __________ __________ or momentarily flash the __________ __________.

3. For flight in VFR conditions at night, you are required to have at least __________ minutes of fuel after the first point of intended landing.

4. To see an object clearly at night, you should look
   a. directly at the object.
   b. 5° to 10° away from the object.
   c. 45° away from the object.
   d. in quick scanning movements.

5. During a night flight, you see a steady red light and a flashing red light ahead. The other aircraft is
   a. crossing from right to left.
   b. crossing from left to right.
   c. approaching head on.
   d. headed away from you.

6. During a night flight, you see a steady white light, a steady green light, and a flashing red light. The other aircraft is
   a. approaching head on.
   b. approaching, but will pass from right to left
   c. flying away from you and will cross from left to right.
   d. flying away from you and will cross from right to left.

SAMPLE ORAL QUESTIONS

1. Describe the visual illusions associated with night flying, and how to overcome them.

____

____

____

____

____

____

____

____

____

____

1. Autokinesis results from staring at a single light against a dark background, such as a ground light or bright star. After a few seconds, the light will appear to move, and can affect aircraft control. This can be prevented by scanning and referring to the instruments. Night myopia occurs when the eyes automatically focus on a point three to six feet in front of you. Finding and focusing on distant light sources helps prevent this. Landing illusions at night include the natural tendency to fly a lower-than-normal approach. However, bright runway lights or a wide runway can produce the illusion of being too low. You can counteract these illusions by taking advantage of a visual approach slope indicator system to verify your landing approach.

2. Your cones adapt quite rapidly to changes in light intensities, but your rods do not. Rods can take up to 30 minutes to fully adapt to the dark. However, a bright light can destroy your night vision almost immediately. If this happens your rods will need another 30 minutes to adapt again.

2. Explain the process of dark adaptation.

____

____

____

____

____

____

____

____

3. FARs require all aircraft that fly from sunset to sunrise to have operable position lights. These include a red light on the left wingtip, a green light on the right wingtip, and a white light on the tail. A red or white anticollision light is also required. Furthermore, a landing light is required if the aircraft is operated for hire.

3. Briefly describe the types of required aircraft lighting.

____

____

____

____

____

____

____

____

ADDITIONAL QUESTIONS

4. Describe the function of the cones and rods.
5. Describe private pilot currency requirements to carry passengers at night.

EXERCISE ANSWERS

1. left, white, right
2. position lights, landing light
3. 45
4. b
5. a
6. c

REFERENCES

JEPPESEN:

Private Pilot Manual/Video – Chapter 10A
Private Pilot Maneuvers/Video – Maneuver 30

FAA:

Aeronautical Information Manual
Federal Aviation Regulations
Airplane Flying Handbook (FAA-H-8083-3)
Pilot's Handbook of Aeronautical Knowledge (FAA-H-8083-25)
Medical Handbook for Pilots (AC 67-2)
Pilot's Operating Handbook and FAA-Approved Airplane Flight Manual

POSTFLIGHT PROCEDURES

A. TASK: AFTER LANDING, PARKING, AND SECURING (ASEL and ASES)

REFERENCES: FAA-H-8083-3; POH/AFM.

Objective: To determine that the applicant:

1. Exhibits knowledge of the elements related to after landing, parking and securing procedures.
2. Maintains directional control after touchdown while decelerating to an appropriate speed.
3. Observes runway hold lines and other surface control markings and lighting.
4. Parks in an appropriate area, considering the safety of nearby persons and property.
5. Follows the appropriate procedure for engine shutdown.
6. Completes the appropriate checklist.
7. Conducts an appropriate postflight inspection and secures the aircraft.

Objective: To determine that the applicant:

1. **Exhibits knowledge of the elements related to after landing, parking and securing procedures.**

AFTER LANDING

Most pilots maintain a high level of vigilance throughout a flight, as well as during the landing. However, the flight is not over after landing. You have to resist the common tendency to relax during the landing roll. After touchdown, hold a straight course on the runway and correct for headwind, crosswind, or tailwind effects with proper elevator and aileron response.

After you slow to taxi speed, exit the runway without delay at the first available taxiway or as instructed by ATC. Stop the aircraft after clearing the runway, complete all necessary checklist items, and change to ground control frequency when advised by tower.

Although you are required to clear the runway after turning off, you are not authorized to cross other runways, taxiways, or ramps until cleared by ATC. When you do receive a clearance from ATC to taxi to the ramp, you are cleared to cross all runway and taxiway intersections.

When taxiing, the carburetor heat control knob should be pushed full in unless carburetor heat is absolutely necessary. When the carburetor heat knob is pulled out, air entering the engine is not filtered.

TAXIING

In spite of the good visibility and ground maneuvering provided by nosewheel aircraft, it is generally poor technique to use excessively high power settings, to taxi at high speeds, or to control the direction and taxi speed with the brakes. Keep taxi speeds slow and use minimal braking.

PARKING

After taxiing to the ramp there are typically two ways to park an aircraft. One way is to taxi the airplane into its designated parking spot and shut down the engine. However, because of the proximity of other aircraft, this procedure may not be possible. In this situation, you should taxi the aircraft near the intended parking spot, shut down and secure the engine, and use a towbar to maneuver the aircraft into parking. Since pushing and/or pulling on some aircraft without a towbar can cause structural damage, you should consult the Pilot's Operating Handbook (POH) and FAA-Approved Airplane Flight Manual.

SECURING THE AIRPLANE

Once an airplane is parked, the best precaution against damage from strong or gusty winds is to tie the aircraft down properly. To do this you should place chocks in front of and behind the main wheels. Furthermore, you should secure all flight controls to prevent them from being blown by the wind.

Before leaving the aircraft, set the parking brake according to requirements established by the fixed base operator (FBO). Most FBOs also require you to secure the aircraft with tiedown ropes or chains. When doing this, secure the tiedowns without slack, but not tight. Too much slack allows the aircraft to jerk against the ropes or chains, and too little slack may permit high stresses to be placed on the aircraft. The tail tiedown should also be secure, but not so tight that it raises the nose of the aircraft.

CLEANUP

Check the interior of the aircraft after it is secured. Make sure all switches are off and that trash, papers, and flight planning items are removed from the cabin area. Install the pitot tube cover, if applicable, and place the propeller in a horizontal position to lessen the possibility of damage to another taxiing aircraft's wingtip.

HAND SIGNALS

As a private pilot, you must be familiar with the standard hand signals used by ramp personnel during ground operations. However, keep in mind that, even though you are being directed, you are responsible for the safe operation of your aircraft. [Figure 12-1]

DEPLANING PASSENGERS

As the pilot in command, you are responsible for the safety of your passengers. Part of this responsibility includes ensuring passenger safety after a flight. For example, passengers should remain seated with seat belts fastened until the aircraft is stopped. Prior to allowing anyone to depart the aircraft, the engine should be shut down and secured. As an added precaution to make sure the magnetos are off, remove the ignition key. Furthermore, you should scan the immediate area for other aircraft that could create a hazard, and take the appropriate measures to warn your passengers of such hazards.

2. Maintains directional control after touchdown while decelerating to an appropriate speed.

- Touching down on the runway doesn't mean that the flight is over. You have to resist the common tendency to relax during the landing roll.
- After touchdown, hold a straight course on the runway and correct for headwind, crosswind, or tailwind effects with proper elevator and aileron response.
- Don't attempt to exit the runway while still at a high speed. Make sure the airplane slows to an appropriate speed before attempting to turn off the runway.

3. Observes runway hold lines and other surface control markings and lighting.

- Always observe the runway hold lines and other surface control markings. Review all of these markings periodically, particularly when flying to unfamiliar airports.
- The examiner will expect you not only to know what the hold lines and surface markings mean, he will also be watching you as you taxi to see if you understand and comply.
- If you are unsure what a surface marking means, ask the appropriate air traffic control before continuing further.

4. Parks in an appropriate area, considering the safety of nearby persons and property.

- Taxi the aircraft into the parking area using a safe taxi speed.

Figure 12-1. Some of the more common hand signals are shown here. You should review them periodically, especially during the early portion of your flight training program.

- Use a towbar whenever maneuvering an aircraft between other aircraft.
- Pushing or pulling some aircraft without a towbar is prohibited, since structural damage may occur. Consult the POH for specific details.

5. Follows the recommended procedure for engine shutdown and securing the cockpit and the airplane.

- Prior to engine shutdown, perform a mag check to verify the magnetos are properly grounded.
- When shutting down the engine, always follow the appropriate checklists.

6. Completes the appropriate checklist.

- You are required to complete all appropriate checklists.

7. Conducts an appropriate postflight inspection and secures the aircraft.

Carefully complete all appropriate postflight procedures, and checklist items. Discrepancies noted during the flight should be written up in appropriate maintenance records. This is particularly true with any problem that could affect the airworthiness of the aircraft.

- Before leaving the aircraft, secure it with tiedown ropes or chains.
- Place chocks in front of and behind the main wheels and release the parking brake (if set).
- Secure all flight controls with control locks to prevent them from being blown by the wind.
- Install the pitot tube cover, if applicable.

EXERCISES

1. To correct for the effects of quartering crosswinds, while taxiing you must use both__________________ and __________________ control inputs.
2. The carburetor heat control knob should be pushed full _____ after landing.
3. When the carburetor heat control is pulled full out, in the hot position, air entering the engine is _____.
4. _______________(True, False) Although it is good practice to use checklists during preflight and engine starting, there is no need to use a checklist for engine shutdown.
5. Before pushing or pulling on any part of an aircraft, consult the ________________________________.
6. Aircraft control surfaces may be damaged during high winds or gusty conditions if you do not use a _____. when you secure the aircraft.

SAMPLE ORAL QUESTIONS

1. Describe the correct carburetor heat control knob response after landing.

____

____

____

____

____

____

2. Briefly explain the significance of after-landing checklists.

____

____

____

____

____

____

1. After landing, the carburetor heat control knob should be pushed full in during all ground operations unless heat is absolutely necessary. When the knob is pulled out to the "Hot" position, air entering the engine is unfiltered.

2. You must use after-landing checklists (or abbreviated checklists) from the Pilot's Operating Handbook and FAA-Approved Airplane Flight Manual. These checklists act as reminders of important steps that must be done to ensure the safe operation of the aircraft. It is not recommended that you rely only on memory in the cockpit, because it is extremely easy to overlook some checklist items.

3. Discuss some of the safety considerations associated with deplaning passengers.

____

____

____

____

____

____

3 You must accept responsibility for the safety of your passengers. When the aircraft is stopped, ensure that you shut down and secure the engine before you deplane any passengers. Carefully scan for other aircraft or vehicles in the immediate area that could create a hazard, and take appropriate measures to protect your passengers.

4. What precautionary measure can be taken to identify the accidental activation of the ELT?

____

____

____

____

____

____

4. Before you shut down the aircraft radios, tune to a frequency of 121.5 and listen for the ELT signal.

ADDITIONAL QUESTIONS

5. What action should be taken with the transponder after landing?
6. State two reasons why it is advantageous to place the wing flaps in the up, or retracted, position after landing.
7. What action should be taken if you have a brake failure while taxiing back to the parking area?
8. Be able to explain and/or demonstrate all hand signals used by ground personnel.

EXERCISE ANSWERS

1. elevator, aileron
2. in
3. unfiltered
4. False
5. Pilot's Operating Handbook
6. control lock

REFERENCES

JEPPESEN:

Private Pilot Manual/Video — Chapters 4A and 4B

Private Pilot Maneuvers/Video — Maneuvers 3 and 5

FAA:

Airplane Flying Handbook (FAA-H-8083-3)

Pilot's Operating Handbook and FAA-Approved Airplane Flight Manual

Aeronautical Information Manual

ABBREVIATIONS

Throughout the study guide you will find typical aeronautical abbreviations and acronyms. We have attempted to identify most, especially unique ones, when first used. However, if you begin studying in Chapter 5, for example, you may come across an unfamiliar abbreviation or acronym. The following, although by no means a complete listing, may be useful:

A

A/FD — Airport/Facility Directory
AC — Advisory Circular
ADF — automatic direction finder
ADIZ — air defense identification zone
ADM — aeronautical decision making
AFSS — automated flight service station
AGL — above ground level
AIM — Aeronautical Information Manual
AIRMET — Airman's Meteorological Information
ALD — Available landing distance
ALS — approach light system
ARTCC — air route traffic control center
ARTS — automated radar terminal system
ASEL — airplane single-engine land
ASOS — automated surface observation system
ASR — airport surveillance radar
ATA — actual time of arrival
ATC — Air Traffic Control
ATD — actual time of departure
ATE — actual time enroute
ATIS — automatic terminal information service
AWOS — automated weather observing system
AWW — severe weather forecast alert

C

CAS — calibrated airspeed
CAT — clear air turbulence
CDI — course deviation indicator
CG — center of gravity
C_L — coefficient of lift
CRM — crew resource management
CTAF — common traffic advisory frequency
CW — continuous wave NDB signals
CWA — center weather advisory

D

DA — density altitude
DF — direction finder
DG — directional gyro
DME — distance measuring equipment
DR — dead reckoning
DUATS — direct user access terminal system
DVFR — defense visual flight rules

E

EFAS — enroute flight advisory service
ELT — emergency locator transmitter
ETA — estimated time of arrival
ETD — estimated time of departure
ETE — estimated time enroute

F

FA — area forecast
FAA — Federal Aviation Administration
FARs — Federal Aviation Regulations
FCC — Federal Communications Commission
FDC — Flight Data Center
FD — winds and temperatures aloft forecast
FL — flight level
FSS — flight service station

G

GPS — Global Positioning System
GS — groundspeed

H

HF — high frequency
HIRLs — high intensity runway lights
HIWAS — hazardous inflight weather advisory service
hPa — hectoPascal
HSI — horizontal situation indicator
HVOR — high altitude VOR

I

IAS — indicated airspeed
ICAO — International Civil Aviation Organization
IFR — instrument flight rules
ILS — instrument landing system
IMC — instrument meteorological conditions
in. HG — inches of mercury
IR — IFR military training route
ISA — International Standard Atmosphere

K

KIAS — knots indicated airspeed
KTAS — knots true airspeed

L

L/MF — low/medium frequency
LAA — local airport advisory
LAHSO — land and hold short operations
LAT — latitude
LF — low frequency
LIRLs — low intensity runway lights
LLWAS — low level wind shear alert system
LONG — longitude
LORAN — long range navigation
LVOR — low altitude VOR

M

mb — millibars
MB — magnetic bearing
MEF — maximum elevation figure
METAR — aviation routine weather report
MH — magnetic heading
MIRLs — medium intensity runway lights
MOA — military operations area
MSAW — minimum safe altitude warning
MSL — mean sea level
MTR — military training route
MULTICOM — frequency used at airports without a tower, FSS, or UNICOM

N

NAS — National Airspace System
NAVAID — navigational aid
NDB — nondirectional radio beacon
NFCT — non-federal control tower
NOAA — National Oceanic and Atmospheric Administration
NORDO — no radio, in reference to lost communications
NOS — National Ocean Service
NOTAM — notice to airmen
NTSB — National Transportation Safety Board
NWS — National Weather Service

O

OAT — outside air temperature
OBS — omnibearing selector
OTS — out-of-service

P

p.s.i. — pounds per square inch
P-factor — an element of asymmetrical thrust
PA — pressure altitude
PAPI — precision approach path indicator
PCL — pilot controlled lighting
PIC — pilot in command
PIREP — pilot report
POH — Pilot's Operating Handbook
PTS — Practical Test Standard

R

r.p.m. — revolutions per minute
RAIL — runway alignment indicator lights
RB — relative bearing
RCO — remote communications outlet
REIL — runway end identifier lights
RMI — radio magnetic indicator
RNAV — area navigation
RVR — runway visual range
RVV — runway visibility value

S

s.m. — statute mile
SAR — search and rescue
SD — Radar weather report
SFL — sequenced flashing lights
SIGMET — significant meteorological information
SPECI — aviation selected special weather report
SR—SS — sunrise — sunset
SVFR — special VFR

T

TACAN — tactical air navigation
TAF — terminal aerodrome forecast
TAS — true airspeed
TC — true course
TEL—TWEB — telephone access to TWEB
TIBS — telephone information briefing service
TRSA — terminal radar service area
TVOR — terminal VOR
TWEB — transcribed weather broadcast

U

UHF — ultra high frequency
UNICOM — aeronautical advisory staion
UTC — Coordinated Universal Time (Zulu time)

V

VASI — visual approach slope indicator
VFR — visual flight rules

VHF — very high frequency
VHF/DF — VHF direction finder
VMC — visual meteorological conditions
VOR — VHF omnidirectional receiver
VOR/DME — collocated VOR and DME navaids
VORTAC — VOR and TACAN collocated
VOT — VOR test facility
VR — VFR military training route

W

WA — AIRMET
WAC — World Aeronautical Chart
WCA — wind correction angle
WILCO — understand and will comply
WS — SIGMET
WST — convective SIGMET
WW — severe weather watch bulletin

Abbreviated format also applies to some FAA references. For example, an Advisory Circular such as AC 61-23, may be referenced without the title of the AC or the suffix letter. The full title of AC 61-23 is, "Pilot's Handbook of Aeronautical Knowledge,'' and the current edition, which is indicated by the letter suffix, is 61-23B. However, a note in the PTS indicates that the latest revision should be used. References to FARs are also shortened to include only the Part number and not the title. FAA references included in the Private Pilot PTS and in the Study Guide include:

FAR Part 61	Certification: Pilots and Flight Instructors
FAR Part 91	General Operating and Flight Rules
AC 00-6	Aviation Weather
AC 00-45	Aviation Weather Services
AC 61-13	Basic Helicopter Handbook
AC 61-21	Flight Training Handbook
AC 61-23	Pilot's Handbook of Aeronautical Knowledge
AC 61-27	Instrument Flying Handbook
AC 61-84	Role of Preflight Preparation
AC 67-2	Medical Handbook for Pilots
AC 91-13	Cold Weather Operation of Aircraft
AC 91-55	Reduction of Electrical Systems Failure Following Engine Starting